Practical Parallel Computing

Journal Special Issue

Volume 3 Issue 6 of the International Journal

CONCURRENCY: PRACTICE AND EXPERIENCE

Edited by
Geoffrey C. Fox, Syracuse University, USA

This selection of papers was first presented at a conference held in Capri, Italy in June, 1990.

Practical Parallel Computing
Status and Prospects

Edited by

Paul Messina
California Institute of Technology, USA

and

Almerico Murli
University of Naples, Italy

JOHN WILEY & SONS
Chichester · New York · Brisbane · Toronto · Singapore

Other Wiley Editorial Offices

John Wiley & Sons, Inc., 605 Third Avenue,
New York, NY 10158-0012, USA

Jacaranda Wiley Ltd, G.P.O. Box 859, Brisbane,
Queensland 4001, Australia

John Wiley & Sons (Canada) Ltd, 22 Worcester Road,
Rexdale, Ontario M9W 1L1, Canada

John Wiley & Sons (SEA) Pte Ltd, 37 Jalan Pemimpin #05-04,
Block B, Union Industrial Building, Singapore 2057

A cataglogue record for this book is available from the British Library.

ISBN 0 471 93182 9
ISSN 1040-3108

Typeset by Text Processing Department, John Wiley & Sons Ltd, Chichester, UK
Printed in Great Britain by Galliard (Printers) Ltd, Great Yarmouth, UK

Concurrency
PRACTICE AND EXPERIENCE

AIMS AND SCOPE

Recent developments in technology have stimulated the development of **concurrent** computers. These machines consist of a collection of processors connected in a network—or alternatively a collection of processors sharing access to a common memory. These include both general purpose MIMD and SIMD architectures and special purpose systems such as neural networks. Optical and dataflow hardware can be expected in the future. There are now several commercially available concurrent computers and an increasing number of microprocessor chips specifically designed to permit the construction of parallel computers varying in size from PC add-in boards with a few processors up to 64000-processor supercomputers.

These machines are being successfully applied in a wide range of application areas especially in science and engineering. This is producing a substantial amount of practical experience in those problems which parallelize well and the features of hardware and systems software needed to use concurrency effectively. There are also new computational methods, such as cellular automata and massively parallel neural networks, which are particularly suited to concurrent execution. At present, there is no journal that brings this work together. Results, if published at all, are scattered throughout specialized technical journals. This journal will therefore focus on practical experience with concurrent machines, especially:

- Concurrent solutions to specific problems
- Concurrent algorithms and computational methods
- Programming environments, operating systems, and tools
- New languages
- Performance design, analysis, models and results

The papers will all have a practical or phenomenological emphasis.

Updated information—The practical experience central to the journal will evolve more rapidly than the basic concurrent algorithms and approaches. Thus, we will consider for publication short addenda to previously published papers which provide significant and clearly presented additional practical experience, e.g. performance of a new parallel computer, that naturally augments the published paper.

EDITOR

Professor Geoffrey C. Fox, *Northeast Parallel Architectures Centre, Syracuse University, 111 College Place, Syracuse, NY 13244-4100, U.S.A.*
Telephone: (315) 443 1723; Fax: (315) 443 1973; e-mail: gcf@ nova.npac.syr.edu.

ASSOCIATE EDITORS

Professor A. J. G. Hey, *Department of Electronics and Computer Science, University of Southampton, Southampton SO9 5NH, U.K.*
Dr Paul Messina, *California Institute of Technology, Mail Stop 158-79, Pasadena, CA 91125, U.S.A.*

EDITORIAL BOARD

Dr Donald M. Austin,
University of Minnesota, U.S.A.

Dr Jacob Barhen,
Jet Propulsion Laboratory, Pasadena, U.S.A.

Dr William J. Camp,
Sandia National Laboratories, U.S.A.

Dr Enrico Clementi,
IBM Corporation, U.S.A.

Dr Erik DeBenedictis,
NCUBE Corporation, U.S.A.

Professor Dennis Duke,
Florida State University, U.S.A.

Dr W. M. Gentleman,
National Research Council of Canada, Canada

Dr Milton Halem,
Goddard Space Flight Center, U.S.A.

Professor Per Brinch Hansen,
Syracuse University, U.S.A.

Professor Ken Kennedy
Rice University, U.S.A.

Professor H. T. Kung
Carnegie Mellon University, U.S.A.

Dr Lennart Johnsson,
Thinking Machines Corporation, U.S.A.

Dr David May
INMOS Ltd, U.K.

Professor Oliver McBryan
University of Colorado, U.S.A.

Dr Raul Mendez
Institute for Supercomputing Research, Japan

Dr Steve Otto
Oregon Graduate Institute, U.S.A.

Dr George Paul
IBM, U.S.A.

Professor Dan Reed
University of Illinois, U.S.A.

Professor Joel Saltz
ICASE, U.S.A.

Professor Martin Schultz
Yale University, U.S.A.

Dr Danny Sorensen
Rice University, U.S.A.

Professor D. J. Wallace
University of Edinburgh, U.K.

Dr Andy White
Los Alamos National Laboratory, U.S.A.

Professor Hans Zima
University of Vienna, Austria

List of Contributors

G. Anagnostou   Ocean Engineering, MIT, Cambridge, MA, USA

E. Appiani   RSB Department, Elletronica San Giorgio, Elsag Bailey SpA, Genova, Italy

H. Berryman   Institute for Computer Applications in Science and Engineering, NASA Langley Research Center, Hampton, VA, USA

D. Bianco   RSB Department, Elletronica San Giorgio, Elsag Bailey SpA, Genova, Italy

A. Chatterjee   Experimental Systems Laboratory, Microelectronics and Computer Technology Corp. (MCC), Austin, TX, USA

J. Demmel   Mathematics Department, Computer Science Division, University of California, Berkeley, CA, USA

P.F. Fischer   California Institute of Technology, Pasadena, CA, USA

G.C. Fox   Northeast Parallel Architectures Center, Syracuse University, Syracuse, NY, USA

J.R. Henderson   University of Edinburgh, Scotland

Y. Hung   Experimental Systems Laboratory, Microelectronics and Computer Technology Corp. (MCC), Austin, TX, USA

A. Khanna   Experimental Systems Laboratory, Microelectronics and Computer Technology Corp. (MCC), Austin, TX, USA

S.P. Kumar   Boeing Computer Services, Seattle, WA, USA

Y. Maday   Laboratoire d'Analyse Numerique, Universite Pierre et Marie Curie, Paris, France

I.G. Main   University of Edinburgh, Scotland

G. Marcenaro   DIST, University of Genoa, Genoa, Italy

D.C. Marinescu   Computer Science Department, Purdue University, West Lafayette, IN, USA

L. Merlo   RSB Department, Elletronica San Giorgio, Elsag Bailey SpA, Genova, Italy

P. Messina   Caltech Concurrent Supercomputing Facilities, California Institute of Technology, Pasadena, CA, USA

A. Murli   University of Naples, Naples, Italy

M.G. Norman   University of Edinburgh, Scotland

A.T. Patera   Mechanical Engineering, MIT, Cambridge, MA, USA

I.R. Philips   Boeing Computer Services, Seattle, WA, USA

J.R. Rice   Computer Science Department, Purdue University West Lafayette, IN, USA

L. Roncarolo   RSB Department, Elletronica San Giorgio, Elsag Bailey SpA, Genova, Italy

E.M. Rønquist   Nektonics, Cambridge, MA, USA

J. Saltz   Institute for Computer Applications in Science and Engineering, NASA Langley Research Center, Hampton, VA, USA

S.R. Sipcic   Department of Aerospace and Mechanical Engineering, Boston University, MA, USA

M. Tistarelli   DIST, University of Genoa, Genoa, Italy

D.J. Wallace   University of Edinburgh, Scotland

J. Wu   Institute for Computer Applications in Science and Engineering, NASA Langley Research Center, Hampton, VA, USA

T. Westbrook   Department of Aerospace and Mechanical Engineering, Boston University, MA, USA

CONTENTS

VOLUME 3 NUMBER 6

DECEMBER 1991

continued

CPEXEI 3(6) 499–742 (1991)
ISSN 1040-3108

CONTENTS

VOLUME 3 NUMBER 6   DECEMBER 1991

Editorial

On 3–7 June 1990, the conference 'Parallel Computing: Achievements, Problems and Prospects' was held in Capri, Italy. The goals of the conference were:

- to assess the progress made in the 1980s in parallel computation for scientific applications and to examine trends in large-scale computations as we enter the 1990s;
- to provide an opportunity for discussion among the researchers and some of the well-known experts in the field of parallel computing.

Ninety-two papers and posters were presented by participants from fourteen countries. The presentations covered the areas of parallel computer architectures, operating systems and software environments, algorithms and their implementations, mathematical software, and large-scale scientific applications. This issue consists of fourteen papers based on invited talks as well as a few contributed presentations. The papers selected are those that best surveyed and summarized achievements in various aspects of parallel computing or that described particularly noteworthy applications and software environments.

Parallel computing has gained even more momentum in the brief period since the conference was held. It appears that 1990 was a turning point for parallel computing. The debate has shifted from whether parallel computers are worthwhile to what are the best software environments, programming models, and hardware architectures. The United States government has launched the High Performance Computing and Communications Program and similar initiatives are taking shape in Europe, Japan and other countries. Consortia of user institutions are being formed around large parallel computers, such as the Caltech-led Concurrent Supercomputing Consortium for the Intel Touchstone Delta System. Significantly more powerful commercial systems are being introduced over the next few months. Even companies that traditionally produced vector computers have launched major development programmes for massively parallel computers.

We extend our thanks to all the conference participants for their fine contributions and to the many sponsors who provided the financial support that made the conference possible.

ALMERICO MURLI
University of Naples
Naples, Italy

PAUL MESSINA
California Institute of Technology
Pasadena, CA, USA

1040–3108/91/060499–01$05.00

CONCURRENCY: PRACTICE AND EXPERIENCE, VOL. 3(6), 501–524 (DECEMBER 1991)

Parallel computing in the 1980s—one person's view

PAUL C. MESSINA

Caltech Concurrent Supercomputing Facilities
158–79 California Institute of Technology
Pasadena, CA 91125, USA

SUMMARY

This paper is a survey of activities related to parallel computing that took place primarily during the 1980s. The major areas covered are hardware, software, and performance measurement and characterization. Emphasis is on identifying the major milestones of the decade and on commercial computers rather than present a comprehensive survey of the field. The material is treated from the user's point of view.

1. INTRODUCTION

This paper is a broad survey of activities related to parallel computing that took place primarily during the 1980s. The major areas that are covered are hardware, software, research activities, performance measurements and characterization, and production uses of parallel use. In no case is there an attempt to present a comprehensive list or survey of all the work that was done in that area. Rather, the attempt is to identify some of the major events during that decade. Emphasis is placed on commercial products and on issues that users tend to care about, rather than on those of interest to people who design parallel computer hardware or software.

There are two major motivations for creating and using parallel computer architectures. The first is that parallelism is the only avenue to achieve vastly higher speeds than are possible now from a single processor. Table 1 demonstrates dramatically the rather slow increase in speed of single-processor systems for one particular brand of supercomputer, CRAYs, the most popular supercomputer in the world. Figure 1 shows a more comprehensive sample of computer performance, measured in operations per second, from the 1940s extrapolated through the year 2000.

Table 1. CRAY cycle times

Year of introduction	Model name	Cycle time in nanoseconds
1976	CRAY 1	12.5
1982	CRAY X-MP	9.5
1985	CRAY 2	4.1[a]
1988	CRAY Y-MP	6.5

[a] Instructions could only be issued every other cycle so the effective cycle time is 8.2 nanoseconds.

1040–3108/91/060501–24$12.00
©1991 by John Wiley & Sons, Ltd.

Received 3 July 1991
Accepted 18 September 1991

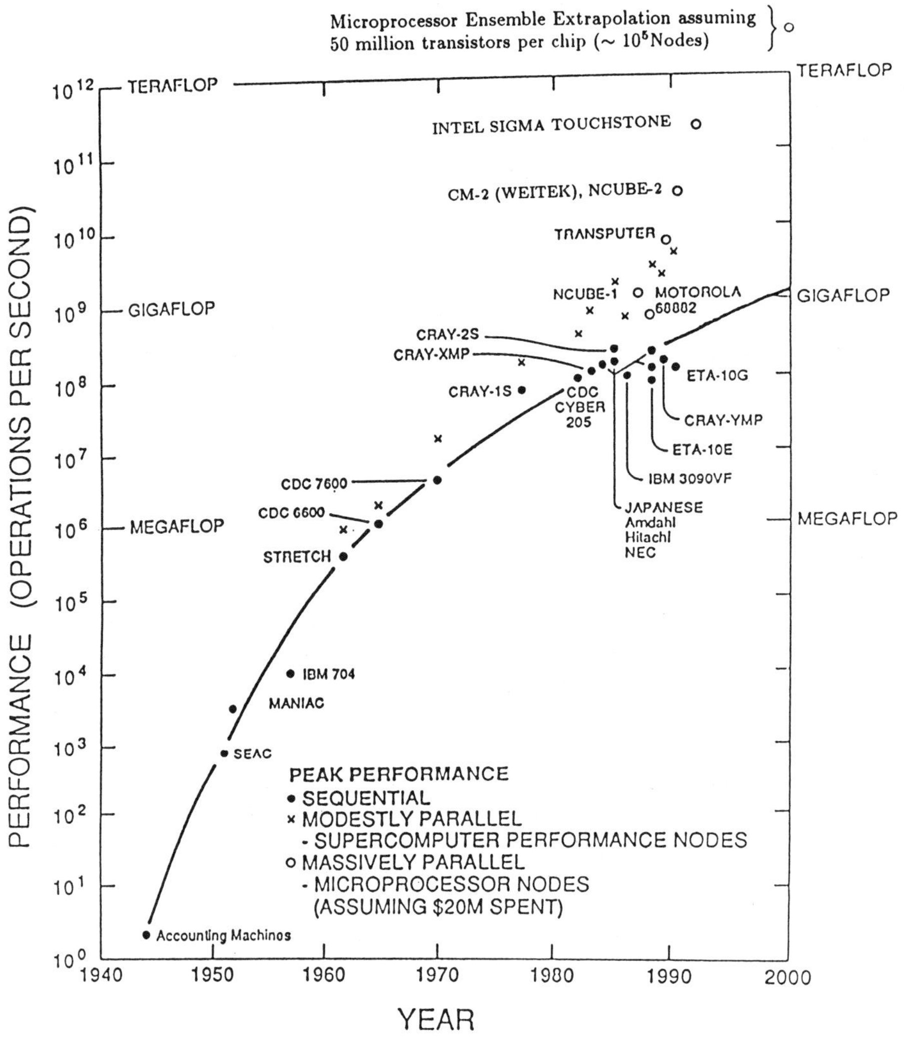

Figure 1. Historical trends of peak computer performance

A second motivation for the use of parallel architectures is that they should be considerably cheaper than sequential machines for systems of moderate speeds, that is, not necessarily supercomputers but instead minicomputers or minisupercomputers would be cheaper to produce for a given performance level than the equivalent sequential system.

At the beginning of the 1980s, the goals of research in parallel computer architectures were to achieve much higher speeds than could be obtained from sequential architectures and to get much better price performance through the use of parallelism than would be possible from sequential machines. This paper describes activities during the 1980s towards those goals and assesses the progress made towards achieving them.

2. HARDWARE TRENDS

2.1. Parallel scientific computers before 1980

There were several parallel computers before 1980, but they did not have a widespread impact on scientific computing. The activities of the 1980s had a much more dramatic impact. Still, a few systems stand out as having made significant contributions that were taken advantage of in the 1980s. The first is the ILLIAC IV [1]. It did not seem like a significant advance to many people at the time, nor did it to me, perhaps because its performance was only moderate, it was difficult to program, and had low reliability. The best performance that was achieved was two to six times the speed of a CDC 7600. This was obtained on various computational fluid dynamics codes. For many other programs, however, the performance was lower than that of a CDC 7600 which was the supercomputer of choice during the early and mid-1970s. The ILLIAC was a research project, not a commercial product, and it was reputed to be extremely expensive so that it was not realistic for others to replicate it. While the ILLIAC IV did not inspire the masses to become interested in parallel computing, hundreds of people were involved in its use and in projects related to providing better software tools and better programming languages for it. In the end, hundreds of people first learned how to do parallel computing on the ILLIAC IV. Many of those people went on to make significant contributions to parallel computing in the 1980s.

The ILLIAC was an SIMD computer—single instruction, multiple data architecture. It had 32 processing elements, each of which was a processor with its own local memory, and the processors were connected in a ring. High-level languages such as Glypnyr and Fortran were available for the ILLIAC IV. Glypnyr was reminiscent of Fortran and had extensions for parallel and array processing.

The ICL Distributed Array Processor (DAP) [2] was a commercial product; a handful of machines were sold, mainly in England where it was designed and built. Its characteristics were that it had either 1 K or 4 K one-bit processors arranged in a square plane, each connected in rectangular fashion to nearest neighbors. Like the ILLIAC IV, it was an SIMD system. It had to be front-ended by an ICL mainframe. The ICL DAP was used for many real university science applications. The University of Edinburgh, in particular, used it for a number of real computations and physics, chemistry and other fields [3,4]. The ICL DAP had a substantial impact on scientific computing culture, but primarily in Europe. ICL did try to market it in the United States, but was never effective in doing so; the requirement that the host had to be an expensive ICL mainframe was a substantial negative factor.

A third important commercial parallel computer in the 1970s was the Goodyear Massively Parallel Processor (MPP) [5,6 (pp. 157–166)]. Goodyear started building SIMD computers in 1969, but all except the MPP were sold to the military and to the Federal Aviation Administration for air traffic control uses. However, in the late 1970s, Goodyear produced the MPP which was installed at Goddard Space Flight Center, a NASA research center, and was used for a variety of scientific applications. The MPP attracted attention because it did achieve high speeds on a few applications, speeds that, in the late 1970s and early 1980s, were remarkable—measured in the hundreds of megaflops in a few cases. The MPP had 16 K one-bit processors, each with local memory and was programmed in Pascal and Assembler. As an aside, it is interesting to note that the attention that the MPP attracted in the late 1970s was nothing compared to the attention that the Thinking Machines Corporation Connection Machine got in the mid- to late 1980s.

So my choice for three significant scientific parallel computers of the 1970s are the ILLIAC IV, the ICL DAP, and the Goodyear MPP. Note that they were all SIMD computers. The DAP and the MPP were fine-grain systems based on single-bit processors, whereas the ILLIAC IV was a large-grain SIMD system. The other truly significant high-performance computer of the 1970s was the CRAY 1, which was introduced in 1976. The CRAY 1 was, of course, a single processor vector computer and as such it can also be classified as a special case of an SIMD computer because it had vector instructions. With a single vector instruction, one causes up to 64 data pairs to be operated on. In summary, there were significant and seminal activities in parallel computing in the 1970s both from the standpoint of design and construction of systems and in the actual scientific use of the systems. However, the level of activity of parallel computing in the 1970s was modest compared to what followed in the 1980s.

2.2. Early 1980s

In contrast to the 1970s, in the early 1980s it was MIMD (multiple instruction, multiple data) computers that dominated the activity in parallel computing. The first of these was the Denelcor Heterogeneous Element Processor (HEP). The HEP attracted widespread attention despite its terrible cost performance. Part of the reason for the attention was perhaps that people at leading institutions, such as Bill Buzbee (then at Los Alamos National Laboratory), saw that the HEP had interesting hardware features and showed interest in it; this attracted widespread attention to the HEP. The HEP was a commercial product that grew out of an Army procurement that was originally designed to produce a hybrid (that is, a combination analog and digital computer), not a parallel computer. The Denelcor HEP was acquired by several institutions, including Los Alamos, Argonne National Laboratory, Ballistic Research Laboratory, and Messerschmitt in Germany. Messerschmitt was the only installation that used it for real applications. The others, however, used it extensively for research on parallel algorithms. The HEP hardware supported both fine-grain and large-grain parallelism. Any one processor had an instruction pipeline that provided parallelism at the single instruction level. Instructions from separate processes (associated with separate user programs or tasks) were put into hardware queues and scheduled for execution once the required operands had been fetched from memory into registers, again under hardware control. Instructions from up to 128 processes could share the instruction execution pipeline. The latter had eight stages; all instructions except floating-point divide took eight machine cycles to execute. Up to 16 processors could be linked to perform large-grain MIMD systems. The HEP had an extremely efficient synchronization mechanism through a full–empty bit associated with every word of memory. The bit was automatically set to indicate whether the word had been rewritten since it had last been written into and could be set to indicate that the memory location had been read. The value of the full–empty bit could be checked in one machine cycle. Fortran, C, and Assembler could be used to program the HEP. It had a Unix environment and was front-ended by a minicomputer. Because Los Alamos and Argonne made their HEPs available for research purposes to people who were interested in learning how to program parallel machines or who were involved in parallel algorithm research, hundreds of people became familiar with parallel computing through the Denelcor HEP [7].

A second computer that was important in the early 1980s, primarily because it exposed a large number of computational scientists to parallelism, was the CRAY X-MP/22, which was introduced in 1982. Certainly, it had limited parallelism, namely only two processors, but still it was a parallel computer. The CRAY X-MP preceded almost all other standard commercial products in that it had more than one processor and was designed to be used as a parallel computer by applications. Since it was at the very high end of performance, it exposed the hardcore scientific users to parallelism, although initially mostly in a negative way. The low level of parallelism in the hardware, plus computer center policies that made the use of the parallelism typically more expensive than sequential computing, made parallel computing seem undesirable. In other words, there was not enough payoff in speed or cost to compensate for the effort that was required to parallelize a program so that it would use both processors: the maximum speed-up would, of course, only be two. Typically, it is less than two and the charging algorithms of most computer centers generated higher charges for a program when it used both processors than when it used only one. In a way, though, the CRAY X-MP multiprocessor legitimized parallel processing, although restricted to very large grain, very small number of processors. The IBM 3090 series, a few years later, had the same effect; the 3090 can have up to six vector and scalar processors in one system. Memory is shared among all processors.

By far the most significant and influential parallel computer system of the early 1980s was the Caltech Cosmic Cube [8], developed by Charles Seitz and Geoffrey Fox. A 64-node system was operational in 1983. Smaller systems were developed even earlier. The hypercube provided a dramatic demonstration that multicomputers could be built quickly, cheaply, and reliably. In terms of reliability, for example, there were two hard failures in the first 560,000 node hours of operation—that is, during the first year of operation. Its performance was low by today's standards, but it was still between five and ten times the performance of a DEC VAX 11/780, which was the system of choice for academic computer departments and research groups in that time period. The manufacturing costs of the system was $80,000, which at that time was about half the cost of a VAX with a modest configuration. Therefore, the price performance was on the order of 10 to 20 times better than a VAX 780. Furthermore, it was clearly a scalable architecture, and that is perhaps the most important feature of that particular project. Finally, the Caltech project inspired several industrial companies to build commercial hypercubes. These include Intel, NCUBE [6], Ametek [9], and Floating Point Systems Corporation. About two years after the 64-node Caltech Cosmic Cube was operational, there were commercial products on the market and installed at user sites.

Another MIMD system that attracted a great deal of attention during that period was the New York University Ultracomputer [10] and a related system, the IBM RP3 [11, 12]. These systems were a serious attempt to design and demonstrate a shared-memory architecture that was scalable to very large numbers of processors. They featured an interconnection network between processors and memories that would avoid hot spots and congestion. The fetch-and-add instruction that was invented by Jacob Schwartz [13] would avoid some of the congestion problems in omega networks. Unfortunately, these systems took a great deal of time to put together and it was the late 1980s before the IBM RP3 existed in a usable fashion. At that time, it had 64 processors but each was so slow, by today's standards, that it attracted comparatively little attention. The architecture

is certainly still considered to be an interesting one, but many fewer users were exposed
to these systems than other designs that were constructed more quickly and put in places
that allowed a large number of users to have at least limited access to the systems for
experimentation.

2.3. Mid-1980s

During this period, many new systems were launched by commercial companies, and
several were quite successful in terms of sales. The two most successful were the Sequent
and the Encore [6 (pp. 111–126)] products. Both were shared-memory, bus-connected
multiprocessors of moderate parallelism. The maximum number of processors on the
Encore was 20; on the Sequent, initially 16 and later 30. Both provided an extremely
stable Unix environment and were excellent for time sharing. As such, they could be
considered VAX killers since VAXes were the time-sharing system of choice in research
groups in those days. The Sequent and the Encore provided perhaps a factor of 10
better cost performance, as well as considerably higher total performance than could be
obtained on a VAX at that time. For smaller jobs, for time sharing, and for learning to do
parallel computing, those systems were extremely useful and fairly widely sold. Perhaps
the most impressive aspect of the systems was their reliability in both hardware and
software. They operated without interruption for months at a time, just as conventional
minisupercomputers did. Their UNIX operating system software was familiar to many
users and, as mentioned before, very stable. Unlike most parallel computers whose system
software requires years to mature, these systems had very stable and responsive system
software from the beginning.

Another important system during this period was the Alliant [6 (pp. 35–44)]. The
initial model featured up to eight vector processors, each of moderate performance but
when used simultaneously providing performance equivalent to a sizable fraction of
a CRAY processor. A startling feature at the time was a Fortran compiler that was
quite good at automatic vectorization and also reasonably good at parallelization. These
compiler features coupled with its shared memory made this system relatively easy to
use and to achieve reasonably good performance. The Alliant also supported the C
language, although initially there was no vectorization or parallelization available in C.
The operating system was, as usual, Unix-based, but at first the Alliant was not always
responsive and stable under load. In the first year or two after its introduction, when
the user workload reached six or eight users the system would frequently bog down.
Because of its reasonably high floating-point performance and ease of use, the Alliant
was one of the first parallel computers of that period that was used for real applications.
The Sequent and Encore, as was mentioned, were used primarily for experimenting with
parallel computing or for time-sharing, in which case the users themselves were not
doing any parallel computing. They were merely running on one processor out of many
in the system. The Alliant, however, tended to be purchased more by groups that wanted
to do medium-sized computations, perhaps even computations they would normally do
on CRAYs. The Alliant's price performance was good enough to make it attractive.
Although the systems were more expensive than say the VAXes of the time, they were
not so expensive as to be beyond the ability of a group to purchase.

Advances in compiling technology made wide-word machines an interesting and
commercially viable architecture. The Multiflow and Cydrome systems both had

compilers that did quite a good job of exploiting very fine-grain parallelism and of scheduling floating-point pipelines within the processing units. Both these systems attempted to get parallelism at the instruction level from Fortran programs—the famous so-called dusty decks that might have convoluted logic and thus be very difficult to vectorize or parallelize in a large-grain sense. The price performance in these systems was the attraction. Multiflow did sell a reasonable number of systems, although it later went out of business. Cydrome did not stay in business long; perhaps it was introduced a little bit too late. These systems had an image problem in that they could not cite very high peak speeds. Their strength was that the achievable speed of these systems ought to be pretty good and that, after all, is what counts to the user. However, many people are fascinated by high peak speeds; they therefore, tended to ignore the wide-word machines although they were cost-effective and had good performance for actual application programs. On the other hand, because these systems did not scale to very high levels of performance, they were relegated to the superminicomputer arena. An important contribution they made was to show dramatically how far compiler technology has come in certain areas. The Multiflow compiler was interesting enough that Intel Corporation recently bought its compiler for possible use on their i860 microprocessor.

As was mentioned earlier, hypercubes were produced by Intel, NCUBE, Ametek, and Floating Point Systems Corporation in the mid-1980s. Of these, the most significant product was the NCUBE with its high degree of integration and a configuration of up to 1024 nodes [14,15]. It was pivotal in demonstrating that massively parallel MIMD medium-grain computers are practicable. NCUBE featured a complete processor on a single chip, including all channels for connecting to the other nodes so that one chip plus six memory chips constituted an entire node. They were packaged on boards with 64 nodes so that the system was extremely compact and was air-cooled, and, after initial problems were solved, the hardware was also reliable. Caltech had an early 512-node system and soon afterwards Sandia National Laboratories installed the 1024-node system. A great deal of scientific work was done on those two machines and they are still in use. The Sandia machine, in particular, with its 1024 nodes got the world's attention by demonstrating for several applications speed-ups of 1000 on its 1024 node system [16]. This was particularly significant because it was done during a period when there was active debate as to whether MIMD systems could provide speed-ups of more than a hundred. Amdahl's law [17] was cited as a reason why it would not be possible to get speed-ups greater than perhaps a hundred, even if one used 1000 processors.

Towards the end of the mid-1980s, transputer-based systems [18,19], both large and small, began to proliferate, especially in Europe but also in the United States. The T800 transputer was like the NCUBE processor, a single-chip system with built in communications channels, and it had respectable floating-point performance—a peak speed of nearly two megaflops and frequently achieved speeds of one-half to one megaflop. They provided a convenient building block for parallel systems and were quite cost-effective. Their prevalent use at the time was in boards with four or eight transputers that were attached to IBM PCs, VAXes or other workstations. The acceptance of transputers was hampered initially by the language situation: Occam was the only language available. Although it is an elegant language that appealed to some people and was used for many real time and embedded applications [20], most scientific users wanted Fortran and C. Eventually, these were provided. By the late 1980s there were good native Fortran and C compilers, and they made transputers much more appealing to scientific users. Because of financial problems, the transputer family of microprocessors did not proceed to faster models beyond the T800 as would normally have been the case. Other microprocessor families tend to double in performance every year or year and a half, and bring out a new version perhaps every other year. The successor to the T800 will not be available until 1992. Still, the transputer-based systems, especially those based on boards in PC systems, provided an easy and inexpensive way for people to experiment with small levels of parallelism in a distributed memory environment and to use them as development machines for programs that would later be run on bigger systems such as the Intel and NCUBE hypercubes.

2.4. Late 1980s

By the late 1980s, truly powerful parallel systems began to appear. The Meiko system at Edinburgh University is an example of such systems. By 1989, that computer had 400 T800s [21]. The system was being used for a number of traditional scientific computations in physics, chemistry, engineering, and so on [20]. The system software for transputer-based systems had evolved to resemble the message-passing system software available on hypercubes. Although the transputer's two-dimensional mesh connection is in principle less efficient than hypercube connections, for systems of a typical size (only a few hundred processors), the difference is not significant for most applications.

Three new SIMD fine-grain systems were introduced in the late 1980s: the CM-2, the MasPar, and a new version of the DAP. The CM-2 is a version of the original Connection Machine [22,23] that has been enhanced with optional Weitek floating-point units, one for each 32 single-bit processors, and optional large memory. In its largest configuration, such as is installed at Los Alamos National Laboratory, there are 64K single-bit processors, 2048 64-bit floating-point processors, and eight gigabytes of memory. The CM-2 has been measured at 5.2 gigaflops running the unlimited Linpack benchmark solving a linear system of order 26,624. It has attracted widespread attention both because of its extremely high performance and its relative ease of use [24–26]. For problems that are naturally data parallel, the CM Fortran language and compiler provide a relatively easy way to implement programs and get high performance. More will be said about the language situation in a separate section of this paper.

The MasPar and the DAP are smaller systems that are aimed more at excellent price performance than at very high levels of performance. The new DAP is front-ended by Sun workstations or VAXes. This makes it much more affordable and compatible with modern computing environments than when it required an ICL front end. DAPs have been built in ruggedized versions that can be put into vehicles, flown in airplanes, and used on ships, and have found many applications in signal processing and military applications. They are also used for general scientific work. The MasPar is the newest SIMD system. Its architecture constitutes a nice evolutionary approach of fine-grain SIMD combined with floating-point hardware.

Two hypercubes became available just as the decade ended. The second generation NCUBE, popularly known as the NCUBE-2, and the Intel iPSC/860. The NCUBE-2 can be configured with up to 8K nodes; that configuration would have a peak speed of 27 gigaflops. Each processor is still on a single chip along with all the communications channels, but it is about eight times faster than its predecessor—a little over three megaflops. Communication bandwidth is also a factor of eight higher. The result is a potentially very powerful system. The NCUBE-2 has a custom microprocessor that is instruction compatible with the first generation system. The largest system known to have been built to date is a 1024 system installed at Sandia National Laboratories. The unlimited size Linpack benchmark for this system yielded a performance of 1.91 gigaflops solving a linear system of order 21,376.

The second hypercube introduced in 1989 and first shipped to a customer (Oak Ridge) in January 1990, the Intel iPSC/860, has a peak speed of over seven gigaflops. While the communication speed between nodes is very low compared to the speed of the i860 processor, high speeds can be achieved for problems that do not require extensive communication. For example, the unlimited size Linpack benchmark on the largest configuration iPSC/860, 128 processors, gave a speed of 1.92 gigaflops when solving a system of order 8600.

The iPSC/860 features the Intel i860 microprocessor which has a peak speed of 60 megaflops full precision and 80 megaflops 32-bit precision. In mid-1991, a follow-on to Intel iPSC/860, the Intel Touchstone Delta System, reached a Linpack speed of 11.9 gigaflops for a system of order 25,000. This was done on 512 i860 nodes of the Delta System. This machine has a peak speed of 32 gigaflops and eight gigabytes of memory and is a one-of-a-kind system built for a consortium of institutions and installed at California Institute of Technology. The Delta uses a two-dimensional mesh connection scheme with mesh routing chips instead of a hypercube connection scheme. A successor to the iPSC/860 and the Touchstone Delta will be the Intel Touchstone Sigma System. The Sigma will have a connection scheme similar to that of the Delta. The Sigma will be a commercial product and is expected to be introduced in 1992. Its maximum configuration will be 2,048 nodes. It will use a second-generation version of the i860 microprocessor and is expected to have a peak speed of 150 gigaflops.

Other systems worth noting that became available in the late 1980s are in the parallel area, Myrias SPS-2 and the BBN TC2000, popularly known as the Butterfly 2. The Myrias SPS-2 was a large-grain MIMD system that featured system software that gave a shared-memory image to the user program, while the BBN TC2000 has hardware-supported shared memory.

The Myrias SPS-2 was a distributed-memory computer with nodes that used the Motorola 60820 processors with 68882 floating-point units. This choice of processor meant that even a system with 256 nodes had relatively low performance. The interesting part about the Myrias was the approach to system software and languages. In the area of programming languages, there was almost complete focus on one specific language construct added to Fortran, namely the PARDO, for parallel DO loops. Through this construct, one could in principle do data parallel computation with all the actual parallelization done by the compiler and operating system. In particular, the operating system would send data to the node where it was needed for processing. It would do so dynamically during the execution of a program so that, to a user, there was a shared-memory programming model using the PARDO. No explicit synchronization or other parallelization had to be done; data were sent to the nodes of the system as needed. Obviously, in some cases this approach might lead to thrashing, that is, of data repeatedly going back and forth among the nodes as it is referenced by different nodes. In some cases, however, computations have a pattern in which, after an initial flurry of transfer of data among the nodes, a substantial amount of computation is done on the data, and only after much computation is there a requirement to transfer the data again. Based on work done by Oliver McBryan at the University of Colorado Boulder, it did appear that the system software was fairly efficient at doing these data transfers and providing the programming model described above. However, very few systems were installed and the company is no longer in business.

The BBN TC2000 is another important system introduced in the late 1980s. Like the Myrias, it provides a shared-memory programming environment, but in this case the environment is supported by hardware. It uses a multistage switch based on crossbars that connect processor memory pairs to each other [6 (pp. 137–146), 27]. The BBN TC2000 uses Motorola 88000 Series processors. The ratio of speeds between access to data in cache, in the memory local to a processor, and in some other processor's memory, is one, three and seven approximately. Therefore, there is a noticeable penalty for using another processor's memory, but it is not a huge penalty. While few large configurations of this system have been sold, two are in highly active and visible places; namely, Argonne National Laboratory and Lawrence Livermore National Laboratory. Argonne has a 45-processor system and Livermore a 126-processor system. The architecture is scalable to 500-plus processors, although none has been built of that size. Each processor can have a substantial amount of memory, and the operating system environment is reasonably good. Therefore, this system is one of the few commercial shared-memory MIMD computers that can scale to large numbers of nodes. As this article went to press, the BBN Corporation announced the termination of its parallel computer activities.

Finally, the vector computers continued to become faster and to have more processors. The CRAY Y-MP can have up to eight processors and there are a number of installations with that configuration. A few people have even used the Y-MP as an eight-processor parallel computer and obtained good speeds. The peak speed of the system is over 2.6 gigaflops. There are configurations with up to a gigabyte of memory, which is a significant amount for CRAY systems. The cycle speed is six nanoseconds, about half of that of the original CRAY 1.

Control Data marketed and sold a few of the ETA-10s. These also are vector oriented systems with multiple processors and a large global memory supplemented by a local memory at each processor. As the name implies, the peak speed of a full configuration ETA-10 was 10 gigaflops with each of the eight processors having a peak speed of about 1.25 gigaflops.

By the late 1980s, several highly parallel systems were able to achieve high levels of performance—the Connection Machine Model CM-2, the Intel iPSC/860, the NCUBE-2, and, early in the decade of the 1990s, the Intel Touchstone Delta System. The peak speeds of these systems are quite high and, at least for some applications, the speeds achieved are also high, exceeding those achieved on vector supercomputers. As noted above, the currently fastest CRAY system is a CRAY Y-MP with eight processors, a peak speed of 2.6 gigaflops, and a maximum speed observed for applications of two gigaflops. In contrast, the Connection Machine Model CM-2 has achieved over five gigaflops for some real applications [28]. There are some new Japanese vector supercomputers with a small number of processors, but a large number of instruction pipelines, that have peak speeds of over 20 gigaflops. The NEC SX-3/12 has achieved 4.2 gigaflops on the unlimited Linpack benchmark. However, little performance data is available on these systems since they are very new and are currently only installed in Japan.

In summary, the 1980s saw an incredible level of activity in parallel computing, much greater than most people would have predicted. Even those projects that in a sense failed;

that is they were not commercially successful or, in the case of research projects, failed to produce an interesting prototype in a timely fashion, even those were useful in that they exposed many people to parallel computing at universities, at computer vendors, and at commercial companies such as Xerox, DuPont, General Motors, United Technologies, many aerospace companies, and oil companies.

3. AN ASSESSMENT OF HARDWARE PROGRESS

There are some interesting trends in the field of large-scale computing as they evolved in the 1980s. For example, six companies produced new conventional vector oriented supercomputing supercomputers in the 1980s: Cray, ETA/CDC, Fujitsu, Hitachi, IBM, and NEC. The number of companies that produced new parallel high-performance computers in the 1980s is much greater, at least 20. Included in this list are Intel SSD, BBN, NCUBE, FPS, Denelcor, Thinking Machines, MasPar, Saxpy, Multiflow, DAP, CHoPP, Astronautics, IBM, Evans and Sutherland, Ametek, Meiko, Suprenum, Myrias, Cydrome, and others. Is the number of companies that produced parallel computers so much greater because less capital investment is required to develop a new parallel supercomputer than a new vector one, or is it that parallel computer companies have neglected major items like I/O, good system software, and reliability? If the latter is the case, then the real price performance of parallel computers is not yet known.

Europe has had substantial impact on parallel computing. Whereas in the case of vector supercomputing Europe has had essentially no impact, in the case of parallel computing the DAP, the Transputer, various Esprit projects and the Manchester Dataflow Machine, have all had substantial impact, worldwide, not only in England or in Europe [29]. The Suprenum project in Germany and the APE project in Italy can also be counted among the leading European efforts.

To date, parallel computers have been most successful in mid-range performance rather than at the top end. In other words, there are many VAX and Convex killers, but not many CRAY killers. This is changing in the early 1990s, but throughout the 1980s the top vector supercomputers could not be surpassed by parallel machines.

There are some additional parallel computers in the wings, about to emerge in the early 1990s. Among these are Kendall Square, Intel's iWARP, Motorola's Monsoon, and Tera. All of these are MIMD systems with the Monsoon being a dataflow computer, following a design by Arvind at MIT. In fact, the Monsoon is a joint project between Motorola and MIT. Kendall Square and Tera are shared-memory MIMD systems with reportedly very high levels of both scalability and absolute performance. The iWARP is a distributed-memory MIMD system, but will have extremely high performance communications between the processing nodes.

While most of the commercially successful parallel computer companies have had products in the mid-range of performance, there are now a number of machines that can compete at the very top end of performance. We are able to get gigaflops now on some applications on some computers. In almost all cases, to get a gigaflop or more, more than one processor is used. Systems that can achieve over a gigaflop include the CRAY Y-MP, the CRAY 2, the ETA-10, the six- and twelve-processor IBM 3090s, Hitachi S820/80, the NEC SX2 and SX3, the Fujitsu VP1400 and VP2600. The latter four machines, all Japanese vector supercomputers, are uniprocessor (except for the NEC SX3), but have multiple instruction pipelines for each processor, in some cases, many such pipelines.

If we define hypothetical one-gigaflop and five-gigaflop clubs that can be joined only by computer systems that have reached one- or five-gigaflop performance in some real application, we see an interesting difference in the composition of the membership of those clubs. At the end of the decade of the 1980s, the one-gigaflop club would include CRAY Y-MP, CRAY 2, NEC SX2, Fujitsu VP1400, Hitachi S820/80, IBM 3090J-600 Tandem, the Intel iPSC/860, and the Connection Machine Model 2. Notice that only the last two systems are massively parallel; all others are moderately parallel or, in some cases, uniprocessors. As of mid-1991, the NEC SX3 and the NCUBE-2 would certainly join that list as well. However, the five-gigaflop club in the 1980s would include only the Connection Machine Model CM-2. By mid-1991, the Intel Touchstone Delta System could join it, as could the NEC SX3. The latter has four processors. So in the five-gigaflop club, the membership is quite small to date, but more massively parallel systems than conventional vector supercomputers belong to it. It is true that there are others that could be in the one- or five-gigaflop clubs if big enough configurations were built. The NCUBE 2 with the maximum number of processors, 8192, has a 27-gigaflop peak speed. Surely there are applications on which over five gigaflops would be reached with a large enough NCUBE 2, one with either 4096 or 8192 processors.

An obvious prediction one could make is that the 10-gigaflop club will be populated primarily by massively parallel computers, at least in the early 1990s.

Although there have been many computer companies involved in parallel and high-performance computing products in the 1980s, it is the case that many have already gone out of business as well. While one normally worries about whether parallel computer companies can stay in business, perhaps the situation now is that it is unclear whether high-performance computers in general, regardless of architecture, are commercially viable. After all, ETA is now out of business and neither of the two Cray companies, Cray Computer Company and Cray Research, are considered to be terribly healthy financially at present.

There is a big industry in parallel computers compared to 1980. In 1980, the only commercial products were the Denelcor HEP, the ICL DAP, and the Goodyear MPP. Some of the commercial parallel computer companies are doing well. Sequent and Teradata are considered to be healthy financially, and both have a customer base that is business oriented as opposed to scientific and engineering oriented. Sequent, for example, has over 6000 systems installed. Alliant and Convex also seem to be healthy financially at present, in their minisupercomputer niche; they each have installed several hundred systems. Thinking Machines also appears to be successful. For others of the current survivors, it is not clear how long they will stay in business.

Many companies have gone out of business or have withdrawn parallel product lines, including Cydrome, Multiflow, Denelcor, FPS, Evans and Sutherland, Saxpy, CHoPP, SCS, American Supercomputer, and Astronautics. Still, many computer companies remain in the parallel computer business. It may be that the overall appetite for computing in society as a whole is growing enough for more companies to stay in business than was the case for traditional supercomputer companies.

4. TRENDS IN ARCHITECTURES

At the beginning of the 1980s, scalability was a prime concern. Apart from a few experts in architecture, most people were not certain that it would be possible to build computer systems that would scale to large numbers of processors and very high performance. Now, the scalability of several different architectures is assured. Many such machines are operational. This is a major breakthrough that occurred in the 1980s. In the early to mid-1980s, people were also preoccupied with the significance of many architectural details. One issue of this type that is still actively investigated is hypercube versus mesh connection schemes for distributed-memory computers. In general, however, people have come to realize that it is the major architectural features that matter the most, for example, shared versus distributed memory. In the latter case, the shared-memory programming model is still being sought; design of hardware and software to provide it is still an area of intense activity. Note that it is the shared-memory programming model that many people try to provide as opposed to providing a physical shared-memory architecture. The experience gained through building IBM's RP3 and BBN TC2000 indicates that large, multi-stage processor memory networks are difficult and expensive to build. On the other hand, limited experience on the Myrias SPS-2 indicated that software can do a reasonable job of providing a shared-memory model on a distributed-memory architecture. New systems that will be introduced in the early 1990s, such as Tera and Kendall Square, will address these issues as well. In some cases, cluster architectures are being tried, that is, architectures that combine groups of small numbers of shared-memory processors that are linked by communications channels such as is the case for distributed-memory systems. Multicomputers with nodes with four or eight processors per board which share memory are being contemplated. A future Intel product is likely to have this configuration with each of the nodes with four or eight processors on each board being connected through a mesh connection scheme. There are also more elaborate cluster architectures, such as the Cedar architecture from the University of Illinois [30], which is a research product, not a commercial system, however.

So, shared versus distributed memory is one of the architectural features that is still under active study and debate. A second one is the issue of SIMD versus MIMD. The Connection Machine Model 2 made this an interesting question because it demonstrated high performance and good price performance coupled with significant ease of use. The new version of the DAP and the MasPar also contribute to making the study of SIMD versus MIMD an important one. Geoffrey Fox [31] has estimated that 50% to 70% of scientific computations are well suited to SIMD, and this estimate has fueled the debate about which is the better architecture and whether one will become dominant over the other. It is not clear that one must become dominant over the other. Perhaps both SIMD and MIMD architectures will find their niche and both will survive and be well represented through commercial products. It is, however, likely that the greater flexibility of the MIMD systems will give them the edge.

While the performance of a massively parallel machines is finally coming up to expectations, there are features that still need attention. These include the balance between computation and communication speed, or between computation and memory latency for other shared-memory machines, which is still not good in many cases. Ratios have not gotten better over the last few years. For example, the Intel iPSC/860 has a ratio of communication time to calculation time that is extremely high—measured in the hundreds. The latency or startup time for communication or for memory access is still very high. In the early 80s, the Denelcor HEP had elaborate latency-hiding hardware. Perhaps future systems will as well. In the meantime, the latency is quite high. A third area that needs attention is input/output. More of the parallel systems are planning to have, or already have, HIPPI interfaces—800 megabit per second interfaces. However, even these are not likely to be fast enough, and in any case, the actual speed achieved is by no means 800 megabits a second. Finally, host systems (for those computers that require an external host) still tend to be much too slow for the machines that they serve. In some cases, they are unable to support enough disk space for a true supercomputer. So all four of these features still require much more attention in terms of commercial products for massively parallel architectures.

Special-purpose computers are appealing and, in areas such as image processing and signal processing, have been quite successful. In general scientific areas, QCD computers are also apparently successful. The Caltech hypercube, incidentally, started out with QCD as its major target application so in a sense it was intended to be a QCD machine; of course, it turned out to be much more general-purpose than QCD. The Columbia University QCD machine has achieved six gigaflops. The IBM GF11, also designed for QCD, has run at over five gigaflops; and there are plans in Italy for the APE-100 which, in its 1991 configuration, is expected to reach six gigaflops but grow to a 200-gigaflop level in 1993. For other scientific applications, special-purpose computers have not yet proved to be effective.

4.1. Hardware Hall of Fame for the 1980s

The author's candidates for machines that should be in the Hardware Hall of Fame for machines that were basically produced in the 1980s, are the following five systems. The first is the Cosmic Cube from Caltech. It showed that one could design, build, and use parallel systems quickly. It was used for applications from the very beginning and it inspired many commercial products, perhaps more than any other design. The second system would be the Sequent. It was the first effective VAX killer, for VAXes running Unix that is. It was very solid and much cheaper, and was a commercial success. It provided a good environment for learning to do parallel programming. The third would be not so much a system, but the Transputer or systems based on transputers. The transputers gave power to the masses in the sense that a few could be put on a single board and installed in PCs or workstations. They were designed for use in multicomputers, have low latency for communications, and thus represent a major breakthrough. The fourth system I would vote to put in the Hardware Hall of Fame would be the NCUBE. It was the first computer to have a 1024-node MIMD system, and it was used by Sandia National Laboratories at Albuquerque to show, convincingly, that the 1000-node 'barrier' presented by Amdahl's law does not exist. That is, it was used to show speed-ups of over 1000 on a 1024-node system for several small but real scientific applications. Finally, the CM-2 should be voted in because it was the first massively parallel machine to beat convincingly vector supercomputers, such as the CRAYs, and because it proved to be relatively easy to use for data parallel applications and thus helped to do away with the myth that massively parallel computers are very difficult or almost impossible to use.

The communities of people who used shared-memory and distributed-memory parallel computer architectures have historically been separate and have had little appreciation for each other. No significant progress has been made towards narrowing the gap between those two communities. The programming model that each has used has been different, and the implementation issues, in terms of getting good algorithmic performance, have also tended to be different, such as, emphasis on very cheap synchronization, on locking of sections of code in shared-memory environments versus very fast and low latency communications in the distributed-memory implementations. However, as massively parallel computers of both kinds evolve, those issues will become more similar. In addition, languages like Fortran 90 [32] may also tend to blur the difference from the user's standpoint. One reference out of many in this field, for an excellent tutorial and survey of parallel computer architectures, can be found in the February 1990 *IEEE Computer Magazine* in an article by Ralph Duncan.

5. SOFTWARE

A gross generalization can be made that there is good software on low and medium performance systems (uninteresting to those who are preoccupied with the highest performance levels) such as Alliant, Sequent, Encore, Myrias, and Multiflow systems, while there is poor quality software in the highest performance systems. In addition, there is little or no software aimed at managing the system and providing a service to a diverse user community. There is typically no software that provides information on who uses the system and how much, that is, accounting and reporting software. Batch schedulers are typically not available. Controls for limiting the amount of time interactive users can take on the system at any one time also are missing. Ways of managing the on-line disks are non-existent. In short, the system software provided with the high-performance parallel computers is at best that which would be suitable for systems that would be used by a single person or a small, tightly knit group of people.

5.1. Languages and compilers

In contrast, in the area of computer languages and compilers for those languages for parallel machines, there has been a significant amount of progress, especially in the late 1980s, for example [33]. In February of 1984, the Argonne Workshop on Programming the Next Generation of Supercomputers was held in Albuquerque, New Mexico [34]. It addressed topics such as

- data versus control synchronization;
- are minor extensions to existing languages, such as C and Fortran, adequate or should new languages be designed and adopted;
- should some minimal parallel-oriented capabilities be added to Fortran now (even then, in early 1984, it was thought that Fortran 8X was about to be frozen into a standard).

Many people came to the workshop and showed high levels of interest, including leading computer vendors, but not very much happened as a result of the workshop in terms of real actions by compiler writers or standards-making groups. By the late 1980s, the situation had changed. Now the Parallel Computing Forum is healthy and well attended by vendor representatives. The Parallel Computing Forum was formed to develop a shared-memory multiprocessor model for parallel processing and to establish language standards for that model beginning with Fortran and C. In addition, the ANSI Standards Committee X3 formed a new technical committee, X3H5, named Parallel Processing Constructs for High Level Programming Languages. This technical committee will work on a model based upon standard practice in shared-memory parallel processing. Extensions for message passing based parallel processing are outside the scope of the model under consideration at this time. The first meeting of X3H5 was held on 23 March, 1990.

It appears that, finally, there are efforts under way to standardize language issues for parallel computing, at least for certain programming models. In the meantime, there has been progress in compilers. Compilers provided with Alliant computers, and the ones provided on Multiflow machines before it went out of business, can be quite good at producing efficient code for each processor and relatively good at automatically parallelizing. On the other hand, compilers for the processors that are used on multicomputers generally produce code for the floating-point hardware that does not use the processor hardware efficiently. Typically, these compilers do not perform even the standard optimizations that have nothing to do with fancy instruction scheduling, and they do not do any automatic parallelization for the distributed-memory computers either. While automatic parallelization for distributed-memory, as well as shared-memory systems, is a difficult task, and it is clear that it will be a few more years before good compilers exist for that task, it is a shame that so little effort is typically invested in producing efficient code for single processors. There are known compilation techniques that would provide a much greater percentage of the peak speed on commonly used microprocessors than is currently produced by the existing compilers.

As for languages, despite much work and interest in new languages, in most cases people still use Fortran or C with minor additions or calls to system subroutines. The language known as Connection Machine Fortran or CM-Fortran is an interesting exception. It is, of course, based largely on the array extensions of Fortran 90, but is not identical to that. One might note that CM-Fortran array extensions are also remarkably similar to those defined in the Department of Energy Language Working Group Fortran effort of the early 1980s [35]. Fortran 90 itself was influenced by the LWG Fortran; in the early and mid-1980s, there were regular and frequent interactions between the DOE Language Working Group and the Fortran Standards Committee. A recent variant of Fortran 90 designed for distributed-memory systems is Fortran 90D [36]. As the new decade begins, it appears that the most activity is on variants of Fortran for scientific and engineering computing on massively parallel machines of all architectures.

Other languages that have seen some use include Linda [37,38] and Strand [39], but relatively few applications have been implemented in those languages and one does not detect a change in that situation. A more recent language effort is Program Composition Notation (PCN) that is being developed at the Center for Research on Parallel Computation (an NSF Science and Technology Center) [40]. PCN is a parallel programming language in its own right, but additionally has the feature that one can take existing Fortran and C functions and subprograms and use them through PCN as part of a PCN parallel program. PCN is a very new language and it is too early to tell to what extent it will become popular and widely used. PCN is in some ways similar to Strand which is a dataflow-oriented logic language in the flavor of Prolog.

5.2. Tools

Substantial efforts have been put into developing tools that facilitate parallel programming, both in shared-memory and distributed-memory systems, e.g., [41–43].

For shared-memory systems, for example, there is SCHEDULE [44], MONMACS, and FORCE. MONMACS and FORCE both provide higher-level parallel programming constructs such as barrier synchronization and DO ALL that are useful for shared-memory environments. SCHEDULE provides a graphical interface to producing functionally decomposed programs for shared-memory systems. With SCHEDULE, one specifies a tree of calls to subroutines and SCHEDULE facilitates and partially automates the creation of Fortran or C programs (augmented by appropriate system calls) that implement the call graphs. For distributed-memory environments, there are also several libraries or small operating systems that provide extensions to Fortran and C for programming on such architectures. A subset of MONMACS falls into that camp. More widely used systems in this area include Cosmic Environment Reactive Kernel [45], Express [46], and PICL [42]. These systems provide message-passing routines in some cases, including those that do global operations on data such as Broadcast. They may also provide facilities for measuring performance or collecting data about message traffic, CPU utilization, and so on. Some debugging capabilities may also be provided. These are all general-purpose tools and programming environments, and had been used for a wide variety of applications, chiefly scientific and engineering, but also non-numerical ones.

In addition, there are many tools that are domain-specific in some sense. Examples of these would be the Distributed Irregular Mesh Environment (DIME) by Roy Williams [47,48] and the ELLPACK partial differential equation solver developed by John Rice and his research group at Purdue. DIME is a programming environment for calculations with irregular meshes; it provides adaptive mesh refinement and dynamic load balancing. There are also some general-purpose tools and programming systems, such as Sisal from Livermore (which provides a dataflow-oriented language capability) and Parti [49–51] (which facilitates, for example, array mappings on distributed memory machines).

None of the general-purpose tools has emerged as a clear leader. Perhaps there is still a need for more research and experimentation with such systems.

6. RESEARCH ON PARALLEL COMPUTING

The level of activity in research related to parallel computing has grown significantly during the 1980s. For example, the number of papers submitted to journals, the number of books, and even the number of journals themselves, has grown tremendously during the decade. One specific example that illustrates this trend is the number of papers submitted to the annual International Conference on Parallel Processing. In 1980, 170 papers were submitted to ICPP; in 1983, the number was 240; in 1986, 400; in 1988, 590.

Another measure of research activity is the number of computing facilities that serve as experimental facilities for research on parallel computing. Facilities such as the Argonne Advanced Computing Research Facility, which was the first of its kind, now number at least in the dozens and perhaps in the hundreds worldwide. Given that each such facility is used by tens to hundreds of people, one can see that many researchers have turned their attention to parallel computing issues.

There has been more progress than most people expected in the area of algorithms. Parallel algorithms have been developed for many of the fundamental computations that arise in science and engineering. Most of these algorithms are not really new algorithms, but rather are modified versions of sequential algorithms. On the other hand, it is not clear how many of those algorithms will scale to efficient utilization of an arbitrarily large number of processors. Especially those that work on shared-memory machines may have been executed only on a fairly small number of processors. In addition, although the algorithms have been developed and implemented for many of the fundamental computations, libraries of mathematical software for parallel machines are still not available for almost all parallel computers. One exception would be a small but good beginning by Thinking Machines Corporation in a subroutine library for its Connection Machines.

It appears that parallel computing has provided a motivation for much more interaction between computer science research and the field of supercomputing or high-performance computing. When supercomputing was done exclusively on vector computers, very few computer scientists were interested in contributing to improving the supercomputing environment whether in hardware architecture or compilers. Parallel computers, however, provide something that is interesting to computer scientists and that can benefit very much from methods that computer scientists have been developing. It may be that in the 1990s there will finally be closer working relationships between computer science research efforts and computational scientists, i.e., people who do large-scale computations on high-performance machines for science and engineering applications. Certainly, the computer science community has been involved in parallel computing for a long time. ICPP, for example, has been held yearly for 20 consecutive years. Research areas such as graph theory, compiler technology, networking technology, parallel algorithms and implementations, new languages for parallel computers, and visualization tools all are of interest to computer scientists and extremely useful for parallel computers. The NSF Center for Research on Parallel Computation led by Ken Kennedy of Rice University also provides evidence that some computer scientists are interested in the needs of scientific users. There is strong coupling between the applications scientists and the computer scientists in the research carried out by that center. Los Alamos and Lawrence Livermore National Laboratories have each been interested in functional programming and dataflow architectures for their long-term potential of making parallel computing easier. Even those branches of computer science research may affect real scientific users in the long run.

7. PERFORMANCE MEASUREMENT AND CHARACTERIZATION

The most important single development in this area in the 1980s was the availability of the CRAY X-MP hardware monitor. This hardware monitor made it possible to obtain exact counts on the number of operations done during program execution, such as the number of floating-point instructions executed. In this way, it was possible for a user to measure precisely on any run (for the first time in a widely used scientific computer) the rate of floating-point operations achieved. The measurements are done by hardware and do not add a significant overhead to the execution. Most previous hardware monitors required special set-up to gather the data.

One reason this development was important is that it dispelled myths that existed about the speed of CRAYs. Once one could measure the actual megaflop rate of programs, it was seen that most programs were getting around 10% of the peak speed of the CRAYs. Second, it made megaflops an accepted single number for use in measuring the performance for scientific and engineering programs. While some people feel that this is a bad measurement, it does have many advantages. It provides a speed measurement that is independent of the application or the size of a given problem that is being solved for a particular program. It factors out non-useful work, such as looping instructions, and provides a measurement for what are typically the items of interest, namely, the arithmetic operations that are carried out. Since other computers in general do not have hardware monitors of this type, a common practice nowadays is to run a program on a CRAY X-MP or CRAY Y-MP, measure the megaflop rate, and then use that rate to convert timings on other machines into megaflop rates. An example of the extent to which the flop rate has become an accepted way of measuring performance is that the recent High Performance Computing Initiative in the United States is also known as the teraflop initiative. It sets as a goal the development of systems able to sustain teraflop per second performance on real applications by the end of the 1990s.

Measurement of performance became a much more important and active area during the 1980s. Certainly, the famous Linpack performance measurements [52] have become ubiquitous and frequently featured on the front page of popular publications such as the *Wall Street Journal* and the *New York Times*. Until recently, however, Linpack was oriented to measurement of sequential programs only.

During the 1980s, interest in performance analysis increased, partly because, as architectures became more complicated, it was recognized how important it would be to be able to predict the performance of new systems before they were built [53]. At the same time, it was more important to measure and characterize performance on existing systems because the ratio of peak to actual performance could now be several orders of magnitude. However, performance analysis was made more difficult by the large number of variables that can effect performance in highly parallel systems. There was also an increased awareness of the difficulty of avoiding biases in measuring performance and of considering properly all the factors that affect performance. There were and are many projects aimed at getting a better understanding of performance measurement, carrying out performance measurements on many different systems, and even attempting to characterize performance. Some specific projects worth mentioning include the PERFECT Club [54] conceived and led by David Kuck at the University of Illinois at Urbana, which is oriented largely at measuring the performance of large application programs on high-performance systems. There is a strong emphasis towards vector-oriented computers, but some of the work is also done on parallel systems. The long-range goals of Perfect include building up an understanding of fundamental computations that are used in different application fields, for example, solving sparse linear systems in fields such as chemical engineering and electronic circuit design, and a large database of performance information both at the entire application level and at the kernel level for many different computers. A long-range goal is to characterize the variables and factors that affect performance on different computer architectures for different application classes. The Perfect Club includes over a dozen institutions who are active in its work at the present.

In the late 1980s, from approximately 1987 onwards, there were several projects initiated aimed specifically in measuring the performance of parallel computers. At Caltech, a project began in 1987 [55] to take approximately six university research programs that had been used in real applications on parallel computers at Caltech and to measure their performance on a variety of computers including the leading shared-memory parallel computers and distributed-memory systems. Some measurements were also carried out on the Connection Machine CM-2. As a reference point, the same programs were also run on leading supercomputer systems, chiefly, the CRAY X-MP,

CRAY-2, and the ETA-10. A major objective of that project was to gain very quickly an understanding of how the commercial parallel computers of the time compared in overall performance for real applications with the leading supercomputer systems of the same vintage. Scalability issues were also addressed in that problems of different sizes were run on different numbers of processors of the various systems. The largest MIMD system used in this study, in terms of number of processors, was the first-generation NCUBE at Caltech with 512 processors. The applications included some that parallelize quite well, such as QCD, and ones that rely heavily on solution of linear systems of equations and on fast Fourier transforms, as well as some applications that did not parallelize terribly well, such as missile tracking. The project also gained insight on the ease or difficulty of use of the various computer systems. Anthony Hey, at Southampton University, England, started a similar effort called Genesis a year or two later [56,57]. It also has gathered information on the performance of parallel computers for a number of application programs. NASA Ames has put together a collection of benchmark programs of particular interest in the aerodynamics field. Some are oriented at measuring vectorization while others are also oriented towards measurement of parallel computer performance. Oak Ridge [58] has measured performance primarily on distributed-memory systems and largely in the area of linear algebra, and there are many more such efforts, e.g. [59–61]. For example, people working in specific disciplines who have reasonably portable programs have, as a by-product of porting their applications from one system to another, measured the performance of, typically, a reasonably simple problem in their discipline area on many different systems. An example of this is Viktor Decyk's work [62,63] in plasma physics; he has measured the performance of a one-dimensional plasma physics code on approximately 40 computers, including several parallel computer systems. Hardware measurement projects are still rare, but there are some efforts including a small one at the National Institute of Science and Technology (the former National Bureau of Standards) and a custom hardware measurement add-on for an Intel iPSC/2 at the University of Wisconsin Madison.

Finally, one indication of the level of interest in the field of performance measurement is that there are now several prizes given for achieving certain levels of performance. One of the first was the Alan Karp prize, which was a one-time prize given for the first program to achieve a speed-up of 200 on a real application on a real parallel computer. Gordon Bell also established what is now a series of prizes for achievements, such as best price performance, absolute top speed, and parallelism. For example, in a paper also presented at the Capri conference, there is a description of work by Myczkowski which won the 1990 Gordon Bell prize for absolute top speed, achieving 5.6 gigaflops on the Connection Machine CM-2.

7.1. Performance characterization

A number of concepts have proved to be useful for characterizing performance of computer systems. The concept of speed-up and its related concept of efficiency, while it was first enunciated in the 1970s, became well-known in the 1980s. Amdahl's Law [17], formulated in 1967, has also proved to be a useful and widely used formula that clearly shows some of the fundamental issues in both vector computing and parallel computing. Hockney has introduced additional useful quantities, such as $n_{1/2}$ and r_∞, that are useful in describing the performance of computer systems. Fox's analyses based on t_{comm} and t_{calc} proved to be fundamental and of practical importance as well [64]. By simply considering the ratio of the time it takes for a parallel computer system single processor to perform arithmetic computations and the time it takes to transfer one word of information from one node of a distributed-memory system to another, one obtains an excellent predictor of the efficiency that can be obtained on distributed memory systems. Different formulas have to be used for different types of computations, but with this key ratio one can make a good prediction of the efficiency that can be achieved on such systems.

Another concept that has proved to be very relevant to the massively parallel computer architectures is something I will refer to as Moler's Law which was, as far as I know, first formulated by Cleve Moler and was later popularized by John Gustafson [16] and his group at Sandia National Laboratories Albuquerque. Basically, this law involves a memory-scaled speed-up, that is the speed-up that one achieves by increasing the size of the problem as one increases the number of processors so that maximum use is made of memory at all times. This is in contrast to running a fixed-size problem on varying numbers of processors of a parallel computer. This approach makes sense because presumably one uses a massively parallel system because one has a very large problem. To measure the performance of a massively parallel system on a small problem is in a sense inappropriate because the problem was too small for the system. Some people do not like memory-scaled speed-up because it does not fit their applications (they may not be big enough to warrant use of massively parallel systems) or because they feel it is unreasonably restrictive to require that their applications must have large grain size to get good performance. There is some follow-on work of this general type in the context of the Perfect Club that is being done by George Cybenko and others at the Center for Supercomputer Research and Development (CSRD) at the University of Illinois at Urbana.

In summary, there are only a few key concepts developed so far in the area of performance characterization, but these concepts are useful for understanding and presenting the performance that is measured on various systems, and in some cases, the concepts can also be used to predict performance of computer systems.

8. SUMMARY

There was remarkable progress during the 1980s in most areas related to high-performance computing in general, and parallel computing in particular. There are now substantial numbers of people who use parallel computers to get real applications work done, in addition to many people who have developed and are developing new algorithms, new operating systems, new languages, and new programming paradigms and software tools for massively parallel and other high-performance computer systems. It was during this decade, especially in the latter half of the decade, that there was a very quick transition towards identifying high-performance computing strongly with massively parallel computing. In the early part of the decade, only large, vector-oriented systems were used for high-performance computing. By the end of the decade, while most such work was still being done on vector systems, some of the leading-edge work was already being done on parallel systems. This includes work at universities and research laboratories, as well as in industrial applications. By the end of the decade, oil companies, brokerage companies on Wall Street, and database users were all taking advantage of parallelism, in addition to the traditional scientific and engineering fields.

There is still a frustrating phenomenon of neglect of certain areas in the design of parallel computer systems, including ratios of internal computational speed versus input and output speed, and speed of communication between the processors in distributed-memory systems. Latency for both I/O and communication is still very high. Compilers are often still crude. Operating systems still lack stability and even the most fundamental system management tools. Nevertheless, much progress was made.

By the end of the 1980s, higher speeds than on any sequential computer were indeed achieved on the parallel computer systems, and this was done for a few real applications. In a few cases, the parallel systems even proved to be cheaper, that is, more cost-effective than sequential computers of equivalent power—this despite a truly dramatic increase in performance of sequential microprocessors, especially floating-point units, in the late part of the 1980s. So, both key objectives of parallel computing—the highest achievable speed and more cost-effective performance—were achieved and demonstrated in the 1980s.

REFERENCES

1. R. W. Hockney and C. R. Jesshope, *Parallel Computers*, Adam Hilger, Bristol, UK, 1981.
2. C. R. Jesshope and R. W. Hockney, 'The DAP Approach', in *Infotech State of the Art Report: Supercomputers*, Vol. 2, pp. 311–329, Infotech Intl. Ltd, Maidenhead, UK, 1979.
3. D. J. Wallace, 'Numerical simulation on the ICL distributed array processor', *Phys. Rep.*, **103**, 191 (1984).
4. D. J. Wallace, 'Scientific computation on SIMD and MIMD machines', invited talk at Royal Society Discussion, Edinburgh, preprint 87/429, 1987.
5. K. E. Batcher, 'MPP: A high speed image processor', in *Algorithmically Specialized Parallel Computers*, Academic Press, New York, 1985.
6. W. J. Karplus (ed.), *Proceedings of the Third Conference on Multiprocessors and Array Processors, Simulation Series*, Vol. 18/2, The Society for Computer Simulation, San Diego, 1987.
7. *Proceedings of the Workshop on Parallel Processing using the Heterogeneous Element Processor*, S. Lakshmivarahan (ed.), The University of Oklahoma, 1985.
8. C. L. Seitz, 'The Cosmic Cube', *Communications of the ACM*, **28**, 22 (1985).
9. C. L. Seitz, W. C. Athas, C. M. Flaig, A. J. Martin, J. Seizovic, C. S. Steele and W.-K. Su, 'The architecture and programming of the Ametek Series 2010 multicomputer', in G. C. Fox (ed.), *Proceedings of the Third Conference on Hypercube Concurrent Computers and Applications*, Vol. 1, pp. 33–36, ACM Press, New York, 1988.
10. A. Gottlieb, 'An overview of the NYU ultracomputer project', in *Experimental Parallel Computing Architectures*, J. J. Dongarra (ed.), North-Holland, Amsterdam, 1987.
11. G. F. Pfister *et al.*, 'The IBM research parallel processor prototype (RP3): introduction and architecture', in *IEEE 1985 Conference on Parallel Processing*, 1985.
12. F. Darema, 'Applications environment for the IBM research parallel processor prototype, RP3', in *ICS 87, International Conference on Supercomputing*, C. Polychronoupolos (ed.), Springer-Verlag, New York, 1987.
13. J. T. Schwartz, 'Ultracomputers', *ACM TOPLAS*, **2**, 484 (1980).
14. J. Palmer, 'A VLSI parallel supercomputer', in *Hypercube Multiprocessors*, M. T. Heath (ed.), SIAM, Philadelphia, 1986, pp. 19–26.
15. NCUBE Corporation, *NCUBE User's Handbook*, Beaverton, Oregon, 1987.
16. J. L. Gustafson, G. R. Montry and R. E. Benner, 'Development of parallel methods 1024-processor hypercube', *SIAM Journal on Scientific and Statistical Computing*, **9**, 609–638 (1988).

17. G. M. Amdahl, 'Validity of the single approach to achieving large-scale computing capabilities', in *AFIPS Conference Proceedings 30*, AFIPS Press, Montvale, NJ, 1967, p. 483.
18. I. M. Barron, P. Cavill, D. May and P. Wilson, 'The Transputer', *Electronics*, **56**, 109 (1983).
19. A. J. G. Hey, 'Practical parallel processing with transputers', in G. C. Fox (ed.), *Proceedings of the Third Conference on Hypercube Concurrent Computers and Applications*, Vol. 1, pp. 115–121, ACM Press, New York, 1988.
20. J. Wexler (ed.), 'Developing transputer applications', in *Proceedings of the 11th Occam User Group Technical Meeting*, IOS, Amsterdam, 1989.
21. D. Wallace, K. Bowler and R. Kenway, 'The Edinburgh Concurrent Supercomputer: Project and applications', in *Proceedings of the Third International Conference on Supercomputing*, Vol. II, L. P. Kartashev and S. I. Kartashev (eds), International Supercomputing Institute, Inc., p. 200, 1988.
22. W. D. Hillis, *The Connection Machine*, MIT Press, Cambridge, Massachusetts, 1985.
23. W. D. Hillis, 'The Connection Machine', *Scientific American*, **256**, 108 (1987).
24. W. D. Hillis and G. Steele, 'Data parallel algorithms', *Communications of the ACM*, **29**, 1170 (1986).
25. W. D. Hillis and J. Barnes, 'Programming a high parallel computer', *Nature*, **326**, 27 (1987).
26. B. M. Boghosian, 'Computational physics on the Connection Machine: massive parallelism—a new paradigm', *Computers in Physics*, **4**, 14–33 (1990).
27. 'Butterfly Products Overview', BBN Advanced Computers, Inc., 10 Fawcett Street, Cambridge, Massachusetts, 1987.
28. R. G. Brickner and C. F. Baillie, 'Pure Gauge QCD on the Connection Machine', *International Journal of High Speed Computing*, **1**, 303–320 (1989).
29. I. S. Duff, 'Supercomputing in Europe—1987', in *Lecture Notes in Computer Science, Supercomputers*, Vol. 297, E. N. Houstis, T. S. Papatheodorou and C. D. Polychronoupolos (eds), Springer-Verlag, New York, 1987, pp. 1031–1041.
30. D. J. Kuck, E. S. Davidson, D. H. Lawrie and A. H. Sameh, 'Parallel supercomputing today and the Cedar approach', *Science*, **231**, 967 (1986).
31. G. C. Fox, 'What have we learned from using real parallel machines to solve real problems?', in *The Third Conference on Hypercube Concurrent Computers and Applications*, Vol. 2, 897–955, ACM Press, New York, California Institute of Technology Report C^3P-522, January 1988.
32. Min-You Wu and Geoffrey C. Fox, 'Compiling Fortran 90 programs for distributed memory MIMD parallel computers', Syracuse Center for Computational Science Technical Report SCCS-88, CRPC-TR91126, C3P-948b, 1991.
33. 'Fortran-Plus Language', Active Memory Technology, 16802 Aston Street, Suite 103, Irvine, California 92714, 1987.
34. 'Proceedings for the Argonne Workshop on Programming the Next Generation of Supercomputers', B. T. Smith, J. J. Dongarra and P. C. Messina (eds), Argonne National Laboratory, Technical Report ANL/MCS-TM-34, 1984.
35. C. Wetherell, 'Language Working Group FORTRAN Manual', Collaborative Technical Report FORT-82-1. Available from the National Technical Information Service, US Department of Commerce, 5285 Port Royal Road, Springfield, Virginia 22161.
36. G. C. Fox, S. Hiranandani, K. Kennedy, C. Koelbel, U. Kremer, C.-W. Tseng and M.-Y. Wu, 'Fortran D language specification', Rice Center for Research in Parallel Computation, CRPC-TR90079 Technical Report, SCCS-42, C3P-949, 1990.
37. D. Gelernter, 'Multiple tuple spaces in Linda', in *Proceedings of Parallel Architectures and Languages, Europe*, Vol. 2, Springer-Verlag, LNCS, 1989.
38. S. Ahuja, N. Carriero and D. Gelernter, 'Linda and friends', *Computer*, **19**, 26–34 (1986).
39. I. Foster and S. Taylor, 'Strand: New concepts in parallel programming', Prentice Hall, Englewood Cliffs, NJ, 1990.
40. K. Mani Chandy and S. Taylor, 'A primer for program composition notation', California Institute of Technology Technical Report, CRPC-TR90056, 1990.
41. L. Clarke and G. Wilson, 'Tiny: An efficient routing harness for the INMOS transputer', *Concurrency: Practice and Experience*, **3**, John Wiley, Chichester, 1991, pp. 221–245.
42. V. S. Sunderam, 'PVM: a framework for parallel distributed computing', *Concurrency: Practice and Experience*, **2**, 315–340 (1990).

43. R. A. Whiteside and J. S. Leichter, 'Using Linda for supercomputing on a local area network', in *Proceedings of Supercomputing '88*, IEEE Computer Society Press, Washington, 1988.
44. F. B. Hanson and D. C. Sorensen, 'The SCHEDULE parallel programming package with recycling job queues and iterated dependency graphs', *Concurrency: Practice and Experience*, **2**, 33–53 (1990).
45. C. L. Seitz, J. Seizovic and W.-K, Su, 'The C programmer's abbreviated guide to multicomputer programming', Caltech Computer Science Technical Report CS-TR-881-1, 1988.
46. ParaSoft, 'EXPRESS: a communication environment for parallel computers', 1988.
47. R. D. Williams, 'DIME: a programming environment for unstructured triangular meshes on a distributed-memory parallel processor', in *The Third Conference on Hypercube Concurrent Computers and Applications*, Vol. 2, pp. 1770–1787, ACM Press, New York, California Institute of Technology Report C^{3}P-502, January 1988.
48. R. D. Williams, 'Supersonic flow in parallel with an unstructured mesh', *Concurrency: Practice and Experience*, **1**, 51–62 (1989).
49. J. Saltz, R. Mirchandaney, R. Smith, D. Nicol and K. Crowley, 'The PARTY parallel runtime system', in *Proceedings of the SIAM Conference on Parallel Processing for Scientific Computing*, Society for Industrial and Applied Mathematics, Philadelphia, 1987.
50. J. Saltz, H. Berryman and J. Wu, 'Multiprocessor and runtime compilation', *Concurrency: Practice and Experience*, accepted for publication, 1991.
51. H. Berryman, J. Saltz and J. Scroggs, 'Execution time support for adaptive scientific algorithms on distributed memory machines', *Concurrency: Practice and Experience*, **3**, 159–178 (1991).
52. J. J. Dongarra, 'Performance evaluation of various computers using standard linear equations software in a Fortran environment', Argonne National Laboratory Technical Report, MCS-TM-23, 1988.
53. 'An agenda for improved evaluation of supercomputer performance', report to the National Academy of Sciences, National Academy Press, Washington, DC, 1986.
54. M. Berry, D. Chen, P. Koss, D. Kuck, S. Lo, Y. Pang, R. Roloff, A. Sameh, E. Clementi, S. Chin, D. Schneider, G. Fox, P. Messina, D. Walker, C. Hsiung, J. Schwarzmeier, K. Lue, S. Orszag, F. Seidl, O. Johnson, G. Swanson, R. Goodrum and J. Martin, 'The PERFECT Club Benchmarks: effective performance evaluation of supercomputers', *International Journal for Supercomputing Applications*, **3**, 5 (1989).
55. P. Messina, C. F. Baillie, E. W. Felten, P. G. Hipes, D. W. Walker, R. D. Williams, W. Pfeiffer, A. Alagar, A. Kamrath, R. H. Leary and J. Rogers, 'Benchmarking advanced architecture computers', *Concurrency: Practice and Experience*, **2**, 195–256 (1990).
56. A. J. G. Hey, 'Concurrent supercomputing in Europe', in *The Fifth Distributed Memory Computing Conference*, Vol. II, D. W. Walker and Q. F. Stout (eds), IEEE Computer Society Press, Washington, 1990, pp. 630–646.
57. C. J. Scott (ed.), 'GENESIS', Report of the state of the art and evaluation group, Southampton University, 1989.
58. T. H. Dunigan, 'Performance of the INTEL iPSC/860 hypercube', Oak Ridge National Laboratory Technical Report, ORNL/TM-11491, 1990.
59. R. K. Sato and P. N. Swarztrauber, 'Benchmarking the Connection Machine 2', in *Proceedings of Supercomputing '88*, Vol. I, IEEE Computer Society Press, Washington, 1988, p. 304.
60. D. C. Grunwald and D. A. Reed, 'Benchmarking hypercube hardware and software', *Hypercube Multiprocessors*, M. T. Heath (ed.), SIAM, Philadelphia, 1987.
61. O. A. McBryan, 'Connection Machine application performance', in *Proceedings of the Conference on Scientific Applications of the Connection Machine*, Horst D. Simon (ed.), World Scientific Publishing Co., Teaneck, NJ, 1989, p. 94.
62. V. K. Decyk, 'Revised benchmark timings with particle plasma simulation codes', University of California, Los Angeles Technical Report PPG-1111, 1987.
63. V. K. Decyk, 'Benchmark Timings with Particle Plasma Simulation Codes', *Supercomputer*, **27**, 33 (1988).
64. G. C. Fox, M. A. Johnson, G. A. Lyzenga, S. W. Otto, J. K. Salmon and D. W. Walker, *Solving Problems on Concurrent Processors*, Vol. I: *General Techniques and Regular Problems*, Prentice Hall, Englewood Cliffs, NJ, 1988.

CONCURRENCY: PRACTICE AND EXPERIENCE, VOL. 3(6), 525–539 (DECEMBER 1991)

ES-Kit: an object-oriented distributed system

ARUNODAYA CHATTERJEE, ARJUN KHANNA AND YING HUNG
Experimental Systems Lab
Microelectronics and Computer Technology Corporation (MCC)
Austin, TX, USA

SUMMARY

This paper describes the design, implementation, and performance of ES-Kit, a distributed object-oriented system being developed by the Experimental Systems Project at the Microelectronics and Computer Technology Corporation. The operating system consists of a kernel and a set of Public Service Objects which dynamically extend the functionality of the kernel by providing several traditional operating system services when required by application objects. Applications for the ES-Kit environment are written in GNU C++ and do not require additional language primitives for distributed execution. Initial performance results from a representative set of applications indicate that the object-oriented paradigm provides a powerful solution to distributed programming.

1. INTRODUCTION

ES-Kit is an open set of software and hardware building blocks that may be readily assembled to produce a heterogeneous, object-oriented, distributed system. A highly modular design approach makes it possible to rapidly prototype high-performance, experimental distributed environments. A uniform reference mechanism provides transparent communication and synchronization for a wide range of tightly and loosely coupled machines, relieving the programmer from worrying about specific architectural and machine-dependent details.

The availability and performance of hardware components have dramatically improved in recent years. Coupled with an ever-increasing demand for greater performance, the result has been a veritable explosion in the number of experimental architectures and systems being proposed and explored. During the development of new experiments and prototypes, significant portions of the research budget, both in terms of time and expense, are frequently consumed in creating an experimental environment, to the point that often the actual experiment itself becomes secondary to the development of the 'test frame'[1].

ES-Kit technologies provide a design framework within which researchers may design and conduct experiments without being overwhelmed by the details of an entire system's implementation. As a result, ES-Kit is expected to reduce the time and cost to conduct architectural experiments in a high-performance system environment. An essential characteristic of ES-Kit is the application of a distributed, object-oriented approach to system design, which has lead to the development of highly modular functional blocks that can be assembled to define a wide spectrum of hardware and software architectures.

Currently, ES-Kit runs on a the Motorola MC88000-based ES-Kit hardware, a network of Sun3 and Sparc workstations, the Motorola Delta Multicomputer, the Sequent Symmetry, and a network of MAC IIs running AUX. Several applications covering a wide

1040–3108/91/060525–15$07.50
©1991 by John Wiley & Sons, Ltd.

Received 23 October 1990
Accepted 20 August 1991

range of computational models have been developed which have been used to validate the design of the ES-Kit system, and to provide benchmarks for continued development.

Section 2 discusses the language support provided by the object-oriented paradigm. This section highlights language features which permit an essentially sequential language like C++ to efficiently support distributed execution *without* additional keywords or language constructs at the user level. Section 3 discusses the kernel and its major functions. The kernel is minimally defined (or 'under-specified'), allowing easy modification and experimentation. Section 4 introduces 'the other half'—traditional operating system services which are provided through Public Service Objects. This design encourages easy extension and alteration without loss of functionality or performance. Section 5 describes the programming environment for ES-Kit, and briefly touches on the performance of the kernel. In Section 6 we offer a discussion of the pros and cons of our approach to programming a distributed system. Section 7 concludes this paper.

2. OBJECT-ORIENTED LANGUAGE SUPPORT

The development of software for distributed systems is a complex task. One of the goals of the Experimental Systems Project was to provide an environment where some of the burdens of distributed program development could be lifted from the shoulders of the programmer. This in turn thrust forward two important requirements: a paradigm powerful enough to support the notions of concurrency and parallelism as natural behavior rather than as extensions of sequential uniprocessor environments, and a transparent interface for low-level messaging and synchronizing functions. The object-oriented paradigm plays a central role in meeting these two requirements.The object-oriented approach itself has been the subject of a fair amount of recent research, as attested to by several object-oriented systems[2], and more than 20 object-oriented languages developed over the last few years[3].

This section briefly discusses the important features of object-oriented programming that have been exploited by ES-Kit to develop a sound environment for distributed program development and execution. GNU C++[4,5] is an object-oriented language based on C, and has been used to implement a majority of the ES-Kit software. It will be used to illustrate some specific ideas; however, the concepts discussed here are general enough and may be applied to other object-oriented languages as well. Recently much has been said about the power and usefulness of object-oriented paradigms for uniprocessor programming. Here, we shall focus our attention on the advantages offered by object-oriented programming to distributed systems. Four ideas that typify object-oriented languages are:

- data-encapsulation
- inheritance
- data abstraction
- late binding

Data encapsulation promotes modularity and provides a natural bias towards data locality and uniformity of data access. Before explaining how this is achieved, we provide a few informal definitions. A *class* is the type definition of an object; it consists of the definitions of data structures and a set of procedures, called *methods*, which operate on the data. An *object* is an *instance* of a class and contains the actual data. Methods provide the only external means to access or alter the data in an object. This forces the programmer to partition the problem into independent classes, each of which have clearly defined interfaces provided by their methods. By restricting data access through method invocation, data encapsulation creates a convenient single interface for object interaction. For instance, in the case of a `stack` class, the class might provide methods to `pop` and `push` items. The user of a `stack` object may only invoke these methods to request services but may not alter the state of the stack directly. This paradigm discourages the use of shared global data. Locality of data access is increased because the data and its operators are two parts of an object, which is a single entity. It may be noted that data encapsulation in object-oriented languages has several similarities to monitors[6,7].

Most importantly, data encapsulation provides a higher motivation for problem partitioning, based on the partitioning of functionality and usage, rather than on minimization of communication cost, maximization of concurrency, or other such objective functions commonly used in parallel program development. It is believed that a sound partitioning strategy based on the principles of data encapsulation will intuitively, although not trivially, lead to the development of efficient distributed programs.

Inheritance has traditionally been touted as a means of increasing the reusability of code. Class definitions may be hierarchical. Often two classes share much of the same code, in this case the shared code can be made a base class, and different classes can be derived from the base class. The derived class inherits the code in the base class and adds the differentiation unique to the new class. In ES-Kit, inheritance, together with operator overloading (explained below) provides the primary mechanism for transparent synchronization and communication. A base class is defined with operators and methods to perform inter-object communication. A user derives his class hierarchy from this base class, thereby inheriting a transparent mechanism for synchronization and communication. Section 3.1 explains this in some detail.

Data abstraction provides the programmer with a tool for creating and using new types. The purpose of creating new types is to provide a concrete definition of a concept that otherwise has no specific counterpart among the built-in types. To make the new type as usable and in a sense, as complete as any built-in type, several operators may be redefined (or *overloaded*) for the new type. For instance, for a user-defined type `complex`, the '+' operator may be overloaded to perform addition in complex arithmetic.

While this may be dismissed as a form on syntactic sugaring, it is very powerful in its ability to abstract complex behaviors in terms of simple consistent interfaces. In the context of distributed systems, it implies that non-local operations may take on the feel and syntax of local operations without requiring arbitrary additions and extensions to the language. Several important aspects of distributed programming have been implemented using overloaded operators in the ES-Kit environment. Object creation and deletion is achieved through overloading the *new* and *delete* operators, thereby relieving the programmer of object placement and mapping issues. Inter-object communication is achieved by overloading the *pointer-to-member-function* operator, $\rightarrow()$. This leads to a location-independent uniform access mechanism for all objects. By overloading *conversion* operators, results of remote invocations are returned to objects through a variety of synchronization alternatives in a highly transparent manner. Details of these processes appear in the next section.

Late binding delays the binding of meaning to an entity as late as possible, usually at run time. In the ES-Kit environment, late binding is used to achieve remote execution of a method. This is performed by using the *virtual* function call mechanism. An object with virtual methods has a *vtable*, which is a table of pointers to virtual functions. When an object on one node invokes a method of an object on another node, only the value of the method-id of the invoked method is bound at compile time. At run time, this method-id is transmitted to the other node, where it is used to index into the vtable, so as to provide the address of the required method. This furnishes a mechanism by which remote execution in distributed systems is made possible without requiring the manipulation of remote code addresses. In addition, it makes feasible another late binding strategy—that of *dynamic loading*. Dynamic loading of class code implies that all code for all classes need not always be loaded on all nodes. At run time, a class is loaded on to a node when it becomes necessary to construct the first object of that type on the node. This in turn greatly enhances the efficiency of memory management and the overall scalability of the system. Further, it permits the selection of nodes at run time.

3. THE KERNEL

The kernel is a small set of statically linked objects[8] that are instances of classes implemented in GNU C++. The kernel performs message management, memory management, method execution, and synchronization. All other services are provided through dynamically linked Public Service Objects, discussed in Section 4. The object-oriented implementation of the kernel makes experimental modification relatively easy. The kernel supports distributed, object-oriented execution. A copy of the kernel resides at each node of the distributed system.

The ES-Kit kernel is a reactive kernel. This means that the execution of applications is driven by messages. The kernel 'reacts' to messages by providing the infrastructure necessary to execute a method. The kernel checks for the arrival of messages, performs a task switch to start (or re-start) a method in an object, and finally returns for more messages when an object either finishes execution of a method or blocks. Method execution may block to wait for a remote value. Alternatively, non-blocking method invocation is allowed through the use of futures[9,10].

3.1. Class hierarchy in the kernel

The kernel makes extensive use of the language features of C++ to implement global naming, mutually exclusive object execution, remote method calls, and synchronization. Figure 1 shows the class hierarchy in the kernel. The *handle* class forms the base class from which all other classes are derived. A handle is a globally unique identifier, and is used by the remote method invocation process to locate an instance. A handle has four fields: a *node-id*, an *application-id*, a *class-id*, and an *instance-id*. These fields are assigned by the kernel to an object at the time of its creation. On a node, all objects have identical node-ids. Objects belonging to an application have the same application-id. Similarly, all instances of the same class share a common class-id. An object uses the handle of another object to invoke its methods. This is very similar to the use of an object pointer in traditional C++. Unlike pointers, handles are consistent across the different address spaces of the nodes, and hence are easily passed as arguments to method calls.

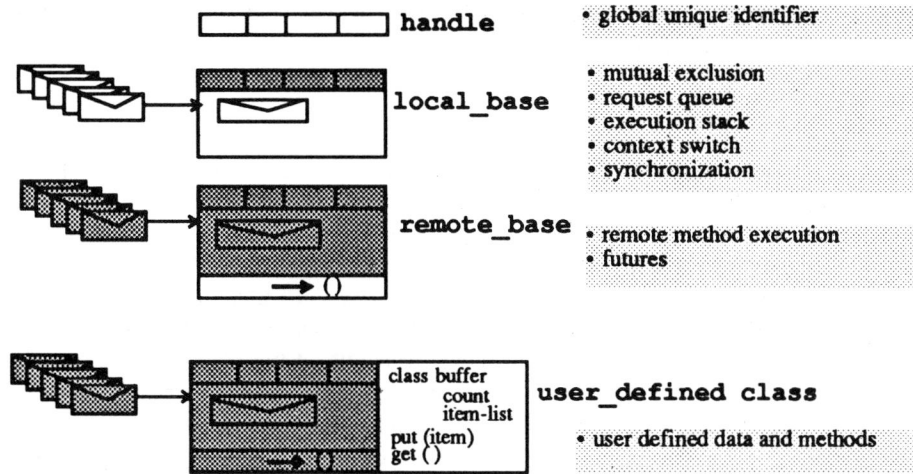

Figure 1. Class hierarchy in the ES-Kit kernel

The *local-base* class is derived from handle. It has instance variables and methods to provide mutual exclusion, context switching and synchronization. A lock ensures that only one method may be active within an object at any time. A request queue is provided to queue requests for an active object. A local-base object can access its execution context, enabling restart of blocked objects. Each executing local-base object has an associated execution stack. The cost of starting up a lightweight process essentially consists of the cost of creating this stack and the cost of context switching, which are together in the range of a few hundred machine instructions.

The next step in the class hierarchy is the *remote-base* class. The *pointer-to-member-function*, →(), is overloaded by this class. This class forms the base class for all application objects. The remote method invocation process is described in some detail in the following subsections.

3.2. Method invocation

Consider a simple example of a producer–consumer problem consisting of producer objects, a buffer object, and consumer objects. When a producer object desires to send an item to the buffer object, it invokes a method of the buffer, with the item as an argument. The buffer updates its state, and stores the item, returning a '1' if successful, and a '0' otherwise. In GNU C++, this exchange would correspond to the following piece of code at the producer:

```
int result = Buffer->put(Item);
```

In the ES-Kit environment, the *same* piece of code performs the tasks of communication and synchronization even if the producer and the buffer objects reside on two different nodes. In fact, the code is independent of the location of the invoking and invoked objects. The same holds for the syntax of the invoked method at the buffer object. This is made possible by overloading the method invocation operator, which is formally called the *pointer-to-member-function* operator. The next three subsections deal with the details of method invocation.

3.3. Messaging

Returning to the example of the producer–consumer problem, let us assume that a Producer and the Buffer are on nodes N1 and N2 respectively. Figure 2 is a pictorial representation of the messaging involved as a result of a remote method invocation; it is a four-step process. In step 1 the definition of the overloaded →() creates a *request* message at the invoking object. The GNU C++ operator →() is a quaternary operator. The arguments provided by the compiler are, in the following order: the object pointer, the vtable index of the method being invoked, the length of the argument list, and the actual argument list. These arguments are placed in a message, whose header contains the handle of the invoked object. Return information to be used by the response message is also included in the message. The execution of the invoking object on node N1 is blocked when the message is mailed, and its context is saved. The kernel resumes it owns reactive execution. Upon receiving a request message at node N2 (step 2 in Figure 2), the handle of the object is de-referenced to determine a pointer to the local instance. The status of the instance is then checked. If the instance is already executing, the request message is enqueued on the request list associated with the instance. This mechanism provides implicit mutual exclusion and guarantees that method execution is strictly in order of message arrival at the object. If the instance is not active, a stack is allocated for it and the arguments are transferred from the message to the stack. The vtable index is used to locate the method code, and control is switched to the method. There is one exception to the rule that method execution is strictly in order of message arrival at the object; it arises when an object uses *method locking* primitives supplied by the ES-Kit kernel to selectively lock/unlock its methods. Method locking is discussed in greater detail in Section 3.5.

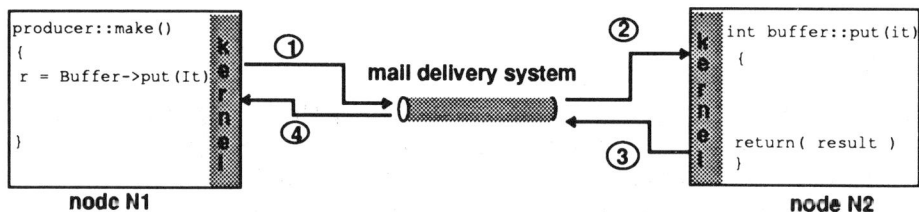

Figure 2.   Remote method invocation

When the remote method terminates on node N2, the return values are placed in a *response* message. The kernel resumes control and mails the response message back to the invoking object (step 3 in Figure 2). The kernel then checks for enqueued messages on the instance's request list. When all queued requests from the list are depleted, the kernel deactivates the instance. Meanwhile, on node N1, the response message is processed (step 4 in Figure 2) to determine the status of the invoker. If the invoker is blocked (as in the scenario explained above), its execution is resumed.

Each node of the ES-Kit system has its own *mail-box*. To send a request message from node N1 to the Buffer object amounts to performing an efficient name search for Buffer. Recall from Figure 1, the object Buffer is derived indirectly from the handle class. Therefore, for the purposes of mailing the request message, the unique address of Buffer is in fact a part of the object itself. This handle information is included in the header of the request message. The node-id part of the handle is used by the message delivery system to route the message to the mail-box of node N2. At this stage, the kernel at node N2 de-references the three remaining fields of the handle to extract a pointer to Buffer.

3.4. Parallelism

If the situation explained above were the only available communication scenario, only one object in the system would be active at a given time. At the time of making the invocation, Producer was active. Buffer becomes active as soon as it receives the message, and remains active until it sends the response message back to Producer. During this time, Producer is waiting for the result and so, is passive. When the result has been received by Producer, it becomes active. This model is called the *sequential* object-oriented model by Bal, Steiner and Tanenbaum[3]. To enable multiple active objects, they identify four possibilities:

- spontaneous activity without receiving a message
- allow the invoked object to continue execution after returning results
- allow the invoker to proceed with execution in parallel with the invoked object
- invoke methods of several objects at once

The first possibility is not very useful unless it can be undertaken in a controlled manner. The result of constructing a new object may be considered a special case of this situation, and is dealt with in the Section 3.6. The second possibility calls for the initiation of an independent thread of execution at the invoked object, which can continue after returning results to the invoked object. Thus, Buffer may wish to return a 'success' to Producer, and then proceed to process the new item, as a result of which *it* may invoke a method from a queue of waiting consumers. In ES-Kit, this facility is available through the *reply-point* mechanism.

The third possibility is perhaps the most widely used form of parallel execution, and encompasses the non-blocking (sometimes called asynchronous) send of message-passing languages[7], as well as *parbegin*[11] and *cobegin*[12–14] type constructs of concurrent languages. Further, the fourth possibility for parallelism[3] which consists in making multiple invocations to several objects at once hinges on the invoker being able to proceed after the making the first invocation. The basic requirement for all these is a mechanism by which the invoker can synchronize with the arrival of a result at any time after making the invocation. In the ES-Kit, this is achieved by using a *future*[15,10]. If the invoker desires, the kernel gives a future to the invoker in immediate response to an invocation. The invoker blocks only when it requires the return value from the invocation, *and* the invocation has not yet responded.

The two main functions of a future are invocation and evaluation. In Code Segment A, Producer makes an invocation to Buffer, but now proceeds with its own execution. When

Producer requires the result of the invocation, it evaluates the future, as shown in Code Segment B. Future evaluation is performed by overloading the conversion operators, rather than by explicit claim functions. At the time of evaluation, if the result is not yet available, Producer will have to wait. However, if Buffer has already returned the result, Producer will continue without blocking.

```
future fu;
fu = Buffer->put(Item);
// do some useful work here in
// parallel with invocation
                            Code Segment A
```

```
// time to evaluate future
int result = fu;



                            Code Segment B
```

```
future fs;
fs += part_B->simulate(t1, A);
fs += part_C->simulate(t1, A);
fs += timer->start(t2-t1);
fs.select_all();
                            Code Segment C
```

Multiple invocations may be made by using the '+=' operator for invocation. For instance, in a simulator, an invoker may start multiple simulations as shown in Code Segment C. There are several predefined methods for synchronizing with the results of multiple invocations. Simple evaluation of the future (as in Code Segment B) results in an order of evaluation that is identical to the order in which results of the multiple invocations become available at the evaluating object's node. By indexing into the future (*future[i]*), specific evaluations can be effected in any desired order. The *future.select_all()* method provides barrier synchronization. The *future.wait()* method returns the invocation number of the available result. These predefined methods can be used to meet fairly complex synchronization requirements.

Another interesting and powerful feature of futures is that they are first-class objects, and can therefore be passed as arguments to, or returned as results from method invocations. In the example in Code Segment C, the effect of evaluating the future after the `timer` expires may also be achieved by passing the future `fs` as an argument to `timer`, and having the `timer` evaluate `fs` at the appropriate time. In this case, the original invoker is completely relieved from all responsibility of synchronizing with the results of the first two invocations.

3.5. Method locking

Method locking primitives allow an object to selectively disable(enable) execution of its methods based on its internal state. If a request message is received for a locked method of an instance, the kernel enqueues the message on a request list associated with that instance. It should be noted that locking a method does not mark the object as completely busy: messages for the unlocked methods of an object execute in the order in which they are received even while some methods in the object are locked.

Method locking is powerful because it allows an object to overrule, based on its dynamic state, the guarantee provided by the kernel that method execution is strictly in order of message arrival at the object. This point is best illustrated by returning to the producer–consumer example. A simple extension would be to allow the buffer object to lock the method put in the event of an overflow condition, and lock the method get when an underflow condition exists. Further, let us assume that the method put is locked and the buffer object receives two messages in the following order: a message to put followed by a message to get a data item. Since the method put is locked, the kernel enqueues this message on the buffer object. As a result, the method get is executed before put (the buffer object could unlock the method put from within the body of get).

It is appropriate to mention that method locking routines are provided as private methods of an instance in order to help prevent synchronization races.

3.6. Object creation

Dynamic object creation greatly enhances the expressiveness of a paradigm in its ability to represent a wider class of problems. In C++, a new object may be created by using the *new* operator. The creation of an object involves two steps: memory allocation for the new object, and the initialization of its state. In distributed environments, there is a third requirement which in fact must be satisfied before the two other steps: the specific target node on which the object is to be created must be known at the time of object creation. In the ES-Kit environment, the user may fully specify this target node, may specify certain constraints in terms of its relation to other nodes and objects, or may simply leave the entire business of node selection up to the kernel. The *new* operator is overloaded for the *remote-base* class to accept additional arguments about the identity of the target node. After the target node is selected, a message is sent to the kernel at that node to create the instance. If this object is the first instance of that particular class on the target node, the code for the class is dynamically loaded and linked by the remote node's kernel at this time. The correct version of the code for a class is found by a *librarian* Public Service Object, as explained in Section 4.2. This is followed by invocation of the *constructor* of the object, which is a special method to initialize the state of the object.

In this respect, object creation may be viewed as a specialized method invocation in which the method invoked is always the constructor. The invoker is the creator of the object, and remains blocked during the invocation of the constructor. When the constructor finishes execution, the handle of the newly constructed object is returned to the creator. The creator may now use this handle to invoke other methods of the object, and may pass the handle on to other objects for the same purpose.

Creating a large number of instances of a class derived from the *remote-base* class is a synchronous operation because the object being constructed does not return its handle to the creating object until it has finished construction, forcing the creating object to remain blocked. Two simple extensions are under review that would make object creation more efficient (from the perspective of the creating object). The first extension is to have the operator *new* return a future. Evaluation of the future would cause the creating object to block pending return of the handle from the object being constructed. Although, this approach adds asynchrony to instance creation consistent with the ES-Kit distributed model, it is inconsistent with the semantics of instance creation in ANSI C++ where a constructor must return a pointer to the type of the object being constructed. Another possibility is that the creating object would receive the handle to the object being constructed *before* it (i.e., the new object) finished construction. The kernel on the node on which the new object is to be constructed would determine the fields for the handle, mark the object as being constructed, and mail the handle back to the creating object before scheduling the actual construction of the new object. This scheme is not completely asynchronous, although the time period that the creating object must wait for the return of the handle can be considerably reduced. The advantage of this scheme, is that it conforms to the semantics of ANSI C++.

4. PUBLIC SERVICE OBJECTS

The ES-Kit kernel has been kept as small as practicable and does not offer many traditional operating system services. Instead, most operating system services are modularized in software in the form of dynamically linked objects that extend the functionality offered by the kernel. Each module constitutes a 'virtual resource' such as a file, system name server, etc. By encapsulating all but the most basic services of an operating system outside the kernel, the experimenter gains by:

- controlling not only the kinds of services but also the algorithms and policies used to implement those services
- being able to rapidly configure a modular operating system in an experimental environment
- restricting malicious access to the kernel by exporting a limited set of kernel symbols to the PSO domain (and not the application domain)

The use of PSOs is consistent with the object-oriented paradigm that is used throughout the ES-Kit implementation. Using the concepts of inheritance, delegation and specialization, the user may derive from a standard PSO provided by ES-Kit or redefine the methods in them to customize and extend the services offered via the PSO. Like other application level objects, PSOs may be created using the *new* operator. Similarly, an object may access a PSO using the method call operator and the appropriate handle.

Before starting a new application, ES-Kit loads a standard set of PSOs for the application. These PSOs encapsulate system services such as input, output, and naming services etc. In order to make standard services globally accessible, a copy of the handles corresponding to each of these PSOs is distributed on every node spanned by an application. Thus, each application object may access these global services using the method call operator and the appropriate handle.

The next two subsections briefly review the functionality of two PSOs: the *application manager* PSO, and the *class librarian* PSO.

4.1. The application manager PSO

The *application manager* PSO provides the necessary support for starting and terminating applications in the ES-Kit environment. The application manager validates the new application, and makes an informed decision based on the load conditions at various nodes in order to select an optimal node on which to start the new application. Additionally, there is a set of problems associated with managing applications on an attached distributed system. For example, application objects executing on ES-Kit nodes should be able to access environment variables as they are defined on the user's UNIX front-end. Further, the capability to perform input and output operations on the front-end must be associated with each application object. Finally, interrupts from the front-end must be faithfully communicated to an application executing on the ES-Kit nodes. These issues provide the motivation for the design of the *application manager* PSO. By implementing the application manager as a PSO, and not a part of the kernel, ES-Kit reserves for researchers the flexibility to determine the policies that control how applications are managed in their respective environments.

4.2. The class librarian PSO

As mentioned earlier, an application may request the kernel to construct an instance of a class using the *new* operator. During this process, at some point, the kernel must 'know' the path in the user's file system where it can load the executable corresponding to the new class. Further, it must assign an application-unique class-id to the class mnemonic.

The *class* librarian PSO has been designed to address these requirements. An instance of the librarian is associated with the kernel. This serves as the *master librarian* and it maintains entries for standard class definitions that are available to every application. The *application manager* creates a librarian for each application. The application librarian is responsible for assigning class-ids as well as locating the executable code corresponding to each class instantiated from within an application (a protocol enables an application librarian to obtain information about standard classes from the master librarian). Additionally, the application librarian provides a means by which the user may determine the class search order for a given application (conceptually, this is similar to the way the file search order may be changed by redefining the path variable in a UNIX environment). The librarian PSO allows object code to be *cross loaded* among the nodes of an application: when a class needs to be loaded on a node where it does not previously exist, the kernel on that node queries the application librarian to determine which node may have earlier loaded the class. If such a node exists, the class code is then copied from there to the required location across the message fabric. Cross loading offers a significant performance improvement when object code is transferred using a high-speed message interconnect between the nodes of a multicomputer *vis-à-vis* loading the code via the UNIX front-end (the ES-Kit message fabric allows peak data rates of 20 Mbytes per second. As a comparison the Ethernet offers a peak data rate of 10 Mbits per second).

Several other PSOs have been designed and implemented. They include a file object, a file manager, an interval timer, an environment PSO, an interrupt handler, etc. The reader is referred to[16] for a more thorough treatment of the current library of PSOs.

5. PROGRAMMING IN THE ES-KIT ENVIRONMENT

The general ES-Kit programming environment consists of a collection of services and facilities that provide an integrated environment for object-oriented system and application development. The components of the programming environment are distributed across the logical ES-Kit system model. The ES-Kit system model consists of three components: a programmer's front-end, the ES-Kit host, and ES-Kit nodes. The user initiates, monitors, and controls application programs from the front-end system. The ES-Kit host connects to the front-end systems using UNIX Internet sockets, and to the ES-Kit nodes through appropriate special-purpose interfaces (if all nodes are UNIX workstations, Internet network sockets are used, and no additional hardware is required). In practice, the user front-end, the ES-Kit host, and an ES-Kit node may be the same physical platform.

Several applications have been developed to aid the integration of the run-time ES-Kit environment as well as to serve as functional regression tests for the ongoing development of the system software. The application suite includes: Parallel Quicksort, a Mandelbrot Set demonstration, an element by element finite element solver, the BRL ray tracing package, a three-dimensional electrochemistry migration/diffusion model (collaboration with the City University of New York), behavioral simulation of circuits using VHDL (collaboration with the University of Cincinnati), penetration mechanics applied to the modeling of collisions of solid bodies (collaboration with Sandia National Labs), and finally an Actor-based system implemented on top of ES-Kit (Virginia Polytechnic Institute).

Inter-nodal application level message overhead has been the focus of ongoing experimentation and analysis. One important experiment measures the total elapsed time for round trip short message pairs (4 bytes), in which the first message invokes a remote object method, and the second returns a future-valuation result to the invoking object. Current versions of ES-Kit technology support round trip latency of about 210 microseconds between pairs of 88K ES-Kit nodes[17].

6. DISCUSSION

We offer this discussion based on the salient points of this paper. They are: the choice of C++ to program a distributed system, applicability of the constructs offered by the language to problems of distributed systems such as synchronization, messaging etc., and finally the notion of Public Service Objects.

The choice of C++. We have made extensive use of features offered by C++ to implement distributed functionality without extending the language. For example: the ability to overload operators such as *new* has allowed us to implement remote object creation in a manner consistent within the framework of the language, overloading the '$\rightarrow$()' operator has facilitated implementation of transparent messaging, the ability to overload operators has proved central to the implementation of futures for synchronization. Inheritance has been used extensively in the design of the kernel.

Encapsulation combined with virtual functions has proved useful in accommodating heterogeneity in specific modules.

Since C++ was designed as a programming language for a single address space, providing the entire suite of C++ functionality in a distributed system is a difficult task. The major problems are:

- pointers may be dereferenced only on the node on which they originate
- passing objects by reference in remote method calls
- passing deep objects, i.e., objects with embedded pointers, as arguments to remote method calls

In the absence of a shared global address space (sometimes an unrealistic assumption in large distributed systems) there are at least two approaches to dealing with pointers. The first is to extend a simple C++ pointer to encapsulate the node address to which the pointer refers. Thus, dereferencing this pointer on a node other than its origin would generate a fault, at which time the underlying system could transfer the data (pointed to) from the original to the remote node. For the purposes of this discussion we call these extended pointers 'smart pointers'. The second approach is to restrict the use of pointers to classes that will not be distributed, or passed, across nodal boundaries.

There are several constraints on the use of smart pointers in a distributed system. One significant concern is that smart pointers must be implemented outside the domain of ANSI C++ for compatibility reasons. Implementing smart pointers would therefore necessitate a customized preprocessing stage. Another concern is that implementing smart pointers would severely limit the ability to link with standard C++ libraries.

In any case, providing smart pointers is not sufficient to address the issues of passing objects by reference or passing deep objects as arguments to remote method calls. These issues form the basis of ongoing research. A complete analysis of the aforementioned problems, and possible solutions to them, are beyond the scope of this paper.

Restricting the use of pointers to classes that never cross a nodal boundary is an impracticable solution for the obvious reason that it places an even greater onus on the shoulders of the application programmer.

Public service objects. PSOs provide the capability to dynamically configure an operating system. This has proved to be extremely useful as we have experimented with different files systems (encapsulated as PSOs), and often made large-scale changes to the policies encapsulated in the application manager and the librarian without having to recompile the kernel. Future research in object persistence will allow more symmetric mechanisms to create PSOs that can be shared across application domains.

7. CONCLUSION

The research described in this paper was conducted as part of the Experimental Systems Project at MCC. The project was funded largely by DARPA for a period of three years, starting December 1987. The main charter of the project was to deliver an open set of hardware and software modules that could be readily assembled to produce multi-node object-oriented systems.

Perhaps the most important result of the ES-Kit research is the determination that a distributed, object-oriented approach is appropriate for high-performance experimentation. The object-oriented approach allows researchers to isolate the experimental facets of a system, while at the same time facilitating the integration of custom architectures or subsystems into an experimental framework.

The Extensible Software Platform Project (ESP) at MCC continues research in the area of distributed, heterogeneous, object-oriented systems. ESP research is focused in the following areas:

- Providing improved resource allocation algorithms as well as object-migration[18].
- Design and implementation of a distributed debugger for a heterogeneous, object-oriented system.
- Design of an ESP preprocessor to improve distributed programming semantics using ANSI C++.
- Dynamic reconfiguration in response to failures.

ACKNOWLEDGEMENTS

The authors wish to gratefully acknowledge the efforts and support of all members of the Experimental Systems Project at MCC. The architecture and design of the ES-Kit kernel is by Bill Leddy. Kim Smith is responsible for the execution environment, and much of the later design iterations of the kernel.The GNU C++ compiler was developed by Michael Tiemann. This work was partly funded by DARPA under contract MDA972-88-C-0013 with the Microelectronics and Computer Technology Corporation.

REFERENCES

1. K.S. Smith and R.J. Smith, 'The experimental systems project at the microelectronics and computer technology corporation', *Proceedings Hypercube and Concurrent Computer Applications*, pp. 709–713, 1989, Monterey, CA.
2. A.S. Tanenbaum and R.V. Renesse, 'Distributed operating systems', *ACM Computing Surveys*, **17**(4), pp. 419–470 (1985).
3. H.E. Bal, J.G. Steiner and A.S. Tanenbaum, 'Programming languages for distributed computing systems', *ACM Computing Surveys*, **21**(3), pp. 261–322 (1989).
4. B. Stroustrup, *The C++ Programming Language*, Addison-Wesley, Reading, MA (1988).
5. M. Tiemann, 'User's guide to GNU C++', MCC Experimental Systems Technical Report ACA-ESP-099-88 (1988).
6. P. Brinch Hansen, 'Concurrent programming concepts', *ACM Computing Surveys*, **5**(4), pp. 223–245 (1973).
7. C.A.R. Hoare, 'Monitors: an operating system structuring concept', *Communications of the ACM*, **17**(10), pp. 549–557 (1974).
8. W.J. Leddy and K.S. Smith, 'The design of the experimental systems kernel', *Proceedings Hypercube and Concurrent Computer Applications*, 1989, Monterey, CA, pp. 737–743.
9. A. Chatterjee, 'Futures: a mechanism for concurrency among objects', *Proceedings of Supercomputing 1989*, Reno, NV, pp. 562–567.
10. K.S. Smith and A. Chatterjee, 'A C++ environment for distributed application execution', *Proc. C++ at Work-90*, 1990, Secaucus, NJ, pp. 137–144.
11. E.W. Dijkstra, 'Cooperating sequential processes', in *Programming Languages*, F. Genuys (ed.), Academic Press, New York (1968).

12. P. Brinch Hansen, 'Edison: a multiprocessor language', *Software Practice and Experience*, **11**(4), pp. 325–361 (1981).
13. B.L. Liskov and R. Scheifler, 'Gaurdians and actions: Linguistic support for robust distributed programs', *ACM Transactions on Programming Languages and Systems*, **5**(3), 381–404 (1983).
14. A. van Wijngaarden, B.J. Mailloux, J.L. Peck, C.H.C. Koster, M. Sintzoff, C.H. Lindsey, L.G.L.T. Meertens and R.G. Fisker, 'Revised report on the algorithm language ALGOL 68', *Acta Informatica*, **5**, 1–3 (1975), pp. 1–236.
15. R. Halstead, 'Multilisp: a language for concurrent symbolic computation', *ACM Transactions on Programming Languages and Systems*, **4**, pp. 501–538 (1985).
16. A. Khanna, 'Public service objects to extend the ES-Kit kernel', *Proceedings Hypercube and Concurrent Computer Applications*, 1989, Monterey, CA, pp. 744–750.
17. R. Shah, S. Lamb and R.J. Smith, 'Performance characterization of ES-Kit distributed systems', *Proceedings Fifth Distributed Memory Computing Conference*, 1990, Charleston, SC, pp. 1276–1283.
18. A. Chatterjee, 'Resource allocation in object-oriented distributed systems: a proposed solution', MCC Technical Report, ACT-ESP-025-90, non-confidential.

CONCURRENCY: PRACTICE AND EXPERIENCE, VOL. 3(6), 541–557 (DECEMBER 1991)

The EMMA2 multiprocessor operating system

E. APPIANI, D. BIANCO, L. MERLO, L. RONCAROLO

Central Research Department
Elsag Bailey SpA
Via Puccini 2
16154 Genova, Italy

SUMMARY

The EMMA2[1] parallel architecture is a network of nodes, named 'Regions': each region is based on two shared-memory hierarchical bus levels, on which a large series of monocpu, multicpu and specialized I/O boards can be inserted, grouped in 'Families'.

Its typical applications are image processing, pattern recognition and artificial intelligence, characterized by intensive computation requirements, real-time constraints and good price–performance ratio for building large industrial systems. This paper presents the main characteristics of the EMMA2 parallel operating system, highlighting the internal organization and mechanisms offering the parallel co-operation model for user programs.

Section 1 briefly introduces the overall hardware architecture. It allows application partitioning into parallel independent subsystems, on two levels of computation: the lower level (family) is dedicated to massive number crunching, while the upper (region) permits the interaction of these lower machines.

Section 2 deals with the system software environment, based on a host–target configuration: the host is mainly devoted to machine control, system monitoring, program development and debugging in a multi-user environment.

Sections 3, 4 and 5 describe respectively the fundamental concepts of the operating system internal organization and the basic mechanisms with respect to the machine architecture; the basic functions that constitute the internal layers and services; the resulting parallel programming and co-operation model and the typical mapping rules of algorithms to this architecture, completed with some examples of their functionalities.

The most important aspect of the EMMA2 operating system is the fact that it offers a uniform interface to user tasks, independently of their allocation on the target machine. Objects managed by system services can be referred to via logical names. Code for system services is distributed among processors and resides on a private read-only memory. The operating system's data reside in shared memory only for system functions that need to be distributed, while private functions are based on different copies of data in private memories.

Section 6 gives more details on the most relevant EMMA2 industrial applications, also showing their mapping to the parallel architecture and some performance-related information. Section 7 contains a brief outline of the novel architecture currently in development and of the subsequent OS improvements.

In conclusion, we report some considerations about the present status of the EMMA2 system, compared with some other well-known architectures, and about research efforts for its future evolution.

1. INTRODUCTION

A very challenging and interesting endeavour is the design of parallel architectures capable of meeting very strict requirements of performance (both in terms of machine

---

[1] EMMA is a registered trademark of Elsag—Elettronica San Giorgio.

1040-3108/91/060541–17$08.50

Received May 1991
Accepted August 1991

instructions per second and data transfers), of versatility (capacity to support different applications such as speech, image recognition or SAR processing), of cost with respect to constraints imposed by the market and, lastly, of a suitable development environment to support user applications in an economic and efficient way.

Although we could design architectures well matched to the applications needs, this is hardly ever justifiable on an industrial basis. What we have been trying to do in the EMMA2 project is to design a system with sufficient generality to support different applications and lines of products. In our experience, the development environment and the parallel reference model for user applications are absolutely vital for the use of parallel machines with large granularity, like the multiprocessor EMMA2.

In this article we will concentrate on the aspects concerning the parallel operating system and much less on the hardware itself. The explanation of the OS internal structure will help in the understanding its properties. We will also describe the development environment and the reference model for applications, i.e., the virtual machine as viewed by the programmer and the services offered by the OS in order to support that model.

2. MULTIPROCESSOR ARCHITECTURE OVERVIEW

The EMMA2 is a distributed shared memory parallel processing system, consisting of a multilevel, tree-like, hierarchical structure and currently employed in a wide variety of real-time and computationally intensive applications. The innermost level of this hierarchy is the processing element (PE), an Intel iAPX286 CPU, possibly coupled with some standard or custom coprocessors[2,8].

At the top level, EMMA2 is a net of multiprocessor machines named 'Regions', including a host computer node, connected to each other by high-speed parallel links, with unconstrained topology. The EMMA2 region consists of a set of multiprocessor machines named 'Families' sharing a common memory address space and a common bus.

The address spaces of the two domains, region and family, are separated and both consist of a set of local memories belonging to the modules residing on the buses. Furthermore each EMMA2 PE possesses also a private memory area; on this layered structure, applications can mix efficiently their own data locality and shareability[7].

The homogeneity of the two buses allows insertion of processing and specialized modules with the same interface. Differences are external to their PEs while private features are quite similar thus offering a uniform model to programmers; this feature is enforced by OS abstraction.

2.1. Memory address spaces and processor hierarchy

The physical memory address space, 16 Mbytes for the 286, is divided into three partitions for each processor: the Private one, visible to all PEs and containing private RAM, EPROM and devices (including coprocessors); the Family one, visible to PEs interfaced to a Family, with the collection of Family shared RAMs and memory-mapped devices; and the Region one, visible to all PEs interfaced to the Region, with the collection of Region shared RAMs and devices.

Every PE can access at least two partitions: its Private one, and the Region or Family one. Only Family supervisor PEs (the 'P1's previously presented) have visibility to all partitions and can act as active bridges between their respective Families and the Region.

Both Region and Family spaces enforce the principle of 'address locality': although being shared, each local RAM allows a privileged access from the related PE (PE residing on the same board) providing almost the same performance of the private RAM. This feature improves data parallel algorithms when shared data can be statically partitioned among parallel tasks: in this case, the Region or Family bus is mostly engaged during initial or final data transfers, remaining free during computation.

2.2. EMMA2 Modules

The most important EMMA2 modules are (see Figure 1):

    P1   (monoprocessor family supervisor)
    PN   (multiprocessor family module)
  IRCU   (inter Region high-speed communication module)
  ELAN   (SCSI I/O adapter, Ethernet LAN controller)
  HCSM   (high-capacity dual-port memory).

Some EMMA2 hardware architectural features are the basis of internal mechanisms and services of the OS.

General bus features

Both region and family buses support 32-bit wide, 10 MB/s data cycles, with distributed arbitration.

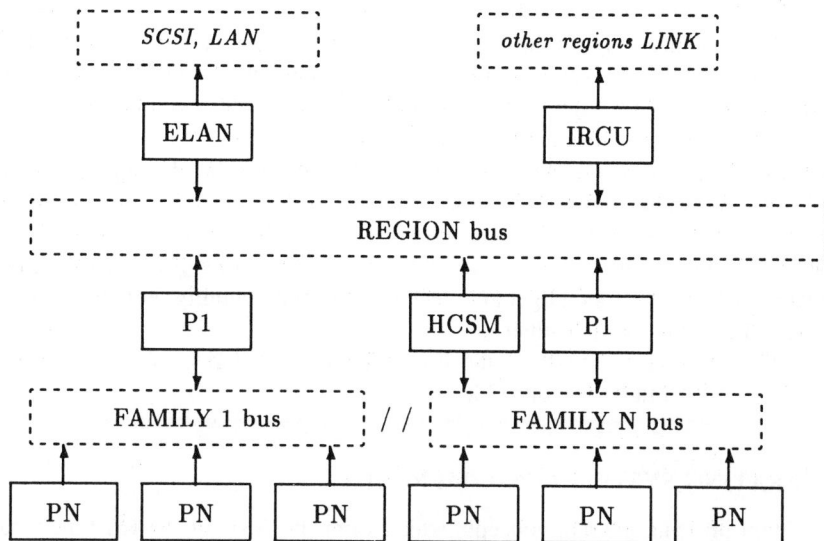

Figure 1. EMMA2 hardware architecture

Self-configuration and fault tolerance

Control and Status registers globally accessible on a bus allow identification and control of any system module thus supporting the initial dynamic self-configuration and diagnostic checks.

Memory position and sharing

Both the address spaces are filled in with the local memories of residing boards, each one taking a different position and length. Memory locality is achieved with distribution and direct access from any related processor, thus improving local computation efficiency. The OS enforces locality by handling different areas separately for both user and internal services. Hardware support to 32-bit parallelism and non-interruptable bus operations, provides efficient block data transfers.

Interprocessor interrupts

The hardware architecture supplies for each bus four kinds of interprocessor interrupts, with single or broadcast destination. Together with shared memory they are the basic means for multiprocessor control.

3. SYSTEM SOFTWARE ENVIRONMENT

The problem of programming this multiprocessor hierarchical architecture is generally quite complex, because parallelism is explicitly controlled, architecture is expandable and aimed to very high throughput, both in computational and communicational aspects. For these reasons, users require a sophisticated environment with high-level tools for programming, debugging and tuning applications[5], directly in the target real-time context[6].

In order to meet these requirements, EMMA2 system software includes a host environment for handling machine supervision and program development. EMMA2 supervision is based on the host multi-user environment, providing commands and debugging services with high-level interfaces and transparent communication with the target, where a run-time resident OS is available to user tasks.

Support for program development has more emphasis on debugging and tuning applications within their real behaviour than on their static generation. In particular, the system has a high-level debugger with a multi-window interface. Its multi-tasking characteristic permits the simultaneous control over many tasks of the same application, everywhere allocated on the target architecture, with full visibility on their co-operation, while running in the real machine[3].

After this brief presentation of the host support, in the rest of the paper we will concentrate on the multiprocessor OS.

4. OPERATING SYSTEM FUNDAMENTALS

This section presents internal concepts which form the basis of the OS functionalities: initial design guidelines, system data structures, and the common models which influence the internal implementation of all subsystems, described later.

All basic choices try to achieve tight correlation between the OS and the parallel architecture, particularly for: code and data allocation, use of virtual memory, machine and resource description, and basic co-operation mechanisms.

OS code is Eprom resident on all processors, with identical base properties, plus board-dependent extensions. OS data reside in local or private databases, according to the scope of the related service. This strategy of allocation is replicated on each bus.

Virtual memory management is based on the 286 model[8]. A Global Descriptor Table (GDT) for each processor refers to system objects, while one Local Descriptor Table (LDT) for each task provides separation among user spaces. The Interrupt Descriptor Table (IDT) contains real-time service handlers and tasks. Also multi-tasking follows the 286 support conventions, internally employing the direct context switch.

A Configuration Data Base (CFDB) for each bus, containing the hardware description, is generated during the initial startup and is enriched with software parameters during the dynamic OS initialization. All the other data are created according to user tuning. Such data are: packet pools for internal communication handling and arrays of items corresponding to various kinds of OS objects.

The user tasks can refer to system objects *by name*, initially for creating them, and later for association with existing ones. In this way, no physical hardware knowledge is imposed on applications, which are given back *identifiers*, for quick reference. OS handles concurrency by means of three rising protection levels: inside a task, by disabling asynchronous events; inside a processor, by disabling interrupts; inside a bus, by using a lock mechanism to allow mutual exclusion.

System commands management is commonly handled by FIFO queues. There are three main internal implementations: Asynchronous System Traps queued in the task system stack (AST); request queueing to continuously delivered services, by double-linked command lists (queue/wake mechanism); finally, send and dispatch real-time Inter-Processor Commands (IPC). All OS functions which need dynamic data buffers, use an internal support for physical memory handling, thus making possible server chaining in data transfers.

5. OPERATING SYSTEM INTERNAL COMPONENTS

This section discusses in detail the main subsystems of the OS, describing both their own functionalities and their mutual relationships, all relying on the already described fundamentals[7].

We can start from the analysis of a processor's internal behaviour and then examine the scope and the effects of its actions, especially with respect to other processors. This analysis also shows how the subsystems' interactions can result in the global multiprocessor dynamic.

For the sake of real-time efficiency, EMMA2 OS emphasizes private processing instead of multiprocessing; this can sound strange, but it means that every processor acts as a private agent, accessing shared services and data only when necessary. This is possible thanks to the presence of private memories and devices, giving each processor a good level of independency.

We can examine and classify the different levels of scope of the OS actions which any task may require, hiding from it the topological complexity of the architecture. Every action type may terminate with a rescheduling operation on the issuing processor.

Private action

This requires access to objects private to the processor; it may imply interrupt disabling.

Local (bus common) action

This means access to a shared object, common to all processors connected to a region or family bus. No co-operation is required from other processors, but it may imply the locking mechanism.

Interprocessor action

This consists in requesting an active service on a target processor residing on the same bus, because of the need to perform a scheduling operation or other private action on the second processor. It certainly implies a local action, at least for filling in a message, followed by sending an interrupt to the target processor, this being the only possibility of influencing its state of execution. Remote communication and control inside a region, but with a broader scope than a bus, involve one or more intermediate actions of this type.

We can now show the composition and organization of independent subsystems.

Task scheduling subsystem

Task scheduling is private to each EMMA2 processor and its main function is to determine which task should be executed by a processor and giving control to it. The Scheduler basic policy is the well-known multi-priority round-robin with task preemption. The ability to do interrupt scheduling, through direct task activation via the IDT, reduces interrupt service latency, which is a fundamental requirement in real-time systems.

Scheduling primitives make it possible to influence any task in the system using the internal IPC mechanism. Some tasks on each processor perform system services related to different subsystems.

Memory management subsystem

The EMMA2 Memory Management subsystem has the following functions:

- physical memory management
- control of segment descriptors and of descriptor tables
- data sharing management
- support for memory-mapped devices and I/O

The EMMA2 physical memory is seen as a set of memory areas, handled with a first-fit extent strategy. Virtual memory subsystem dynamically manages descriptors in GDTs and LDTs also performing privilege level and segment-type protection.

Since tasks' virtual spaces are separated, segment sharing is obtained by replying the same physical description in different LDTs and maintaining control over the repetition number. Segment identification is based on logical names.

Moreover, the Memory Management subsystem gives support for accessing memory areas associated with physical devices, obeying to the same rules of physical memory visibility, through the *Resource Segments* system service, again referenced by means of a naming convention. Finally, this subsystem provides support for creating, deleting, fixing in memory, mapping and unmapping dynamic data system buffers.

Task synchronization subsystem

Task synchronization is provided by the scheduling subsystem and by three different services named respectively *Event Flags*, *Asynchronous System Traps* (ASTs) and *Signals*.

— *Event Flags.* Each application task can be associated with clusters of binary events named *Event Flags* shareable on the same bus whose association is based on logical names. Any group of tasks can achieve the most typical forms of multiprocessor synchronization through: the state of any event flag (starting many tasks), the state of a counter (barrier wait), a numerical message (individual identity signalling).

— *ASTs.* Through the ASTs mechanism a task can associate a procedure with the occurrence of asynchronous events, thus making it possible to wait for multiple events.

— *Signals.* Signals are task-to-task impulsive events. Any receiving task can trigger such events by associating their arrival with ASTs and/or Event Flags.

Interprocessor and inter-region communication subsystem

This part of the OS is devoted to the basic and closer multiprocessor interactions and communications, and to the host–target and inter-region routing system. Special actions related to the system IPC solicitations are directly associated with commands handled by a first set of service tasks on any processor. They execute the primary actions, manage tasks's answers and dispatch to the proper server other classes of I/O, control, debug and communication commands.

A second set includes many system servers allocated in the neuralgic interconnection points giving transparent user access to distributed non-local resources. In particular, a system process describes and collects all instantaneous requests that need extra-region routing. This way, a high traffic rate, deriving from a multiprocessor structure, can be sustained more easily.

On the inter-region communication board, two system drivers with a full-duplex message/frame-based protocol, dispatch incoming requests inside the region, and send extra-region messages. These system communication facilities are also extended to any *Family* task by means of a dedicated server. This process completes the set of system communication processes, with the internal inter-bus transport of requests.

All the servers are system tasks that use the dynamic packet pool resources, different FIFO queueing mechanisms, and the memory management and task synchronization subsystems.

Input-output and file management susbystem

This subsection of the OS attends to the management of all input–output requests, concurrently with the applications and the physical I/O drivers. User interface characteristics are: the synchronous or asynchronous I/O models, the independence of the kind and the allocation of the physical device (local or remote), and the possibility of inserting new drivers in the system.

Two primary classes of I/O devices can be defined:

- host peripherals with remote access via host link (*host file system, terminals, printers, mailbox*)
- EMMA2 peripherals with local or inter-bus access (*fast file system, serial lines, special devices, inter-task mailbox*)

The I/O subsystem consists of many service tasks (logical and physical *drivers*), requested by means of a uniform target interface that connects user channels to the peripheral devices, activates I/O requests, and finalizes them with data transfer and status report. The I/O system concentrates I/O channel characteristics in dynamic tables inside the task system stack. User I/O requests are internally queued to Unit Control Blocks (UCB), which are intermediate system structures between tasks and drivers, that are retrieved by logical names in peripheral tables self-configured at system startup.

Depending on the complexity of the device, one or two driver levels can manage it. The internal file system, for instance, is based on different system tasks, that support respectively the multiprocessor user task front-end and the physical device operations, with block cacheing and contiguous files. Benefits in performance may also be obtained, by replicating this structure in order to meet the desired requirements of transfer rate and mass storage capacity.

A special device class consists of some modules to interface in real-time the multiprocessor with external fields, like image acquisition CCD devices and fast parallel link to graphics VME-bus-based boards. *Mailbox* software drivers also support the 'message send–receive' paradigm, which complements, and takes advantage of, the 'shared-memory' one.

Relationships with the other subsystems and system resources are similar to those used by the communication subsystem.

Dynamic task loading susbystem

This operating subsystem allows dynamic and flexible application loading on the target architecture; tasks can refer to the OS through virtual memory without linking any static code.

The creation of new user tasks is carried out by a system task, the *Loader Master*, present in every processor; the mechanism is based on progressive hand-shaking with another active counterpart, the *Loader Assistant*. This constitutes the initial core of the process being created, getting it ready when all its environment and system resources have been prepared and passing it control definitively.

Two main creation modes are supported: the pipelined loading of different task subsets, targeting single tasks to single processors, and the parallel loading of identical task subsets, targeting the same task to multiple processors. Any task can create other processes on the target, with no father/child 'thread' relationship, as the corresponding host command.

The loading subsystem uses the I/O component to access the file containing user code from both host and EMMA2 private file systems, eventually in an automatic way. Consequently all lower subsystems are involved.

6. PARALLEL MODELS

Here we present the run-time environment from the programmer's point of view, pointing out the parallel model and the features relevant to all services. The basic aim of the EMMA2 programming environment was to provide adequate support for industrial applications, whose important needs are:

- to execute regular algorithms for long periods with sustained high performance;
- to combine close control over task co-operation and machine resources with a virtual object model and clear mechanisms;
- to be defined and programmed by people expert in algorithms but not necessarily in parallel programming formalisms and methods.

6.1. Parallel programming model

A synthetic definition of the EMMA2 parallel programming model might be: concurrent sequential processes with shared data. This is usual in MIMD machines with shared memory and sequential processors. Parallel cooperation is achieved through the insertion of OS calls in standard languages for the 286 microprocessor; the development unit is the task, an independent execution of a program[1].

The main features of our development model are: use of standard languages instead of parallel ones or special formalisms; static development unrelated with run-time co-operation; support for both loose and tight parallelism; avoidance of dynamic *multi-threading* inside each task; operational access to system objects much faster than initial creation or association[3].

An important point is the contemporary support of two fundamental models based on the sequential programming paradigm:

- *data* parallelism, usually supported on other systems at fine grain level, but also at task grain, with dynamic creation of multiple threads inside a program, each one executing the same portion of code on a different subset of common data;
- *functional* parallelism, usually supported at task grain with some loose co-operation among independent tasks, executing different programs.

An industrial application generally employs both models, being composed of different functional stages in pipelined execution, some of which internally require data parallelism for speeding up computation. Functional parallelism is implicit in our programming model, based on independent co-operating tasks.

Some points are worth making about EMMA2 support of data parallelism, especially in comparison with the multi-threaded model. In our system, such parallelism is obtained by loading identical tasks (i.e., based on the same executable programs) on different processors, with static or dynamic shared data.

In the multi-threaded model, programmers must in any case 'think parallel', and share workloads by explicitly coding the serial and parallel parts. The only extra effort required to use the data parallel model in EMMA2 is separation of the 'master' algorithm, equivalent to the serial part, and the 'slave' one, namely the part to be replicated, into separated programs: the master will instantiate a single task, while the slave will be replicated as much as needed.

In conclusion, the efficient EMMA2 support of repetitive algorithms derives from parallel code replication on processors, with private independent execution, instead of 'forked' and 'joined' threads.

6.2. General algorithm–architecture mapping rules

Here are some rules for good application mapping to an EMMA2 region. Any application should be divided into functions, namely different jobs and roles that contribute to the final result. In most cases, these are stages with pipelined execution. Examples will be shown later when presenting some applications. Some functions can be implemented with single tasks, for instance when managing a single device or dispatching messages and data, while others require parallel implementation due to their large computational requirements.

Single-task functions can be mapped to Region or Family PEs, depending on optimization of device allocation or data transfer. Parallel functions, instead, should be mapped to a Family by placing their computing tasks on PNs and the co-ordinating task (for interfacing with other functions and executing the serial part of the algorithm) on the Family P1. Data exchange with the Region and other Families are managed by this task, directly or through dual-ported high capacity memories (HCSM).

Currently, such mapping schemes are not generated or guided by automatic tools; however, the uniformity and the machine virtualization offered by OS run-time interface make it possible to run applications on reduced configurations (also for initial debugging) or with suboptimal mapping to target Regions. Performance monitoring tools help to adjust the mapping and eventually increase the configuration until the desired performance is achieved.

The typical usage of private and shared memories derives from the suggested task mapping. Region shared memories are for data with global meaning in the EMMA2 node application, and are shared among different function co-ordinators and single tasks located on Region PEs. Family shared memories are mostly devoted to common data of data parallel functions located on each Family.

On both Region and Family, shared data relevant to a task should be placed on the local memory area of the PE running the task: this service is provided by the OS in a transparent way. Finally, private memories are devoted to user tasks' code and private data, to be accessed without contention among PEs; if the same task runs on different processors, such code and data will be replicated.

6.3. Run-time co-operation model

We can now describe the most important co-operation modes offered to user tasks. Since the development model is based on independent programs activated as task entities, the run-time behaviour essentially depends on relationships among tasks and with the external world. We have grouped all services in basic co-operation 'methods', listed below in order of increasing coupling.

They can involve pure synchronization, pure data exchange or a combination of the two. Every method has also a scope, namely the architectural subset in which the mechanisms involved can take place. The scope decreases as the coupling increases. There are no particular elements of novelty in these five methods in themselves, except the fact that they all are present in the same operating system[1].

Communication with the external world

Data exchange + synchronization. Scope: the whole system (including the host computer). Relevant information: peripheral names and access modes.

This method consists of the interaction with peripherals and devices of different kinds, either located on the host or on the target machine. The related OS services are the I/O and the File System. The method can allow the distribution of the application over many communicating nodes (i.e., *user host programs*).

Task-to-task communication

Data exchange + synchronization. Scope: the whole system. Relevant information: mailbox logical names and usage modes.

This method consists of exchanging messages among tasks by using mailboxes. Since mailboxes are treated as virtual peripherals on EMMA2, the I/O System is again the related service. It allows data exchange when machine topology does not allow memory sharing, and in any case when an user wishes to achieve a loose co-operation. The method is suited to functional parallelism.

Task-to-task synchronization

Pure synchronization. Scope: the target system. Relevant information: task names and identifiers.

This method consists of directly affecting the scheduling state of other tasks through their run-time identifiers. Tasks using this synchronization mode can be located anywhere on the target machine, without requiring shared space. The method is adaptable to various situations, but is particularly suited to functional parallelism, since the tasks do not necessarily share data and interact on the base of mutual knowledge of their identities.

Use of synchronization objects

Pure synchronization. Scope: an EMMA2 bus (region or family). Relevant information: names of event clusters and event numbers.

Within this method, a set of tasks located on the same bus can join a common synchronization object, provided by the *Event Flags* service. Like the previous one, the method applies to a variety of situations. However, its scope and mechanisms make it particularly suited for supporting data parallelism. In fact, this co-operation mode does not require explicit knowledge of the tasks involved and provides information and mechanisms for dynamically partitioning a common workload.

Data sharing

Pure data exchange. Scope: an EMMA2 bus. Relevant information: *Global Segment* logical names, lengths and pointers.

This last method is fundamental on every shared-memory architecture; on EMMA2, it relies on the *Global Segments* service. Data sharing can apply to static or dynamic data; access is achieved by using static variable names or dereferencing the acquired pointers. No implicit synchronization is involved in memory sharing, which is normally associated with some synchronization method.

6.4. Behaviour examples of some user functionalities

In this section we report two representative examples of user programming functionalities, describing their subcomponents, in order to explain how these can be achieved in the EMMA2 system.

Task synchronization with the 'one-to-many' model

A common synchronization mechanism adopted by applications is the 'one-to-many' model in a configuration of one master task and *n* slave tasks.

The first action to be undertaken is the association to an Event Flags Cluster in order to access a common area for synchronization. In this case, the OS could decide whether to create a new cluster getting the first free entry in the Event Flags Clusters Data Base (EFCDB) or to perform a simple association by incrementing the counter of tasks associated to the cluster in an already existing EFCDB entry.

After this 'attach' operation each task is returned a progressive identifier that might be used to label the task among the synchronization group. Internally this operation implies the association of the processors to a broadcast family reserved to the OS for this purpose. Actions involved:

- the slave tasks set themselves 'waiting for a global event flag', and the OS enables the interprocessor interrupt used for this synchronization service
- the master task then sets this global event flag to start the slave tasks
- the event is marked as set in the corresponding EFCDB entry
- the proper IPC interrupt is sent to the reserved broadcast family
- all the processors that are associated to that broadcast family, and whose IPC interrupt is enabled, execute an interrupt procedure that awakens all the tasks of the processor that are waiting for a global event flag
- the slaves execute the primitive epilogue checking if they have been awakened for the right reason and, in this case, slave tasks can resume their execution leaving the barrier.

Executing steps and breakpoints for debugging user programs

This user action example is chosen to highlight the host–target interaction mechanism, performing control without interfering with parallel dynamics, through the communications subsystem. Actions involved:

- the interactive user indicates the source code line where to break its program, by a host debugger command

- the symbolic address of the source line is translated into code physical address, filling a specific communication command, and is sent via mailbox to the host link process
- through the link/drivers communication subsystem, the command is delivered to the correct processor and task, that were waiting for debug instructions
- a system AST is executed in the task context, replaces the instruction code at the breakpoint address with system exception trap code, and resumes the task
- at breakpoint, the system exception handler restores the instruction code, stops the task, and answers the host debugger with a similar communication packet
- again the communication subsystem, on inverse routing, will inform the host debugger user with the packet confirming the breakpoint reached.

Note that many IPC command services, required on every multiprocessor communication and to force AST scheduling actions, were omitted for clarity.

7. EMMA2 PARALLEL INDUSTRIAL APPLICATIONS

The fields in which EMMA2 is currently used are mail sorting and document processing, with address and character recognition in real time; satellite image acquisition and filtering; stereo-imaging and motion analysis; speech recognition; artificial intelligence and expert systems. The following subsections are related to three classes of EMMA2 applications, highlighting some examples with related implementation details[4].

7.1. OCR systems and office automation

Elsag Bailey's most important industrial system in character pattern recognition is the mail sorting system (SARI), employed in many postal plants, in Italy and abroad, for automatic determination of the destination (zipcode), based on the optical acquisition of the mail address.

A letter travels on a mechanical transport system and an optical sensor capture its image, digitizes it, and then feeds it to a recognition system for extraction of full address information. After the image is recognized, the letter is finally routed by the same mechanical system, in the right destination stack. A Multiline, Reader/Optical Character Recognition system (MLR–OCR) requires variable document-processing times, which strongly depend on the address contents.

The MLR–OCR performs its task by means of several pipelined processing steps, thus becoming capable of handling up to 45,000 images/hour. An EMMA2 configuration, consisting of one Region and three Families, with a total of about 100 PEs and 66 ALA coprocessors, implements the recognition process.

A second application in information processing is a document automatic recognition and archiving system (SLAM) that handles alphanumeric machine or handwritten characters on different kinds of forms, and that is currently used by many administrative departments for medical, financial and tax applications, as well as by Deutsche Bundespost cheques service.

Document forms are transported by a mechanical unit, under an optical high-resolution sensor. Document images are compressed, and then entered the first processing stage of an EMMA2 system, that is also fed with a parametric representation of the form fields position and characteristics.

In the first stage, compensation of form skew and other geometrical preprocessing functions are carried out, then output field lines are sent to the second stage, where a preliminary character segmentation and normalization is performed. The last stage provides a massive recognition process, returning images and strings to the host, where partial strings and related images go to the 'videocoding' stage, on human-assisted operative stations.

The high data-entry rate (6000 forms/hour), and the complexity of forms with handwritten fields may require an EMMA2 configuration with a Region and two Families containing up to 55 PEs, handling five active documents in pipeline.

The evolution of this class of systems will lead to a distribution of the acquisition, recognition and archiving functions, in different heterogeneous processing nodes, in order to support many PC workstations, by using local area networks with specialized EMMA2-based OCR servers.

7.2. Machine Vision and Robotics

Image processing is present also in a second application class with scene analysis and recognition which is employed in industrial systems or research projects for artificial machine vision. Current computer vision systems barely achieve real-time performance, without providing flexibility and future improvements at any processing level (high-level scene analysis, objects recognition and low-level imaging).

An example is a real-time robot vision system, in which images are filtered by a preliminary 'edge-detection' stage. The subsequent image representations are inserted into a relational database in terms of topological features, as well as pictorial-geometric description. Final merged regions are suitable for a polar description that allows the shape recognition process to be invariant to rotation, translation, and scaling.

The EMMA2 hardware configuration is made up of one Region and two Families, with a total of 39 PEs interfaced to a flexible assembly cell. The vision algorithm is identically replied on all PEs, while the monitor of the assembly cell resides in a P1 module.

Another application of this class concerns the realization of automatic systems for mail sorting able to detect and to locate reliably the position of the mailpiece address block, which may be written in non-standard fonts. This task of Address Block Location (ABL), can be accomplished by systems that use all the early vision techniques developed so far: edge extraction, binarization, region growing, colour transforms and so on.

The system we developed is composed of two main sections: the image analysis system (IAS) and the knowledge-based system (KBS). The former performs all computation tasks on raw image data in order to produce a description of their most relevant features; the latter matches the information previously obtained against *a priori*, empirical and statistical knowledge, coded in form of rules, able to deal with fuzzy and approximate data.

The required throughput is 12 letters/s, 5 flats/s and 1 IPPs/s, supported by an EMMA2 system configured with one Region of four to five Families, respectively for image input, low resolution preprocessing, optional low-resolution morphological filtering, high resolution processing and KBS processing. The maximum configuration can include 130 PEs.

7.3. SAR processing

An interesting recently emerged field of multiprocessor application is satellite image processing and remoted data sensing by use of Synthetic Aperture Radar (SAR) equipment. In this kind of sensor, each signal is an amplitude and phase measure of the electromagnetic field, scattered in a large number of high resolution elements, instead of a traditional single resolution element employed in optical and infrared sensors.

The SAR image processor executes a two-dimensional, separable and commutative correlation, carried on using FFT doppler algorithm. The ERS-1 (European Remote Sensing Satellite) specifically requires an input data rate of 100 Mbit/s, an output data rate of 40 Mbit/s, and a computation speed of about 1.3 gigaOPS. Such SAR image processing on a conventional VAX 11/780 would perform at speeds about 1500 to 2000 times less than real-time acquisition rate. Executing in the EMMA2 environment, speed increases to 30–100 times less than real-time reference rate.

In this multiprocessor realization, a four-stage pipeline carries out the following tasks: raw data input and range compression, azimuth spectral analysis, azimuth compression and image data output. The EMMA2 configuration needed includes one Region and two Families, with a total of 86 PEs.

8. NOVEL ARCHITECTURE AND OS EVOLUTION

Evolution trends are driven by precise system requirements: enhancing the parallel programming environment application software; improving run-time processing and communication perfomance, to reduce the final configuration costs; realizing an open architecture, facilitating the insertion of third-party components, like digital signal processors or RISC coprocessors, and integrating the system with industry-standard environments.

Interoperability with heterogeneous machines, and the CISC–RISC coprocessing capability, could guarantee application benefits when employing the EMMA2 multiprocessor as a standard component of complex and distributed processing systems. In this way, its signal processing engine service can be factorized into multiple cooperative nodes, while the inheritance of external high-level functionalities, can smooth its natural technological obsolescence.

The EMMA2 architecture will become a 32/64-bit machine based on the Intel microprocessor line, with global improvements in machine features, aiming at increasing the uniformity and the common address space visibility, while maintaining the distributed memory approach. Internally, a dataflow-oriented twin busses structure, reflecting the present one, but with direct access among Families, will reduce the communication overhead, maintaining computational locality and concentrating multiprocessor interactions and fast DMA transfers over global bus features for control-oriented dedicated messages.

New modules under development will belong mainly to two system functions, the PN multiprocessing engine and the communication I/O module. PN modules will have both Region and Family interface capability, local shared memory split among PEs, and a distributed DMA facility. I/O modules will present the same whole system visibility, with an internal modular hardware structure, decoupling standard from device-dependent parts.

Connectivity among host and EMMA2 nodes will be improved by local area network extensions, while higher programming layers will overlap both the host and the target environments, making it easier to develop programs with parallelism and distribution of concurrent functions.

9. CONCLUDING REMARKS

EMMA2 OS has been in use for some years at many sites in Italy and abroad; new applications are under development, as well as constant improvements to system software. Reports from programmers and operators are encouraging for both development costs and final performance; the low failure rate shows an acceptable robustness of target hardware and system software.

9.1. Comparison with similar architectures

A comparison in terms of absolute performance with today's architectures would not make sense, since many current CPUs develop the same computing power of many 286s, which have a 16-bit architecture and a clock of 10 MHz on EMMA2.

In the mid-80s, when EMMA2 was developed, some commercial parallel machines were already available but, in our opinion, not suited to our needs. Two well-known systems of that time are Alliant FX/8 (eight Computational Elements based on custom extensions of M68020; 32 Mbytes shared memory; Concentrix operating system; Fortran 8X) and Sequent Balance (30 Processors based on NS32032; 16 MBytes shared memory; Dynix operating system; Fortran 77 with parallel extensions).

Both had the advantages of architectural uniformity, 32-bit CPUs, cache policies, Unix-like environments and standard languages enriched for easy parallelization of programs. However, a survey of their main features[6] show that they are particularly suited to parallel execution of number-crunching programs, for instance scientific calculus or simulation, which require efficient support of languages, floating-point computation, data sharing and standard I/O.

Industrial applications for image understanding, character recognition, robotics, SAR processing and others, instead, require: little or no floating-point computation, using predominantly integer or bit-wise custom operations; flexible and scalable machines, ranging from few processors to hundreds; real-time services; efficient data block transfers; and the capability to interact not only with standard peripherals, but also with sensors, controllers and mechanical devices.

EMMA2 satisfied these requirements with its ability to combine common architectural properties (hierarchy, scalability, memory distribution, uniform and real-time OS services, transparent communications and I/O) and custom solutions to particular problems (interaction with field devices, high capacity dual-port memories, custom coprocessors). Besides, the cost/performance ratio (about 2,000 dollars for each PE, delivering 1 MIPS) was better than other commercial parallel processors of the mid-1980s.

9.2. Future activities

Future activities will mainly deal with the hardware/software architecture and the programming model. As explained before, EMMA2 will become a machine based on the

32-bit Intel microprocessors and with global improvements in machine features, aiming to increase the uniformity and the common address space visibility.

Major benefits, both in terms of system efficiency and of applications support, will come from the new architectural features: system uniformity and high level modelling, to help fast prototyping; base system framework, with its protected environment, to maintain and improve real-time operating system functionalities; and DSP/RISC coprocessing capabilities, in order to better accomplish typical signal processing functions.

The base programming model will rely on the current one, with a simplified structure for some internal parts described in this paper, but higher programming layers will overlap on both the host and target environments, to enhance parallelism and program development support. Research will be also carried out on language notation and integration of distributed systems, with both sequential and logic paradigms.

REFERENCES

1. E. Appiani, High performance with medium-grained parallelism: EMMA2 architecture and its operating system, *Proceedings of International Conference on Parallel Processing and Applications*, L'Aquila (1987), pp. 23–32, Scuola Superiore G. Reiss Romoli, L'Aquila (1987).
2. E. Appiani, B. Conterno, V. Luperini and L. Roncarolo, 'EMMA2, a high-performance hierarchical multiprocessor', *IEEE Micro*, February, 42–56 (1989).
3. E. Appiani, D. Bianco, L. Briano, L. Grattarola and L. Merlo, 'The EMMA2 system software environment', *International Conference on Supercomputing Tools for Science and Engineering*, Pisa (1989), Franco Angeli, Milano (1990).
4. D. Bianco and V. Luperini, 'The EMMA2 parallel processor and its industrial applications', *First International Exhibition and Conference on RISC–Transputer Architecture and Application*, RISC 90, Karlsruhe (1990), pp. 137–145.
5. Z. Cvetanovic, 'The effects of problem partitioning, allocation, and granularity on the performance of multiple-processor systems, *IEEE Transactions on Computers*, C-**36**, 421–432 (1987).
6. R.G. Babb II, *Programming Parallel Processors*, Addison-Wesley, Reading, MA (1988).
7. K. Hwang and Faye A. Briggs, *Computer Architecture and Parallel Processing*, McGraw-Hill, New York (1984).
8. *iAPX286 Programmer's Reference Manual*, Intel Corp., Santa Clara, CA (1985).

Portable tools for Fortran parallel programming

SWARN P. KUMAR AND IVOR R. PHILIPS

Boeing Computer Services
PO Box 24346, M/S 7L-22
Seattle, WA 98124-0346, USA

SUMMARY

This paper presents a survey of some of the tools, techniques, and constructs for the development of portable, multitasked Fortran programs. The study mainly focuses on existing software tools that implement different approaches to achieving portability of multitasked Fortran programs for local and shared memory multiprocessor computers. However, some proposed approaches are also included. It appears that while each approach enjoys some advantages and suffers some disadvantages, at present, the development and use of portable multitasking tools is in its infancy, and thus no one system is clearly superior. Indeed, we expect that, for the foreseeable future, these and perhaps other techniques will all be actively pursued.

1. INTRODUCTION

The emergence of a wide variety of multiprocessor computer systems (e.g. CRAY X/Y-MP[5], Alliant FX/Series[2], Sequent Balance and Symmetry Systems[17], Intel iPSC[11], BBN Butterfly[4], Connection Machine[10]) is accompanied by the need for suitable programming tools and models to make efficient use of these systems. Because the technology of parallel computation is so new, most commercial systems have been delivered with very little software support other than the addition of a few extensions to the standard programming languages Fortran and C.

Two of the main issues in parallel computation are:

- Complexity: parallel programs are much more difficult to design and debug than their scalar counterparts. This is due to the complex synchronization and data scoping issues involved. User's needs range from taking an existing scalar code and, with no code changes, have it run efficiently on a parallel architecture, to designing parallel code by explicitly employing multi-tasking (and vector) concepts.
- Transportability: a wide variety of parallel architectures are now available commercially, ranging from mini-supercomputers to full supercomputers. From a user's viewpoint, it is often desirable to have a multi-tasked code developed on one computer type run efficiently, with no coding changes, on a different computer type.

There is need for as much automatic parallelism as possible. A large class of users—generally, those who are primarily scientists or engineers—wish to concentrate on the technology aspects of their particular problems; not on expending considerable programming effort explicitly multi-tasking their code. For such users, the tools must not become more important than the problem being solved. The Alliant FX/Series currently caters to this class of users by automatic vectorization and multi-tasking of Do loops in a

---

1040–3108/91/060559–14$07.00
Received 23 October 1990
Revised 4 June 1991

Fortran code. Kuck and Associates[14] have developed an automatic Do loop parallelizer, called KAP, for the Sequent computer systems.

It is clear, however, that further large increases in speed are possible if code, originally designed for scalar architectures, is reworked to take explicit advantage of parallelism. A significant class of users is willing to expend further effort to gain such increases in speed. They are willing to exploit parallelism by explicitly reworking their Fortran codes but would like to do it in such a way that a program that has been multi-tasked on one computer will execute efficiently on a different parallel architecture. This requirement for portability immediately precludes the use of vendor-specific parallel extensions to Fortran 77.

This study mainly focuses on the existing software tools that implement different approaches to achieving portability of multi-tasked Fortran programs. They are:

(1) The SCHEDULE[7] package that allows users to structure Fortran programs as a system of statically or dynamically allocated processes by explicitly inserting calls to SCHEDULE subroutines in their code.

(2) The FORCE[12] package of macros that are inserted into Fortran code and are then interpreted by a preprocessor to produce standard Fortran 77 enhanced by machine-specific compiler directives.

(3) A conceptual package named Parallel Fortran[3] of compiler directives, called the Language Layer for Concurrency, that would help compilers identify parallel constructs that currently resist automatic analysis.

(4) The Parallel Computing Forum (PCF)[15], a mixed organization of parallel computer vendors and others interested in parallel constructs are developing a common set of parallel Fortran extensions.

(5) The Linda[1,9] set of operators that conceptually could be added to many programming languages—Fortran or C, for example—to turn them into parallel programming languages.

(6) The Strand[8,18] parallel programming environment based on parallel semantics (concurrent logic programming) that allow parallel streams to be mapped directly into executable Strand code to take advantage of the available parallel hardware.

The rest of the paper is divided as follows: Section 2 describes the SCHEDULE package. An overview of the FORCE package is given in Section 3. Section 4 discusses the Parallel Fortran compiler directives for multi-tasking. Section 5 contains a discussion of the PCF. Section 6 contains a discussion of the Linda operators as applied to Fortran. Section 7 contains a discussion of the Strand parallel programming tools. Section 8 concludes the document.

2. SCHEDULE

SCHEDULE is a package of Fortran-callable subroutines designed to permit the writing of portable, multiprocessing programs. The SCHEDULE package was developed by Jack Dongarra and Danny Sorensen[7] of Argonne National Laboratory.

The SCHEDULE package is designed for parallelism at the subroutine level. Thus, Fortran DO loops cannot be parallelized without significant modification of the original program. However, offsetting this disadvantage, a SCHEDULE program can call existing, unmodified Fortran subroutines. This protects investment in previous (scalar) software.

The SCHEDULE package also has the capability to log library events with a trace file created at the end of a run. This trace file can be used to create a graphical representation of the multi-processing activity performed and debugging.

To implement the concept on a particular computer, a machine-specific version of SCHEDULE must be made available as a part of the operating system. SCHEDULE is at present implemented on the Alliant FX/8, CRAY-2, Sequent Balance and Symmetry, Sun, and Encore computer systems.

2.1. The SCHEDULE approach

SCHEDULE requires the user to define tasks (consisting of subroutines that are independently executable) and the data dependencies between the tasks. SCHEDULE, in conjunction with the local operating system, then schedules the tasks for parallel execution appropriately.

The design of a SCHEDULE program thus proceeds in several stages:

(a) Identify parallel structures. That is, identify subroutines that can be executed in parallel with other subroutines.
(b) Identify data dependencies. That is, for each subroutine from step (a), determine how its inputs depend on the prior completion of the other subroutines, and which of its outputs are required as inputs for the subsequent execution of other subroutines.

   This set of subroutines and data dependencies determines the parallel execution of the program. It may be that an existing program is already structured in such a way that a large degree of parallelism can be obtained with no essential change of the underlying algorithms or code. However, in many cases, algorithms and code will have to be significantly modified to take advantage of parallelism. This is true for all scalar code being executed in a parallel environment using the various extensions to Fortran described in this paper.
(c) Write a Fortran code using the SCHEDULE extensions. This is done by calling SCHEDULE subroutines to define tasks. Each task consists of a user subroutine name, from step (a), and its actual arguments, together with the data dependency information from step (b). The programmer must also provide a unique positive number for each task.

As a result of steps (a), (b), and (c), a program will be produced that can be run in either serial or parallel mode.

SCHEDULE operates by considering each task as a node in a dependency graph. Thus, in Figure 1, tasks T_1, T_2, and T_4 have no dependencies on predecessor tasks and could begin executing immediately. Task T_3 cannot start until tasks T_1 and T_2 complete. Task T_5 cannot start until tasks T_3 and T_4 complete. Tasks T_6 and T_7 cannot start until task T_3 completes.

SCHEDULE will not start executing a task until all the predecessor dependencies have been satisfied—that is, all the inputs from predecessor tasks have been calculated. Initially, in a well-formed program, it is clear there must be at least one task that can

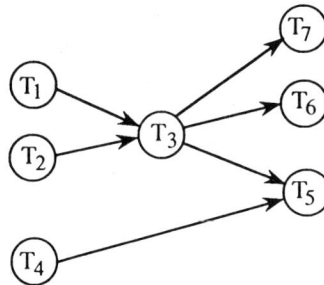

Figure 1. Example of a data dependency graph

start executing. When SCHEDULE completes a task, the predecessor dependencies of all task nodes that depend on it are decremented by 1.

When a task is complete, SCHEDULE then selects one of the remaining tasks that now have no unsatisfied predecessor dependencies, continuing until all tasks have been executed. In a well-framed program this process will always be possible.

The number of virtual processors to work on a program segment may be set dynamically. Generally, it is advisable to set the number of virtual processors so as to not exceed the number of actual processors available on a system. Both static and dynamic task scheduling is possible and tasks may also spawn one sublevel of processes. The reader is referred to Reference 7 for further information.

2.2. Comments on SCHEDULE

SCHEDULE is a portable parallel programming tool suitable for both local and shared memory multi-processor systems. Some other advantages of the SCHEDULE package are:

- Both static and dynamic scheduling of processes are allowed.
- It has the capability of executing parallel programs in serial mode.
- It can spawn parallel processes at the nested level other than DO loops.
- Existing (scalar) libraries of subroutines can be called in parallel without any modifications.
- It supports both functional and data decomposition parallelism.
- Graphical display tools for debugging purposes are provided.

The SCHEDULE tool however, is not a final solution to the portable parallel programming problem. This has been stated by the authors of the package. SCHEDULE basically provides users a portable way of structuring Fortran programs as a system of statically or dynamically allocated processes. Parallelism is only permitted at the subroutine level. Fine-grained parallelism is not possible. The burden of specifying the communication between processes, by the data dependency graph, is on the user. Process management is also explicitly done by the user. The SCHEDULE approach also involves a complicated set of primitives. Too much responsibility for managing the parallel execution may not be attractive to many engineers and scientists in the computational community.

The basic concept behind SCHEDULE has provided a good starting point for the development of other such tools. Mark Seager and his collegues at Lawrence Livermore National Laboratory started the software package libCray.a[6] and GMAT[18], Cray-compatible tools for the Alliant FX/8 computer, with SCHEDULE-based concepts.

3. THE FORCE

The FORCE is a macro preprocessor that provides a set of directives to Fortran. The directives permit small- and large-grain parallelism in a shared-memory multiprocessor environment. The FORCE was designed by Harry Jordan and his students at the University of Colorado[12].

In the FORCE environment, parallelism is achieved by defining a fixed number of processes at the beginning of program execution (the fixed number could be one). All processes then are active from the beginning to the end of the program with each process having access to the complete program. Each process, however, can perform different parts of the total work with various synchronization constructs controlling their flow.

The FORCE is implemented at present in a Unix-based environment on the Alliant FX/8, Multimax Encore, Sequent Balance, and the CRAY-2 parallel/vector computers.

3.1. The FORCE approach

At the beginning of a FORCE program, all processes start to execute the program. To control their flow, barriers and critical regions are inserted into the program. Unlike SCHEDULE, the processes are anonymous to the programmer and have no individual identification. Thus, there is no direct process synchronization or management required of the programmer. A barrier or critical region can be inserted around any section of executable code that is contained within a single program unit.

The code within a barrier does not execute until all the processes reach the beginning of the barrier. When this occurs, one process is arbitrarily selected to execute the code within the barrier. When the selected process completes execution of the code within the barrier all processes then start executing the code following the end of the barrier.

The code within a critical region must be executed by each process, one at a time.

In a FORCE program, variables and COMMON blocks may be declared to be either PRIVATE or SHARED. The default is PRIVATE. Each process gets its own copy of PRIVATE variables and COMMON blocks. Consequently, when a process changes a PRIVATE entity the change is confined to that process. The values of the corresponding entity in the other processes remains unaltered. By contrast, shared variables are available to all processes. If any process changes a shared variable that change affects all other processes subsequently referencing that variable. The concept of shared and private variables assists in keeping the processes anonymous to the programmer—variables do not have to be explicitly associated with processes.

There are several other FORCE directives, controlling the flow of processes, added to standard Fortran 77. The parallel CASE statement defines blocks to be executed in parallel by arbitrary processes. There are two kinds of parallel DO statements. The first form assigns processes to perform the calculation within the DO systematically, based on the DO indices. This form should be used when the times needed to complete the calculations are essentially independent of the value of the DO index. The second form is driven by the availability of processes. This second form involves more processor synchronization activity and should be used when the time to perform to calculations within the DO block depends strongly on the value of the DO index. Each of the parallel DO statements may be nested two deep.

Not all of the FORCE's constructs have been given here. For more information the reader is referred to Reference 12.

The FORCE may be readily transported to new shared-memory parallel environments. Mutual exclusion and process counting are sufficient to implement most of the FORCE's parallel constructs.

3.2. Comments on the FORCE

The FORCE is a portable (shared memory multiprocessor) programming tool for parallel execution of many processes all working to solve a single problem. The highlights of the package are:

- Process management is invisible to the user. Processes are created and terminated at the top of the program hierarchy.
- Parallelism using a generic synchronization mechanism.
- Program independence of the number of processes specified.
- It is highly suitable for tightly coupled parallel programming.
- The ease of programming (small set of primitives to learn).
- Parallel constructs are allowed at any level of the program hierarchy. Hence both coarse- and fine-grained parallelism are supported.
- Existing (scalar) libraries of subroutines can be called in parallel.
- Correctness of program execution can be tested with one process, independently of effects due to improper synchronization.
- It supports primarily data decomposition parallelism—as compared to functional decomposition.

A major weakness in the set of FORCE macros (it its present version) is that it does not efficiently support functional decomposition parallelism of a program—an often-desired feature at the upper levels of a program's hierarchy. Harry Jordan and his group have suggested the macro *Resolve* (since the macro *Pcase* allows only one process to execute each of the parallel functions) which will resolve the Force into components executing different parallel code sections. The implementation of *Resolve* is complicated by the conflicting demands of generality and efficiency (that is, if complete independence from the number of processes is required). It is our understanding that an implementation of the *Resolve* macro, which will produce process rescheduling at every possible deadlock point, and is still efficient when the number of processes exceeds the number of components, is under development at the University of Colorado.

4. PARALLEL FORTRAN

Since Fortran is the first choice for a programming language in most physical science and engineering applications, vendors and researchers in the supercomputing community are making a serious effort to provide parallel processing within Fortran. Unfortunately, many of the basic constructs of standard Fortran strongly conflict with the most obvious primitives of parallel processing. Clifford Arnold and his associates[3], have announced the development of a set of compiler directives to alter Fortran for parallel processing without any formal language extensions.

The basic aim of this approach was to extend the Fortran standards informally by compiler directives without violating the ANSI language definition. The goal was to develop a strategy that allows the compiler to generate multitasking code for a larger context than DO loop nests.

4.1. The parallel Fortran approach

The proposed approach (for the solution of parallel computational problems) is that of the so-called language layer for concurrency. This high-level layer for concurrency is used to implement parallel concepts such as: *do all, do parallel, common, task common* in Fortran itself. It is claimed that the compiler directives used for development will be portable and will allow efficient code to be generated for a large variety of shared memory or other parallel architectures.

The goal is to help the compiler understand code sequences and generate multi-tasking code in situations that currently resist automatic analysis. Code segments that are parallelizable, where the rate of computing to I/O is greater than $9:1$, are the prime targets for this approach. The idea is to make maximum usage of the compiler's analysis capability while allowing a user to provide the extra information needed to assist in more complete parallelization.

The approach is based on a set of optional user directives for multitasking. The compiler interprets them in order to dispose of problems inhibiting automatic parallelization. If the directives are not interpreted, the code will run serially on one processor. If the directives are used but not all of barriers to parallelization are removed, the compiler will generate uniprocessor code with appropriate diagnostics about the remaining problems. These diagnostics will inform the user of the additional multitasking directives needed to generate parallelized code.

The general form of a multitasking directive used in this approach is:

$$C\#MTL \; directive[(arg_1,...,arg_n)]$$

The set of directives includes: *INITIALIZE, SETTINGS, BEGIN PARALLEL, END PARALLEL, PARALLEL DO, END PARALLEL DO, SHARE, GET, PUT, BARRIER, WAIT, BROADCAST, MULTIPLE BLOCK, NEXT BLOCK, END MULTIPLE BLOCK, GUARD, END GUARD.*

The *share* directive informs the compiler of COMMON blocks that are to be shared among processes within a particular *begin parallel...end parallel* section. The *parallel do* directive instructs the compiler to partition candidate DO loops into tasks that will execute in parallel, *end parallel* do marks the end of a parallel do structure. The *get* directive tells the compiler to get data from a portion of an array contained in a shared COMMON block and put it in a task's local array of the same name. The *put* directive performs the reverse function. For a more detailed description of these directives see Reference 3.

4.2. Comments on parallel Fortran

This appears to be a good direction to investigate. it provides a set of multi-tasking directives that are clear, comprehensive, and portable. However, as yet, no implementations have occurred. Practical experience is needed before this proposal can be fully evaluated.

5. THE PARALLEL COMPUTING FORUM (PCF)

(PCF) was organized by Bruce Leasure of Kuck and Associates[15]. It consists of members from various computer vendors and users interested in the development of a set of portable extensions, for parallel programming, to Fortran and C. The forum has been meeting regularly for several years to define such parallel extensions.

5.1. The PCF approach

PCF has extended Fortran 77 by adding *parallel constructs*. The set of parallel extensions to Fortran 77 described below is based on a PCF draft dated 21 January 1990. It should be realized that the draft standard is subject to change.

(1) A program is executed, in parallel, by one or more processes working in collaboration.
(2) A single process (the base process) begins execution of a program. When the process encounters a parallel construct, the system may assign extra processes (a team) to enter the construct and assist in its execution. The base process may, at the operating systems discretion, assist in the execution of the parallel construct. The number of extra processes involved is determined by the operating system. The only control the programmer has is that a maximum number of processes may be specified. At any time, as long as there is work remaining to be done, the system may assign extra processes to the team executing a parallel construct.
(3) Each process in a team begins execution of the parallel construct with the first statement of the construct.
(4) There are special constructs called work sharing constructs, except for the code in a work sharing construct, all processes in a team execute all parts of the parallel construct redundantly.

    For a work sharing construct, the operating system determines which members of the teams will participate in its execution.

    Each participating process performs some part of the required work. Note the distinction from a parallel construct where each process in a team will execute the code redundantly.

    When a participating process completes its assignment it will wait at the end of the work-sharing construct for the rest of the participants to complete their work. However, if there is more unassigned work to be performed in the *work-sharing* construct then the process may be assigned to perform some portion of that work.

    When all the work in a work-sharing construct is completed all the participating processes can then resume execution of the next statement in the code
(5) When all the processes in a team have completed their work, the base process,

which waits at the end of the parallel construct for this to occur, continues execution of the next statement. The processes in the team do not perform any further work.

(6) Nested parallelism may occur when the member of a team itself encounters a parallel construct. In this case, the above process is repeated recursively, with the team member that encountered the parallel construct itself becoming a base member for a team of associated processes.

(7) An object may be labelled private or shared. If an object is labelled private then each process in a team has its own copy of the object. If an object is shared then each process on the team shares the object's storage with the base process. The default is shared. Thus, if a process changes the value of a private object, that is a local change for that process only and other processes in the team do not see this change in their copy of the object. The converse is true for shared objects.

Some of the parallel constructs in the language are LOCK, UNLOCK, CRITICAL SECTION, PARALLEL DO, PARALLEL SECTIONS, PRIVATE, SHARED. The PARALLEL DO and the PARALLEL SECTIONS are examples of work-sharing constructs.

5.2. Comments on PCF

In September 1989 the PCF became an American National Standards Committee—X3H5: Parallel Processing Constructs For High-Level Programming Languages.

The parallel computing extensions to standard Fortran 77 are entirely within the spirit of Fortran, giving the programmer detailed control over parallelism. However, the programmer must give meticulous attention to process synchronization and data-sharing issues. A parallel program will almost always be more complex to write and debug than its non-parallel equivalent.

6. LINDA

Linda is a parallel programming tool based on an associative object memory model. It provides parallelism in Fortran (and other programming languages) in a particularly simple manner by providing an additional set of four operations. A Linda program consists of a collection of objects occupying a region called *tuple space*. Programs write and read n-tuples (of various lengths) of data into tuple space. Tuple space is a shared environment accessible to all parts of a program. In addition, special n-tuples can be launched into tuple space that consist of a set of n functions that are to be evaluated. This n-tuple becomes a separate task that, when it completes execution, resolves itself into an n-tuple of values in the tuple space. Arbitrary nesting of Linda operations is permitted. Thus, a Linda task can itself launch Linda tasks.

6.1. The Linda approach

In Linda, parallelism is achieved by creating a tuple space of data and processes. There are no explicit synchronization constructs in Linda. Processes create and consume entities in tuple space. Once a tuple is in the tuple space there is no communication back to the process that created it.

There are only four constructs in Linda, two for adding entities to tuple space and two for reading entities in tuple space.

The OUT($e_1,e_2, \ldots ,e_n$) construct evaluates $e_1,e_2, \ldots ,e_n$ and then adds the resulting n-tuple of values ($e_1,e_2, \ldots ,e_n$) to tuple-space, where $e_1,e_2,\ldots ,e_n$ are each expressions. Thus OUT(`point`, x, y) and OUT(x, SQRT(1.- x**2), 1., `CIRCLE`, `SHADE`) would add a 3-tuple and a 5-tuple, respectively, to the tuple space.

The EVAL($f_1,f_2, \ldots ,f_n$) construct adds a process to the tuple-space, where $f_1, \ldots ,f_n$ are each user-defined functions. The process may be executed in parallel with any other process in the tuple space. The program does not wait for the process to complete but goes on to the next statement. Thus EVAL(`bearing`, 23, f(x,y), g(z)), (where f and g are user-defined functions, creates a separate process that, when it executes, will evaluate the four expressions in the tuple (the first two evaluations are trivial, being constants) and add the resulting 4-tuple to tuple space. The process will be added to the list of processes waiting to be executed. The order of selection of processes for execution is indeterminate.

The IN and RD constructs both read data from tuple-space. The only difference is that IN removes the item from the tuple space while RD leaves it behind for possible subsequent reading by other parts of the program. They both function by pattern matching. The form is IN($\alpha_1, \ldots, \alpha_n$), where each α_i is either a constant or a variable name. The effect of this operation is to search the tuple space for an entity that matches the pattern specified (in position and value) by the constant α_is. When such an entity is found, the values of the variable α_is are set to the corresponding values in the item found in the tuple space.

The matching entity will then be removed from the tuple space. If such an entity is not found in the tuple space the processor executing the IN operation will suspend until success eventually occurs.

The RD construct functions similarly, except that the matching entity, when found, is not removed from the tuple space.

There is no ordering in tuple space. So that the order of defining processes via EVAL does not specify an execution order. Also, the order of writing entities into tuple space bears no connection with the order in which they may be found by an IN or a RD operation.

6.2. Comments on Linda

Linda was initially defined by David Gelernter et al.[1], and then subsequently refined by Gelernter, Carriero, Chandron, and Chang[9].

When compared with the other methods presented here, Linda is striking in its simplicity—the programmer does not have to consider the synchronization of processes. Observe that the Linda constructs cannot stand by themselves; they must be embedded in a high-level language—Fortran or C, for example.

An unanswered question is efficiency. Until we have access to a Fortran version of Linda we cannot answer this question.

7. STRAND

Strand is the most radical departure from the Fortran style of thinking of any of the concepts presented here. It is based on concurrent logic programming[19]. Because of its differences from Fortran, we will present the basic concepts of Strand in more detail than we have done for the other methods described in this paper. It is still, however, far from a complete description of Strand.

7.1. The Strand approach

The data structures in Strand are called terms. They are of four basic types:

(1) Numbers: integers or real. For example, 347, 23.96.
(2) Strings: sequences of characters delimited by single or double quotes. For example, 'cat', "Dog*@!".
(3) Variables: sequences of characters and numbers. They must begin with a capital letter or an underscore (_). For example, Altitude, X_32. Unlike Fortran, a variable may only be assigned once.
(4) Structures: these are collections of data items (which could themselves be structures). There are two basic types of structures:
    (a) Tuples: these are n-ary trees, represented as a set of data items enclosed in braces. For example, {'abc', {3, 4.2}, 79}. This is a 3-ary tree containing a 2-ary tree as an element.
    (b) Lists: these are binary trees in which each element is denoted by [Head|Tail]. For example, ['abc | [{3, 4.2} | [79| [ ]]]]. Note the empty list, [ ]. For convenience, this can be written as ['abc', {3, 4.2}, 79].

A Strand program consists of a *pool* of interacting processes and a set of *rules*. Strand executes a program by randomly selecting a process from the pool of unexecuted processes and determines if it can be *reduced* (described below). If it can, it is removed from the pool of processes and the process *commits*. This continues until no processes are left in the pool.

A process is defined as a term of the form

$$p(T_1, \ldots, T_n) \qquad (n \geq 0)$$

where p is the process name and $T_1, \ldots, T_n$ is the process data state (The Ts are similar to the Fortran concept of subprogram arguments.) A process receives a local copy of the data state. Note that, unlike Fortran, a process may be referenced with different numbers of arguments. Thus the pair p/n identifies the process definition.

Programs are defined as a set of *rules*. Each rule defines a single action (depending on the initial data state). This is different from Fortran, where the definition of a subprogram is contained in one program body. For example, a Fortran subprogram that had a two-way branch in it would be represented in Strand as two rules—one for each branch.

To define a rule, a concise notation is used:

$$H :- G_1, \ldots, G_m \mid B_1, \ldots, B_n. \qquad m,n \geq 0$$

where H is the rule *head* and has the same form as a process, :- is the *implies* operator, the Gs are the rule *guard*, and the Bs are the rule *body*.

Before a process can be reduced (removed from the pool of processes) two preconditions must be satisfied. The first is *matching*. That is the data structure of the process must match (in number, position, and data type) the data structure of some rule head. Secondly, each element of the rule guard specifies a logical condition that must be satisfied by the process data state before the rule will be executed. The guards correspond to Fortran IF tests.

If these two conditions are satisfied, the invoking process is removed from the pool of unexecuted processes, it *changes state* to one of $B_1,\ldots,B_n$ (selected randomly), and *forks* the remaining $(n - 1)$ B processes (that is, it adds them to the pool of unexecuted processes).

The following simple example illustrates some of the strand concepts. This Strand program will find the maximum element in a list and put it in M. The program is intended to illustrate the Strand philosophy—not to demonstrate the most efficient way such a problem could be solved in Strand.

```
%  R1  Initialize with the first element
max([X | Xs], M) :-
  max1(Xs, X, M).


%  R2  Replace the maximum to date
max1([Y | Ys], Q, M) :-
  Y >= Q |
                Q1 := Y,
                max1(Ys, Q1, M).


%  R3  Examine next element
max1([Y | Ys], Q, M) :-
  Y < Q |
                max1(Ys, Q, M).


%  R4  Set Global maximum
max1([ ], Q, M) :-
  M := Q.
```

Table 1 shows a possible execution sequence for this program. It can be seen that a Strand program is driven by data availability, not process synchronization.

Table 1

Step	Process chosen	Result	Process pool	Comments
0	—	—	max([7, 1, 9], M)	Only R1 can be applied
1	1	Change state	max1([1, 9], 7, M)	Only R3 can be applied
2	1	Change state	max1([9], 7, M)	Only R2 can be applied
3	1	Change state & fork	Q1:=9, max1([ ], Q1, M)	Either process can be selected
4	2	Change state & fork	Q1:=9, M:=Q1	Apply intrinsic assignment
5	1	Terminate	M:=9	Apply intrinsic assignment
6	1	Terminate	Empty and $M = 9$	Program terminates

If the process pool initially was max($[7, 1, 9]$, $M1$), max($[3, 6, 1, 2]$, $M2$), max($[M1, M2]$, M), then the program could interleave the selection of the three sets of processes generated by each of the original max processes. The final result will, of course, be that $M = 9$.

Using the ability to define data structures, Strand processes can interact with existing code written in Fortran (and other languages). This permits the reuse, in the Strand environment, of the large investment already made in existing Fortran code.

We appreciate the assistance provide to us by Timothy G. Mattson of Strand Software Technologies Inc. Any errors in the description of Strand in this paper are, of course, the fault of the authors.

If multiple processors are available they may all be selecting processes from the pool of unexecuted processes. This is how parallelism may be achieved in Strand. In fact, Strand has specific directives for defining common structures for parallel architectures. Thus, a ring or a torus of processors may be defined and processes may be directed to execute on different processors. In the preceding second example above, two or more processors could be used to process the sets of max processes being generated.

7.2. Comments on Strand

Strand is based on the work of Foster and Taylor[8] and is currently available from Strand Software Technologies Inc.[18].

While Strand, of the ideas presented here, is the furthest conceptually from Fortran, it is straightforward once the different philosophy is grasped. It has the advantage of permitting the use of existing code in other languages—Fortran and C, for example. It is available for Apollo, COGENT, Encore Multimax, Intel iPSC2 and iPSC860, Macintosh, Next, Sequent, Sun computers, and transputer-based systems.

8. CONCLUSIONS

An analytical overview of portable multi-tasking tools (presently available) for parallel Fortran programming is presented. The four most commonly used methods for developing portable multi-tasking programming tools: (i) a multitasking library, (ii) compiler directives, (iii) extending the Fortran language, and (iv) using Fortran as a subset of a higher level language, are covered.

At present, it does not seem possible to draw conclusions about which one of the techniques presented here will prevail. The main factor determining this will be the availability of the tool on a wide variety of multiprocessor systems, ease of use, and efficiency. We will address the last two issues in a subsequent paper. We expect all the approaches defined here to be vigorously pursued.

Finally, we note that there is ordinarily some performance degradation when using the portable multi-tasking tools described in this report—some performance is sacrificed for the sake of portability. This issue has not been addressed here and deserves careful investigation in the future.

REFERENCES

1. S. Ahuja, N. Carriero and D. Gelernter, 'Linda and her friends', *IEEE Computer*, No. 19, 26–34 (1986).

2. Alliant Computer Systems Corporation, *Alliant FX/Series, Product Summary*, Acton, MA, June, 1985.
3. Clifford Arnold, *ETA Systems Multiprocessing Library Specifications*, ETA Systems Inc. (Internal Report) (1987).
4. BBN Inc., *The Butterfly Parallel Processor*, (BBN Report) May, 1986.
5. Cray Research, Inc., *Multitasking User Guide*, Document #SN 0222, Cray Research, Inc. (1986).
6. Kent Crispin and Robert Strout, *NSYSLIB Library Reference Manuals*, LCSD 912, Lawrence Livermore National Laboratory (1985).
7. Jack Dongarra and Danny Sorenson *SCHEDULE: Tools for Developing and Analyzing Parallel Fortran Programs*, ANL/MSC TM 86, Argonne National Laboratory, Math. and Computer Science Division (1986).
8. Ian Foster and Steven Taylor, *STRAND: New Concepts In Parallel Programming*, Prentice Hall, Englewood Cliffs, NJ (1990).
9. D. Gelernter, N. Carriero, S. Chandran and S. Chang, 'Parallel programming in Linda', *Proceedings of the 1985 International Conference on Parallel Processing*, IEEE Computer Society, 255–263 (1985).
10. W. D. Hillis, *The Connection Machine*, The MIT Press, Cambridge, MA.
11. Intel Scientific Computers Inc., *The iPSC Multiprocessor*, Beaverton, OR.
12. Harry Jordan *et al.*, *Force User's Manual*, Department of Electrical and Computer Engineering, University of Colorado (1986).
13. Bruce Kelly, *MAT: Multitasking Analysis Tool*, LCSD 347, Lawrence Livermore National Laboratory (March, 1986).
14. Kuck and Associates, *KAP: KAP/Sequent User's Guide*, Kuck and Associates Inc., Champaign, IL (1989).
15. Parallel Computing Forum, *PCF Fortran: Language Definition*, version 1, B. Leasure, Editor, 16 August (1988).
16. Mark Seager *et al.*, *Graphical Multiprocessing Analysis Tool (GMAT)*, Lawrence Livermore National Laboratory, document #ISCR 87 2 (1987).
17. Sequent Computer Systems, *Guide to Parallel Programming* (1987).
18. Strand Software Technologies, *A General Purpose Programming System for Concurrent Computers*, Watford, Hertfordshire, UK.
19. S. Taylor, *Parallel Logic Programming Techniques*, Prentice Hall, Englewood Cliffs, NJ (1989).

CONCURRENCY: PRACTICE AND EXPERIENCE, VOL. 3(6), 573–592 (DECEMBER 1991)

Multiprocessors and run-time compilation

JOEL SALTZ, HARRY BERRYMAN AND JANET WU

Institute for Computer Applications in Science and Engineering
NASA Langley Research Center
Hampton, VA 23065, USA

SUMMARY

Run-time preprocessing plays a major role in many efficient algorithms in computer science, as well as playing an important role in exploiting multiprocessor architectures. We give examples that elucidate the importance of run-time preprocessing and show how these optimizations can be integrated into compilers. To support our arguments, we describe transformations implemented in prototype multiprocessor compilers and present benchmarks from the iPSC2/860, the CM-2 and the Encore Multimax/320.

1. INTRODUCTION

1.1. Overview

In many algorithms, data produced or input during a program's initialization plays a large role in determining the nature of the subsequent computation. When the data structures that define a computation have been initialized, a preprocessing phase follows. Vital elements of the strategy used by the rest of the algorithm are determined by this preprocessing phase.

To effectively exploit many multiprocessor architectures, we may also have to carry out run-time preprocessing. This preprocessing will be referred to as *run-time compilation*. The purpose of run-time compilation is not to determine which computations are to be performed but instead to determine how a multiprocessor machine will schedule the algorithm's work, how to map the data structures and how data movement within the multiprocessor is to be scheduled. In this paper, we specifically address problems for which computational patterns can be predicted when values assigned to key data structures are known. These problems include computations on non-uniform meshes, sparse direct factorization which does not involve pivoting and sparse iterative linear solvers.

Values obtained during program execution can affect the nature and degree of potential concurrency. *Run-time compilation may be needed to identify and exploit concurrency.* Complex heterogeneous memory hierarchies characterize virtually all multiprocessor architectures with more than a few dozen processors. Primary memory is divided among processors. To obtain data from other portions of the primary memory of the multiprocessor, we typically need to access a communications network. *Program performance can be dramatically affected by the scheduling of data movement among processors.*

There has been much research carried out on methods for run-time parallelization as well as run-time workload and data partitioning. Most parallelization and

1040–3108/91/060573–20$10.00
©1991 by John Wiley & Sons, Ltd.
Received 23 October 1990
Revised 4 March 1991

problem partitioning methods explicitly or implicitly specify patterns of interprocessor communication. When patterns of computation are determined by data structures initialized during program execution, traditional compiler techniques cannot possibly carry out these partitioning and scheduling operations. Only recently have methods been developed that can integrate the kinds of run-time optimizations mentioned above into compilers and programming environments.

In this paper, we survey recent work on run-time compilation methods targeted towards several different multiprocessor architectures. We describe run-time compilation research targeted towards MIMD shared and distributed memory architectures that has been carried out by the authors, (Section 2 and Section 3). We also describe run-time compilation methods targeted towards the CM-2, developed by Dahl[10] (Section 4).

In the remainder of this introduction, we set the stage for the remainder of this this paper by citing describing preprocessing methods used for several classes of uniprocessor algorithms. In these uniprocessor algorithms, execution-time preprocessing is used to determine key aspects of the computational strategy.

In Section 2, we describe and benchmark several compiler-linked methods for detecting parallelism during program execution. These run-time parallelization methods are described in the context of shared memory architectures. In Section 3, we describe run-time compilation methods that have proved useful for solving unstructured problems on distributed memory architectures. We describe and benchmark a prototype compiler that allows us to efficiently carry out irregular patterns of data access on distributed arrays. These distributed arrays can be partitioned between processors in an arbitrary manner. Finally, in Section 4, we describe and benchmark software designed by Reference 10 to support irregular data reference patterns on the CM-2.

1.2. Algorithmic execution-time preprocessing

In many efficient approaches to solving problems in computing, data produced or input during program execution plays a large role in determining computational patterns. Examples include:

- most searching and sorting problems
- critical path analysis
- game tree and decision tree manipulations
- direct and iterative sparse linear system solvers

Once an appropriate subset of the input (or generated) data is available, it is frequently worthwhile to perform some preprocessing. This preprocessing can take many forms, but results of the preprocessing determine vital elements of the strategy used by the remainder of the algorithm. A simple example of this is the method of interpolated binary search. The number of computations required for a simple binary search of a sorted list depends on the values of the elements in the list and on the value of the key. We can preprocess the sorted list and use the distribution of element values in the list to produce an interpolation function that is used to direct the search. It is frequently possible to amortize the cost of preprocessing. In the interpolated binary search example, once preprocessing is carried out, we can used the interpolation function to search for a sequence of different keys.

Some other examples of well known algorithms that carry out preprocessing to determine vital elements of the strategy used by the remainder of the algorithm are:

(a) Creation of indices to speed data base retrieval where indices are created to allow the use of efficient search methods on many different data base keys[32].
(b) Generation of threaded binary search trees where extra links are added to a binary tree to speed tree traversal[16].
(c) Matrix reordering and symbolic factorization used in sparse direct linear equation solvers. In such problems, the number and pattern of computations in a sparse matrix factorization is determined by the order in which steps in the factorization are carried out. In many cases it is possible to use the non-zero structure of a matrix to predetermine the order in which computations will be carried out and to allocate the memory needed to store the resulting factored matrix[12].

In each of these examples, the results of a single preprocessing computation can be used to solve any member of a class of structurally similar problems. In the data base example, the creation of an index can be followed by an arbitrary number of queries. Once a threaded binary search tree is generated, the resulting data structure can be used in an arbitrary number of tree traversals. A symbolic matrix factorization can be used to speed the factorization of any matrix with a given pattern of non-zero entries.

Run-time compilation techniques attempt to discover how to maximize the performance of algorithms on multiprocessors. Since these methods are particularly useful in algorithms whose computational patterns depend on values assigned to data structures during program execution, a significant preprocessing cost is frequently involved. In run-time compilation, we are also often able to amortize costs of preprocessing among a number of structurally similar computational phases.

2. RUN-TIME PARALLELIZATION FOR SHARED MEMORY ARCHITECTURES

Run-time parallelization is perhaps the most obvious form of multiprocessor run-time compilation. Parallelization carried out during compilation is necessarily conservative. If a compiler cannot figure out how to generate a correct parallelizing loop transformation, loop iterations have to be performed sequentially. Many loop nests defy compile-time parallelization because dependency patterns are determined by variables or arrays initialized during program execution. One way of carrying out run-time parallelization is to analyze the inter-iteration dependency pattern in a loop nest to identify *wavefronts* of concurrently executable loop iterations. Using a form of run-time preprocessing, we transform a loop nest with inter-iteration dependencies into a sequence of parallel loops. Execution time preprocessing is frequently used to parallelize sparse numerical algorithms, such as those arising in sparse direct and iterative linear solvers[2,4,26,11,1].

Typically, programmers need to explicitly code the procedures that carry out the necessary run-time preprocessing. It is possible to produce a *run-time parallelization* program transformation that generates code designed to perform run-time loop parallelization. In this section, we review the approaches described in References [29] and [30]. Related runtime parallelization methods are described in References [37] and [38]. The compiler transforms a loop into *two* separate code segments. The first code segment, the *inspector*, finds sets of independent loop iterations while the second code segment, the *executor*, carries out the scheduled work. Run-time parallelization transformations have been implemented in a prototype compiler targeted at shared memory machines[31]. Run-time compilation only handles a subset of the possible types of run-time parallelization. Our transformations only apply to loop nests in which inter-iteration dependencies do not depend on the results of computations carried out within the loop nest. There are a number of algorithms that merge the process of identifying and performing concurrent work. It seems likely to us that it will be possible to produce compiler transformations that generate hybrid inspector/executors for more fully dynamic algorithms, but we will not address this issue further in this paper.

To clarify the scheme, we now present a simple example. A simple sequential program is presented in Figure 1. Note that right-hand side references to array y use a level of indirection. The inspector used to perform run-time parallelization (Figure 2) is simply a topological sort. This sort can be generated from the parse tree produced by the loop in Figure 1. The inspector in Figure 2 is sequential but can be parallelized using the principles to be described later in this section. Once the wavefront corresponding to each index is known, we can sort the indices in order of increasing wavefront number to produce the array schedule. The inspector also initializes a pointer array count. Array count contains the address in schedule of the beginning of each wavefront. Loop iterations corresponding to wavefront *i* are found in schedule between count(i) and count(i+1)-1.

```
do i=1,N

    y(i) = a(i)*y(ia(i)) + b(i)*y((ib(i)))

end do
```

Figure 1. *Sequential code to be parallelized*

```
wf(1:N) = 0

do i=1,N

    wf(i) = max(wf(i),wf(ia(i)),wf(ib(i))) + 1

end do

Use wf() to produce schedule(), a list of indices in order of increasing
wavefront number
```

Figure 2. *Parallelizing inspector*

The executor in Figure 3 is a sequence of parallel do loops that run over consecutive wavefronts obtained by the inspector from the sequential code in Figure 1. Note that to obtain the correct solution in the executor we need to maintain *two* copies of the array y found in the sequential code. In Figure 3 we call these copies y and ynew.

```
do phase = 1, np

    parallel do i=count(phase),count(phase+1)-1
        ii = schedule(i)

        if(ia(ii).lt.ii) then tmp1 = ynew(ia(ii))
        else tmp1 = y(ia(ii)) endif

        if(ib(ii).lt.ii) then tmp2 = ynew(ib(ii))
        else tmp2 = y(ib(ii)) endif

        ynew(ii) = a(ii)*tmp1 + b(ii)*tmp2

    end parallel do

end do

y(1:n) = ynew(1:n)
```

Figure 3. Parallelizing executor

In evaluating the usefulness of run-time parallelization, the cost of the preprocessing must be taken into account. In Reference 31 we present timings obtained from the run-time parallelization transformation applied to sparse lower triangular solves. On an 18-processor Encore Multimax/320, a single processor required 241 milliseconds to solve a lower triangular system obtained from an incomplete factorization of one of the Boeing Harwell test matrices. On 16 processors of the Multimax, the inspector required 100 milliseconds and the executor required 23 milliseconds. In many situations, we can amortize the cost of an inspector because we need to repeatedly carry out a given pattern of computations. For instance, in iterative linear systems solvers we may need to repeatedly solve the same sparse triangular systems with different right-hand sides.

A variety of trade-offs can be made between the costs and benefits of preprocessing. We can dispense with reordering loop iterations into concurrent wavefronts and still be able to exploit parallelism to a degree by using a *preprocessed doacross* transformation[29]. In a doacross construct[9], loop iterations are partitioned between processors in a striped fashion and synchronization calls are introduced so that computations from some loop iterations can be overlapped. Doacross loops typically make use of *a priori* knowledge of inter-iteration dependencies to carry out needed inter-iteration synchronizations. It is possible to carry out a relatively small amount of run-time preprocessing and postprocessing that eliminates the need for *a priori* knowledge of dependencies. On machines with snooping caches (such as the Multimax/320), it is efficient to synchronize using shared arrays. The following is a sketch of some of the transformations involved in generating preprocessed doacross loops, a much more detailed description may be found in Reference 29. A shared array ready is initialized to NOTDONE. When a left-hand side array element i is calculated, ready(i) is set to DONE. Processors needing to use an updated value of array element i busy wait on ready(i) until ready(i) is set to DONE. In *preprocessed doacross loops*, we need to maintain two copies of shared arrays that appear on the left-hand side of expressions during the computation. After the loop is completed, the two shared array copies need to be reconciled.

The run-time initialization and postprocessing in the preprocessed doacross loop are relatively inexpensive compared to the preprocessing costs incurred by a parallelizing inspector (e.g. Figure 2). For the above-cited lower triangular solve involving the incompletely factored Boeing Harwell test matrix, the preprocessed doacross loop requires 45 milliseconds. This can be compared to the 23 milliseconds required to carry out the run-time parallelized solve and the 100 millisecond preprocessing time of the inspector.

Run-time parallelization can be carried out on a variety of architectures. In this paper, we discuss run-time parallelization only in the context of shared memory architectures; a discussion of run-time parallelization for distributed memory machines is found in Reference 28.

3. RUN-TIME COMPILATION FOR DISTRIBUTED MEMORY MACHINES

3.1. Distributed memory inspectors and executors

In distributed memory machines, large data arrays need to be partitioned between local memories of processors. These partitioned data arrays are called *distributed arrays*. We follow the usual practice of assigning long-term storage of distributed array data to specific memory locations in the distributed machine. A processor that needs to read an array element must fetch a copy of that element from the memory of the processor in which that array element is stored. Alternately, a processor may need to store a value in an off-processor distributed array element. Local copies of off-processor distributed array elements are stored in hash tables called *hashed caches*. Run-time procedures carry out the movement of data between processors and manage the above-mentioned hash tables.

In distributed memory MIMD architectures, there is typically a non-trivial communications latency or startup cost[7]. For efficiency reasons, information to be transmitted should be collected into relatively large messages. The cost of fetching array elements can be reduced by precomputing what data each processor needs to send and to receive.

In Figure 4, we outline the preprocessing we performed to implement a parallel loop on a distributed machine. The distribution of parallel loop indices to processors determines where computations are to be performed. We assume that all needed distributed arrays have been defined and initialized and that loop iterations have been partitioned between

```
Each processor P:

    — preprocesses its own loop iterations
    — Records off-processor fetches and stores in hashed cache
    — Finds send/receive calls required for data exchange
      1. P generates list of all off-processor data to be fetched
      2. Other processors tell P which data to send
      3. Send/receive pairs generated and stored
```

Figure 4. Inspector for parallel loop on distributed memory multiprocessor

processors. Using the hashed cache to record off-processor fetches and stores allows us to recognize when more than one reference is being made to the same off-processor distributed array element, so that only one copy of that element need be fetched or stored.

During our inspector phase, we carry out a set of interprocessor communications that allows us to anticipate exactly which send and receive communication calls each processor must execute so that all interprocessor data transmission is correctly carried out. By contrast, if individual fetches and stores were to be carried out during the actual computation, things would be much more awkward. For example, in such a case processor A might obtain the contents of a distributed array element which is not on A by sending a message to processor B associated with the array element. Processor B would be programmed to anticipate a request of this type, to satisfy the request and to return a responding message containing the contents of the specified array element.

Once preprocessing is completed, we are in a position to carry out the necessary communication and computation, Figure 5 outlines the steps involved. The initial data exchange phase follows the plan established by the inspector. During preprocessing, each processor finds out which distributed array elements need to be transmitted. When a processor obtains copies of off-processor distributed array elements, the copies are written into the processor's hashed cache. Once the communication phase is over, each processor carries out its computation. Each processor uses locally stored portions of distributed arrays along with off-processor distributed array elements stored in the hashed cache. When the computational phase is finished, distributed array elements to be stored off-processor are obtained from the hashed cache and sent to the appropriate off-processor locations.

- Before loop or code segment

    1. Data to be sent off-processor read from distributed arrays
    2. Send/receive calls transport off-processor data
    3. Data written into hashed cache

- Computation carried out

    — off-processor reads/writes go to hashed cache

- At end of loop or code segment

    1. Data to be stored off-processor read from hashed cache
    2. Send/receive calls transport off-processor data
    3. Data written back into distributed arrays for longer-term storage

---

Figure 5. Executor for parallel loop on distributed memory multiprocessor

There are many situations in which simple, easily specified distributed array partitions are inappropriate. For instance when we compute using an unstructured mesh, we attempt to partition the problem so that each processor performs approximately the same amount of work and so that the communications overhead is minimized. Typically, it is not possible to express the resulting array partitions in a simple way. If we allow an arbitrary assignment of distributed array elements to processors, the data structure used to describe the partitioning will have the same number of elements as the distributed array.

In order to access an array element, we need to know where the element is stored in the memory of the distributed machine. We use a distributed *translation table* defined by a partitioning algorithm, to describe the mapping. When a distributed translation table is used to describe array mappings, inspectors must be modified so that they access the distributed table. Using an irregular array mapping *does not alter the form of the executor*. The modifications to be made to an inspector are outlined in Figure 6.

```
Each processor P:

    — Preprocesses its own loop iterations
    — Records off-processor fetches and stores in hashed cache
    — Consults distributed translation table to
       * Find location in distributed memory for each off-processor
         fetch or store
    — Finds send/receive calls required for data exchange
       1. P generates list of all off-processor data to be fetched
       2. Other processors tell P which data to send
       3. Send/receive pairs generated and stored
```

Figure 6. Inspector for parallel loop using irregular distributed array mapping

3.2. Languages and tools for irregular problems

Programs designed to carry out sparse direct and iterative methods also typically require many of the optimizations described in Section 3.1. Some examples of such programs are described in References 3, 19, 15 and 4. Williams[36] describes a programming environment (DIME) for calculations with unstructured triangular meshes using distributed memory machines. In Reference 36, collections of distributed array accesses are translated into an efficient set of inter-node messages. The DIME programming environment embodies many of the principles discussed in Section 3.1. The optimizations discussed in the last section can be incorporated into distributed compilers. Run-time compilation for distributed machines was proposed in Reference 27; this description was in the context of the Crystal language. Distributed memory run-time compilation was expanded upon in Reference 21, which outlines the principles behind the Parti project. A more detailed description of the concepts behind distributed memory run-time compilation is found in References 28 and 22. The idea of splitting a loop into an inspector and executor and integrating this into a compiler was also developed independently as part of the KALI project[18]. Other compiler projects have also proposed run-time resolution of communications on distributed machines[8,24,25]. These compilers do not carry out the kinds of run-time optimizations of the sort found in Parti and KALI.

We have designed a set of procedures or primitives that do the work needed to implement inspectors and executors. We have also designed and implemented a model compiler that recognizes a subset of Fortran with extensions (ARF, ARguably Fortran). The ARF compiler generates inspector and executor loops with embedded primitives. We will now briefly describe the extensions that we have added to Fortran 77 to create the

ARF language. Distributed arrays are declared in ARF source. These distributed arrays can either be partitioned between processors in a regular manner (e.g. equal-sized blocks of contiguous array elements assigned to each processor), or in an irregular manner. An ARF user declares a mapping into distributed memory for each distributed array. When an array is to be partitioned in an irregular fashion, mapping information is specified in a regularly distributed integer array. Element i of the integer array specifies the processor to which element i of the distributed array is to be mapped. Examples are shown below.

```
S1 distributed regular using block real k(SIZE)
S2 distributed regular using block integer map(SIZE)
S3 distributed irregular using map real y(SIZE).
```

S1 declares that k is a real array, distributed in a regular block manner, S2 declares that map is an integer array, also distributed in a regular block manner. S3 declares a real array y whose distribution is to be determined by the distributed integer array map; distributed array element $y(i)$ is stored on processor $map(i)$. In the examples we give in this paper, all integer arrays used to specify irregular mappings were produced by hand-coded partitioning procedures and then passed to an ARF routine.

Embedded primitives include communications procedures designed to support irregular patterns of distributed array access. Other primitives that involve interprocessor communication initialize distributed translation tables or access distributed translation tables to find the location of irregularly mapped distributed array data. Primitives also support the maintenance of hashed caches. (Recall from Section 3.1 that hashed caches store copies of off-processor distributed array data.) There are also Parti primitives that perform accumulations to off-processor distributed array elements.

Another addition to Fortran 77 is the *on clause*. The on clause was originally implemented in KALI[17]. It is a mechanism by which the user has control over distributing the iteration space or work load among processors. *Distribute do* is an ARF language extension, this implies that the loop iterations in a given do loop should be distributed between processors. In the next section we use two examples to illustrate the transformations and optimizations performed by the ARF compiler. These message-passing Fortran codes were generated by the ARF compiler.

ARF was developed as a platform that allowed us to develop the transformations required to embed Parti primitives. Consequently, the ARF compiler recognizes only a small subset of Fortran.

3.3. Code generation by the ARF compiler

The ARF compiler transforms an ARF program into a target program which incorporates the primitives needed to efficiently carry out the distributed computation. The kernels we present here have been coded in ARF, compiled and run on an iPSC/860; in Section 3.3.2 we will present performance data obtained from both kernels.

3.3.1. Sparse block matrix vector multiply

In Figure 7 we present an ARF program that carries out a block sparse matrix vector multiply. This kernel was obtained from an iterative solver produced for a program

```
... partition generated outside procedure ...

S0 distributed regular using block integer partition(n)
S1 distributed irregular using partition real*8 x(4,n),
                                    y(4,n),f(4,4,maxcols,n)
S2 distributed irregular using partition integer cols(9,n), ncols(n)

 ... initialization of local variables ...

S3 distribute do i=1,n on partition

        do j=1,ncols(i)
S4        do k=1,4
            sum = 0
S5          do m = 1,4
S6            sum = sum + f(m,k,j,i)*x(m,cols(j,i))
            enddo
          y(k,i) = y(k,i) + sum
          enddo
        enddo

enddo
```

Figure 7. ARF sparse block matrix vector multiply

designed to calculate fluid flow for geometries defined by an unstructured mesh[33]. The matrix is assumed to have size 4 by 4 blocks of non-zero entries. Statements S4 and S5 are loops that sweep over the non-zero entries in each block.

The current implementation partitions only one dimension, the last dimension of the array. The Parti primitives, however, do support a broader class of array mappings[6]. Thus partition describes the partitioning of the last dimension of the irregularly distributed arrays x, y, cols, ncols and f declared in statements S1 and S2. The information in partition is used to make calls to primitives that initialize the distributed translation tables. The distributed translation table contains the processor assignment information specified by partition, along with information to specify the memory location of each element of an irregularly distributed array.

The partitioning of computational work is specified in statement S3 by an *on clause*. In this example, distributed array partition is used to specify which loop iterations are to be carried out on each processor. The reference x(m,cols(j,i)) in S6 may require off-processor references. ARF must consequently generate an inspector to produce a schedule and a hash table to handle accesses to the distributed array x. A reference to the irregularly distributed array f occurs in statement S6. Note that distributed array f is irregularly distributed using array partition and that partition is also used by the on clause to partition loop iterations in S3. It can therefore be deduced that the reference to f in statement S6 is on-processor. partition specifies how distributed array elements and loop iterations are to be distributed between processors. A separate partitioning routine generates partition. In this paper, we simply assume that array partition is passed to the sparse matrix vector multiply kernel after having been generated elsewhere.

The ARF compiler generates an inspector and an executor to run on each processor. The work of the inspector is carried out on each processor as follows:

Call Parti procedure *build-translation-table* using the mapping defined by array partition. Procedure *build-translation-table* generates distributed translation table $T_{partition}$.

Call Parti procedure *dereference* to find processor assignments, PA and local indices, LA for consecutive references to $x(m,cols(j,i))$. Procedure *dereference* uses the distributed translation table $T_{partition}$ to find the processor and memory locations of distributed array data that have been mapped to processors using distributed array *partition*.

Pass PA and LA to Parti procedure *scheduler*, generate schedule S.

Use PA and LA to set up hash table H.

The executor generated by ARF on processor P is depicted in Figure 8. In Figure 8 we use Fortran 90 notation where appropriate to enhance readability. Off-processor elements of x are gathered using Parti procedure *gather-exchanger* and placed in a previously allocated hash table H (step I Figure 8). Values from x are obtained from H or from local memory as is appropriate (step IIa, Figure 8). Arrays PA and LA are used to distinguish local from off-processor array accesses. In step IIb, we accumulate to y. Note that the

```
 I. call gather-exchanger using schedule S to obtain off-processor elements
    of x

    gather-exchanger places gathered data in hash table H

    count = 1

II. for all rows i assigned to processor P

    do j=1,ncols(i)
       do k= 1,4
          sum = 0
IIa.      if PA(count) == P then
              vx(1:4) = x(1:4,LA(count))
          else
              Use PA(count), LA(count) to get vx(1:4)
              from hash table H
          endif
          do m=1,4
              sum = sum + f(m,k,j,i)*vx(m)
          end do
IIb.      y(k,i) = y(k,i) + sum
       end do
       count = count + 1

end loop over rows
```

Figure 8. *Executor generated from ARF for sparse block matrix vector multiply* declarations in S1 and S3 in Figure 7 allow the compiler to determine that accumulations to y are local.

3.3.2. Compiler performance on two unstructured kernels

In this section, we present the execution times on 32-processor and 64-processor Intel iPSC/860 machines, obtained from the block matrix vector multiply kernel as well as execution times from another, more complex kernel that arose in an unstructured code. This kernel, to be referred to here as *fluxroe*, computes convective fluxes using a method based on Roe's approximate Riemann solver[34,35]; the kernel is discussed in some detail in Reference 6. Both the block matrix vector multiply and the fluxroe kernel arise from iterative algorithms. In these tests, both kernels were translated into ARF and compiled. It should be noted that syntax recognized by the compiler differs in a number of minor ways from the ARF syntax described above.

In these experiments, we used two different unstructured meshes:

(1). A 21,672-element mesh generated to carry out an aerodynamic simulation involving a multi-element airfoil in a landing configuration[20].
(2) A 37,741-element mesh generated to simulate a 4.2% circular arc airfoil in a channel[14].

In all the cases presented below, each unstructured mesh was partitioned by recursive orthogonal dissection[13].

For the experiments described in this section, we used either a 32-processor iPSC/860 machine located at ICASE, NASA Langley Research Center, or a 128-processor iPSC/860 machine located at Oak Ridge National Laboratories. The processors in both machines had 8 megabytes of memory. We used the Greenhill 1.8.5 Beta version C compiler to generate code for the 80860 processors.

In Table 1 we present:

- inspector time—the time required to carry out the inspector preprocessing phase.
- computation time—the time required to perform computations in the iterative portion of the program.
- communication time—the time required to exchange messages within the iterative portion of the program.

The inspector time includes the time required to set up the needed distributed translation table as well as the time required to access the distributed translation table when carrying out the preprocessing in the inspector. In these experiments, the ratio of the time required to carry out the inspector to the computation time required for a single iteration ranged from a factor of 0.7 to a factor of 3.6. Most of the preprocessing time goes to setting up and using the distributed translation table. For instance, consider the block matrix vector multiply on 64 processors using the 21,672 element mesh. The total preprocessing cost was 122 milliseconds, of which 111 milliseconds went to translation table related work.

We can define parallel efficiency for a given number of processors P as the sequential time divided by the product of the execution time on P processors times P. The sequential time was measured using a separate sequential version of the each kernel run on a single node of the iPSC/860. In Table 1 we depict under the heading of *single sweep efficiency*,

Table 1. Performance on different number of processors

nprocs nprocs	inspector time(ms)	comp. time(ms)	comm. time(ms)	single sweep efficiency	amortized efficiency
Block matrix vector multiply—21,672-element mesh					
32	148	49	9	0.15	0.55
64	122	25	9	0.10	0.48
Block matrix vector multiply—37,741-element mesh					
32	200	85	10	0.19	0.59
64	150	42	9	0.14	0.54
Fluxroe—21,672-element mesh					
8	231	310	24	0.40	0.69
16	162	157	21	0.34	0.65
32	135	80	22	0.19	0.57
64	172	41	19	0.12	0.48
Fluxroe—37,741-element mesh					
8	393	534	23	0.41	0.70
16	249	269	18	0.36	0.68
32	191	156	23	0.28	0.62
64	203	69	14	0.17	0.59

the parallel efficiencies we would obtain if we were to preprocess the kernel each time we carried out calculations. In reality, preprocessing time can be amortized over multiple mesh sweeps. If we neglect the time required to preprocess the problem in computing parallel efficiencies, we obtain the second set of parallel efficiency measurements, the *amortized efficiency* presented in Table 1. The amortized efficiencies for 64 processors ranged from 0.48 to 0.59, while the single sweep efficiencies ranged from 0.10 to 0.17.

In the experiments depicted in Table 1, the time spent computing is at least a factor of 2 greater than the communication time. The amortized efficiencies are, however, impacted by the fact that the computations in the parallelized codes are carried out less efficiently than those in the sequential program. The parallel code spends time accessing the hashed cache. It also needs to perform more indirections than the sequential program.

3.3.3. Overheads associated with Parti primitives

To elucidate the communications costs incurred by the Parti scheduler and data exchange primitives, we measured the time required to carry out the Scheduler, Gather Exchanger and Scatter Exchanger procedure calls and compared them to the hand-coded version of iPSC/860 supplied sends and receives; the sends and receives communicated the same amount of data as the Parti procedures. In the experiment we performed two processors repeatedly exchange information using either gather exchangers or scatter exchangers. We measured the time required to carry out the scheduler, scatter and gather exchanger primitives and the iPSC/860 supplied send and receive pairs programmed to communicate the same quantity of data as transported by the Parti data exchangers. In Table 2 we depict the results of these experiments. We present the time (in milliseconds) required to carry out the requisite data exchange using send and receive messages. We then present the ratio between the time taken by Parti primitive calls and the time taken by the equivalent send and receive calls. Table 2 only presents Gather Exchange and Scheduler calls. The Scatter Exchange calls were also timed, the results of which were virtually identical to those of the corresponding Gather Exchange call.

Table 2. Overheads for Parti scheduler and gather exchange primitives

Number of data elements	Send receive time (ms)	Gather exchange (ratio)	Scheduler (ratio)
100	0.5	1.0	2.1
400	1.0	1.1	1.4
900	1.8	1.1	1.3
1600	2.9	1.2	1.3
2500	4.3	1.2	1.1
3600	6.0	1.2	1.0

4. RUN-TIME COMPILATION IN SIMD MACHINES—THE COMMUNICATIONS COMPILER

Irregular problems can cause serious performance degradation on the CM-2[5]. It turns out that this performance degradation can be ameliorated by a form of run-time compilation. Denning Dahl has developed a set of software facilities for the Connection Machine (CM-2) that are designed to handle applications that exhibit fixed irregular patterns of communication[10]. One procedure called the *communications compiler*, schedules interprocessor communications. The communications compiler decomposes an irregular communications pattern into a sequence of simple, inexpensive data transfers. The other procedure a *mapping facility* maps graphs generated from a communication pattern onto the CM-2. In this paper, we will focus our attention on the communications compiler.

4.1. CM 2 communications architecture

A p processor CM-2 may be regarded as a $log_2(p) - 4$ dimensional hypercube in which each edge of the hypercube is identified with a CM chip. Each pair of CM chips is connected by a single bit wide data path. A p processor CM-2 has $log_2(p) - 5$ Weitek floating-point accelerators. Two CM chips are associated with each Weitek chip, a *sprint* chip is used to provide the needed interface between the CM chips and the Weitek accelerators. It proves to be convenient to think of the CM-2 as a $log_2(p) - 5$ dimensional hypercube each node of which contains two CM chips, a sprint chip and a Weitek chip. In the rest of this paper, we will refer to this collection of four chips as a *sprint node*. It should be noted that each pair of CM-2 nodes are connected by a *pair* of single bit wide data paths.

When we program using the PARIS parallel instruction set[23], data in the 32 processors associated with each CM-2 node is stored in bit-serial format. Because the floating-point processors require data to be in 32-bit word-oriented format, the coupling between the bit serial processors and the floating-point chip requires a data transposition. Thus, even though all floating-point computation is carried out by the 32-bit floating-point processors, the memory of each sprint node is fragmented into 32 separate segments.

A PARIS program is written in a manner that assumes the existence of an unlimited number of virtual processors. Interaction between virtual processors is carried out by passing messages. When a pair of communicating virtual processors are assigned to different sprint nodes, messages must traverse the intervening links. When communicating virtual processors are assigned to the same node, no communication along hypercube links is required.

The communication compiler[10] is a set of procedures used to schedule irregular communication patterns on the CM-2. Each processor calls the communication compiler scheduler and lists the processors with which communication is to take place. The communications compiler produces a schedule which is used to determine how messages will be routed through the hypercube channels. The architecture is able to make use of all hypercube links simultaneously. In a single router cycle, the CM-2 system software is able to carry out a bidirectional message transfer along each of the two links between each sprint node.

Messages are assigned to wires independently at each sprint node. An *assignment graph* is used to match messages with outgoing hypercube links. For each communication cycle, this assignment processes corresponds to picking links from a graph with two disjoint sets of nodes (i.e. a bipartite graph). The first set of assignment graph vertices represent messages that either

(1) originate in the sprint node,
(2) originate elsewhere and must be forwarded to their ultimate destination.

These vertices are called *message vertices*. The second set of assignment graph vertices consist of the $log_2(p) - 5$ *pairs* of hypercube links associated with each sprint node. These vertices are called *hypercube link vertices*. Constraints on this assignment problem are:

(1) when a message has been assigned to a hypercube link, it cannot be moved over any other hypercube link during a given cycle,
(2) once a hypercube link has been assigned to a message, it cannot transmit any other message during a given cycle, and
(3) hypercube link assignments always decrease the Hamming distance to a message's destination.

An a-edge is drawn from a message vertex M to a link vertex L when we route the message represented by M over the hypercube link represented by L. The communication compiler uses a heuristic assignment algorithm that attempts to maximize the number of messages sent during each communications cycle[10]. The degree ρ of an a-edge E of the assignment graph is defined as the sum of the number of a-edges leading out from E's message vertex and the number of a-edges leading out from E's hypercube link vertex. The algorithm begins by computing ρ for each a-edge. The a-edge S in the assignment graph with the smallest value of ρ is chosen. All a-edges that terminate on S's message or link vertex are removed and the process is repeated until all a-edges in the assignment graph have been chosen or eliminated.

4.2. Test problems

We present a set of benchmarks to characterize the performance of the communications compiler. A *synthetic mesh* was defined in the following way. A square mesh in which each point was linked to four nearest neighbors was incrementally distorted. Random edges were introduced subject to the constraint that in the new mesh, each point still required information from four other mesh points.

The following assumptions are inherent in our mesh generator:

(1) The problem domain consists of a 64 by 128 mesh of points which are numbered using their row major or natural ordering.
(2) Each point is initially connected to its four nearest neighbors.
(3) Each link produced in the above step is examined, with probability q the link is replaced by a link to a randomly chosen point.

4.3. Experimental results

We use our synthetic meshes to compare the performance of the communications compiler to the performance of other CM-2 communications mechanisms. An 8192 processor Connection Machine-2 was configured as a 64 by 128 torus. The mesh was mapped onto the torus in the obvious manner. A sweep over the mesh was then performed using the following communication mechanisms:

(1) Get: the standard CM-2 general router is called four times, once for each of the four off-processor data elements needed by each processor.
(2) Compiled get: communications compiled using the communications compiler; the communications compiler preprocessor was called four times, once for each of the four off-processor data elements required by each processor. The data delivery procedure is called four times during each mesh sweep.
(3) Compiled gather: communications compiled using the communications compiler; a single call to the communications compiler preprocessor handles each processor's four data requests. For each iteration, a single data delivery function carries out all communication.
(4) NEWS: CM-2 communications procedures that transmit information using mesh embedded into hypercube by binary reflected gray code. NEWS was only used to benchmark the completely uniform mesh ($q = 0$).

The results of these benchmarks are depicted in Figure 9. In these experiments we carried out sweeps over meshes generated by varying q from 0.0 to 0.5. For the uniform mesh ($q=0$), we used all four communications mechanisms described above. For the synthetically generated irregular meshes, we used the standard CM get, the compiled get and the compiled gather. Let T_{NEWS} represent the the time required by the CM-2 to to sweep over a regular mesh ($q=0$) using the NEWS mechanism; T_{NEWS} was equal to 0.80

milliseconds. In Figure 9, we compare T_{NEWS} with the time taken by the CM-2 to sweep over irregular meshes using the standard CM get (T_{GET}), the compiled get (T_{CGET}) and the compiled gather ($T_{CGATHER}$). For the regular mesh, T_{GET}, T_{CGET}, and $T_{CGATHER}$ were factors of 15.4, 2.2 and 1.1 times larger than T_{NEWS}. As q increased, the performance of the mesh sweep degraded significantly with all three routing mechanisms tested. For $q = 0.5$, T_{GET}, T_{CGET}, and $T_{CGATHER}$ were factors of 22.6, 4.4 and 2.7 times larger than T_{NEWS}. It is clear that run-time compilation techniques can play an important role in reducing communications costs for irregular problems on SIMD machines. The computational cost of the simulated annealing based communications compiler is, however, extremely high.

The construction of the communication schedule took anywhere from 1 to 13 *seconds*. The amount of time required for scheduling depends on the number of router cycles

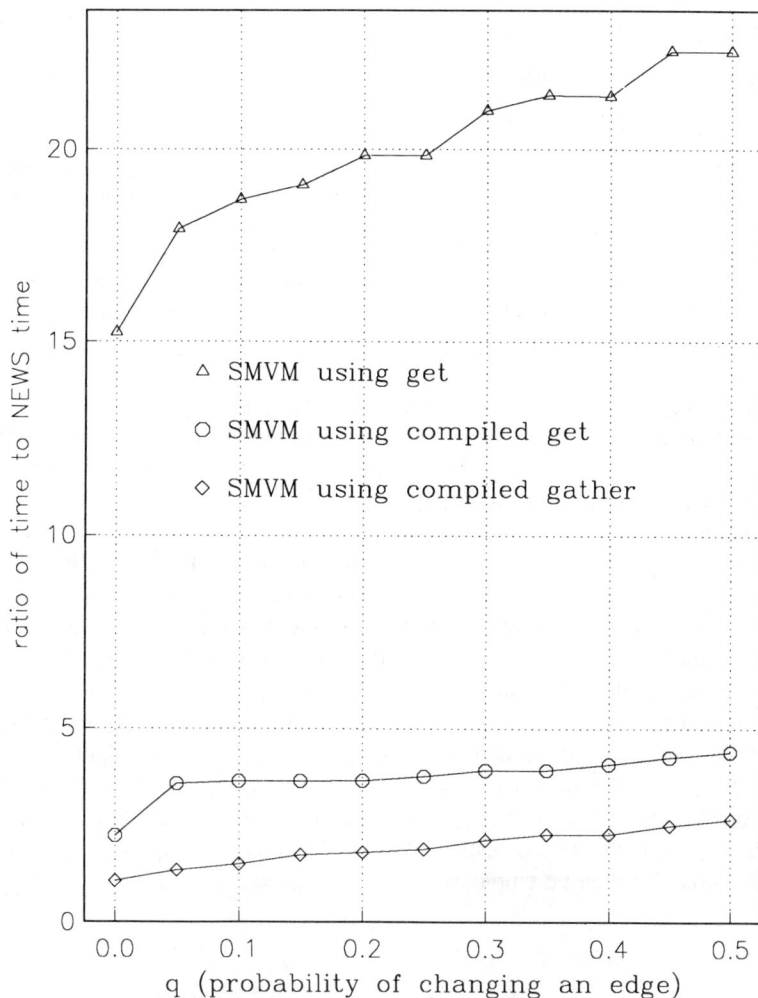

Figure 9. *Effect of communications compiler—synthetic workload*

needed to transmit all necessary data. As we would expect, the time required to construct the communications schedule increases with q.

5. CONCLUSIONS AND FUTURE WORK

Execution-time preprocessing plays a major role in many efficient algorithms in computer science. Run-time preprocessing also plays an important role in exploiting multi-processor architectures. Examples of such preprocessing include run-time parallelization, run-time aggregation and scheduling of remote distributed array accesses and execution time data and workload partitioning. We have surveyed examples of how optimizations of this type can be integrated into compilers. We have also presented specific benchmarks that document, on a range of multiprocessor architectures, the importance of various types of run-time compilation.

We have described three different types of compiler-linked run-time preprocessing targeted towards three different multiprocessor architectures. We have described:

(1) run-time parallelization for bus based shared memory multiprocessors,
(2) conversion of irregular patterns of data fetches into matched pairs of send and receive calls for distributed memory multiprocessors, and
(3) conversion of irregular patterns of data fetches into a prescheduled pattern of store and forward nearest neighbor hypercube data swaps for SIMD multiprocessors.

There is great scope for additional work in this area. For instance, most of the optimizations described in Section 3 are motivated either directly or indirectly by the high communication latencies typically found in distributed memory computers. Because we can anticipate all of the interprocessor communications that will be needed in carrying out a loop, we have the information we need to schedule interprocessor communications to reduce overheads due to contention. As we have seen in Section 4, scheduling of interprocessor communication has already been shown to be an important optimization for some SIMD architectures. We expect this to also turn out to be a fruitful optimization for distributed memory MIMD computers.

It appears that there is substantial scope for improvement in the heuristic used by Dahl to schedule CM-2 interprocessor communications (Section 4). Preliminary work by our group appears to indicate that it is possible to develop improved heuristics able to schedule communications patterns seen in unstructured mesh computations. It also seems to be quite likely that it will be possible to reduce the high preprocessing overheads.

Another potentially promising form of run-time preprocessing involves integrating work and data partitioning procedures into compilers. Computations can be characterized by patterns of data dependency. Procedures that partition data structures and computational work take these dependency patterns into account. It is possible to design program transformations that generate procedures which output a record of the dependency patterns in a loop nest[21]. Standardized partitioning programs that use these data structures can then be employed.

ACKNOWLEDGEMENTS

We wish to thank Dimitri Mavriplis and David Whitaker for supplying us with unstructured meshes, and to David Whitaker and P. Venkatkrishnan for allowing us to use computational kernels from their codes. We would also like to thank Adam Rifkin for helping to code the partitioning algorithms and for carrying out iPSC/860 timings. We would like to thank the Advanced Computing Laboratory at at Oak Ridge National Laboratory for allowing us to use their 128 node iPSC/860 and Ravi Mirchandaney and Bob Voigt for their helpful comments on the manuscript.

This work is supported under NASA contract NAS1-18605, and NSF grant ASC-8819374.

REFERENCES

1. G. Alaghband, 'Parallel pivoting combined with parallel reduction', *Parallel Computing Journal*, **11**(2), 201–221 (1989).
2. E. Anderson and Y. Saad, 'Solving sparse triangular linear systems on parallel computers', *International Journal of High Speed Computing*, **1**, 73–95 (1989).
3. C. Ashcraft, S. C. Eisenstat and J. W. H. Liu, 'A fan-in algorithm for distributed sparse numerical factorization', *SISSC*, **11**, 593–599 (1990).
4. D. Baxter, J. Saltz, M. Schultz, S. Eisentstat and K. Crowley, 'An experimental study of methods for parallel preconditioned krylov methods', in *Proceedings of the 1988 Hypercube Multiprocessor Conference*, Pasadena, CA, January 1988, pp. 1698, 1711, ACM Press, New York, NY.
5. H. Berryman, J. Saltz and W. Gropp, 'Krylov methods with incomplete factorization preconditioners on the cm-2', *Journal of Parallel and Distributed Computing*, **8**, 186–190 (1990).
6. H. Berryman, J. Saltz and J. Scroggs, 'Execution time support for adaptive scientific algorithms on distributed memory machines', Report 90-41, ICASE, May (1990).
7. S. Bokhari, 'Communication overhead on the intel ipsc-860 hypercube', Report 90-10, ICASE Interim Report (1990).
8. D. Callahan and K. Kennedy, 'Compiling programs for distributed-memory multiprocessors', *Journal of Supercomputing*, **2**, 151–169 (1988).
9. R. Cytron, 'Doacross: beyond vectorization for multiprocessors', in *The Proceedings of the ICPP, 1986*, pp. 836–844, IEEE Computer Society Press, Los Alamitos, CA (1986).
10. E. D. Dahl, 'Mapping and compiled communication on the connection machine system', in *Proceedings of the Fifth Distributed Memory Computing Conference*, Charleston, SC, IEEE Computer Society Press, Los Alamitos, CA (1990).
11. I. S. Duff, 'Parallel implementation of multifrontal schemes', *Parallel Computing*, **3**, 193–204 (1986).
12. I. S. Duff and J. K. Reid, *Direct Methods for Sparse Matrices*, Oxford Science Publications, Oxford University Press, New York (1986).
13. G. Fox, M. Johnson, G. Lyzenga, S. Otto, J. Salmon and D. Walker, *Solving Problems on Concurrent Computers*, Prentice Hall, Englewood Cliffs, NJ (1988).
14. A. Rizzi and H. Vivand (eds), 'Numerical methods for the computation of inviscid transonic flows with shock waves—a gamm workshop', in *Notes on Numerical Fluid Mechanics*, **3**, 1–266, Vieweg, Germany.
15. A. George, M. T. Heath, J. Liu and E. Ng, 'Sparse cholesky factorization on a local memory multiprocessor', *SISSC*, **9**(2), 327–340 (1988).
16. E. Horowitz and S. Sahni, *Fundamentals of Data Structures*, Computer Science Press, Rockville, MD (1976).
17. C. Koelbel and P. Mehrotra, 'Compiling global name-space programs for distributed execution', Report 90-70, ICASE (1990).
18. C. Koelbel, P. Mehrotra and J. V. Rosendale, 'Supporting shared data structures on distributed memory architectures', in *2nd ACM SIGPLAN Symposium on Principles Practice of Parallel Programming*, ACM SIGPLAN, March 1990, pp. 177–186, ACM Press, New York, NY.
19. J. W. Liu, 'Computational models and task scheduling for parallel sparse cholesky factorization', *Parallel Computing*, **3**, 327–342 (1986).

20. D. J. Mavriplis, 'Multigrid solution of the two-dimensional Euler equations on unstructured triangular meshes', *AIAA Journal*, **26**, 824–831 (1988).
21. R. Mirchandaney, J. H. Saltz, R. M. Smith, D. M. Nicol and K. Crowley, 'Principles of runtime support for parallel processors', in *Proceedings of the 1988 ACM International Conference on Supercomputing*, St. Malo France, July 1988, pp. 140–152, ACM Press, New York, NY.
22. S. Mirchandaney, J. Saltz, P. Mehrotra and H. Berryman, 'A scheme for supporting automatic data migration on multicomputers', in *Proceedings of the Fifth Distributed Memory Computing Conference*, Charleston, SC, IEEE Computer Society Press, Los Alamitos, CA (1990).
23. *Using the Connection Machine System (Paris)*, Vol. 3, Report ANL/MCS-TM-118, Argonne National Laboratory, June (1989).
24. A. Rogers and K. Pingali, 'Process decomposition through locality of reference', in *Conference on Programming Language Design and Implementation*, ACM SIGPLAN, June 1989, pp. 69–80, ACM Press, New York, NY.
25. M. Rosing and R. Schnabel, 'An overview of Dino—a new language for numerical computation on distributed memory multiprocessors', Tech. Rep. CU-CS-385-88, University of Colorado, Boulder (1988).
26. J. Saltz, 'Aggregation methods for solving sparse triangular systems on multiprocessors', *SIAM J. Sci. and Stat. Computation*, **11**, 123–144 (1990).
27. J. Saltz and M. Chen, 'Automated problem mapping: the crystal runtime system', in *The Proceedings of the Hypercube Microprocessors Conference*, Knoxville, TN, September, SIAM Press, Philadelphia, PA (1986).
28. J. Saltz, K. Crowley, R. Mirchandaney and H. Berryman, 'Run-time scheduling and execution of loops on message passing machines', *Journal of Parallel and Distributed Computing*, **8**, 303–312 (1990).
29. J. Saltz and R. Mirchandaney, 'The preprocessed doacross loop', *Conference on Parallel Processing*, St. Charles, IL. **II**, 174–179 (1991).
30. J. Saltz, R. Mirchandaney and D. Baxter, 'Runtime parallelization and scheduling of loops', in *The Proceedings of the 1st ACM Symposium on Parallel Algorithms and Architectures*, Santa Fe, NM, June 1989, pp. 303–312, ACM Press, New York, NY.
31. J. Saltz, R. Mirchandaney and K. Crowley, 'Run-time parallelization and scheduling of loops', *IEEE Trans. on Computers*, **40**(5), 603–612 (1991).
32. J. D. Ullman, *Principals of Database Systems*, Computer Science Press, Rockville, MD (1982).
33. P. Venkatkrishnan, J. Saltz and D. Mavriplis, 'Parallel preconditioned iterative methods for the compressible Navier–Stokes equations', in *12th International Conference on Numerical Methods in Fluid Dynamics*, Oxford, England, July (1990), Lecture Notes in Physics, 371, K. W. Morton (ed.), Springer-Verlag, Berlin, Germany (1990).
34. D. L. Whitaker and B. Grossman, 'Two-dimensional euler computations on a triangular mesh using an upwind, finite-volume scheme', in *Proceedings AIAA 27th Aerospace Sciences Meeting*, Reno, NV, January (1989).
35. D. L. Whitaker, D. C. Slack and R. W. Walters, 'Solution algorithms for the two-dimensional euler equations on unstructured meshes', in *Proceedings AIAA 28th Aerospace Sciences Meeting*, Reno, NV, January (1990).
36. R. D. Williams and R. Glowinski, 'Distributed irregular finite elements', Tech. Rep. C3P 715, Caltech Concurrent Computation Program, February (1989).
37. V. Krothapalli and P. Sadayappan, 'An approach to synchronization for parallel computing', *Proceedings of the 1988 conference on supercomputing*, St. Malo, 573–581 (1988), ACM Press, New York, NY.
38. C. Q. Zhu and P. C. Yew, 'A Scheme to enforce data dependency on large multiprocessor systems', *IEEE Trans. on Software Eng.*, SE-13(6), 726–739 (1987).

Synchronization and load imbalance effects in distributed memory multi-processor systems

DAN C. MARINESCU AND JOHN R. RICE

Computer Science Department
Purdue University
West Lafayette, IN 47907, USA

SUMMARY

Synchronization is a major cause of wasted computing cycles and of diminished performance in parallel computing. This paper investigates the effects of synchronization upon the performance of iterative methods on distributed memory MIMD machines. A quantitative analysis of the effects of the communication latency and of the load imbalance due to the non-deterministic execution times for iterative methods is presented. This analysis explains the rather poor performance observed often in actual implementations of such methods and suggests better ways to achieve convergence without frequent synchronization.

1. INTRODUCTION

Numerous parallel algorithms and methods require some form of synchronization, or co-ordination of concurrent activities. To synchronize, a processor executing a thread of control may block waiting for the data produced by another thread, or for an external event to occur. There are cases when all the threads of control have to reach a consensus before proceeding to the next step and *global synchronization* is necessary. For example, iterative methods require a processor to exchange boundary values with its neighbors, but only after *all of them* have finished the current iteration.

Synchronization is a major cause of wasted computing cycles and of diminished performance in parallel computing. Synchronization is analogous to stopping at a traffic light: the more red lights that are encountered on a given route, the longer is the time to reach the destination. Avoiding synchronization is equivalent to taking a highway instead of a city street. The method of self-synchronization discussed in Section 3 amounts to traveling on a boulevard at a speed dictated by the 'green wave' to avoid the penalty of red lights.

This paper investigates the effects of synchronization upon the performance of iterative methods on distributed memory MIMD machines. The discussion is restricted to the so-called SPMD execution, when the same program is executed by all the processors of a parallel system on different data subdomains. The SPMD paradigm is widely used because divide and conquer methods are very popular for solving large numerical problems. Moreover, it is fairly difficult to write and debug a large number of different programs, one for each individual computation executing on each of the processing elements of a MIMD machine.

On a distributed memory system the synchronization is done by exchanging messages and its performance depends upon the communication latency. The communication on such a machine is fairly expensive, currently; the time to exchange a short message

1040–3108/91/060593–33$16.50
©1991 by John Wiley & Sons, Ltd.

Received 23 October 1990
Accepted 20 August 1991

between two nearest neighbors is typically equivalent to the time to execute a few hundred floating-point operations. As new generations of distributed memory MIMD machines emerge, the processor bandwidth (the instruction execution rate) increases at a faster rate than the communication speed, therefore the effects discussed in this paper become more and more severe. A possible solution for future machines is to have a a dedicated, very fast communication network for short messages needed for synchronization.

Most iterative methods require global synchronization, an operation which involves the exchange of a large number of messages and it is a source of considerable inefficiency on distributed memory MIMD machines. Yet, explicit synchronization could be avoided if two conditions are met. The computations have to start at the same time and their duration must be the same. But even in the case of SPMD execution the data dependency makes this approach unfeasible. Different processors reach the synchronization point at different times, even in the load balanced case, because they execute different instructions streams and even the execution time of an instruction is data-dependent.

This paper is devoted to a quantitative analysis of the effects of the communication latency and of the load imbalance due to the non-deterministic execution times for iterative methods. This analysis explains the rather poor performance often observed in actual implementations of such methods and suggests better ways to achieve convergence without frequent synchronization.

The paper is focused upon distributed memory MIMD systems because they are emerging as a viable alternative to other computer architectures for solving very large problems in areas like signal processing, structural analysis, fluid mechanics, molecular biology, etc. [2,3]. As an example of a very large problem, consider the molecular replacement real space averaging method described in [17]. To produce an electron density map the method needs considerable computing resources, tens of hours of CPU time of Cyber 205 and enough memory for 3.24×10^9 grid points for a particular algorithm and unit cell dimensions. Dozens of such maps must be computed to determine the structure of one virus.

Distributed memory MIMD systems with hundreds of processing elements, PEs, able to deliver tens of GFlops and with Gbytes of memory have been built. The INTEL Touchstone Delta machine of the Concurrent Supercomputer Consortium is a 2-D mesh with 520 numeric nodes, each with 16 Mbytes of memory and with each processor capable of delivering tens of Mflops. If the current trend continues, it is reasonable to expect that in the mid-90s machines will be available with thousands of PEs able to deliver tens of Tflops and with tens of Tbytes.

Though other types of interconnection networks like multi-stage networks, rings or meshes are used in MIMD systems, the hypercubes are the most common ones. In a hypercube of order L, there are $N = 2^L$ PEs, located in the nodes of a cube in the space of L dimensions. Each node is connected to exactly L other nodes and the maximum distance between any pair of nodes, the number of links to be traversed from one node to the other, is at most L. The overall communication bandwidth of a hypercube increases with its size, since the communication bandwidth is proportioned with the number of links connecting each node with the rest of the cube. When the size of the cube increases by one, from order L to order $L + 1$, the number of processing elements doubles, but the number of links emerging from each node increases only one one. This makes the hypercube machine attractive to build and well balanced in terms of the computation to communication bandwidth ratio. The cost performance ratio of such machines makes them very attractive for many applications. These factors explain the popularity of the hypercubes. Numerous hypercubes have been built and the work reported in this paper was carried out using one of the commercially available machines, an NCUBE/1. Impressive results have been reported using such machines [3], but not all types of parallel numerical computations are suitable for implementations on hypercubes, primarily due to the high cost of communication.

This paper is organized as follows. A fluid approximation for the analysis of data dependencies upon load balance and models for several synchronization structures are discussed in Section 2. Section 3 discusses the effects of communication latency upon synchronization, and finally Section 4 presents performance measurements.

2. LOAD IMBALANCE EFFECTS IN SPMD COMPUTATIONS

The speed-up is defined as the ratio of the execution time with one processor to the execution time with P processors and is a measure of the performance of a parallel computation. To obtain a large speed-up, it is necessary to maintain a high processor utilization; the time the processors are idle needs to be kept as low as possible. To do so, the load assigned to different processors must be balanced. A *static load balancing* in the SPMD execution means to assign to every PE balanced or equal data subdomains with the hope that, during execution, different processors will have dynamic loads close to one another. But, as pointed out earlier, static load balancing does not provide a guarantee of *dynamic load balancing*. Owing to data dependencies, the actual flow of control of different PEs is different; different PEs execute different sequences of instructions and they arrive at a synchronization point at different times. Hence starting computations at the same time on all PEs does not guarantee that they will terminate at the same time, even when their loads are statically balanced. A first objective of the paper is to model the effects of data dependencies upon the load balance and to report upon the actual measurements of the execution times on a particular application. If the study of data dependencies allows us to compute the load imbalance factor Δ (defined in Section 2.1), then methods to reduce the effects of communication latency upon synchronization can be considered. For example, a method of self-synchronization discussed in Section 3.5 proposes that every PE enters the communication period at the end of each iteration only after a time equal to $\mu(1 + \Delta)$ with μ the expected execution time per iteration. Then, an explicit synchronization takes place only every Rth iteration.

From this brief presentation it follows that, even if the effects of data dependencies are relatively minor, and so may increase the actual execution time by only a few per cent, the analysis of these effects is important in order to design schemes which prevent the frequent need for synchronization by requiring processors to enter periods of *self-blocking*.

2.1. Load balance and data dependency in SPMD execution

Consider a parallel computation $\mathcal{C}$ and a multiprocessor system with P identical PEs, $\pi_0, \pi_1, ..., \pi_{P-1}$. It is assumed that the same program is executed by every PE using different data and that $\mathcal{C}$ requires global synchronization. In other words, $\mathcal{C}$ consists of say n subcomputations C_i, $1 \leq i \leq n$ such that any PE, π_0 starts C_{i+1}, only after all PEs have completed C_i. The period when C_i is executing is called the *ith epoch* $\mathcal{E}_i$ of the computation.

For simplicity assume first that communication occurs instantaneously and attempt to quantify the effects of data dependencies upon the traditional measures of efficiency in parallel processing, namely, the processor utilization U, or its dual, the speed-up with P processors

$$S_P = PU \tag{1}$$

Since $U \leq 1$ we have $S_P \leq P$.

To achieve an algorithmic load balance, it is customary to perform an *equipartition* of the data domain, namely, to assign to every PE, π_j a data subdomain $\mathcal{D}_j$ of equal size. First assume that all P data subdomains are identical, they contain the *same* data. If E_i is the time required by an PE to perform C_i, then in absence of any delay due to hardware failures, all PEs are expected to complete C_i, $1 \leq i \leq n$ at the same time, since they have started at the same time. The time required by C_i is denoted as T^i and it is called the *duration of the ith synchronization epoch*. The previous arguments indicate that in case of a strictly deterministic execution time, all PEs can be kept running at all times during the execution of C and then $U = 1$.

When the P processors execute C_i using different data subdomains, the execution time X_j^i of each π_j will depend upon the pair $(\mathcal{E}_i, \mathcal{D}_j)$, it is data-dependent. In general, each PE will execute a different sequence of instructions.

To model the non-determinism due to data dependencies X_j^i, $1 \leq j \leq P$, will be considered independent identically distributed random variables with mean μ_i and variance σ_i for all synchronization epochs, $1 \leq i \leq n$. In this case the duration of the ith synchronization epoch will be a new random variable

$$T^i = \max(X_1^i, \ldots, X_P^i) \tag{2}$$

Clearly, the average processor utilization will be $U < 1$, since some PEs will finish execution of C_i before the others.

As shown in [8], the expected value of T^i can be expressed as

$$E(T^i) = \mu_i(1 + \Delta_i) \tag{3}$$

with

$$\Delta_i = f(P) \cdot g(C_X) \tag{4}$$

with $C_X = (\mu_X)/(\sigma_X)$ and f and g depend upon the actual distribution of X^i and upon the number P of PEs.

For a uniform distribution we have [8]

$$f(P) = \frac{P - 1}{P + 1} \tag{5}$$

$$g(C_X) = C_X \sqrt{3} \tag{6}$$

For the exponential distribution, $g(C_X) \equiv 1$ and $f(P) = \log P + C$ with C is Euler's constant, $C = 0.577$. For the standard normal distribution $g(C_X) \equiv 1$ and

$$f(P) \approx (2 \log P)^{1/2} - \frac{1}{2} (2 \log P)^{-1/2}(\log \log P + \log 4\pi - 2C) \qquad (7)$$

To analyze the effects of data dependencies we propose a *fluid approximation* in which we replace the stochastic duration of a synchronization epoch T^i by its average value $E(T^i)$. In this approximation, the average processor utilization is

$$U = \frac{\sum_{i=1}^{n} \mu_i}{\sum_{i=1}^{n} \mu_i (1 + \Delta_i)} \qquad (8)$$

It is more convenient to compute a load imbalance factor defined as

$$\psi = \frac{\sum_{i=1}^{n} \mu_i \Delta_i}{\sum_{i=1}^{n} \mu_i} \qquad (9)$$

Then the average processor utilization U is related to ψ by

$$U = \frac{1}{1 + \psi} \qquad (10)$$

The computation of ψ is slightly more difficult when the number of PEs in different synchronization epochs is different. The next two sections explore such situations.

2.2. Analysis of two synchronization structures

We discuss two synchronization structures which can be used in conjunction with domain decomposition techniques for solving partial differential equations (PDEs). We restrict our analysis to the effects of load imbalance. The two synchronization structures use at most $N = a^K$ processors. These structures are presented in Figure 1 for the particular case $a = 2$ and $K = 3$. The first structure (Figure 1(a)) is characterized by the following properties:

P1. The computation consists of $K + 1$ epochs and the number of active processors in the ith epoch is $I_i = a^{K-i}$ with $a > 1$. In the first epoch there are $I_0 = N = a^K$ active processors. It follows that $\Delta_i > 0$ for $i > 0$ and $\Delta_K = 0$ since there is only one processor active during the last epoch.

P2. The execution time of all tasks in all synchronization epochs are independent, identically distributed random variables X_{ij} with mean μ_X, variance σ_X and coefficient of variation C_X.

P3. There is a global synchronization among all tasks of a given epoch.

The second structure (Figure 1(b)) is characterized by the following properties:

P1. The same number of active processors as the first structure.

P2. The same assumption on the execution times as for this structure.

P3. Within a given epoch, the tasks are synchronized in groups of a processors. There is no global synchronization between epochs and, as soon as a related set of tasks completes in epoch i, the descendant task commences in epoch $i + 1$.

We believe that the synchronization structures shown in Figure 1 are common among those that arise in parallel computation. We note some applications here to illustrate the variety that exists. We do not attempt to explain them in detail, as that detracts from the object of this paper.

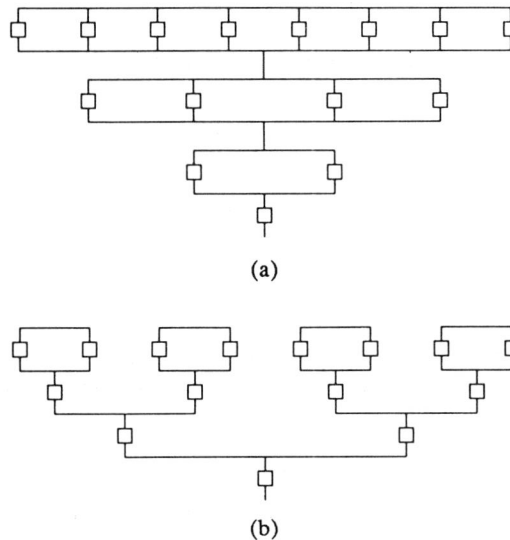

(a)

(b)

Figure 1. The two synchronization structures for $a = 2$ and $K = 3$. The structures are (a) an exponentially decreasing number of processors with rate a, (b) a tree with a processors in parallel at each branch

A principal source is in models of physical phenomena (e.g., heat flows, electromagnetic forces, stresses, air flows) which are modeled by differential equations in 1 to 4 physical dimensions. These phenomena are inherently local in time and space. They are inherently synchronized in time, but loosely synchronized in space; space synchronization comes through the time for effects to propagate through space via local interactions.

Computations modeling these phenomena can exploit this loose coupling in space to achieve parallelism. The principal technique is called *domain decomposition*, where physical space is decomposed into a large number of domains. Since interactions between these domains is local, this allows one to use locally connected computer architectures effectively. See [9–11], [13] and [14] for previous work of ours, which include descriptions of this approach at a fairly high level. The first control structure arises in multi-grid and other multi-level iterations for PDEs, the second arises in divide and conquer methods, e.g., nested dissection. There is an enormous literature [4], [16] on the mathematical analysis of specific instances of this general approach, this is currently one of the most intensively studied areas of numerical computation.

The basic technique is to compute the results in the interior of a particular domain and then communicate the new state to neighboring domains for their use. Important characteristics of such computation are as follows:

(1) The interior computations and data are usually large compared to data to be communicated. One of the objectives of algorithm design is to be sure this is so, it follows naturally if one chooses domain shapes that have small 'surface' compared to 'volume' (e.g., nearly spheres or cubes).

(2) The interior computations are usually similar (use the same program), but rarely identical (have different data) due to variations in shapes, materials, intensities of physical effects, etc.

(3) Synchronization in time is essential. Some models of the physics may compensate for small time asynchronizations locally, and more as domains become separated in space. Many algorithms have an artificial time (e.g., iteration numbering) which has the same characteristics as real world time.

There are other applications such as graphics, image processing, searching unstructured data and text processing where parallelism is inherent in the nature of the problem. The structures considered all occur in specific examples of these applications.

The key ingredients in the analysis of these applications for parallel computations are:

- the ratio γ of computing X_j^i costs to communication costs,

- the ability to partition the problem so processors have equal expected computational loads (the X_j^i have the same mean μ_i), tenitem *

- the distribution of the execution times X_j^i.

In many of the applications, it is practical to allocate the expected computational loads fairly equally. Each processor is assigned an equal volume of space, an equal area of a display or an equal amount of text to typeset. Of course, one can easily construct examples where this allocation is not easy, but even then, one can expect that an effective allocation is made. The distribution of the X_j^i can also vary greatly, but again we expect that many, if not most, applications will have the X_j^i distributed 'tightly' about the mean μ_i. Thus a model assuming a uniform or normal distribution for the X_j^i will be appropriate for many applications.

In Table 1, we present a list of applications along with rough orders for the ratio of computation and communication costs. The entries are only orders of magnitude, numerical factors can vary greatly. The quantity S merely measures the size or 'bulk' of the computation assigned to a processor, it is not the same from line to line, nor is it necessarily a variable that appears in an algorithm for these applications. We see that this ratio increases with problem sizes for all these applications, sometimes dramatically. In machines that can overlap communication with computing, the effective communication cost (the value of β) may be much less than the values indicated in Table 1.

Table 1. *Applications using hierarchical synchronization structures.* The order of magnitude of the computing/communication ratio is given as a function of the size of the computation assigned to a processor

Application	Ratio of computing to communication	
	2 dimensions	3 dimensions
Domain decomposition for PDEs		
• using Gauss elimination (multi-front methods)	$S^4/S = S^3$	$S^7/S^2 = S^5$
• using SOR iteration	$S^3/S = S^2$	$S^4/S^2 = S^2$
• using FFT method	$S^2/S = S$	$S^3/S^2 = S$
• multi-grid iteration	$S^2/S = S$	$S^3/S^2 = S$
Time-dependent PDE solutions		
• explicit methods	$S^2/S = S$	$S^3/S^2 = S$
• implicit methods		
Gauss elimination	$S^4/S = S^3$	$S^7/S^2 = S^5$
iteration	$S^2/S = S$	$S^3/S^2 = S$
• ADI methods	$S^2/S = S$	$S^3/S^2 = S$
Newton iteration for non-linear PDE		
• Gauss elimination	$S^4/S = S^3$	$S^7/S^2 = S^5$
• iteration	$S^3/S = S^2$	$S^4/S^2 = S^2$
• FFT methods	$S^2/S = S$	$S^3/S^2 = S$
Graphics		
• simple display	$S^2/0 = -$	$S^3/0 = -$
• connected displays (contours)	$S^2/S = S$	$S^3/S^2 = S$
• feature extraction	$(S^2 \rightarrow S^3)/S = S \rightarrow S^2$	$(S^3 \rightarrow S^4)/S^2 = S \rightarrow S^2$
Search in amorphous data	$S/1 = S$	
Text processing (Tex, troff)	$S/1 = S$	
Numerical integration	$S^2/1 = S^2$	$S^3/1 = S^3$
Discretization of PDEs	$S^2/S = S$	$S^3/S^2 = S$

The load imbalance costs for the two synchronization structures discussed previously are investigated. It is assumed that the execution times in all synchronization epochs have the same distribution F_X. The strategy is to compute the total load imbalance costs and then the load imbalance factor, ψ, for each structure and for several distributions of the execution times.

The first synchronization structure

Let us denote by $\Delta_{a,K}^{(1)}$, the total load imbalance for the first structure (Figure 1(a))

$$\Delta_{a,K}^{(1)} = \sum_{i=0}^{K-1} \Delta_i \tag{11}$$

The effects of the load imbalance are characterized by $\psi_{a,N}^{(1)}$, which is defined as the ratio of the expected increase of the execution time due to load imbalance, to the parallel execution time in absence of any load imbalance, that is

$$\psi_{a,K}^{(1)} = \frac{\mu_X \Delta_{a,K}^{(1)}}{\mu_X} \left(\frac{1}{(\log_a N + 1)} \right) = \frac{\Delta_{a,K}^{(1)}}{K + 1} \tag{12}$$

The case when $a = 2$ and $K = \log_2 N$ is of special interest. Then

$$\psi_{2,K}^{(1)} = \frac{\Delta_{2,K}^{(1)}}{K + 1} \tag{13}$$

Exact expressions for $\Delta_{a,K}^{(1)}$ can be obtained for the uniform, and the normal distributions of the execution time in each epoch. After presenting these results we give an upper bound for the case when the distribution F_X of X is not known.

The uniform distribution. In this case the ratio of the load imbalance costs to the parallel execution time is given by

$$\psi_{a,K}^{(1)} = C_X \sqrt{3} \, \frac{[K - 2 \times Q_{a,K}]}{K + 1} \tag{14}$$

with

$$Q_{a,K} = \sum_{i=0}^{K-1} \frac{1}{1 + a^i} \tag{15}$$

This expression is derived using the load imbalance cost for a synchronization epoch with a uniform distribution of the execution time

$$\Delta_i = C_X \sqrt{3} \, \frac{l_i - 1}{l_i + 1} = C_X \sqrt{3} \, \frac{a^{K-i} - 1}{a^{K-i} + 1} \tag{16}$$

Then the total load imbalance costs are

$$\Delta_{a,K}^{(1)} = \sum_{i=0}^{K-1} \Delta_i = C_X \sqrt{3}[K - 2Q_{a,K}] \tag{17}$$

Observe that

$$\sum_{i=0}^{\infty} \frac{1}{1 + a}i = \frac{1}{2} \, \Phi_{21} \, (a, -1; -a; 1) \tag{18}$$

with Φ_{21} the basic generalized hypergeometric function. It seems non-trivial to derive exact expressions for $Q_{a,K}$ and we derive bounds for it. We see immediately that

$$\frac{A}{a} \le Q_{a,K} \le A \tag{19}$$

with

$$A = \frac{a^K - 1}{a^{K-1}(a - 1)} = \frac{a}{a - 1} \left(1 - \frac{1}{N} \right) = \frac{a(N - 1)}{N(a - 1)} \tag{20}$$

It follows that

$$C_X \sqrt{3}(K - 2A) \leq \Delta_{a,K}^{(1)} \leq C_X \sqrt{3} \left(K - 2\frac{A}{a} \right) \tag{21}$$

When $a = 2$ and N is large $A \approx 2$. In this case

$$C_X \sqrt{3}(K - 4) \leq \Delta_{2,K}^{(1)} \leq C_X \sqrt{3}(K - 2) \tag{22}$$

To conclude the discussion for the uniform distribution and the first synchronization structure we plot $\psi_{2,K}^{(1)}$ in Figure 2 for the binary case, $a = 2$, and for different values of C_X. For small values, say $C_X = 0.01$, the effect of load imbalance is hardly noticeable. For larger C_X, the load imbalance can add as much as 30% to the parallel execution time when N is large ($N > 2^{32}$).

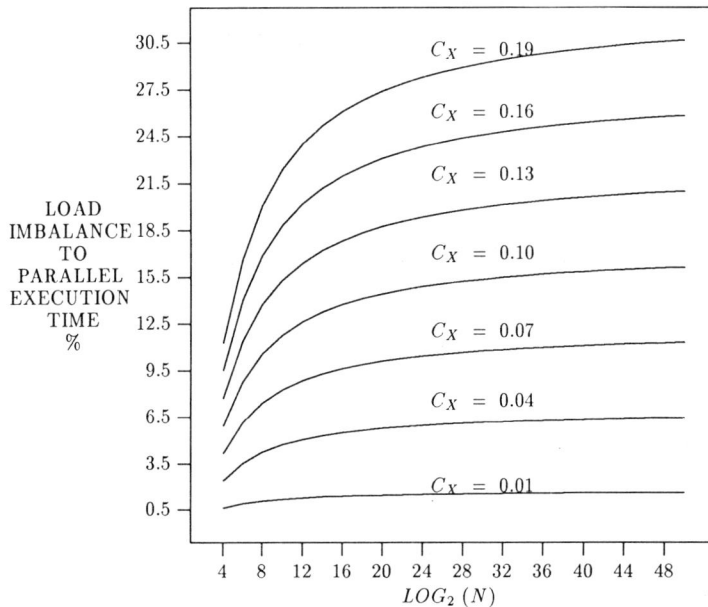

Figure 2. The ratio $\psi_{2,k}^{(1)}$ of load imbalance costs to the parallel execution time in absence of any load imbalance effects as function of the problem size for the first synchronization structure. The execution time has a uniform distribution with coefficient of variation C_X

The normal distribution. Consider first the case of a standard normal distribution. In the Appendix we show that

$$\psi_{a,K}^{(1)} = \frac{1}{K + 1} \left[A(a) \cdot S_1(K) - B(a) \cdot S_2(K) - \frac{1}{2A(a)} \cdot S_3(K) \right] \tag{23}$$

with

$$A(a) = (2 \log a)^{1/2} \tag{24}$$

$$B(a) = \frac{1}{2A(a)} [\log 4\pi - 2C + \log\log a] \tag{25}$$

$$S_1(K) = \sum_{i=1}^{K-1} (K - i)^{1/2} = \sum_{i=1}^{K-1} (i)^{1/2} \tag{26}$$

$$S_2(K) = \sum_{i=1}^{K-1} (K - i)^{-1/2} = \sum_{i=1}^{K-1} (i)^{-1/2} \tag{27}$$

$$S_3(K) = \sum_{i=1}^{K-1} (K - i)^{-1/2} \log(K - i) = \sum_{i=1}^{K-1} i^{-1/2} \log i \tag{28}$$

When $a = 2$, the coefficients A and B have the following values: $A = 0.779$, and $B = 0.3713$.

Let us now consider the case of a (μ, σ) normal distribution. The derivation of the formulas is presented in the Appendix. The ratio of load imbalance costs to the parallel execution time for the first structure of Figure 1 is

$$\psi_{a,K}^{(1)} = \frac{C_X \cdot \mu_X}{K + 1} \left[A(a) \cdot S_1(K) - B(a) \cdot S_2(K) - \frac{1}{2A(a)} \cdot S_3(K) \right] \tag{29}$$

with $A(a)$, $B(a)$, $S_1(K)$, $S_2(K)$, $S_3(K)$ defined previously.

The results are presented in Figure 3. We see that for relative small values of the coefficient of variation, e.g. for $C_X < 0.05$, the load imbalance increases the execution time only slightly by 10% to 20% even for large computations. For larger coefficients of variation the increase in the execution time grows more rapidly with the number N of processors.

An upper bound for a general distribution. We conclude the discussion of the first structure by deriving an upper bound for $\psi_{a,K}^{(1)}$ for the case when the distribution function of X is continuous, strictly increasing. In this case

$$\psi_{a,K}^{(1)} = \sigma_X \times \frac{D_{(a,K)}}{\sqrt{2} \times (K + 1)} \tag{30}$$

with $D_{(a,N)}$ given by the following expressions

$$D_{(a,K)} = \begin{cases} D' & \text{if } K = 2K' \quad (K \text{ even}) \\ D' + \left[a^{K'+1} - \frac{1}{a^{K'}} \right] & \text{if } K = 2K' + 1 \quad (K \text{ odd}) \end{cases} \tag{31}$$

where

$$D' = \frac{1 + \sqrt{a}}{a - 1} \left(a^{K'} - 1 \right) \left[a - \frac{1}{\sqrt{a} a^{K'-1}} \right] \tag{32}$$

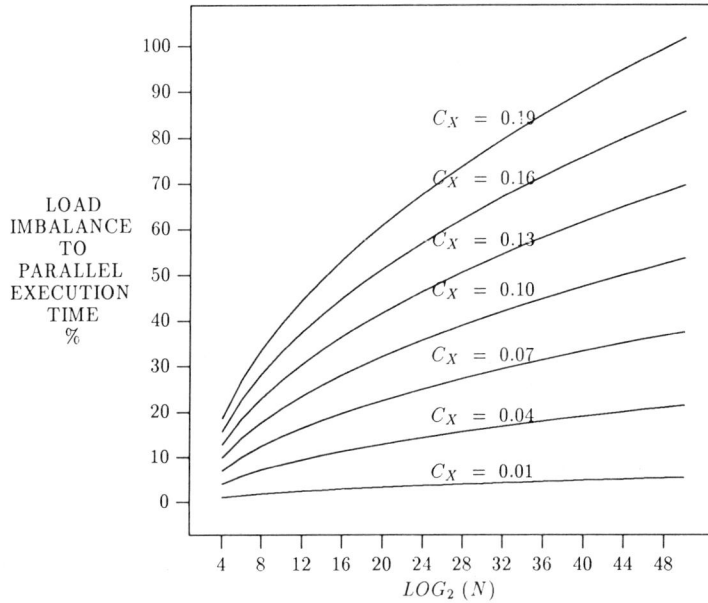

Figure 3. The ratio $\psi_{2,k}^{(1)}$ of load imbalance costs to the parallel execution time in absence of load imbalance effects as function of the problem size for the first synchronization structure. The execution time has a (μ,σ) normal distribution with $\mu = 1$

According to [8] we have

$$\Delta_i \leq C_X \frac{I_i - 1}{\sqrt{2I_i - 1}} \tag{33}$$

In our case $I_i = a^i$ and it can be seen easily that

$$\frac{a^i - 1}{\sqrt{2a^i - 1}} \leq \frac{a^i - 1}{\sqrt{2a^{i-1}}} \qquad \text{for} \quad a > 1 \tag{34}$$

But

$$\frac{a^i - 1}{\sqrt{2a^{i-1}}} = \frac{1}{\sqrt{2}} \left[a\sqrt{a^{i-1}} - \frac{1}{\sqrt{a^{i-1}}} \right] \tag{35}$$

and

$$\Delta_{a,K}^{(1)} \leq \frac{C_X}{\sqrt{2} \, D_{(a,K)}} \tag{36}$$

The second synchronization structure

Consider the second structure presented in Figure 1(b). Call $\Delta_{a,N}^{(2)}$ the total load imbalance cost for this structure.

Proposition. *For any distribution of the execution time the load imbalance cost for the first synchronization structure is an upper bound for the load imbalance cost of the second structure with the same number of elements.*

$$\Delta_{a,K}^{(2)} \leq \Delta_{a,K}^{(1)} \tag{37}$$

The proof is based upon the following observation. For any distribution of the execution time the execution time including any load imbalance effects for the second structure is smaller than the execution time for the first structure. Since the expected execution time of a given processor is the same in both cases it follows that the load imbalance costs for the second case are smaller.

To prove that the execution time for the second structure is always smaller than the one for the first structure let us consider the simple structure presented in Figure 4. Let X_i, X_j, X_k, X_l, X_m and X_n be independent, identically distributed, random variables representing the execution times on processors executing in parallel, subject to synchronization condition as shown in Figure 4.

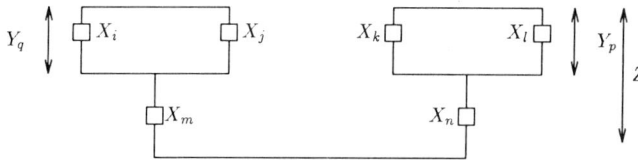

Figure 4.   An element of the synchronization structure in Figure 1(b)

The following expressions give the total execution time, Z, as well as the partial execution times, Y_q, and Y_p:

$$Y_q = \max(X_i, X_j) \tag{38}$$

$$Y_p = \max(X_k, X_l) \tag{39}$$

$$Z = \max[(X_m + Y_q), (X_n + Y_p)] \tag{40}$$

The following inequality follows immediately:

$$Z = \max[(X_m + \max(X_i, X_j)), (X_n + \max(X_k, X_l))] \\ \leq \max(X_m, X_n) + \max(X_i, X_j, X_k, X_l) \tag{41}$$

But $\max(X_m, X_n) + \max(X_i, X_j, X_k, X_l)$ is precisely the execution time for the first structure with four processors active in the first epoch (the corresponding execution time are X_i, X_j, X_k, X_l), and two active in the second epoch (the corresponding execution time are X_m, X_n).

The results presented in Section 2.1 may be used to estimate the load imbalance costs for the second structure. Note that closed form expressions for the distribution function of the parallel execution time can be derived but it is impracticalable to construct them.

3. THE EFFECTS OF COMMUNICATION LATENCY UPON SYNCHRONIZATION

3.1. Communication latency on a hypercube

A simplified model of parallel computations with global synchronization was presented in the previous sections. A serious limitation of the model comes from the assumption that in epoch $\mathcal{E}_k$ all I_k PEs, $\pi_1, \ldots, \pi_{I_k}$ start computing precisely at the same time and the epoch terminates when the last processor in the group completes its execution. Communication does not occur instantaneously; on the contrary, the communication latency between any two processors π_i and π_j is substantial.

For example, according to [5] the time to deliver a short message from node i to node j on an NCUBE/1 can be approximated by

$$\delta_{ij} = 261 + 193 d_{ij} \tag{42}$$

with

δ_{ij} = the transmission latency in μs,

d_{ij} = the Hamming distance between node i and node j. For example $d_{14} = 2$ since 1 = 0001 and $4_{10} = (0100)_2$. The distance d_{ij} represents the number of links to be traversed by a message from the source (i or j) to the destination (j or i) node.

For example, when $d_{ij} = 10$ then $\delta_{ij} \cong 2200$ μs.

The communication is faster on second generation hypercubes. For example on NCUBE/2 with a 20 MHz clock, the time to deliver a short message (2 bytes) from node π_i node π_j is approximately [1]

$$\delta_{ij} = 140 + d_{ij} + \frac{12}{20 \times 10^6} \simeq 140 + d_{ij} \tag{43}$$

with

δ_{ij} = the transmission latency in μs.

140 μs = is the start-up and the close-up time for a connection.

2 μs = is the overhead in routing the packet at every intermediate node along the path.

20·Mbps = the DMA transfer rate.

If $d_{ij} = 10$ then $\delta_{ij} \cong 160\mu$s. Note that this approximation for δ_{ij} does not take into account possible contention for communication links and/or memory with other nodes, but it is an effective delivery time. It takes into account the software overhead associated with VERTEX, the operating system on NCUBE.

3.2. Synchronization and broadcasting on a hypercube

In this section, we assume that a sub-cube of dimension L is allocated to a computation $\mathcal{C}$ which requires global synchronization. Each processor executes the same code, but on different data according to the following pattern. A leader, usually processor π_0, signals the beginning of an epoch and every PE, π_i starts computing and upon termination, signals completion. When π_0 receives completion messages from all π_i, $1 \leq i \leq 2^L - 1$, the next epoch is started.

To analyze quantitatively the effects of communication latency, it is necessary to define precisely the communication patterns involved in global synchronization. In this paper we consider a broadcast-collapse synchronization protocol [18] using the broadcast tree shown in Figure 5. In this protocol, a synchronization epoch starts when π_0 broadcasts a short message signaling the beginning of the epoch. Each processor π_i starts computing as soon as it receives the start-up signal. Each processor sends up a termination signal to its ancestor in the tree when the following two conditions are fulfilled:

(1) It has completed execution.

(2) It has received a termination signal from all its descendants (if any) in the broadcast tree.

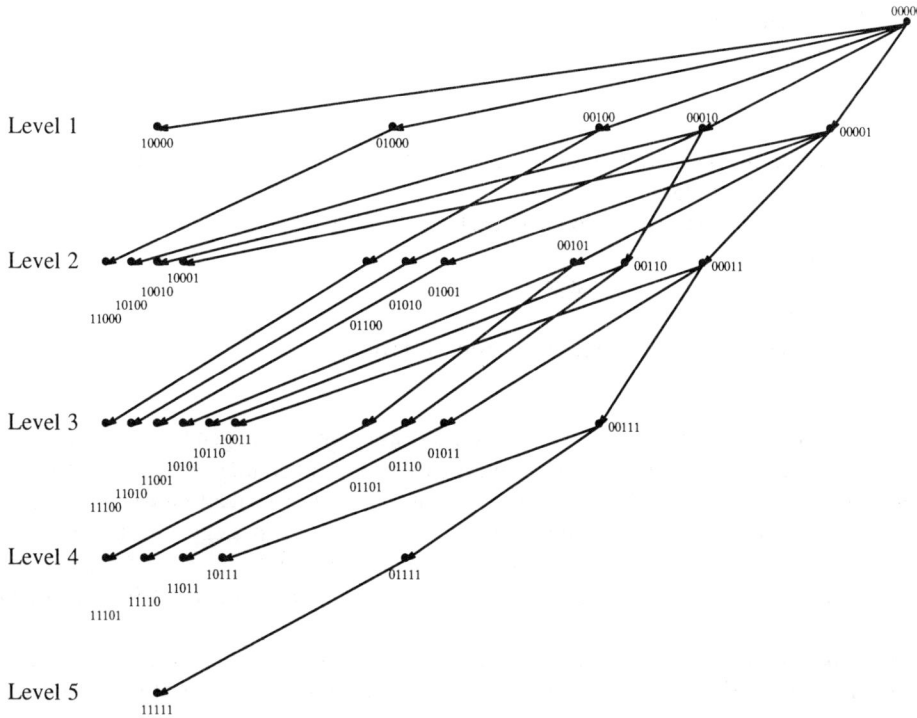

Figure 5. A broadcast tree which allows optimal communication time in distributing or collecting messages

This protocol guarantees that π_0 receives a termination signal if and only if all PEs have signaled termination and there is no contention for communication links, due to signaling of beginning and termination of the epoch.

The tree in Figure 5 has the property that in a cube of order L the number n_ℓ of nodes at level ℓ is

$$n_\ell = \binom{L}{\ell} \qquad 0 \leq \ell \leq L \tag{44}$$

In other words, all nodes at distance ℓ from the root are at level ℓ. It follows that if the communication hardware has a fan-out mechanism which allows a node to send a broadcast message to all its immediate descendants at the same time, then the broadcast tree is optimal in the sense that each node receives a broadcast message from the root at the earliest possible time. If such a fan-out is not supported by the hardware, then the following scheme guarantees that the node at the farthest distance from the root receives the broadcast message at the earliest possible time. A node at level ℓ in the broadcast tree (see Figure 5) sends messages to its descendants at level $\ell + 1$, in the order of the depth of the subtree rooted at that node. For example, π_0 sends the broadcast messages in the following order π_1, π_2, π_4, π_8, π_{16}, since the subtrees rooted at these nodes have their respective depth 4, 3, 2, 1 and 0.

To implement the synchronization protocol described earlier, each PE at level $\ell > 0$ executes repeatedly the following sequence of steps:

```
read start-up message from ancestor_at_level (ℓ − 1) and pass it to the descendants
    execute computation
    for i = 1, number_descendents_at_level ℓ + 1 do
    begin
        read termination_message
    end
    write termination_message to ancestor_at_level ℓ − 1
```

This code assumes a blocking read and a non-blocking write. The generic read statement allows a node to read the termination messages in the order they arrive. If a generic read statement is not available, then the node at level ℓ has to read messages from its descendants at level $\ell + 1$ to minimize blocking. An optimal strategy in this case is to read first from the node with the shortest subtree. For example, π_0 should read in the order π_{16}, π_8, π_4, π_2, π_1, since the corresponding subtrees have the depth 0, 1, 2, 3 and 4 respectively.

Note that in this case the communication time for the collapse mechanism is dependent upon the number of descendants at distance one. A node may have at most L descendants and in our analysis we overestimate the time to read all termination messages as $\delta_1 = L\delta'$ with δ' the time for a read operation which does not block, since the data is already there.

3.3. A first order approximation for the effects of synchronization upon efficiency

To get an estimate of the effect of communication latency in global synchronization upon processor utilization, consider a very simple model based upon the following assumptions.

A1. The computation $\mathcal{C}$ uses a sub-cube of dimension L of a hypercube of dimension N, and there is no interference between the sub-cube allocated to $\mathcal{C}$ and other sub-cubes. No messages other than those needed by $\mathcal{C}$ are routed through the sub-cube.

A2. The execution time of the computation allocated to every processor in epoch i is strictly deterministic, $X^i = E$, $0 \leq i \leq 2^L - 1$.

A3. A broadcast/collapse mechanism is used for synchronization. To signal the beginning of a synchronization epoch the processor at the root of the broadcast tree, π_0 sends a message of the shortest length at time t^s and the message reaches the n_ℓ processors at level ℓ in the broadcast tree at time $t^\ell = t^s + \ell\delta_0$. To signal the termination of the synchronization epoch, the processors at level L send a message of the shortest length at time time $t^L = t^s + L\delta_0 + E$ and the message is processed by π_0 at time $t^{s'} = t^s + E + L(\delta_0 + \delta_1)$. The timing diagram corresponding to this synchronization protocol is presented in Figure 6 for the case $L = 5$.

Since we have assumed strictly deterministic execution times and no communication interference from other sub-cubes, the synchronization protocol described above guarantees that no blocking due to memory and/or link contention will ever occur, and the *duration of a synchronization epoch* is precisely $T_S = E + L(\delta_0 + \delta_1)$. Call $\delta = \delta_0 + \delta_1$. It follows immediately that when assumptions A1–A3 are true, then the average utilization of any processor is

$$U = \frac{E}{T_S} = \frac{E}{E + L\delta} = 1 - \frac{L\delta}{E + L\delta} \tag{45}$$

or

$$U = 1 - \frac{1}{1 + \frac{E}{L\delta}} = 1 - \frac{1}{1 + \beta} \tag{46}$$

with $\beta = E/(L\delta)$ a factor describing the computation to communication time ratio.

For example, when $E = 100\delta$, namely when the computation time is two orders of magnitude larger than communication time, then for a cube of order $L = 10$ it follows that $\beta = 10$ and

$$U = 1 - \frac{1}{11} \simeq 0.89$$

When $E = \delta$ then $\beta = 0.1$ and $U \cong 0.091$.

For the NCUBE/2 we have $\delta \simeq 160$ μs, while the execution time of the fastest instruction is about 50 nanoseconds. It follows that in order to achieve 90% processor utilization on such a hypercube, each PE has to execute $10^2 \times 10^3 = 10^5$ instructions in a synchronization epoch.

The previous analysis can be easily extended to the case when the execution time has a bounded distribution, i.e., when $a \leq X^i \leq b$, and when the broadcast-

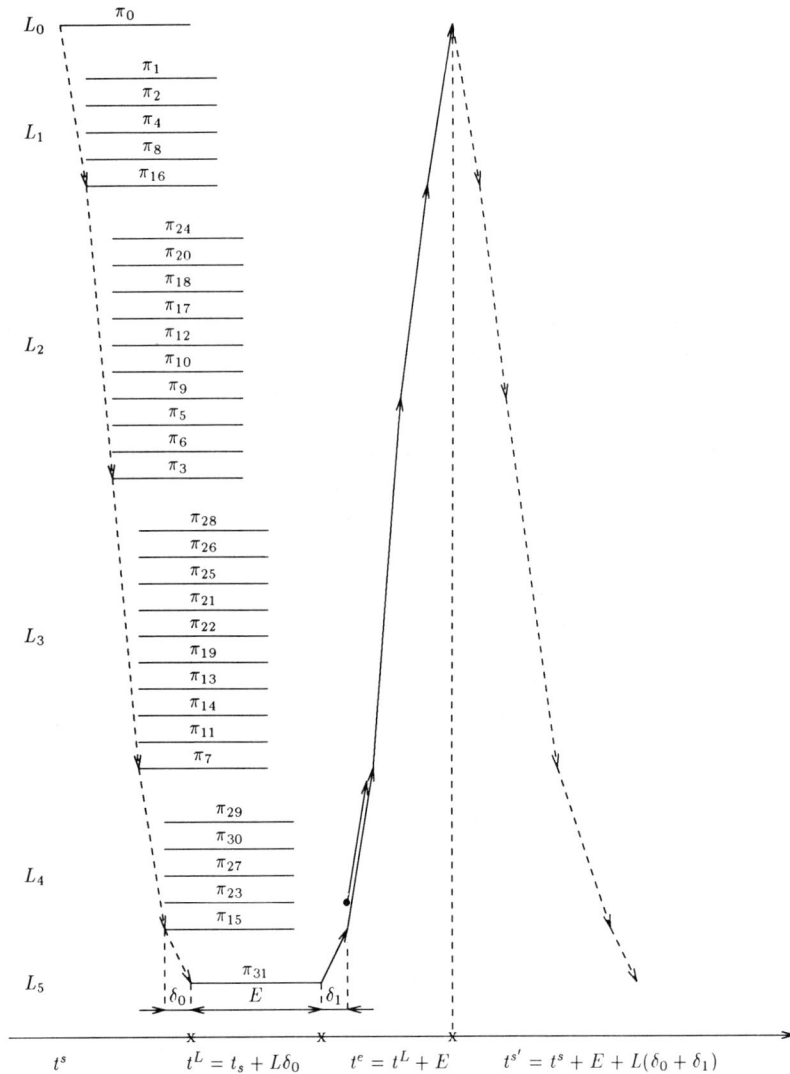

Figure 6. A timing diagram for the case $L = 5$. Broadcast time per level is δ_0, collapse time per level is δ_1, and execution time is deterministic E

collapse time per level satisfies $\delta \geq b - a$. In this case it is guaranteed that communication latency hides all the effects of non-determinancy in execution time. In other words, a processor at level ℓ will always complete its execution no later than the completion messages from all its descendants have arrived, as shown in Figure 6.

Consider processors π_i and π_j with actual execution times a and b, respectively. To complete execution on π_i before receiving all the completion messages, say from π_j, in the worst case scenario we must have the condition $b \leq \delta_0 + \delta_1 + a$ or $\delta \geq b - a$. In this case, the processor utilization is bounded by

$$1 - \frac{1}{1 + \frac{(2^L - 1)a + b}{L}} \leq U \leq 1 - \frac{1}{1 + \beta_b} \tag{47}$$

with

$$\beta_b = \frac{b}{L\delta} \tag{48}$$

To minimize the inefficiency associated with low values of β_b, the following strategy could be used. Rather than assign equal computations to every PE, assign a higher load to processors at lower levels in the broadcast-collapse tree. For example, Figure 6 suggests that in the case of deterministic execution time, the processors at level ℓ can be kept busy for an additional time equal to

$$\tau_\ell = (L - \ell)\delta \tag{49}$$

The computation time for processors at level ℓ is

$$E_\ell = E + (L - \ell)\delta = E \left[1 + \frac{L - \ell}{L\beta} \right] \tag{50}$$

or

$$E_\ell = E \left(1 + \frac{1 - \frac{\ell}{L}}{\beta} \right) \tag{51}$$

This simply means that rather than having an equipartition of the data domain, an optimal balanced assignment would mean assigning different computational loads depending upon the position of the processor in the broadcast-collapse tree.

With this approach all n_ℓ PEs at level ℓ have a utilization

$$U_\ell = 1 - \frac{\ell\delta}{E + L\delta} = 1 - \frac{\ell}{L} \frac{1}{1 + \beta} \tag{52}$$

The average utilization is

$$U^{opt} = \frac{1}{2^L} \sum_{\ell=0}^{L} n_\ell U_\ell \tag{53}$$

and substituting for U_ℓ we have

$$U^{opt} = \frac{1}{2^L} \sum_{\ell=0}^{L} n_\ell U_\ell = 1 - \frac{1}{2^L} \sum_{\ell=0}^{L} \binom{L}{\ell} \left[1 - \frac{\ell}{L} \frac{2}{1 + \beta} \right] \tag{54}$$

$$= 1 - \frac{\sum_{\ell=0}^{L} \ell \binom{L}{\ell}}{L2^L} \frac{1}{1 + \beta}$$

---

or

$$U^{opt} = 1 - \frac{L2^{L-1}}{L2^L} \frac{1}{1+\beta} = 1 - \frac{1}{2} \frac{1}{1+\beta} \tag{55}$$

To evaluate the advantage of this approach, consider the case when

$$E = \delta$$

In this case, using an equipartition of the load, the average processor utilization is

$$U = 1 - \frac{L}{L+1} \tag{56}$$

with $\beta = E/L\delta = 1/L$. Using the optimal load partition the utilization is

$$U^{opt} = 1 - \frac{1}{2} \frac{L}{1+\beta} = 1 - \frac{1}{2} \frac{L}{L+1} \tag{57}$$

For $L = 10$, $U = 0.091$ and $U^{opt} = 0.5455$. The corresponding speed-ups are

$$S = 2^L \cdot U \cong 92$$
$$S^{opt} = 2^L \cdot U^{opt} \cong 546$$

For the case $L = 10$, $E = 100\delta$ considered earlier, we have

$$U = 0.89, \, S = 911$$
$$U^{opt} = 0.976, \, S^{opt} = 1000$$

3.4. Expected processor utilization in iterative methods

The model discussed so far does not take into account communication delays due to the need to update boundary values. If one considers a 2-D problem, we assume that at the beginning of each iteration every PE has to exchange boundary values with at most four PEs holding neighboring data subdomains. This effect can be captured by adding a communication time δ_c to the computation time E. Then the average processor utilization is

$$U = \frac{E}{L\delta + \delta_c + E} \tag{58}$$

with δ and E previously defined and

$$\delta_c = q \times \tau \times \alpha \tag{59}$$

with

q — the number of neighboring data subdomains,

τ — the time to exchange one boundary value with a neighboring subdomain at distance $d = 1$,

α — a factor ≥ 1 determined by the mapping strategy and describing the effects of the distance between nodes upon the communication delay.

Then U becomes

$$U = 1 - \frac{L\delta + q\tau\alpha}{L\delta + q\tau\alpha + E} = 1 - \frac{1}{1 + \beta} \qquad (60)$$

with β defined as

$$\beta = \frac{E}{L\delta + q\tau\alpha} \qquad (61)$$

3.5. A scheme with self-synchronization

Consider now a computation in which global synchronization should occur at every iteration. We present a scheme in which global synchronization occurs only every Rth iteration and during the intermediate iterations each PE attempts a *self-synchronization*. This scheme is illustrated in Figure 7. At time t_0 the leader (π_0) sends a start-up signal. All PEs defer starting the computation until time $t_0' = t_0 + L\delta_0$.

The scheme assumes that each PE knows the expected duration E of its computation time per iteration, and has a good bound Δ on its average load imbalance amount. Thus the PEs are expected to complete their execution by time $t_0'' = t_0' + E + \Delta$ and at this time all PEs start exchanging boundary values. This communication period has a duration of $\delta_c = q \times \tau \times \alpha$ with $\alpha \geq 1$, the factor described above, and τ the time required to exchange one boundary value. For each PE there are q other PEs containing adjacent data subdomain. For 2-D problems we have $q = 4$ and for 3-D problems, $q = 8$. At time t_1 this communication period terminates and a new iteration begins. This scheme could be improved slightly, for example, by having a PE which has not completed the computation by time t_0'' but has finished its communication before time t_1 start the next iteration earlier.

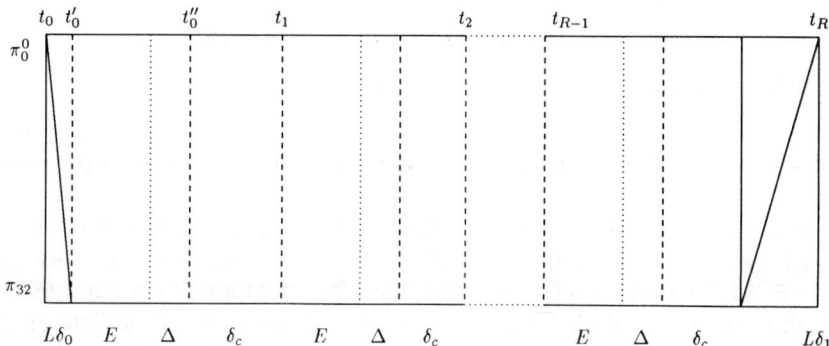

Figure 7. The timing diagram for the self-synchronization scheme. True synchronization is done only every Rth iteration. Here E = expected compute time, Δ = bound on load imbalance, and δ_c = time to exchange boundary values

The processor utilization for this scheme is approximated by the following expression

$$U = \frac{R\mu}{L\delta + R(E + \Delta) + Rq\alpha\tau} \tag{62}$$

or

$$U = 1 - \frac{L\delta + R(\Delta + q\alpha\tau)}{L\delta + R(E + \Delta + q\alpha\tau)} \tag{63}$$

Often $q\alpha\tau \gg \Delta$, and the utilization becomes in this case

$$U = 1 - \frac{1}{1 + \beta} \tag{64}$$

with

$$\beta \cong \frac{L\delta + R(E + q\alpha\tau)}{L\delta + Rq\alpha\tau} \tag{65}$$

Table 2 shows values of speed-up predicted by this model of the self-synchronization scheme. We fix the values $L = 10$, $q = 4$, $\alpha = 2$ and $\tau = \delta$ and vary R, E and Δ. As before, we use the ratio E/δ and also set $\Delta = \gamma E$. The formula for speed-up is then

$$S = \frac{2^L R(E/\delta)}{L\delta + R(q\alpha\tau/\delta + (E/\delta)(1 + \gamma))}$$

$$= \frac{1024R(E/\delta)}{10 + R(8 + (E/\delta)(1 + \gamma))} \tag{66}$$

Some extreme values for the speed-up are:

(1) As $E \to \infty$ then $S \to 1024/(1 + \gamma)$.

(2) As $R \to \infty$ then $S \to 1024(E/\delta)/(8 + (E/\delta)(1 + \gamma))$.

(3) As $R \to \infty$ with $(E/\delta) = 1$, then $S \to 1024/(9 + \gamma) \approx 102$ to 114.

(4) With $(E/\delta) = 1$, $R = 1$, then $S = 1024/(19 + \gamma) \approx 50$ to 54.

Note that $R = 1$ corresponds to ordinary synchronization as discussed in the previous section.

The most significant observation from Table 2 is that there is a regime of operation where self-synchronization is quite effective for increasing performance. This occurs when the E/δ is relatively small, say between 1 and 20. Thus for $E/\delta = 5$ and $\Delta/E = 0.1$, we see that self-synchronization can increase the speed-up from 218 to 380, or about a 75% improvement. As E/δ becomes large, the synchronization cost is small anyway, so self-synchronization only helps a little. When E/δ is very small (1 or less), the best speed-up is already very low so that while the improvement due to self-synchronization is perhaps a factor of 2, the resulting efficiency is still very low.

Table 2. Speed-ups for a self-synchronized iteration on a 1024 processor NCUBE with $L = 10$, $q = 4$, $\tau = \delta$. The values R = number of self-synchronized iterations, (E/δ) = computation to communication ratio, and (Δ/E) = variation of computation are varied as indicated.

Imbalance $(\Delta/E) = 0$
E/δ ratio

R	1	5	20	100	inf
1	54	223	539	868	1023
4	89	331	672	927	1023
10	103	366	707	940	1023
25	109	382	722	945	1024
inf	114	394	732	949	1024

Imbalance $(\Delta/E) = 0.1$
E/δ ratio

R	1	5	20	100	inf
1	54	218	512	800	930
20	89	320	631	850	930
100	102	354	661	861	931
500	108	369	674	865	931
inf	113	380	683	868	931

Imbalance $(\Delta/E) = 0.4$
E/δ ratio

R	1	5	20	100	inf
1	53	205	446	649	731
4	86	293	532	681	731
10	99	320	554	688	731
25	105	333	563	690	731
inf	109	342	569	692	731

Imbalance $(\Delta/E) = 1.0$
E/δ ratio

R	1	5	20	100	inf
1	52	183	354	470	512
20	82	250	406	487	512
100	93	270	418	490	512
500	99	279	424	492	512
inf	103	285	427	493	512

Note that two of the factors kept constant in Table 2 also affect the speed-up substantially. Thus, if $\alpha = 1$ (the optimum value—and often achievable) or $\alpha = 1.5$, then we have the following effects for $E/\delta = 5$ and $\Delta/E = 0.1$. For $\alpha = 1.5$, the speed-up goes from 244 to 466 as R goes from 1 to infinity; for $\alpha = 1.0$, the speed-up goes from 263 to 539 (an improvement of over 100%). This is plausible because reducing α means making the computation more local, which improves the efficiency. The second factor is L, if $L = 13$ instead of 10, then again the computation becomes more local and the efficiency plus the advantage of self-synchronization improves. For the same case $(E/\delta) = 5$ and $\Delta/E = 0.1$, the speed-up increases from 1546 to 3034 or about a 96% improvement due to self-synchronization. With $L = 13$ and $\alpha = 1$, the speed-up for this case increases from 1821 to 4311 or about a 137% improvement.

4. EXPERIMENTAL RESULTS

An experiment to study the performance of iterative methods on a distributed memory system is described in detail in [8]. The experiment uses the parallel ELLPACK (PELLPACK) system developed at Purdue [7], running on a 128 processor NCUBE/1. The TRIPLEX tool set [6], is used to monitor the execution and to collect trace data.

The experiment monitors the execution of the code, implementing a Jacobi iterative algorithm for solving a linear system of equations, an important component of a parallel PDE solver. To ensure a load balanced execution, the domain decomposer, part of the PELLPACK environment, attempts to assign to every PE an equal amount of computation. The experiment was conducted by taking a problem of a fixed size and repeating the execution with a number of PEs ranging from 2 to 128.

The experiment monitors communication events and permits the determination of the time spent by every computation assigned to a PE, called in the following a *thread of control*, in any state. A thread of control can be either *active* (or computing), or *performing an I/O operation* (either reading or writing), or in a *blocked state* (waiting while attempting to read data from another PE). Communication is done strictly by broadcasting and the broadcast-collapse mechanism uses two balanced binary trees rooted at π_0 and π_1, respectively. Every five iterations a convergence test is done to ensure that the computation converges. The time is measured in ticks, and 1 tick = 0.167 milliseconds.

In the following, we discuss the case of a rectangular domain and a 50×50 grid with 64 processors used to solve the problem [8]. Figures 8, 9 and 10 present histograms of the computing times for processors on each of the levels of the broadcast tree. The groupings are PEs O and 1 in Figure 8(a,b), PEs 2 and 3 in Figure 8(c,d), PEs 4 to 7 in 9(a,b), PEs 8 to 15 in 9(c,d), PEs 16 to 31 in 10(a,b), and PEs 32 to 63 in 10(c,d). Figures 11, 12 and 13 present histograms of the blocking time with the same grouping of processors.

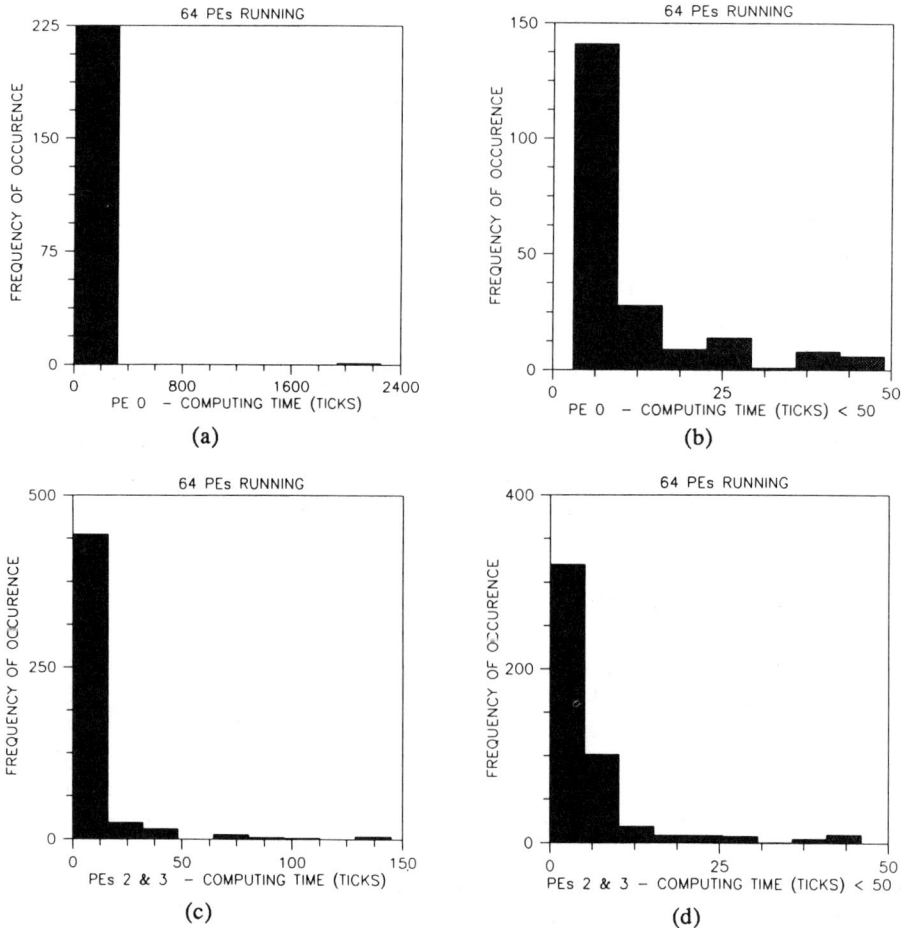

Figure 8. *Histograms of computing time for PE 0, (a) and (b), and PEs 2 and 3, (c) and (d)*

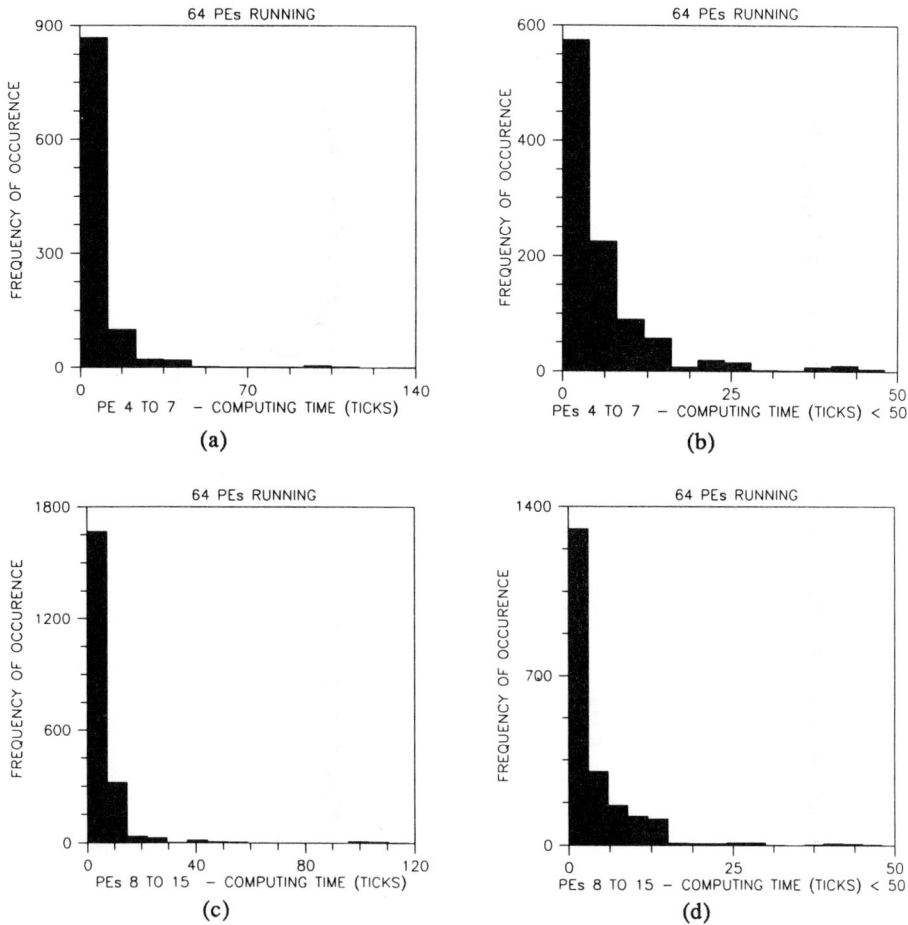

Figure 9. *Histograms of computing time for PEs 4–7, (a) and (b), and PEs 8–15, (c) and (d)*

The computing time for PE O is displayed in Figure 8(a,b). The first shows that most of the computing time is done in slices of 50 ticks or less, but a few slices (less than 2%) take considerably longer. We suspect that these relatively long computing intervals correspond to the convergence tests done every five iterations. A close-up of the computing intervals with length in the 0 to 50 ticks range is presented in Figure 8(b), which shows that about 80% of the computing intervals last less than 10 ticks. The same approach is taken to other groups, the first diagram in each pair presents a histogram of all the computing intervals observed for the group and the second diagrams zooms upon the region with computing intervals of 50 ticks or less.

The following trends are common for all groups of processors. About 98% of the computing intervals are of 50 ticks or less. About 2% of all intervals are higher than 50 ticks; but the duration of these few relatively long computing periods decreases as the level of the group in the broadcast tree increases. For example, these long periods are of about 2000 ticks for level 0 and close to 400 for level 5. Probably close to 80% of all computing intervals are the length of 10 ticks or less. The expected length of a

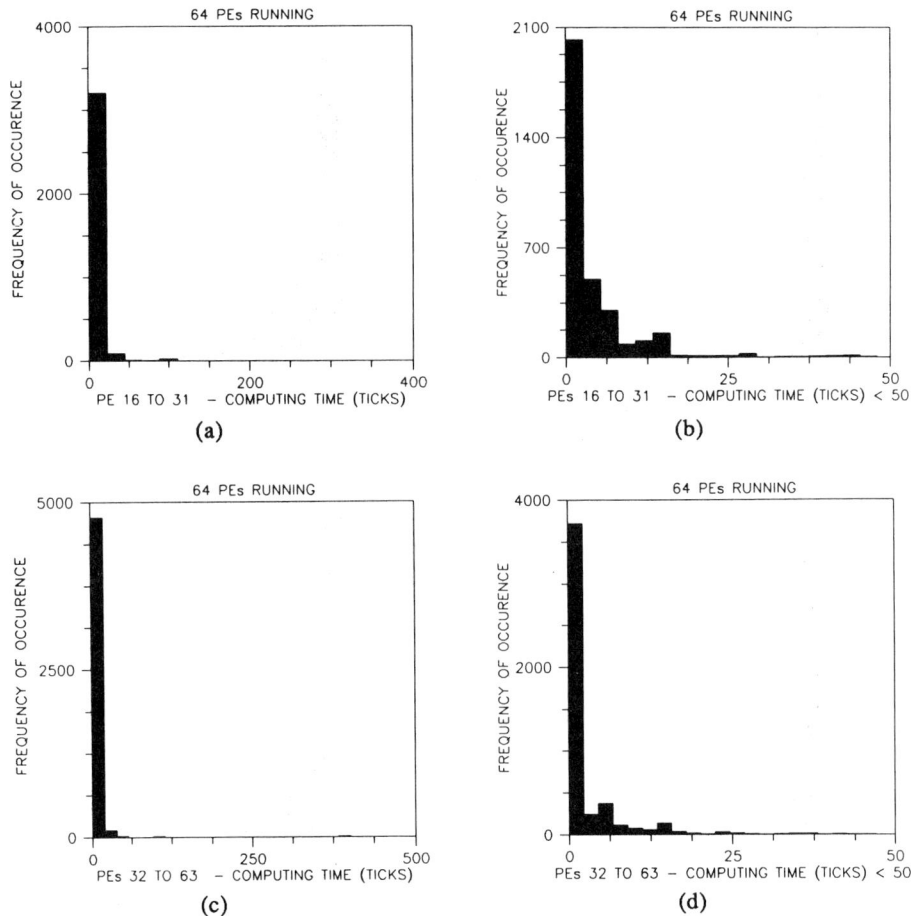

Figure 10. Histograms of computing time for PEs 16–31, (a) and (b), and PEs 32–63, (c) and (d)

computing interval decreases as the group is located at a higher level in the broadcast tree. The distribution of the computing time is bounded, but it is not well approximated with either a uniform or a normal distribution.

Let us now discuss the blocking time intervals. A thread of control enters a blocked state as a result of a READ operation when the data requested are not available in the local buffer associated with the link on which the message is expected. Since communication time, in particular the blocking time, depends upon the actual communication hardware, we have defined and measured the *algorithmic blocking*. The algorithmic blocking is a measure of the amount of time the demand for data at the consumer processor precedes the actual generation of data by the producer processor. The algorithmic blocking is measured as the interval from the instance when a READ is issued by a consumer PE, until the corresponding WRITE is issued by the producer PE. If the WRITE precedes the READ, then the algorithmic blocking is considered to be zero.

The blocking time is always larger than the algorithmic blocking. The non-algorithmic blocking, defined as the difference between the blocking time and the

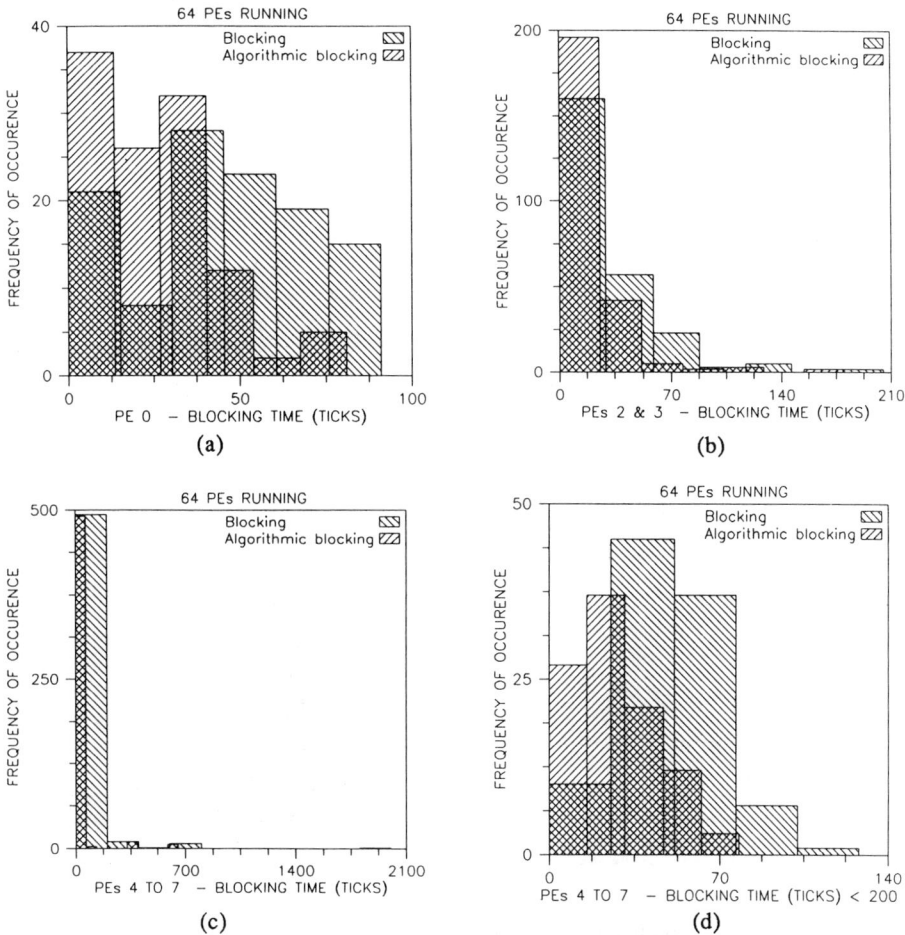

*Figure 11. Histograms showing both total blocking and algorithmic blocking times for PE 0, (a);
PEs 2 and 3, (b); and PEs 4–7, (c) and (d)*

algorithmic blocking time, is a measure of the communication latency. Congestion of the communication network leads to large non-algorithmic blocking times. Figures 11, 12 and 13 present pairs of histograms for the blocking and algorithmic blocking for several groups of processors. Figure 11(a,b) show the blocking time for PE 0 and for PEs 2 and 3. PE 0 exhibits blocking for relatively short periods of time of 100 ticks or less. The effects of communication latency are visible, the algorithmic blocking is about 80% of all blocking intervals of less than 50 ticks, while blocking times larger than 50 ticks occur in about 50% of all cases. PEs 2 and 3 experience longer blocking periods as shown in Figure 11(b). This trend continues for PEs 4 to 7 (Figure 11(c,d)), and PEs 8 to 15 (Figure 12(a,b)), and PEs 16 to 31 (Figure 12(c,d)). For these cases, the histograms of all blocking times in the group and the histogram of blocking times less than 200 ticks are shown in pairs.

Figure 13 presents in more detail the 32 to 63 PE group. The overall histogram in Figure 13(a) is as before and the histogram of the non-algorithmic blocking time is also

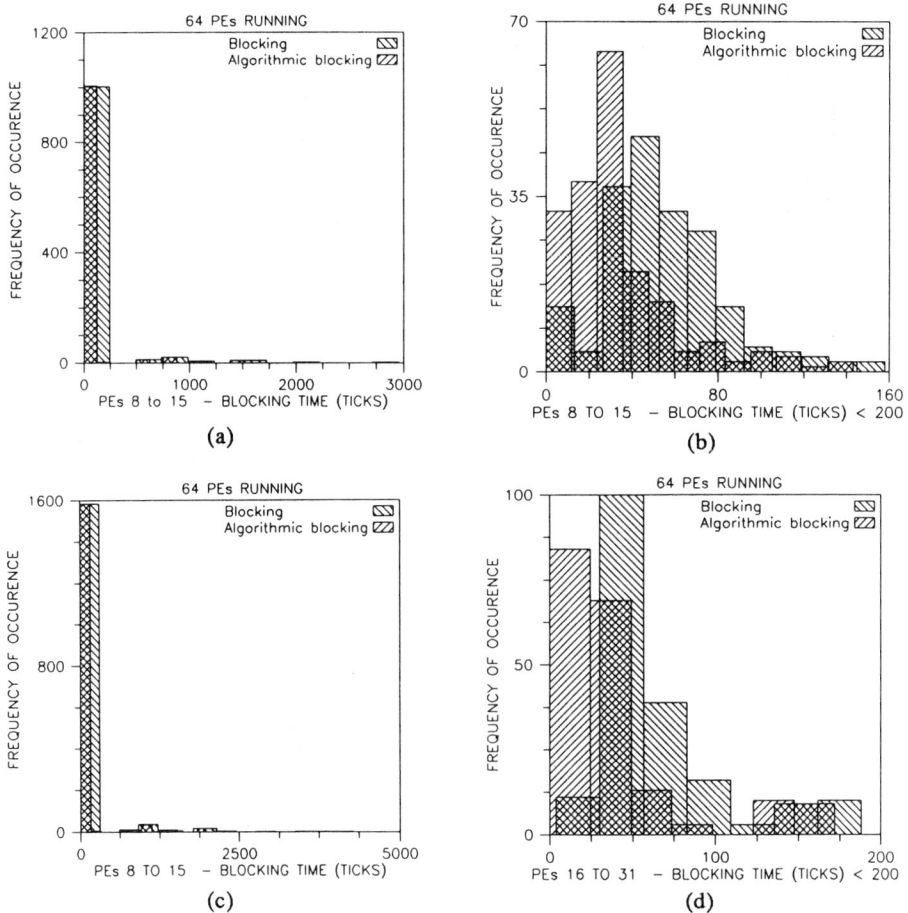

Figure 12. Histograms showing both total blocking and algorithmic blocking for PEs 8–15, (a) and (b), and for PEs 16–31, (c) and (d)

given in Figure 13(d). Their counterparts are given in Figures 13(c) and (b) for the case when the blocking time is less than 200 ticks. Again, we observe an anomaly, namely in a few instances a fairly large blocking interval occurs. A plausible explanation is that these effects are due to the start-up and termination.

5. CONCLUSIONS

The paper reports results on the performance of iterative methods on distributed memory MIMD systems. High communication costs and dynamic load imbalance are responsible for the low speed-up observed in practice for computations which require global synchronization.

Architectural and/or algorithmic approaches may be considered to improve the performance. Architectural solutions, likely to be found in future generations of distributed memory MIMD machines, are to provide either a fast, dedicated communication subsystem for handling short messages for synchronization, or some form of shared memory for semaphores.

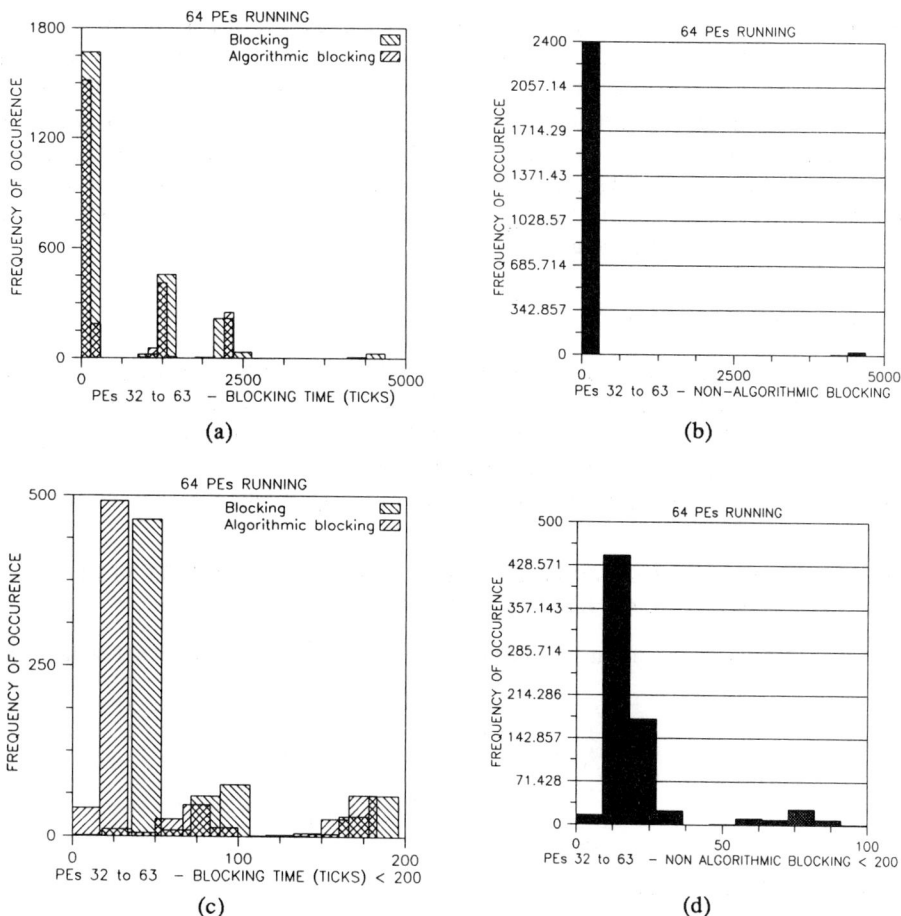

Figure 13. Histograms showing both total blocking and algorithmic blocking for PEs 32–63, (a) and (c), and non-algorithmic blocking for PEs 32–63, (b) and (d)

An algorithmic solution to the problem is to reduce the number of synchronization points in iterative methods. Yet, the numerical convergence is guaranteed only in case of synchronized execution. Therefore, it is desired to eliminate explicit synchronization but have different threads of control co-ordinate their execution implicitly. The self-synchronization method we propose achieves this by estimating the time when all threads of control have completed an iteration. This approach requires an understanding of the effects of the dynamic load imbalance due to non-deterministic execution time, to estimate this time.

This paper is devoted to the study of algorithmic solutions. Section 2 of the paper presents an analysis of the dynamic load imbalance. A load imbalance factor is defined and its upper bounds for different distributions of the execution time are computed. Section 3 analyzes the effects of the communication latency and produces a closed form expression for the expected processor utilization which takes into account the communication latency. Then an algorithm for self-synchronized execution is given. Section 4 presents an experiment involving the parallel ELLPACK system in which detailed information concerning the behavior of all threads of control was collected. These data do not conform to the model developed; there is a bimodal behavior. The first mode involves small delays consistent with our model and are due to expected variations in balance and data dependencies. The second mode involves very long delays due to the global synchronizations required. The long delays (and there are also some intermediate ones) prevent us from validating our model in any statistical sense, but the data does suggest that our model is appropriate for the effects of local variations and irregularities in SPMD computations.

ACKNOWLEDGEMENTS

This work was supported in part by the Strategic Defense Initiative through ARO grants DAAG03-86-K-0106 and DAAL03-90-0107, by the National Science Foundation by grant CCR-8619817 and by the NATO grant 891007. The experimental work reported in Section 4 from [8], is the result of a collaboration with E.A. Vavalis who contributed significantly to performing the experiment and analyzing the results.

APPENDIX: THE LOAD IMBALANCE FACTOR FOR THE FIRST STRUCTURE IN CASE OF A NORMAL DISTRIBUTION

First consider a standard normal distribution. In this case $\mu = 0$ and $\sigma = 1$ which leads to

$$
\begin{aligned}
\Delta_i \approx (2 \log I_i)^{1/2} &- \frac{1}{2} (2 \log I_i)^{-1/2} (\log 4\pi - 2C) \\
&- \frac{1}{2} (2 \log I_i)^{-1/2} (\log \log I_i)
\end{aligned} \tag{A.1}
$$

Since $I_i = a^{K-i}$, Δ_i becomes:

$$
\Delta_i(a,K) \approx A(a)(K-i)^{+1/2} - B(a)(K-i)^{-1/2} - \frac{1}{2A(a)} (K-i)^{-1/2} \log(K-i)
$$
$$
A(a) = (2 \log a)^{1/2} \tag{A.2}
$$

$$
B(a) = \frac{1}{2A(a)} [\log 4\pi - 2C + \log \log a] \tag{A.3}
$$

Then

$$
\Delta_{a,N}^{(1)}(a,K) = \sum_{i=1}^{K-1} \Delta_i \approx A(a) \cdot S_1(K) - B(a) \cdot S_2(K) - \frac{1}{2A(a)} S_3(K) \tag{A.4}
$$

with

$$
S_1(K) = \sum_{i=1}^{K-1} (K-i)^{1/2} = \sum_{i=1}^{K-1} (i)^{1/2} \tag{A.5}
$$

$$S_2(K) = \sum_{i=1}^{K-1}(K-i)^{-1/2} = \sum_{i=1}^{K-1}(i)^{-1/2} \qquad (A.6)$$

$$S_3(K) = \sum_{i=1}^{K-1}(K-i)^{-1/2}\log(K-i) = \sum_{i=1}^{K-1}i^{-1/2}\log i \qquad (A.7)$$

According to Ramanujan [12]:

$$S_1(K) = C_1 + \frac{2}{3}(K-1)\sqrt{K-1} + \frac{1}{2}\sqrt{K-1}+$$
$$+\frac{1}{6}\left[\left\{\sqrt{K-1}+\sqrt{K}\right\}^{-3} + \left\{\sqrt{K}+\sqrt{K+1}\right\}^{-3} + \ldots\right] \qquad (A.8)$$

with

$$C_1 = -\frac{1}{4\pi}\left(\frac{1}{1\sqrt{1}} + \frac{1}{2\sqrt{2}} + \frac{1}{3\sqrt{3}} + \ldots\right) \qquad (A.9)$$

The asymptotic expansion for large value of K can be shown to be

$$S(K) = C_1 + \frac{2}{3}(K-1)\sqrt{K-1} + \frac{1}{2}\sqrt{K-1}+$$
$$+\frac{1}{\sqrt{K-1}}\left(\frac{1}{24} - \frac{1}{1920(K-1)^2} + \frac{1}{9216(K-1)^4} \ldots\right) \qquad (A.10)$$

Then $S_2(K)$ is

$$S_2(K) = C_0 + \sqrt{K-1} + \frac{1}{2\sqrt{K-1}} -$$
$$-\frac{1}{2}\left\{\frac{\{\sqrt{K-1}+\sqrt{K}\}^{-3}}{\sqrt{K(K-1)}} + \frac{\{\sqrt{K}+\sqrt{K+1}\}^{-3}}{\sqrt{K(K+1)}} + \ldots\right\} \qquad (A.11)$$

with

$$C_0 = -(1+\sqrt{2})\left(\frac{1}{\sqrt{1}} - \frac{1}{\sqrt{2}} + \frac{1}{\sqrt{3}} - \frac{1}{\sqrt{4}} + \ldots\right) \qquad (A.12)$$

To evaluate $S_3(K)$ note that

$$\sum_{i=1}^{\infty}i^{-x}\log i = -\zeta'(x) \qquad (A.13)$$

for $1 \le x \le \infty$. $\zeta(x)$ is Riemann's zeta function. It follows that

$$S_3(K) \le -\zeta'(\sqrt{2}) \approx 307.822\,357\,2 \qquad (A.14)$$

When $N = 2^K$, the coefficients A and B have the following values: $A = 0.779$, and $B = 0.3713$.

Finally

$$\psi_{2,K}^{(1)} = 0.779 \frac{S_1(K)}{K+1} - 0.3713 \frac{S_2(K)}{K+1} - 0.6444 \frac{S_2(K)}{K+1} \qquad (A.15)$$

Consider the general case of a (μ, σ) normal distribution. The load imbalance costs for a synchronization epoch with I_i processors active is

$$\Delta_i \cong \sigma_X [(2 \log I_i)^{1/2}) - \frac{1}{2} (2 \log I_i)^{-1/2} (\log \log I_i + \log 4\pi - 2C)] \qquad (A.16)$$

Consequently the ratio of load imbalance costs to the parallel execution time for the first structure is

$$\psi_{2,K}^{(1)} = \frac{\mu_X \sum_{i=1}^{K-1} \Delta_i}{\mu_X (K+1)} = \frac{C_X \cdot \mu_X}{K+1} \left(A \cdot S_1(K) - B \cdot S_2(K) - \frac{1}{2A} \cdot S_3(K) \right) \qquad (A.17)$$

with S_1, S_2, S_3 previously defined.

REFERENCES

1. R. Berry, Private communication.
2. G. Fox, M. Johnson, G. Lyzenga, S. Otto, J. Salmon and D. Walker, *Solving Problems on Concurrent Processors*, Prentice Hall, Englewood Cliffs, NJ (1988).
3. J.L. Gustafson, G.R. Montry and R.E. Brenner, 'Development of parallel methods for a 1024-processor hypercube', *SIAM J. Scientific and Statistical Computing*, 9, 609–638 (1988).
4. R. Glowinski, *Domain Decomposition Methods for Partial Differential Equations*, SIAM Publications, Philadephia (1991).
5. D.E. Heller, 'Performance measurements on the NCUBE/10 multiprocessor', Technical Report, C S Department, Shell Development Company, Houston (1988).
6. E.N. Houstis and J.R. Rice, 'Parallel ELLPACK: an expert system for parallel processing of partial differential equations', *Mathematics and Computers in Simulation*, 31, 497–507 (1989).
7. D.W. Krumme, A.L. Couch and B.L. House, 'The TRIPLEX tool set for the NCUBE multiprocessors', Technical Report, Tufts University (1989).
8. D.C. Marinescu, J.R. Rice and E.A. Vavalis, 'Performance of iterative methods for distributed memory multiprocessors', *Proceedings IMACS 13th World Congress*, 2, 684–685 (1991).
9. D.C. Marinescu and J.R. Rice, 'Synchronization of nonhomogeneous parallel computations', *Parallel Processing for Scientific Computing*, G. Rodrigue (ed.), SIAM Publications, Philadelphia (1989), pp. 362–367.
10. D.C. Marinescu and J.R. Rice, 'The effects of communication latency upon synchronization and load balance on a hypercube', *Proceedings 5th International Parallel Processing Symposium*, IEEE Press, Washington, DC (1991), pp. 18–25.
11. D.C. Marinescu and J.R. Rice, 'Multilevel asynchronous iterations for PDE's', in *Iterative Methods for Large Linear Systems*, D.R. Kincaid and Linda J. Hayes (eds), Academic Press, New York (1990), pp. 193–214.
12. S. Ramanujan, *Collected Papers*, Chelsea Publishing Company, New York, NY (1962).
13. J.R. Rice and D.C. Marinescu, 'Analysis of a two level asynchronous algorithm for PDEs', in *Aspects of Computations on Asynchronous Parallel Processors*, M. Wright (ed.), North Holland, Amsterdam (1989), pp. 23–33.
14. J.R. Rice and D.C. Marinescu, 'Analysis and modeling of Schwartz splitting algorithms for elliptic PDEs', in *Advances in Computer Methods for Partial Differential Equations*, VI

R.S. Stepleman and R. Vishnevetsky (eds), IMACS, Rutgers University, New Brunswick, NJ (1987), pp. 1–6.

15. J.R. Rice, 'Parallel methods for partial differential equations', in *The Characteristics of Parallel Computation*, L. Jamieson, D. Gannon and R. Douglass (eds), MIT Press, Cambridge, MA (1987), pp. 209–231.

16. G. Rodrique, *Parallel Processing for Scientific Computing*, SIAM Publications, Philadelphia, (1989).

17. M. Rossmann, R. McKenna, L. Tong, D. Xia, J. Dai, H. Wu, H-K. Choi and R.E. Lynch, 'Molecular replacement and real space averaging', Purdue University (in preparation).

18. Y. Saad and M.H. Schultz, 'Data communication in hypercubes', Report YALEU/DCS/RR-428, Yale University (1985).

CONCURRENCY: PRACTICE AND EXPERIENCE, VOL. 3(6), 627–653 (DECEMBER 1991)

Physical computation

GEOFFREY C. FOX

Northeast Parallel Architectures Center
Syracuse University
Syracuse, New York 13244-4100, USA

SUMMARY

Physical computation embraces a variety of physical analogies used to tackle non-traditional problems. We describe Monte Carlo and deterministic methods, including simulated annealing and neural networks. Applications include economic change in Eastern Europe, the travelling salesman problem, vehicle navigation, track finding, and parallel computer load balancing. We show how different problems are suitable for the different various approaches to optimization—there is no universally applicable method.

1. INTRODUCTION

Physical computation encompasses a variety of ideas that can be loosely classified as the use of physical analogies or methods from the physical sciences to problems outside their normal domain of applicability. One example is the use of simulated annealing (an idea from physics) in chip routing and placement[1] (a problem in optimization). Another is the use of neural networks (an idea from biology) in learning and pattern recognition (problems in computer science, robotics, etc.). Again, we will show an example of cellular automata (an idea from physics) applied to social change in Eastern Europe (a problem from economics).

The Santa Fe Institute and its articulate spokesman Gell Mann has defined the concept of a complex system.

The need for new options in education and research

The transformation of society by the scientific revolution of the 19th and 20th centuries is about to be overshadowed by even more sweeping changes arising from a growing ability to understand the complex mechanisms which are central to human concerns. *The technology base of the new revolution will be provided by almost unimaginably powerful computers together with the mathematical and experimental tools and associated software which are essential to achieving an understanding of complexity. Complex systems contain large numbers of coupled elements. The strength of the interaction between elements varies with time, space, and the nature of the surrounding environment which may also change with time.* Such systems can adapt to their environments. Examples of adaptive, complex systems include biological evolution, learning, and neural processes, intelligent computers, protein chemistry, much of pathology, and medicine, human behavior, and economics.

Invited Talk at International Conference on Parallel Computing: Achievements, Problems and Prospects, Anacapri, Italy, 3–9 June 1990.

1040–3108/91/060627–27$13.50
Received May 1991
Accepted August 1991

It is becoming increasingly evident that understanding complex systems demands mutually supportive research conducted by scholars representative of a broad spectrum of the intellectual community ranging from mathematics and the natural sciences to the humanities. Society must find new ways to nurture the necessary convergences of academic disciplines and other critical resources. Present-day academic institutions are not well designed to meet this increasingly urgent need.

We can view physical computation as the use of physical methods to describe general complex systems. Note that as used here, 'physical' means 'pertaining to nature' and is broader than just physics. However, this field is particularly relevant as physics has studied large complex systems, albeit those obeying Newton's and other basic laws of physics. For example, in thermodynamics, we find a theory describing large systems in a way that is insensitive to irrelevant microscopic detail. A key feature of physical computation is approaches that naturally tackle large problems; we can anticipate a growing role for physical computation as the growing power of computers allows the simulation of larger and larger systems. Some traditional methods (for discrete optimization) have time complexities that scale exponentially in problem size while physical computation is often essentially linear. The factor of a thousand in computer performance improvement, expected by the year 2000, makes little impact on an exponentially complex algorithm; however, it implies a revolution for an algorithm with linear time complexity.

Optimization is an important applicant of physical computation and Simic originally introduced the term physical optimization[2,3]. Indeed, most physics laws can be formulated variationally as an optimization problem while nature is also involved in optimization. Thus, in the long term, the evolution of the human race is perhaps maximizing some combination of survival and happiness. In the short term, we interpret visual and other sensor information optimally according to our prejudices and experience. These last two analogies lead respectively to genetic and neural net approaches to optimization. Simulated annealing minimizes the (free) energy by Monte Carlo methods and later we will see elastic net and deterministic annealing approaches to optimization. These correspond to non-statistical variational methods from physics applied to optimization. Maximum entropy or information theory leads to similar approaches based on analogies from an engineering field.

Above, we listed several ideas that we collectively call physical optimization. They can be contrasted with other methods for optimization. Heuristics can be considered as an approach motivated by the problem, combinatorial optimization as one from mathematics, and expert systems as one from computer science.

There is no universally good approach to optimization. Each method has different trade-offs in robustness, accuracy, speed, suitability for parallelization, and problem-size dependence. For instance, neural networks do simple things on large data sets and parallelize easily while expert systems do complex things on small data sets and parallelize with difficulty. In nature, we see at least four approaches combining to solve the problem of survival. On the long term, a genetic algorithm is used to evolve people to maximize survival. On the short term, we wish to avoid being eaten by a lion. A relatively simple low-level vision network with largely local connections is used to process the initial image. A learning (learned) back-propagation-like network may be used to distinguish various animals in the scene. A high-level, possibly expert-system-like, reasoning is used to optimize escape procedures after the lion has been identified.

Also note that physical analogies tend to be fundamentally imprecise; when applied to optimization, they find approximate and hopefully good solutions, but not the best. Combinatorial optimization aims for the exact solution. In practice, approximate solutions to large real world problems are all that is required and, indeed, all that is warranted by imprecise data.

In the next section, we describe a novel cellular automata approach to understanding society. The majority of the paper is devoted to optimization and Section 3 describes the basic ideas of physical optimization. Initially, we describe deterministic annealing for clustering in Section 4, and neural networks and simulated annealing for the travelling salesman problem, computer load balancing, and vehicle navigation in Section 5. In Section 6, we develop the elastic network and its relation to neural networks for the same applications. In Section 7, we show that track finding may be tackled by difference approaches in different regimes differing in track and noise density. The final Section 8 looks to the future.

2. PHYSICAL ANALOGIES IN COMPLEX SYSTEM

As mentioned in Section 1, thermodynamics and statistical physics has taught us how to understand large systems built out of many particles interacting with nature's laws. One may speculate that similar behavior may be exhibited by large complex systems composed of members linked in ways distinct from traditional physics. As described in [4 (Ch. 3), 5–7], we successfully applied these ideas to decomposing problems onto a multicomputer. We were able to introduce a concept analogous to temperature and observe phase transitions between different types of problem decompositions onto the computer. We are currently experimenting with such an analogy for society viewed as a complex system of interacting people. In particular, we are exploring the idea that the recent changes in Eastern Europe can be viewed as a phase transition. These are seen in physical systems possessing more than one stable state idealized in Figure 1 with two states m_1 and m_2 whose free energy takes a value $F_i(\lambda)$ as a function of parameter λ. For a magnetic material, λ could be the strength of the external magnetic field or it could refer to an internal coupling strength. For one value $\lambda = \lambda_a$, m_1 may be the equilibrium state, but as λ varies one may find $F_1(\lambda_b) > F_2(\lambda_b)$ with a transition λ_T in between λ_a and λ_b so that m_2 is the ground state at $\lambda = \lambda_b$. One also sees the effect of 'supercooling' where the system is in the wrong (higher-energy) state until a slight disturbance causes it to find its true equilibrium.

We chose to model Eastern Europe not as a bunch of people, but rather in terms of geographical cells as idealized in Figure 2[8]. In a serious simulation, one might cover (Eastern) Europe by a set of some 10^5 cells. Each cell holds a single spin s_i where at the crudest level;

$$
\begin{aligned}
s_i &= +1 \quad &&\text{if cell is communist} \\
s_i &= -1 \quad &&\text{if cell is capitalist}
\end{aligned}
\tag{1}
$$

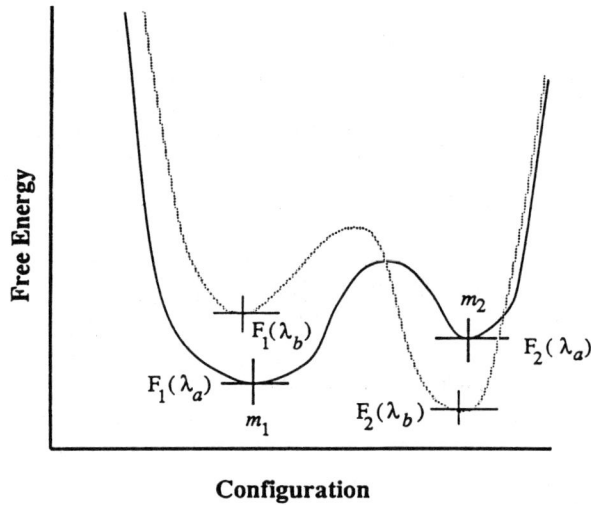

Configuration

Figure 1. The value of the free energy for a typical system as a function of system configuration. The two curves correspond to two values of a parameter λ; $\lambda = \lambda_a$ is solid curve, $\lambda = \lambda_b$ is dashed. The index i of F_i (λ) labels two equilibrium states m_i

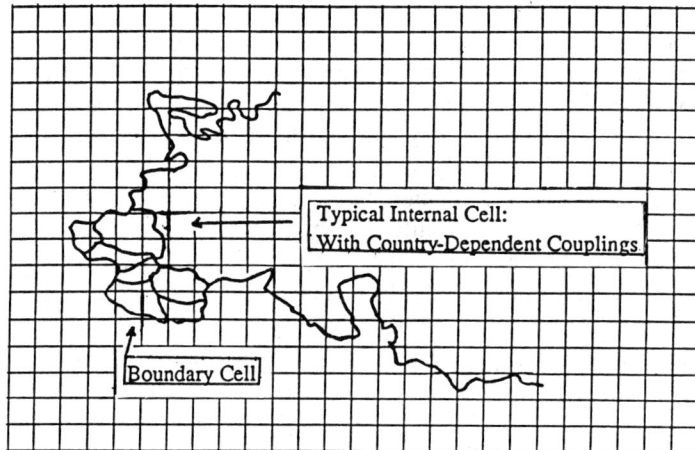

Figure 2. A cellular automata model for Eastern Europe

We model society as governed by a Hamiltonian H that is a function of each s_i where i runs over all the cells. One can speculate on suitable terms to include in H. One possible term would be a nearest-neighbor interaction:

$$H_1 = -J_1 \sum_{\langle ij \rangle} s_i s_j \tag{2}$$

where the interaction between i and j with a positive J_1 tends to force s_i and s_j to line up in order to minimize H_1, i.e., Eastern Europe is a ferromagnetic material. In an unsophisticated culture, only neighboring i and j are linked in equation (2) but with an ever-increasing fashion, the information revolution (phones, TV, networks) links i and j at geographically distant points. Another interesting term would be

$$H_5 = -J_5 \sum_i s_i \qquad (3)$$

This is an external field in the physics analogy with, for instance, the 'Voice of America' broadcasts contributing a negative J_5 tending to force the s_i to negative (capitalist) values. The current model is completed with boundary conditions at Western Europe; a set of dictator spins d_α—'the Warsaw Pact'—which couple to each other and to the people s_i; impurity spins 'Gorbachev', 'Lech Walesa'; and a temperature representing the size of internal fluctuations allowed by the government.

This model is qualitatively reasonable with different societies (USA v. present day China v. Eastern Europe today v. medieval, feudal Europe) showing quite different parameter values.

A different approach to such systems is in terms of chaos and attractors from non-linear dynamical systems[9]. The relation and relative merits of the two approaches is not clear. Both neural networks ($\sim$ cellular automata) and dynamical system models can provide good extrapolations of the time series produced by such complex systems.

3. PHYSICAL OPTIMIZATION

Suppose we wish to minimize

$$E = E(\text{parameters } \mathbf{y}) \qquad (4)$$

where the parameters $\mathbf{y}$ can be continuous, discrete or a mix. We introduce a fake temperature T and set $\beta = 1/T$; in particular cases, we will have a simple physical interpretation of T as, for instance, the scale or granularity at which the problem is formulated. A state of the system is labeled by $\mathbf{y}$ and to each state we associate a probability

$$Pr(\mathbf{y}) = \frac{e^{-\beta E(\mathbf{y})}}{Z}$$

where

$$Z = \sum_{\mathbf{y}} Pr(\mathbf{y}) \qquad (5)$$

As $T \to 0$ or $\beta \to \infty$, the minimum $\mathbf{y}_{\min}$ of E dominates in Z and the probability of this state tends to unity. The basic idea in annealing is to find the minimum $\mathbf{y}_{\min}(T)$ of $F(T)$ for $T \sim 0$ by tracking $\mathbf{y}_{\min}(T)$ from high to low temperatures. Here, $F = E - TS$ is the free energy expressed in terms of original energy E and entropy S. In some cases, Rose has been able to show that $\mathbf{y}_{\min}(T)$ is continuous in T, and computer experiments indicate this is at least approximately true in the cases we look at. Then, this continuation technique should avoid local minima, such as the one shown on Figure 3, as it is easy to find true global minima at high temperatures.

We will describe in the following, four different methods for finding $\mathbf{y}_{\min}(T)$ and tracking it with temperature.

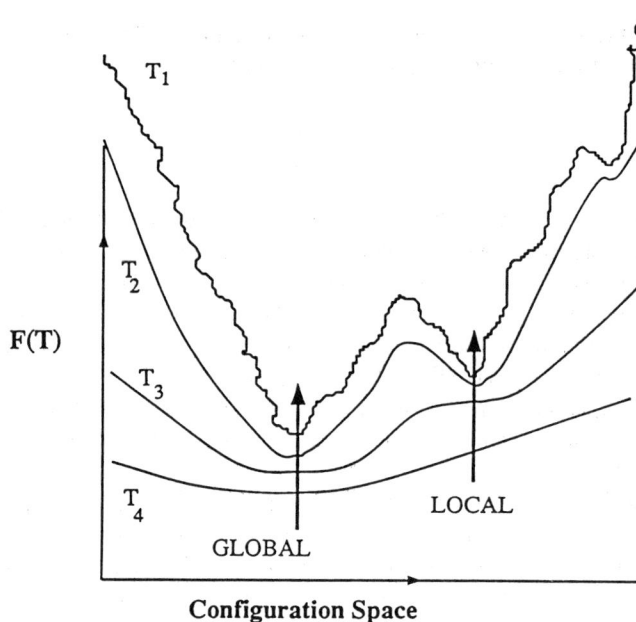

Figure 3. Schematic of the free energy F(T) at a set of temperatures $0 \sim T_1 \langle T_2 \langle T_3 \langle T_4 \sim \infty$

(1) *Simulated annealing.* We find $y_{sample}(T)$ by Monte Carlo as either a mean or a representative of configurations at temperature T. As both the mean and a representative have the same limit as $T \rightarrow 0$, we can use either. This method is the best known and currently most reliable physical optimization method[1]. We view it as the standard of excellence for the three alternative and less well-known methods that we will discuss in this paper. From the point of optimization theory, the other methods are faster as they avoid costly Monte Carlo steps but less reliable, i.e., they are less successful in avoiding local minima. All the methods have the disadvantage that they cannot in practice either guarantee achieving a true global minima or estimate the quality $(F(y_{min}$ (found as $T \rightarrow 0)) - F(y_{min}$ (true))) of solution. Experience has shown that several of these methods give very reliable answers, near to the true minima, for a variety of problems. We remember that these are methods designed to find approximate and not exact minima.

(2) *Deterministic annealing.* Here we just choose a simple heuristic to minimize $F(T)$ at temperature T where one starts with an initial guess for temperature T as the minimum $y_{min}(T+\delta T)$ at higher temperature. This is most effective for cases where y is low-dimensional, i.e., we only have a few degrees of freedom. This can be achieved in some cases by summing over all except a few critical components of y. We discuss this in Section 4. The deterministic approach is familiar in chemistry where particle dynamics and Monte Carlo are both used to find the ground state of a complex molecule. The atoms in the molecule are often found experimentally— say from NMR measurements—and the annealing minimizes a potential containing both physical forces and artificial terms representing agreement of the model with the data. This can be viewed as physical computation addressing the optimization

problem 'what molecule best fits the experimental data and is consistent with chemistry'[11]. A similar idea underlines the molecular dynamics approach to quantum chromodynamics lattice simulations[12–14].

(3) *Neural networks*[15,16]. This could, and probably does, have deep biological significance but here we can 'just' view this method as a calculation of an approximation to $y_{min}(T)$ using the mean field approximation in the case where **y** is discrete. We discuss this in Section 5.

(4) *Elastic network*[17]. We can view this as a similar approach to that of neural networks where an improved mean field strategy is used that incorporates some of the constraints which are used as penalty terms in the neural network method. We discuss this in Section 6.

We illustrate these general ideas with examples in the following sections.

4. DETERMINISTIC ANNEALING FOR CLUSTERING

Consider a set of data points x which we wish to associate into clusters. This type of problem comes up in many applications, but here we will consider physical clusters in a two-dimensional space such as the 360 points shown in Figure 4 and generated by four clusters[18,19].

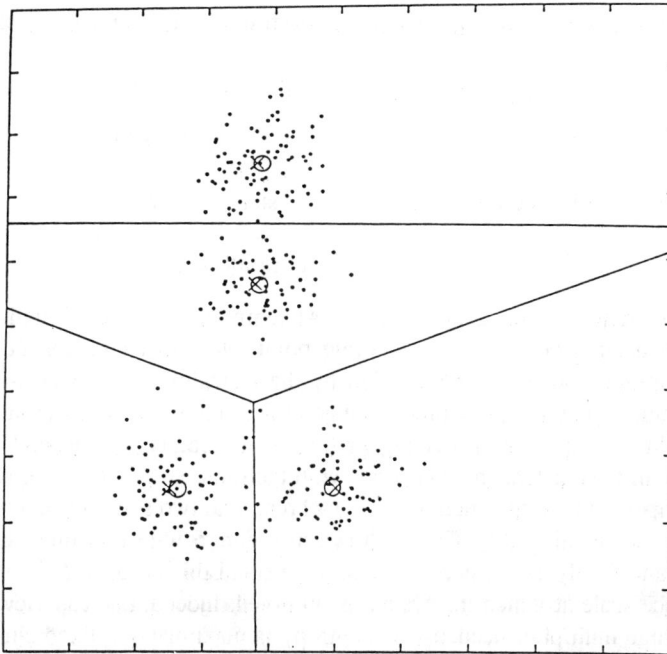

Figure 4. Deterministic annealing clustering of four clusters. The lines are the decision boundaries. The final beta is 0.1, and the final energy is 30.05. ◯—computed cluster mean. X—center of cluster used to generate points x[18]

For each data point x, we assign an energy $E_x(j)$ (cost) for it to belong to the cluster j with mean y_j. We sum over the uninteresting variables that specify the assignment of x to one of the N_c clusters. Then the partition function is

$$Z = \prod_x \sum_{k=1}^{N_c} \exp[-\beta E_x(k)] \tag{6}$$

and the free energy

$$F = -\frac{1}{\beta}\log Z \tag{7}$$

If the clusters were due to Gaussian fluctuations then we can take

$$E_x(j) = |x - y_j|^2 \tag{8}$$

and now the cluster centers are determined by the deterministic annealing condition

$$\frac{\partial F}{\partial y_j} = 0 \tag{9}$$

which gives the implicit equation

$$y_j = \frac{\sum_x x\, Pr(x \text{ in cluster} j)}{\sum Pr(x \text{ in cluster} j)} \tag{10}$$

where y_j also appears on the right-hand side from the expression for the probability;

$$Pr(x \text{ in cluster} j) = \frac{\exp(-\beta|x - y_j|^2)}{\sum_{k=1}^{N_c} \exp(-\beta|x - y_k|^2)} \tag{11}$$

We can solve the implicit equation iteratively starting with

$$y_j(T = \infty) = \text{mean of all 'x's} \tag{12}$$

and gradually reducing the temperature T. At temperature T, we initialize the search for $y_j(T)$ by using $y_j(T + \delta T)$ as a starting point. Note that equation (10) surely has many local minima but these are avoided by the annealing as we can usually find the global minimum easily at high temperature and track it down with lowering temperature. This particular example has a striking pattern in its temperature-dependence. At high temperature, all the clusters are degenerate with the same y_j. As β is increased, one finds a critical temperature (β) at which the clusters break into two sets—again the members of each set have identical y_j[20]. This is shown in Figure 5 with transitions corresponding to 1–2–3–4 and finally 18 clusters. We can understand this because $T^{1/2}$ is proportional to the distance scale at which the system is observed. Indeed, one can view temperature as the Lagrange multiplier needed when entropy is maximized at fixed cluster variance, i.e., a fixed distance scale. Lowering T corresponds to looking at a finer and finer scale and so we need to specify a minimum interesting T. The 18 clusters found in Figure 5 correspond to looking inside the four real clusters. Figure 4 shows that very good results are obtained by this method.

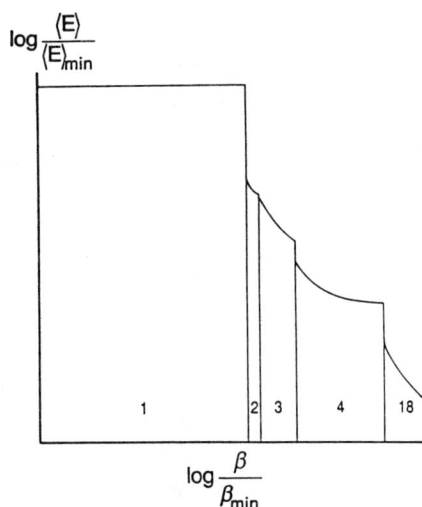

Figure 5. The phase structure of Figure 4 as a function of temperature or $\beta = 1/T$ [20]

In this application, annealing is equivalent to a multiscale approach; we initialize the fine-scale optimization with the results of a coarse-scale analysis. The utility of this approach is known in many fields including the well-known multigrid method for partial differential equations. It also has been applied to vision by Terzopoulos[21–23].

5. NEURAL NETWORKS FOR OPTIMIZATION

Neural networks for optimization were first introduced for the travelling salesman problem (TSP) by Hopfield and Tank[15,16] and although the method is not very effective in this application[24], the basic ideas are important for a range of problems. We will set up the formalism for the TSP and then show how it can be applied to parallel program decomposition (Section 5.2) and navigation (Section 5.3). The application in Section 5.2 is very successful for reasons we will be able to identify, but for the examples in Section 5.1 and Section 5.3, neural networks do not perform well. However, in Section 6, we will give the elastic network extension which gives good results for the TSP and navigation. In the final Section 7, we show that track finding naturally uses either elastic or neural networks but in different domains of the parameter values.

From the point of view of deterministic annealing, elastic and neural networks are similar. They both use mean field approximations to the free energy and deterministic methods to solve the resultant equations.

5.1. The traveling salesman problem

Consider a set of N cities labeled by the integer $p = 1 \ldots N$ and illustrated in Figure 6. We wish to visit each city once and once only in a tour that minimizes the total distance

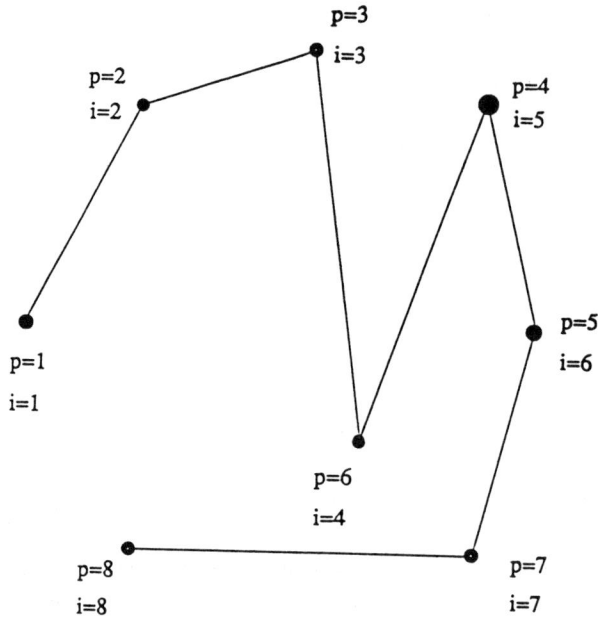

Figure 6. Traveling salesman non-optimal path—a simple TSP indicating labels p(city) and i(time)

traveled. We let $i = 1 \ldots N$ label successive steps of the tour with $p = P(i)$ labeling the city visited at the ith step. Then we need to minimize

$$\sum_{i=1}^{N-1} d_{P(i) P(i+1)} \tag{13}$$

This assignment $(i \rightarrow P(i))$ is the classic NP complete discrete optimization problem which is often used as the standard benchmark for discrete optimization methods. The following examples make it clear that the TSP is not necessarily typical of all such problems and methods that perform poorly on the TSP work well on other (NP complete) optimization problems.

We introduce the neural variables

$$\eta_p^i = \begin{cases} 1 & \text{if p} = P(i) \\ 0 & \text{if p} \neq P(i) \end{cases} \tag{14}$$

and we rewrite equation (13) as

$$E_1 = \sum_{i} \sum_{p,q} d_{pq} \eta_p^i \eta_q^{i+1} \tag{15}$$

where in equation (13) and equation (15), d_{pq} is the distance between cities p and q. We now have a nice quadratic form to minimize as a function of the N^2 neural variables η_p^i. Unfortunately, not all choices of η_p^i are allowed; for this to correspond to a true assignment, one needs to satisfy constraints that each i corresponds to one p and vice versa. These can be written as

$$\sum_i \eta_p^i \eta_q^i = \delta_{pq}$$

$$\sum_p \eta_p^i \eta_p^j = 0 \qquad i \neq j \tag{16}$$

These constraints are implemented by minimizing

$$E = E_1(\text{equation 15}) + \sum [\text{constraints—equation (16)}] \tag{17a}$$

with penalty terms, simple linear or quadratic functions of the forms (equation (16)), which are positive when constraints are violated.

A typical example for a penalty term could be,

$$\sum_{i \neq j} \left[\sum_p \eta_p^i \eta_p^j \right]^2 \tag{17b}$$

Combining equation (17) with the physical optimization framework of Section 3 leads to a traditional statistical physics problem with N^2 'spins' η_p^i governed by an energy function E. The resultant simulated annealing or Monte Carlo approach to this statistical physics formulation does provide an effective approach to the TSP[26].

Here we will study a faster, but less reliable, deterministic method. A well-known approximate method for studying such physics systems is the mean field approximation. Consider an equation such as

$$\langle \eta_r^k \rangle = \sum_{states} \eta_r^k \exp(-\beta E(\eta_1^1 \dots \eta_r^k \dots \eta_N^N))/Z \tag{18}$$

One can calculate this if one linearizes the exponential by approximating any term in E that is quadratic in η by a linear dynamic term multiplied by the 'mean field'—the other 'η's replaced by their mean value. Roughly, one substitutes

$$\eta M \eta \longrightarrow \langle \eta \rangle M \eta \tag{19}$$

With the approximation of equation (19), one can sum over the dynamical variables labeling the states and equation (18) can be converted into a deterministic equation for $\langle \eta_r^k \rangle$. At the desired ground state, $\eta_r^k = \langle \eta_r^k \rangle$ and one finds a deterministic method for finding the minimum of E.

Unfortunately, this method is an approximation and one will find 'illegal' solutions which are not only non-optimal in E but also violate the constraint penalty terms in equation (17). This has made this approach unsatisfactory for even modest ($N \sim 50$) TSP problems[24]. These results are disappointing for the TSP, but we include them as the basic ideas *are* correct and are very successful in related NP complete optimzation problems, as we describe later in this paper.

5.2. Load balancing parallel programs

A similar approach is much more successful in load balancing; although this is also NP complete and formally equivalent to the TSP, there is a natural neural representation that involves no constraints and penalty terms. Here we get non-optimal solutions, but ones that are accurate enough for the problem at hand[61]. This is encouraging as it shows that the difficulty with the TSP neural network is not with a deterministic annealing approach, but rather with the choice of variables. In Section 6, we will change these variables and find good TSP results for deterministic annealing.

The load balancing or (automatic) decomposition problem in parallel programming depends on many issues; the application, the software paradigm and the parallel computer architecture. We have discussed these points elsewhere[27–31] and here we will consider loosely synchronous problems running on a hypercube; we indicate how to generalize to other architectures at the end of this subsection. We can abstract load balancing graph theoretically as illustrated in Figure 7. The application is defined by a graph with M members, labeled by $m = 1 \ldots M$, such that $w(m)$ computational units are needed to 'update' m while the matrix $C(m,m')$ is a measure of information needed to be transmitted from m' to m to update graph node m. We wish to decompose the graph onto $N = 2^d$ processor nodes so as to minimize total execution time. As in Section 5.1, we again have an association problem—this time of $m \rightarrow P(m)$ where P is processor number to which m is assigned. We could, as in equation (14), introduce neural variables $\eta(m,p) = 1$ if $p = P(m)$ and 0 otherwise, but this has difficulties already seen for the TSP. Rather, we write

$$P(m) = \sum_{k=0}^{d-1} 2^k \eta_k(m) \tag{20}$$

and the $Md = M log_2 N$ neural variables $\eta_k(m)$ provide a non-redundant specification of the decomposition. This is to be compared to the MN variables $\eta(m,p)$ in the redundant formulation. Using some technical assumptions, we can now specify the energy of the associated physical system as

$$E = E_{\text{calc}} + E_{\text{comm}}$$

where

$$E_{\text{calc}} = \frac{1}{N} \sum_{m,m'} w(m) w(m') \prod_{k=0}^{d-1} [1 + s_k(m)s_k(m')] \tag{21}$$

$$E_{\text{comm}} = \frac{1}{4} \sum_{m,m'} C(m,m') \sum_{k=0}^{d-1} [1 - s_k(m)s_k(m')]$$

with spins $s_k(m) = 2\eta_k(m) - 1$ taking values of ± 1 (for $\eta_k(m) = 1$ or 0). The physical analogy is particularly good here with E_{calc} (balancing computation on each node) as a short-range repulsion and E_{comm} (minimizing communication) as a long-range attractive force.

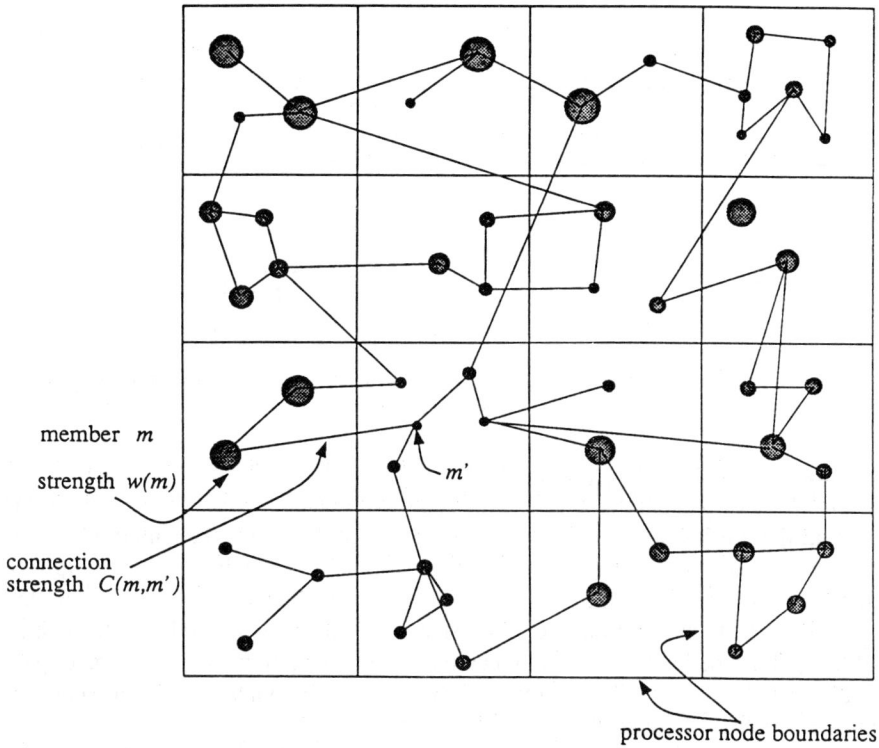

Figure 7. Decomposition as a graph theory problem

Equation (21) can now be used in the physical optimization approach; both the simulated annealing and neural network methods can be applied[61]. Indeed, even in simulated annealing, the elegant neural network choice of variables is preferred to a direct expression of energy E in terms of $P(m)$. As shown in [62], the mean field method developed by Hopfield and Tank for the TSP is directly applicable and gives excellent results. These are comparable in quality to simulated annealing but much faster as one is just solving deterministic equations[61]. As already mentioned, neural networks work well here because the objective function E in equation (21) has no penalty terms.

The neural representation of equation (20) was originally motivated by the hypercube topology. However, it is generally useful and there is an interesting analogy with the clustering method in Section 4. Thus, as shown in Figure 8, the neurons provide a multiscale representation with $\eta_{d-1}(m)$ the coarsest and $\eta_0(m)$ the finest detail. From this point of view, it is clear how to generalize this approach to non-hypercube topologies by using the appropriate hierarchical neural multiscale representation in 'processor space'.

5.3. Navigation

The discussion of the last subsection is confined to essentially static or what we like to call adiabatic problems[31]. More challenging are dynamic problems where one needs to determine for each member, m, the time-dependent processor location $P(m,t)$. We developed a path or string formalism for this generalized problem[28] and realized that

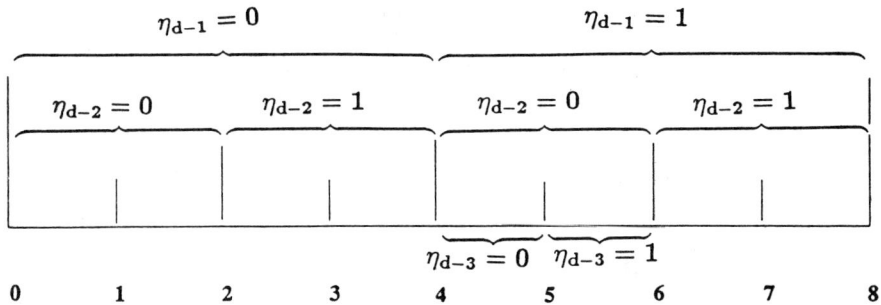

*Figure 8. Multiscale decomposition of processor node space with neural variables. The case d=3
is illustrated*

the methods were similar to those needed for navigation problems. These include two-
and three-dimensional land vehicles and aircraft path planning, and the motion of one or
more multijoint robot arms. In each case, one needs to determine the path of one or more
entities in a target space; this path typically involving minimizing a travel time subject
to constraints involving avoidance of obstacles and collisions between entities. In the
parallel processing application, the target space is formed by the nodes of the computer
with a topology defined by the architecture. In the navigation case, the target space is
typically a two- or three-dimensional physical space although the higher dimensional
configuration space may be used in a robotics example[32].

One can formulate a physical computation approach to navigation using the direct
neural network of Section 5.1, the multiscale representation of Section 5.2 or the path
or elastic net formalism of Section 6. We believe the latter to be most promising, but
we have only completed the analysis using the simple neural representation introduced
in Section 5.1[33–36]. We will briefly discuss this here as it illustrates the main issues
for the more powerful approach based on the methods of Section 6[37].

Consider a vehicle, V, avoiding a missile, M. Introduce two sets of neural variables
$v(\mathbf{x},t), m(\mathbf{x},t)$

$$v(\mathbf{x},t) = \begin{cases} 1 \text{ if vehicle at point } \mathbf{x} \text{ at time } t \\ 0 \text{ if vehicle not at } \mathbf{x} \end{cases} \tag{22}$$

$$m(\mathbf{x},t) = \begin{cases} 1 \text{ if missile at point } \mathbf{x} \text{ at time } t \\ 0 \text{ if missile not at point } \mathbf{x} \end{cases} \tag{23}$$

The motion of the vehicle can be found by minimizing an energy function E embodying
its goals and constraints. This includes a term

$$E_1 = \sum_{\mathbf{x},t} v(\mathbf{x},t)T(\mathbf{x}) \tag{24}$$

where the terrain function T measures the difficulty of driving vehicle at point $\mathbf{x}$.

$$E_2 = \sum_{\mathbf{x},t} v(\mathbf{x},t)[m(\mathbf{x},t-1) + m(\mathbf{x},t) + m(\mathbf{x},t+1)] \tag{25}$$

Minimizing E_2 ensures that vehicle and missile are safely separated!

$$E_3 = \sum_{\mathbf{x},t} v(\mathbf{x},t)|\mathbf{x} - \mathbf{x}_{\text{destination}}| \qquad (26)$$

This term 'attracts' vehicle to its destination $\mathbf{x}_{\text{destination}}$. These terms are not realistic but indicative of the ease with which one can express goals and constraints in this formalism. Our publications give more details and we give, in Figure 9, one example where we determine the path of four vehicles. These must avoid each other and reach their destinations by passage through a narrow 'mountain pass'.

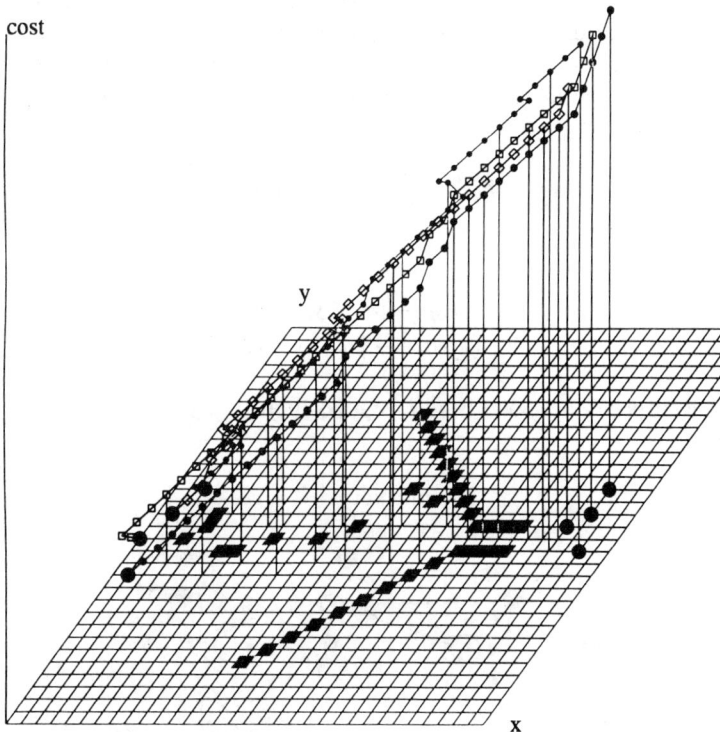

Figure 9. The path produced by the neural network method for four vehicles. The 'cost' (vertical axis) is a measure of travel time and travel in the two-dimensional x-y plane must avoid other vehicles and the shaded obstacles. Circles represent initial positions and the final destinations[41]

We understand now and show in Section 7 that this neural approach is best for the case of very many vehicles. The traditional combinatorial method is fine for one and perhaps two vehicles; the very interesting case of 'several' vehicles is probably best handled by the elastic net method. The redundancy of the neural net $v(x,t) = 0$ at all 'x's not occupied by vehicles—is, just as in the TSP, a major difficulty when the number of vehicles is small.

We stress that the essential point of our approaches is that they scale naturally to problems with many vehicles[38] or robots with many arms whilst the traditional methods have a time complexity of $O(N^l)$ for l degrees of freedom when each of these is discretized into N cells[39].

6. THE ELASTIC NET

6.1. The traveling salesman problem

Durbin and Wilshaw introduced the elastic net approach to the TSP[17,40] as a physically based model that outperformed the neural network method in this case. One 'invents' a physical system whose equilibrium state is the desired minimum path[10]. As shown in Figure 10, we consider an elastic string with beads, labeled i, for each (time) step of the journey. The beads are attracted to each other by a simple elastic force that, in the absence of other constraints, collapses the string to zero length. We start with this at temperature $T = \infty$ when the elastic forces collapse the beads to a point. Each bead i is attracted to each city p by a force

$$F_i^{city,p} = \alpha w_{pi}(\mathbf{x}_p - \mathbf{y}_i)$$ (27)

where

$$w_{pi} = \frac{exp - |\mathbf{x}_p - \mathbf{y}_i|^2/2K^2}{\sum_j exp - |\mathbf{x}_p - \mathbf{y}_j|^2/2K^2}$$ (28)

where city p is at position $\mathbf{x}_p$ and bead i is at position $\mathbf{y}_i$.

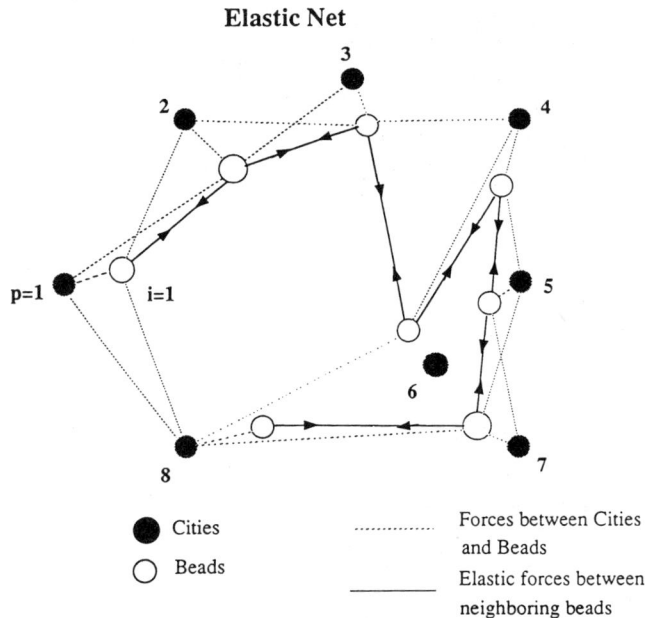

Figure 10. The elastic net for the TSP of Figure 6

The deterministic annealing equation is

$$\mathbf{y}_i \rightarrow \mathbf{y}_i + \Delta \mathbf{y}_i$$

$$\Delta \mathbf{y}_i = \sum_p F_i^{city,p} + \beta K (\mathbf{y}_{j+1} + \mathbf{y}_{j-1} - 2\mathbf{y}_j) \tag{29}$$

including the elastic term together with the force of equation (27). This corresponds to

$$\Delta y_i = -K \frac{\partial E}{\partial \mathbf{y}_i} \tag{30}$$

with the energy function E given by

$$E = -\alpha K \sum_p \log \sum_i \exp(-|\mathbf{x}_p - \mathbf{y}_i|^2/2K^2)$$
$$+ \beta \sum_j |\mathbf{y}_j - \mathbf{y}_{j+1}|^2 \tag{31}$$

The formulation is now similar to that of Section 4 with K playing the role of temperature or equivalently in this case, as for clustering, a position resolution. For large K, equation (31) is minimized with all beads i at the geometric average (center of mass) of the cities

$$\mathbf{y}_i (K = \infty) = \frac{1}{N_{city}} \sum_p \mathbf{x}_p \tag{32}$$

We have exactly satisfied the second term in equation (31) corresponding to the elastic forces between beads and we are surely at a global minimum of E. As K is reduced, we increase the importance of the first term in E which is the constraint that each bead lie near a city (or in the limit $K = T \rightarrow 0$, each bead is on top of). In[40], it is shown that one gets a similar set of bifurcations to that illustrated in Figure 5 as K is lowered and the single global minima splits into several local minima. Empirically, the deterministic annealing ansatz of equation (29), namely:

- Start at $K_0 = T = \infty$,
- Minimize energy E at fixed $K = K_0$ starting with minimum for $K = K_0 + \delta K_0$ and using steepest descent, equation (30),
- reduce K from K_0 to $K_0 - \delta K_0$

tracks the global minimum approximately and gives good solutions to the traveling salesman problem.

6.2. Neural network approach

In Section 6.1, we showed that the TSP could be mapped into a physical computation involving a mechanical system of interacting beads. In Section 5.1, a seemingly different physical analogy was presented with the solution of the TSP corresponding to the ground state of a system of interacting spins η_p^i. Simic has shown that these two approaches correspond to different approximation solution methods for finding the ground state of essentially the same physical system. Here, we will just describe the relation between the approximation methods without the detailed mathematical justification which can be found in[2].

Simic starts with the analogy of Section 5.1 with the energy function of equation (17) which includes penalty terms corresponding to the constraints of equation (16). The degrees of freedom are the redundant set $\{\eta_p^i\}$. Applying the mean field approximation and deterministic annealing to the statistical mechanics based on equation (17), gives rise to the neural network approach. Alternatively, we may choose a 'better' set of degrees of freedom which satisfy exactly some of the constraints of equation (16). Suppose we only consider those physical states $\{\eta_p^i\}$ which exactly satisfy

$$\sum_p \eta_p^i \eta_p^j = 0 \qquad i \neq j$$

$$\sum_i \eta_p^i \eta_p^i = 1 \qquad \text{all } p \tag{33}$$

We are ensuring that each city p corresponds to one and only one time step i but we allow the constraint

$$\sum_i \eta_p^i \eta_q^i = 0 \qquad p \neq q \tag{34}$$

to be violated, i.e., we do not enforce that each time step i be associated with a unique city p. Equation (34) is included as a penalty term in the energy function.

Then Simic derives a new mean field approximation for

$$E = E_1(\text{equation}(15)) + \sum[\text{constraints—equation}(34)] \tag{35}$$

with this restricted phase space. Change variables to

$$\mathbf{y}_i = \sum_p \mathbf{x}_p \langle \eta_p^i \rangle \tag{36}$$

where $\langle \eta_p^i \rangle$ are the mean values of the fields η_p^i in the mean field approximation to equation (35). Then apart from a few technical differences, we find that we have derived the elastic net method expressed in terms of the bead positions of equation (36). The term E_1 gives rise to the elastic forces between beads, and the constraint of equation (34) leads naturally to the potential which gives the forces of equation (27) which attract cities p to beads i. This is reasonable as the constraint of equation (34) is ensuring that each bead i correspond to a single city p.

6.3. Other applications of the elastic net

An important consequence of Simic's results is that we understood better the trade-off between the neural network and elastic network approaches; both correspond to deterministic annealing of an energy function, but with different phase spaces, i.e., different degrees of freedom. Secondly, we can more easily generalize the elastic network from the TSP to other optimization problems[10]. We now briefly show how the problems of Section 5.2 and Section 5.3 fit into this scheme.

As shown in Section 5.2, the neural network approach was very successful in the load balancing application. We do not need to, and indeed cannot, 'improve' it using the ideas of Section 6.2 because there are no constraints in the energy function of equation (21). The neural variables of equation (20) are not redundant like those used for the TSP.

On the other hand, the neural variables of equation (22) and equation (23) used in the navigation problem are redundant and constraints must be satisfied. Thus, we would expect that the direct (Hopfield–Tank) neural network approach can be improved using the ideas of Section 6.2 This is in fact straightforward as shown in[42,43,37]. In fact, the situation is easier than the TSP because we do not need to ensure the two sets of constraints—corresponding to equation (32) and equation (33). Thus, for navigation, each time step t corresponds to a unique position $y_{\text{vehicle}}(t)$ but it is not necessary or generally desirable to ensure that each position be visited once and once only. Thus, one can use Simic's idea directly with the minor technical change that the variables i and p of Section 6.1 need to be interchanged. The resultant physical computation picture for navigation is straightforward and illustrated in Figure 11 for two vehicles with a common source and destination. The degrees of freedom are the positions of the vehicles at discretized time values labelled by an index $i = 1,2\ldots$ The goal of minimum travel time translates into elastic forces between neighboring beads on each path. Other constraints correspond to avoidance of obstacles (this is represented as repulsive forces between obstacles and beads), and avoidance of collisions corresponding to repulsive forces between beads of different vehicles at each time step. The formalism allows the inclusion of many different issues such as variable terrain and vehicles of finite size and these are discussed in[37]. This work is still at an exploratory stage, but we believe it is very promising and can be applied to areas such as robot arm manipulation. There, a similar physical approach has been extensively explored[32], but our elastic network is significantly different as previous approaches have viewed the problem in terms of the 'Newtonian' dynamics of the instantaneous position of the 'vehicle' whereas we use the complete path as the basic degrees of freedom. The advantage of the elastic net approach is that you can ensure that the paths link source and destination whereas the other methods can get trapped with the 'vehicle' (robot arm) evolved in time into a state which cannot (easily) reach the desired destination.

Note that there are two distinct features of physical computation and, in particular, of the elastic net approach to the TSP and other problems. Critical is the choice of degrees of freedom and the idea of the minimization of an energy function E. Secondly, we can use either deterministic or Monte Carlo, or probably better, a mix to find the approximate minimum of E.

We can also relate the elastic network to the deterministic clustering algorithm of Section 4. Indeed, the TSP can be viewed as a special case of clustering where there is but a single point in each cluster. In his thesis[10,44], Rose has shown how the elastic

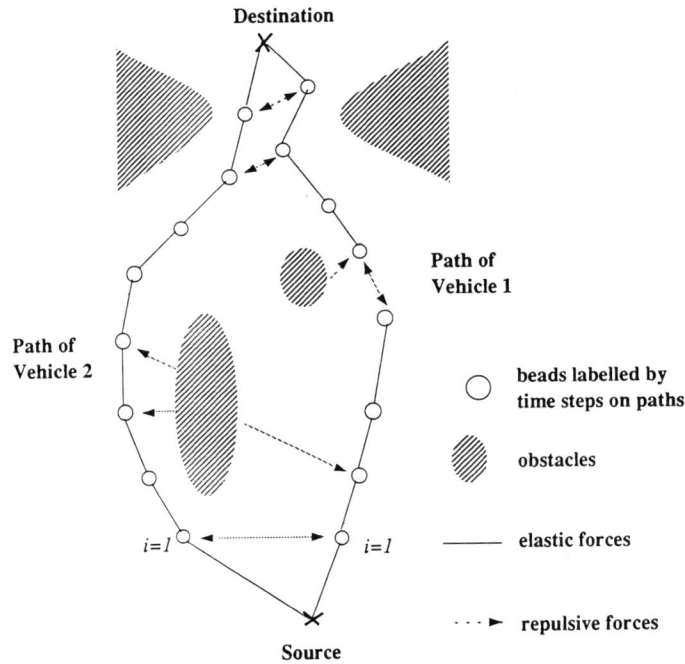

Figure 11. The physical computation picture for navigation in the generalized elastic net approach[37]

network approach can be derived from the formalism given in Section 4. Thus, we find a rather unified picture with different formulations of physical computation being related in a clear fashion.

7. TRACK FINDING

7.1. The problem

Here, we briefly discuss track finding to illustrate the different possible approaches to optimization that we have discussed here. Consider a set of measurements $x_k(t_l) \pm \delta x_k(t_l)$ where we observe the data values x_k at a set of times t_l. This application is present in many different areas of data analysis and signal processing. These applications differ in the number and reliability of the measurements and the number of underlying tracks giving use to these signals. The example in Figure 12(a) shows five tracks in a very noisy environment with many false signals. Other examples differ in the number of tracks (which could vary from one to say 10^5 in a strategic defense application), the complexity (cross overs) of tracks, the noise level, and the number of dimensions—the measurements can be in one, two or three spatial dimensions. The applications also differ in the shape of the tracks; they can be, at their simplest, linear as in Figure 12 or curved as in, say, high-energy physics data analysis, where several hundred particles will bend in a magnetic field as they are produced in a collision in the new SSC (superconducting colliding beams under construction near Dallas).

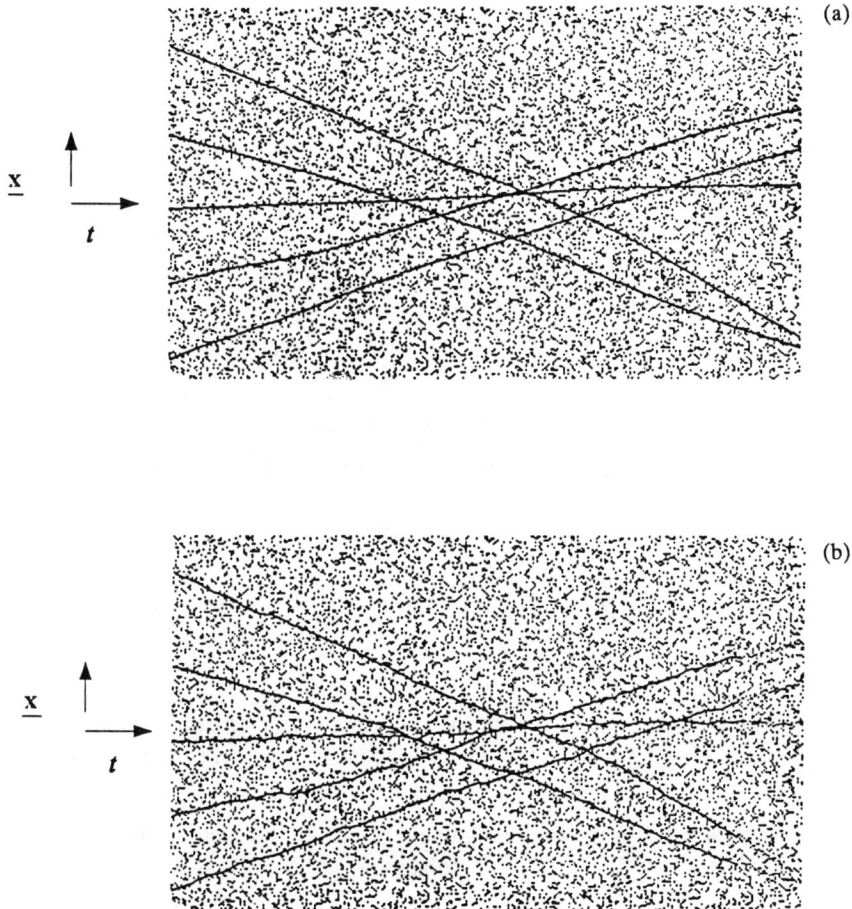

$\underline{x}$ $\uparrow$ t $\rightarrow$ (a)

$\underline{x}$ $\uparrow$ t $\rightarrow$ (b)

Figure 12. (a) The original trajectories plus clutter. (b) The computed trajectories using deterministic annealing[45,46,10]

In each case, one wishes to find an optimal interpretation of the situation given the data measurements $x_k(t_l)$, their errors, and any knowledge or prejudice as to the nature and number of tracks. So we have what is 'just' an (*NP*-complete) optimization problem which can be approached by the many methods, including those discussed here. In the following sections, we discuss appropriate methods in different parameter domains illustrated schematically in Figure 13.

7.2. The Kalman filter approach

When one is finding a relatively small number of tracks in a clean environment, the Kalman filter approach is well developed and optimal[47]. Very crudely, we can explain this as follows. First, one finds all N_{Tr} tracks up to time t_0 and then extends them to

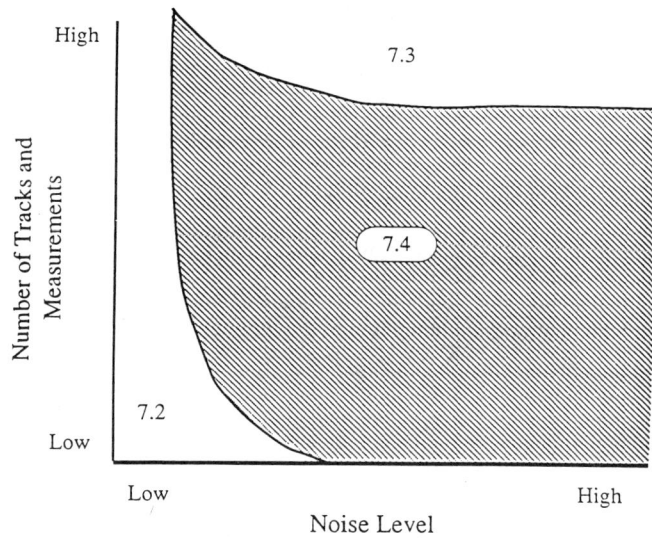

Figure 13. Track finding divided in three regions based on the noise and track complexity level and number of real tracks. The regions are labeled by the sections of this paper in which they are discussed

$t_0 + \delta t_0$ by using $\mathbf{N}_M$ measurements at this later time value. The optimization involves a chi-squared fit following the solution of an assignment problem of the following kind:

- What is the best assignment of the N_M measurements to lie on the extrapolation of the N_{Tr} tracks

(37)

This is solved by combinational or simple heuristic methods. In many cases, it is easy to find good assignments, but in general one is faced by a well-known optimal assignment problem which can be tackled by clever combinational algorithms such as Munkres' method[47–49] with a time complexity of order $O(N_{Tr}^2 N_M)$. Although not *NP* complete (i.e., not exponential in N_{Tr}, N_M), this method is very time-consuming in many important cases even though we have been able to parallelize it effectively[50–52]. The use of neural networks for this case has been discussed in[53], but this does not address the real difficulty. In cases where N_{Tr} and N_M are large, then the problem in equation (37) becomes ill-posed. There are too many ambiguities in the assignment for one to consider a single 'best' solution which matches tracks to measurements. One can and does carry along several possibilities which are resolved by later measurements. However, in general, the strategy of reducing track finding to a single time step matching fails with noisy data or many tracks. Rather, one must go back to the 'original full optimization problem' and view it as a simultaneous optimization over all (many) time values t_l, tracks and measurements $\mathbf{x}_k(t_l)$. In the following two sections, we consider this last possibility from two points of view.

7.3. An analogy with vision

One can consider the global optimization approach combinatorially, and, indeed, this is common in high energy physics data analysis. Indeed, I used it myself in analyzing data from an experiment at Fermilab which had around ten tracks to be found from about one hundred measurements[54]. In many signal processing applications, it is natural to step in time as this is how the data is gathered. In high-energy physics, the relativistic particles form tracks in a few nanoseconds, and the data is naturally gathered together for all time values.

However, the combinatorial approach is clearly limited and breaks down when N_{Tr} and N_M are large. In [55], we noted that track finding is formally equivalent to edge detection in vision problems. The problem of finding tracks on one space and one time dimension, as illustrated in Figure 12, is formally identical to conventional two-dimensional vision. Track finding in two or three spatial dimensions, requires an obvious generalization of vision to three or four dimensions.

We know that combinatorial methods are not effective in vision, but rather one uses methods like neural networks and Hough transforms [56–58]. We have neural variables η $(\mathbf{x}, t)$ which are nonzero when one or more tracks pass through the discretized point $(\mathbf{x}, t)$. Note that the number of neural variables is independent of the values of N_{Tr} and N_M. Thus, as N_{Tr}, N_M increase, the time complexity of a neural network formalism is invariant, whereas that of heuristic and combinatorial increases rapidly, sometimes exponentially. The major problem with the neural network method for the TSP in Section 5.1 was the redundant formalism and corresponding constraints. In this application, we have some constraints corresponding to continuous tracks, but these are easy to implement as a local term in the energy function. We do *not* have the difficult (in Section 5.1) constraints corresponding to uniqueness. Indeed, one usually does not know how many tracks are present and it is an advantage and not a disadvantage of the neural network formalism that it allows any number of tracks.

There has not been much experience with this approach, although initial results are encouraging[59]. It is clear to me that neural networks are the right approach to the case of many tracks in a noisy environment. However, further research and experimentation is needed.

7.4. The elastic net approach

It is also clear to me that for some values of the parameters N_{Tr} and N_M, the elastic net or string (path) approach of Section 6 is appropriate. As shown in Figure 13, this will probably be used in the parameter region that is intermediate between the methods of Section 7.2 and Section 7.3.

At a superficial level, tracking and navigation are the 'same' problem.

- In navigation, we are finding paths in some space respecting the terrain and vehicle behavior, and avoiding obstacles.
- In tracking, we are finding paths in some space respecting the track models and passing through measurements.

Thus, we find that the methods of Section 6.3 are immediately applicable to tracking. The repulsive forces in Figure 12 between obstacles and vehicles are replaced by attractive forces between measurements and tracks. Rose has explored this general approach in [45,46] and obtained excellent results shown already in Figure 12. These ideas are developed more generally in [55] where we note that the elastic net (string) approach is not really an alternative to the neural network method but rather a natural higher level formalism. After preliminary tracks are found from a Hough transform or neural network, this step needs to be followed up by a 'clean-up' stage which labels independent tracks and makes them continuous; the step from the field of track densities $\eta(\mathbf{x}, t)$ which is nonzero at a candidate track, to the discrete set of N_{Tr} tracks $\{\mathbf{x}_i(t)\}$ is non-trivial. The elastic net is an appropriate approach to this higher level labeling problem.

7.5. Summary

We have illustrated by qualitative arguments in one example that there is no uniquely good approach to optimization. A given problem, namely tracking, is best approached by combinatorial, heuristic, neural network or elastic network methods in different circumstances. The last two methods, elastic and neural networks, are characterized by searching for approximate global solutions over the entire data set.

8. CONCLUSIONS

We have shown in this paper how physical analogies can be used in several applications outside the domain of the traditional physics problem. We believe that as we search for the solution of larger and larger problems on more and more powerful parallel computers, these analogies will grow in importance.

ACKNOWLEDGEMENTS

I would like to thank Paul Messina and his colleagues, especially Almerico Murli from the University of Naples, for their warm hospitality and an excellent conference. This work was supported by the Department of Energy (Applied Mathematical Sciences— Grant: DE-FG03-85ER25009), Joint Tactical Fusion Program Office, and the National Science Foundation under Cooperative Agreement No. CCR-8809165; the Government has certain rights in this material.

The collaborations with Wojtek Furmanski, Eitan Gurewitz, Ken Rose, and Petar Simic were essential in crystallizing my ideas in this area. I thank TRW for very helpful discussions about robot manipulation.

REFERENCES

1. S. Kirkpatrick, C. D. Gelatt and M. P. Vecchi, 'Optimization by simulated annealing', *Science*, **220**, 671–680 (1983).
2. P. Simic, 'Statistical mechanics as the underlying theory of 'elastic' and 'neural' optimizations', *Network*, **1**, 89–103 (1990). (Caltech Report C3P-787.)
3. G. C. Fox, 'Approaches to physical optimization', Technical Report C3P-959, California Institute of Technology, April 1991. CRPC-TR91124, SCCS-92, Submitted to *SIAM J. Sci. Stat. Comp.* for publication.

4. G. C. Fox, M. A. Johnson, G. A. Lyzenga, S. W. Otto, J. K. Salmon and D. W. Walker, *Solving Problems on Concurrent Processors*, Vol. 1, Prentice Hall, Englewood Cliffs, NJ (1988).

5. G. Fox and S. Otto, 'Concurrent computation and the theory of complex systems', in M. T. Heath (ed.), *Hypercube Multiprocessors*, SIAM, Philadelphia (1986), pp. 244–268. (Caltech Report C3P-255.)

6. G. Fox, S. W. Otto and E. A. Umland, 'Monte Carlo physics on a concurrent processor', *Journal of Statistical Physics*, **43**(5/6) (1986). (Proceedings of the Conference on Frontiers of Quantum Monte Carlo, September 3–6, 1985 at Los Alamos. Caltech Report C3P-214.)

7. G. C. Fox and W. Furmanski, 'The physical structure of concurrent problems and concurrent computers', *Phil. Trans. R. Soc. Lond. A*, **326**, 411–444 (1988). (Caltech Report C3P-493.)

8. G. C. Fox, 'A complex system model for Eastern Europe', Technical Report C3P-931, California Institute of Technology, June 1990. Unpublished.

9. D. L. Stein (ed.), *Lectures in the Sciences of Complexity*, Vol. 1, Addison-Wesley, Redwood City, CA, lectures edition (1989). Santa Fe Institute Studies in the Sciences of Complexity.

10. K. Rose, 'Deterministic Annealing, Clustering, and Optimization', PhD thesis, California Institute of Technology, December 1990. (Caltech Report C3P-950.)

11. B. R. Brooks, R. E. Bruccoleri, B. D. Olafson, D. J. States, S. Swaminathan and M. Karplus, 'CHARMM: a program for macromolecular energy, minimization, and dynamics calculations', *J. Comput. Chem.*, **4**(2), 187–217 (1983).

12. S. A. Gottlieb, W. Liu, D. Toussaint, R. L. Renken and R. L. Sugar, 'Hybrid-molecular-dynamics algorithms for the numerical simulation of quantum chromodynamics', *Phys. Rev. D*, **35**, 2531 (1987).

13. S. Duane and J. Kogut, 'The theory of hybrid stochastic algorithms', *Nucl. Phys.*, **275**, 398 (1986).

14. S. Duane, A. D. Kennedy, B. J. Pendleton and D. Roweth, 'Hybrid Monte Carlo', *Physics Letters B*, **195**, 216–220 (1987).

15. J. Hopfield and D. Tank, ' "Neural" computation of decisions in optimization problems', *Biol. Cybern.*, **52**, 141–152 (1985).

16. J. J. Hopfield and D. W. Tank, 'Computing with neural circuits: a model', *Science*, **233**, 625 (1986).

17. R. Durbin and D. Wilshaw, 'An analogue approach to the traveling salesman problem using an elastic net method', *Nature*, **326**, 689–691 (1987).

18. K. Rose, E. Gurewitz and G. Fox, 'A deterministic annealing approach to clustering', *Pattern Recognition Letters*, **11**(9), 589–594 (1990). (Caltech Report C3P-857.)

19. K. Rose, E. Gurewitz and G. C. Fox, 'Vector quantization by deterministic annealing', Technical Report C3P-895, California Institute of Technology, May 1990. Submitted to *IEEE Transactions on Information Theory*.

20. K. Rose, E. Gurewitz and G. C. Fox, 'Statistical mechanics and phase transitions in clustering', *Physical Review Letters*, **65**(8), 945–948 (1990). (Caltech Report C3P-893.)

21. D. Terzopoulos, 'Multilevel computational processes for visual surface reconstruction', *Computer Vision Graphics and Image Processing*, **24**, 52–96 (1983).

22. D. Terzopoulos, 'Image analysis using multigrid relaxation methods', *IEEE Trans. Pattern Analysis Machine Intelligence*, **8**, 129 (1986).

23. R. Battiti, 'Real-time multiscale vision on multicomputers,' *Concurrency: Practice and Experience*, **3**(2), 55–87 (1991). Accepted for Publication. Caltech Report C3P-932b.

24. G. V. Wilson and G. C. Pawley, 'On the stability of the travelling salesman problem algorithm of Hopfield and Tank', *Biol. Cybern.*, **58**, 63–70 (1988).

25. C. H. Papadimitriou and K. Steiglitz, *Combinatorial Optimization: Algorithms and Complexity*, Prentice Hall, Englewood Cliffs, NJ (1982).

26. O. Martin, S. W. Otto and E. W. Felten, 'Large-step Markov chains for the traveling salesman problem'. Technical Report C3P-836, California Institute of Technology, August 1989. Submitted to *Operations Research*.

27. G. Fox, A. Kolawa and R. Williams, 'The implementation of a dynamic load balancer', in M. T. Heath (ed.), *Hypercube Multiprocessors*, SIAM, Philadelphia (1987), pp. 114–121. (Caltech Report C3P-328.)

28. G. C. Fox and W. Furmanski, 'A string theory for time dependent complex systems and

its application to automatic decomposition', in G. C. Fox (ed.), *The Third Conference on Hypercube Concurrent Computers and Applications*, Vol. 1, ACM Press, New York, pp. 285–305 (1988). (Caltech Report C3P-521.)

29. G. C. Fox, 'A review of automatic load balancing and decomposition methods for the hypercube', in M. Schultz (ed.), *Numerical Algorithms for Modern Parallel Computer Architectures*, Springer-Verlag (1988), pp. 63–76. (Caltech Report C3P-385.)

30. G. C. Fox and W. Furmanski, 'The physical structure of concurrent problems and concurrent computers', in R. J. Elliott and C. A. R. Hoare (eds), *Scientific Applications of Multiprocessors*, Prentice Hall, Englewood Cliffs, NJ (1988), pp. 55–58. (Caltech Report C3P-493.)

31. G. C. Fox, W. Furmanski and J. Koller, 'The use of neural networks in parallel software systems', *Mathematics and Computers in Simulation*, **31**(6), 485–495 (1989). Elsevier Science Publishers BV (North-Holland). (Caltech Report C3P-642b.)

32. J. Barraguard and J. C. Latombe, 'A monte carlo algorithm for path planning with many degrees of freedom', in *Proceedings of 1990 IEEE Robotics and Automation Conference*, May 1990, Cincinnati (1990).

33. G. C. Fox, W. Furmanski, A. Ho, J. Koller, P. Simic and Y. F. Wong, 'Neural networks and dynamic complex systems'. Technical Report C3P-695, California Institute of Technology, December 1988. Proceedings of 1989 SCS Eastern Conference, Tampa, Florida, March 28–31, 1989.

34. G. C. Fox, E. Gurewitz and Y. Wong, 'A neural network approach to multi-vehicle navigation', Technical Report C3P-833, California Institute of Tehcnology, October 1989. Published in Proceedings of SPIE Conference, Philadelphia.

35. E. Gurewitz, G. C. Fox and Y.-F. Wong, 'Parallel algorithm for one and two-vehicle navigation', Technical Report C3P-852, California Institute of Technology, 1989. Published in the Proceedings of the 1990 IEEE International Workshop on Intelligent Robots and Systems, IROS'90 held in Tsuchiura, Ibaraki, Japan, July 1990.

36. E. Gurewitz, G. C. Fox and Y.-F. Wong, 'Parallel algorithm for one and two-vehicle navigation', in D. W. Walker and Q. F. Stout (eds), *The Fifth Distributed Memory Computing Conference*, Vol. I, IEEE Computer Society Press, Los Alamitos, CA (1990). (Held April 9–12, Charleston, South Carolina. Caltech Report C3P-876.)

37. A. Gandhi and G. C. Fox, 'Physical optimization for navigation and robot manipulation', Technical Report SCCS-43, Syracuse University, 1990. Unpublished.

38. S. T. Jones, 'Solving problems involving variable terrain, Part I: a general algorithm', *BYTE*, February (1980).

39. G. Heinzinger, P. Jacobs, J. Canny and B. Paden, 'Time-optimal trajectories for a robot manipulator: a provably good approximation algorithm', in *Proceedings of 1990 IEEE Robotics and Automation Conference*, May 1990. Cincinnati (1990).

40. A. Durbin, R. Szeliski and A. Yuille, 'An analysis of the elastic net approach to the Travelling Salesman Problem', *Neural Computation*, **1**, 348–358 (1989).

41. G. C. Fox, E. Gurewitz and Y. Wong, 'A neural network approach to multi-vehicle navigation', in D. W. Walker and Q. F. Stout (eds), *The Fifth Distributed Memory Computing Conference*, Vol. I, IEEE Computer Society Press, Los Alamitos, CA (1990), pp. 148–152. (Held April 9–12, Charleston, SC. Caltech Report C3P-910.)

42. G. C. Fox, 'Applications of the generalized elastic net to navigation.' Technical Report C3P-930, California Institute of Technology, June 1990. Unpublished.

43. A. Gandhi and G. C. Fox, 'Solving problems in navigation', Technical Report SCCS-9, Syracuse University, 1990. Unpublished.

44. K. Rose, E. Gurewitz and G. C. Fox, 'Constrained clustering as an optimization method', Technical Report C3P-919, California Institute of Technology, June 1990. Submitted to *IEEE Transactions on Pattern Analysis and Machine Intelligence*.

45. K. Rose, E. Gurewitz and C. Geoffrey Fox, 'A nonconvex cost optimization approach to tracking multiple targets by a parallel computational network', Technical Report C3P-853, California Institute of Technology, 1989. Published in Proceedings of the 1990 IEEE International Workshop on Intelligent Robots and Systems, IROS'90 held in Tsuchiura, Ibaraki, Japan, July 1990.

46. K. Rose, E. Gurewitz and C. Geoffrey Fox, 'A nonconvex cost optimization approach to

tracking multiple targets by a parallel computational network', in D. W. Walker and Q. F. Stout (eds), *The Fifth Distributed Memory Computing Conference*, Vol. I, pages 78–84, 10662 Los Vaqueros Circle, P. O. Box 3014, Los Alamitos, California 90720-1264, 1990. IEEE Computer Society Press, Los Alamitos, CA (1990), pp. 78–84. (Held April 9–12, Charleston, SC. Caltech Report C3P-875.)

47. S. S. Blackman, *Multiple-Target Tracking with Radar Applications*, Artech House, Dedham, MA (1986).

48. F. Burgeios and J. C. Lassalle, 'An extension of munkres algorithm for the assignment problem to rectangular matrices', *Comm. of the ACM*, **14**, 802 (1971).

49. H. W. Kuhn, 'The Hungarian method for the assignment problem', *Naval Research Logistics Quarterly*, **2**, 83 (1955).

50. T. D. Gottschalk, 'Concurrent multiple target tracking', in G. C. Fox (ed.), *The Third Conference on Hypercube Concurrent Computers and Applications*, Vol. 2, ACM Press, New York (1988), pp. 1247–1268. (Caltech Report C3P-567.)

51. T. D. Gottschalk, 'Concurrent implementation of Munkres algorithm', in D. W. Walker and Q. F. Stout (eds), *The Fifth Distributed Memory Computing Conference*, Vol. I, IEEE Computer Society Press, Los Alamitos, CA (1990), pp. 52–57. Held April 9–12, Charleston, SC. (Caltech Report C3P-899.)

52. T. D. Gottschalk, 'Concurrent multi-target tracking', in D. W. Walker and Q. F. Stout (eds), *The Fifth Distributed Memory Computing Conference*, Vol. I, IEEE Computer Society Press, Los Alamitos, CA (1990), pp. 85–88. (Held April 9–12, Charleston, SC. Caltech Report C3P-908.)

53. D. Sergupta and R. A. Iltis, 'A neural-network solution to the data association problem in multiple target tracking', *IEEE Trans. Aerospace and Electronic Systems* (1988). To be published.

54. G. C. Fox, 'Jet production in high-energy Hadron–Proton collisions', *Nuclear Physics B*, **171**, 38 (1980). (With experimental groups at Caltech, UCLA, Chicago Circle, Fermilab and Indiana.)

55. G. C. Fox, 'A note on neural networking for trackfinding', Technical Report C3P-748, California Institute of Technology, March 1989. Unpublished.

56. D. H. Ballard and C. M. Brown, *Computer Vision*, Prentice Hall, Englewood Cliffs, NJ (1982).

57. D. H. Ballard, 'Cortical connections and parallel processing: structure and function', *The Behavioral and Brain Sciences*, **9**, 67–120 (1986).

58. J. Illingworth and J. Kittler, 'A survey of the Hough Transform', *Computer Vision, Graphics and Image Processing*, **44**, 87–116 (1988).

59. R. M. Kuczewski, *Neural Network Approaches to Multi-Target Tracking*, TRW MEAD (1988).

61. R. D. Williams, 'Performance of load balancing algorithms for unstructured mesh calculations', *Concurrency: Practice and Experience* (1991). Accepted for publication. (Caltech Report C3P-913b.)

62. G. C. Fox and W. Furmanski, 'Load balancing loosely synchronous problems with a neural network', in G. C. Fox (ed.), *The Third Conference on Hypercube Concurrent Computers and Applications*, Vol. 1, ACM Press, New York, (1988), pp. 241–278. (Caltech Report C3P-363b.)

CONCURRENCY: PRACTICE AND EXPERIENCE, VOL. 3(6), 655–666 (DECEMBER 1991)

LAPACK: a portable linear algebra library for high-performance computers

JAMES DEMMEL

Mathematics Department and Computer Science Division
University of California
Berkeley, CA 94720, USA

SUMMARY

The goal of the LAPACK project is to design and implement a portable linear algebra library for efficient use on a variety of high-performance computers. The library is based on the widely used LINPACK and EISPACK packages for solving linear equations, eigenvalue problems, and linear least-squares problems, but extends their functionality in a number of ways. The major methodology for making the algorithms run faster is to restructure them to perform block matrix operations (e.g. matrix–matrix multiplication) in their inner loops. These block operations may be optimized to exploit the memory hierarchy of a specific architecture. In particular, we discuss algorithms and benchmarks for the singular value decomposition.

1. INTRODUCTION

The University of California at Berkeley, the University of Tennessee, the Courant Institute of Mathematical Sciences, the Numerical Algorithms Group, Ltd, Rice University, Argonne National Laboratory, and Oak Ridge National Laboratory are developing a transportable linear algebra library in Fortran 77. The library is intended to provide a uniform set of subroutines to solve the most common linear algebra problems and to run efficiently on a wide range of high-performance computers.

The LAPACK library (shorthand for Linear Algebra Package) will provide routines for solving systems of simultaneous linear equations, least-squares solutions of over-determined systems of equations, and eigenvalue problems. The associated matrix factorizations (LU, Cholesky, QR, SVD, Schur, generalized Schur) will also be provided, as will related computations such as reordering of the factorizations and condition numbers (or estimates thereof). Dense and banded matrices will be provided for, but not general sparse matrices. In all areas, similar functionality will be provided for real and complex matrices.

The new library will be based on the successful EISPACK[35,27] and LINPACK[14] libraries, integrating the two sets of algorithms into a unified, systematic library. A great deal of effort has also been expended to incorporate design methodologies and algorithms that make the LAPACK codes more appropriate for today's high-performance architectures. The LINPACK and EISPACK codes were written in a fashion that, for the most part, ignored the cost of data movement. Most of today's high-performance machines, however, incorporate a memory hierarchy[23,29,37] to even out the difference in speed of memory accesses and vectorized floating-point operations. As a result, codes must be careful about reusing data in order not to run at memory speed instead of

---

Received 17 December 1990
Revised 4 June 1991

floating-point speed. LAPACK codes have been carefully restructured to reuse as much data as possible in order to reduce the cost of data movement. Further improvements are the incorporation of new and improved algorithms for the solution of eigenvalue problems[10,20].

LAPACK is designed to be efficient and transportable across a wide range of computing environments, with special emphasis on modern high-performance computers. While we do not hope for LAPACK codes to be optimal for all architectures, we expect high performance over a wide range of machines. By relying on the Basic Linear Algebra Subprograms (BLAS)[22,15,31] the codes can be 'tuned' to a given architecture by efficient—and, in all likelihood machine-dependent—implementations of these kernels. Machine-specific optimizations are limited to those kernels, and the user interface is uniform across machines. We shall also distribute test and timing routines to verify the installation of the LAPACK codes on a particular architecture and to allow for easy comparison with existing software.

In addition to higher speed, LAPACK is designed to provide higher accuracy for a number of problems. We do this by replacing the conventional notion of normwise back-ward error with componentwise relative backward error. This approach better respects the sparsity and scaling structure of the original problem. This leads to new perturbation theory, algorithms and error analysis for a number of problems, and is discussed in section 5 below.

Netlib[18] has demonstrated how useful and important it is for libraries to be easily available, and preferably on line. We intend to distribute the new library in a similar way, for no cost or a nominal cost only.

The rest of this paper is outlined as follows. Section 2 describes the BLAS and explains why their use can speed up algorithms. Section 3 describes block algorithms and shows in some detail how to reorganize the singular value decomposition (SVD). Section 4 contains benchmark results for the SVD and other routines on a variety of machines. Section 5 outlines our general approach to achieving high accuracy. Section 6 reviews the target machines for which LAPACK is designed to run most efficiently. Finally, Section 7 outlines future plans to extend the library, including the challenges faced in adapting the codes to distributed-memory machines.

In addition to that of the author, this represents work of E. Anderson, Z. Bai, J. Barlow, C. Bischof, P. Deift, J. Dongarra, J. DuCroz, A. Greenbaum, S. Hammarling, W. Kahan, L.-C. Li, A. McKenney, D. Sorensen, C. Tomei and K. Veselić.

2. BASIC LINEAR ALGEBRA SUBPROGRAMS

The BLAS were originally introduced in the construction of LINPACK[31]. These BLAS did operations only on vectors of data, such as a dot product or a saxpy (adding a scalar multiple of one vector to another). We refer to these vector–vector operations as Level 1 BLAS. The Level 1 BLAS permit efficient implementation on scalar machines, but the granularity is too low for effective use on most vector or parallel machines.

More recently, higher-level BLAS have been specified that perform operations of higher granularity and so offer more opportunity for optimization on different architectures. The Level 2 BLAS[17] perform matrix–vector operations such as matrix–vector multiplication and rank-one updates. The Level 3 BLAS[16] perform matrix–

matrix operations such as matrix–matrix multiplication, solving triangular systems with multiple right-hand sides, and rank-k matrix updates.

To appreciate why these Level 2 and Level 3 BLAS with larger granularity offer better opportunities for efficiency, one must understand memory hierarchies. All machines (not just supercomputers) have a hierarchy of memory levels—for example, with registers at the top, followed by cache, main memory, and finally disk storage at the bottom. Toward the top of the hierarchy, memory is smaller, more expensive, and faster. Since operations such as multiplication and addition must be done at the top level, data has to move up through the various levels to the top to be processed, and then down again to be stored. The result is that data at higher levels is available only after some delay and (because of memory bank conflicts) may not be available at a rate fast enough to feed the arithmetic units. Clearly, an algorithm that minimizes the memory traffic in the hierarchy will run faster.

One way to measure the amount of this memory traffic is the ratio of flops (floating-point operations) to memory references in an algorithm. The larger this ratio, the longer a piece of data may be kept at the top of the hierarchy on average. Let us use this measure to compare the three operations of saxpy (Level 1 BLAS), matrix–vector multiplication (Level 2 BLAS), and matrix–matrix multiplication (Level 3 BLAS), where all vectors and matrices are of dimension n. Simple counting yields the ratios 2/3 for saxpy, 2 for matrix–vector multiplication, and $n/2$ for matrix–matrix multiplication. The large ratio for matrix–matrix multiply represents a surface-to-volume effect, doing $O(n^3)$ operations on $O(n^2)$ data. Hence, matrix–matrix multiplication offers much greater opportunity for exploiting the memory hierarchy than the lower-level BLAS routines. Table 1 illustrates this fact with some benchmark results.

Table 1. Speed of the BLAS on various architectures (all values are in Mflops)

	Alliant FX/8 (8 processors)	IBM 3090/VF (1 processor)	Cray 2S (1 processor)
Peak speed	94	108	488
Level 1 BLAS	14	26	121
Level 2 BLAS	26	60	350
Level 3 BLAS	43	80	437

Fortran implementations of all the BLAS are available; to get the full benefit, however, the BLAS should be optimized for each architecture. We encourage the computer manufacturers to perform these optimizations; the data in Table 1 are for such optimized implementations. We also expect that the LAPACK project will reveal the need for a few additional basic routines whose performance may need to be optimized for different architectures and may be regarded as extensions to the current set of BLAS (e.g. applying a sequence of plane rotations to a matrix).

3. BLOCK ALGORITHMS

To exploit the Level 3 BLAS, one usually must express the algorithm in terms of operations on submatrices, or 'blocks', as compared to vector- or scalar-oriented operations. We have developed such block routines for Gaussian elimination and Cholesky, QR decomposition (with and without pivoting), the nonsymmetric eigenproblem (both reduction to Hessenberg form and QR iteration), and the symmetric eigenproblem (reduction to tridiagonal form). Work is continuing on block algorithms for the SVD and generalized eigenproblems. See Reference 19 for details. A good survey of block algorithms is in Reference 26. In this section we discuss the SVD in detail.

The singular value decomposition of an m by n real matrix A is a factorization $A = U \Sigma V^T$, where U is m by m and orthogonal, V is n by n and orthogonal, and $\Sigma = \text{diag}(\sigma_1,\ldots,\sigma_s)$ is m by n and diagonal. Here $s = \min(m,n)$ and $\sigma_1 \geq \cdots \geq \sigma_s \geq 0$. The σ_i are called *singular values*, the columns of V the *right singular vectors*, and the columns of U the *left singular vectors*. A similar, somewhat cheaper and more compact version is to take V_1 the first s columns of V, U_1 the first s columns of U, and Σ_1 the top left s by s corner of Σ so $A = U_1 \Sigma_1 V_1^T$.

If m and n do not differ too much in size (are within a factor of, say, 5/3 of one another[28]), then the SVD is computed in two stages as follows. We assume without loss of generality that $m \geq n$. First, we compute orthogonal matrices U_2 and V_2 so that $B = U_2^T A V_2$ where B is s by s and *bidiagonal*, i.e. nonzero only on the main diagonal and on the first superdiagonal. This can be done in a finite number of steps as described below, and requires about $8n^3/3$ flops if A is square.

The second stage computes orthogonal U_3 and V_3 so that $\Sigma_1 = U_3^T B V_3$. This is an iterative scheme which stops when the computed Σ_1 is close enough to diagonal. Altogether we get $A = (U_2 U_3)\Sigma_1(V_2 V_3)^T$, the SVD. The first stage of the algorithm may be rewritten in terms of the Level 2 and 3 BLAS; we describe this below. The second stage is harder to vectorize or parallelize, in particular if one is only interested in computing Σ. Our main algorithm is sequential, and described briefly at the end of Section 5. If only Σ is desired, this part of the algorithm takes $O(n^2)$ flops. Thus, it is asymptotically negligible compared to the first stage. However, as we shall see in Section 4, our current inability to speed up stage two means $O(n^2)$ can dominate $O(n^3)$ for surprisingly large n.

For the rest of this section, we describe the Level 2 and 3 BLAS versions of the reduction to bidiagonal form.

3.1. Reduction to bidiagonal form using Level 2 BLAS

We begin by describing the conventional algorithm, and then show how to rewrite it using Level 2 BLAS. Our basic tool is the *Householder reflection* or *Householder matrix*, an orthogonal matrix of the form

$$H_u = I - 2uu^T \qquad \|u\|_2 = 1 \tag{1}$$

Given a vector x of size n, it costs just $O(n)$ work to compute a vector u such that $H_u x = x - 2u(u^T x)$ has zeros in entries 2 through n. More generally, one can compute a vector u which is nonzero in entries k through n such that Hx is zero in entries $k + 1$ through n. We can use this to reduce A to bidiagonal form as follows.

At the first step we choose u_1 so that the first column of $H_{u_1} A$ is zero below the diagonal, and then v_1 so that the first row of $H_{u_1} A H_{v_1}$ is zero in columns 3 through n. This leaves the zeros in column 1 unchanged.

At the beginning of step i we have pre- and postmultiplied A by $i - 1$ Householder matrices to get $A_{i-1} = H_{u_{i-1}} \cdots H_{u_1} A H_{v_1} \cdots H_{v_{i-1}}$, with zeros below the diagonal in columns 1 through $i - 1$ and to the right of the first superdiagonal in rows 1 through $i - 1$. In step i we choose u_i to zero out below the diagonal in column i of $H_{u_i} A_{i-1}$ and then v_i to zero out row i in columns $i + 2$ through n in $H_{u_i} A_{i-1} H_{v_i}$. Both these multiplications leave previously created zeros unchanged. Finally, at step $n - 1$, we need only premultiply by $H_{u_{n-1}}$.

The basic operation is therefor pre- and postmultiplying a matrix A by Householder transformations H_u and H_v, respectively. This can be done easily with Level 2 BLAS as follows:

    (1) Compute u from the first column of A.
    (2) $x^T = 2u^T \cdot A$ (matrix–vector multiply).
    (3) $A = A - u \cdot x^T$ (rank-1 matrix update).
    (4) Compute v from the first row of A.
    (5) $y = 2A \cdot v$ (matrix–vector multiply).
    (6) $A = A - y \cdot v^T$ (rank-1 matrix update).

The entries of the bidiagonal matrix are byproducts of the computations of u and v. This algorithm is performed by subroutine SGEBD2 in LAPACK.

3.2. Reduction to bidiagonal form using Level 3 BLAS

We now describe how the above algorithm can be changed to use matrix–matrix operations. Briefly, in order to update the first b rows and columns of A, all of A must be read from memory, but only the first b rows and columns written. Thus we may reduce the first b rows and columns of A to bidiagonal form, accumulating the information we need to update the rest of the matrix in m by b work matrices U and Y, and n by b work matrices V and X. Then, using matrix–matrix multiplication, we can compute $A_b = A - UX^T - YV^T$. These two rank-b updates replace the $2b$ rank-1 updates $A - ux^T - yv^T$ in the Level 2 BLAS algorithm.

We describe how U, Y, X and X are computed. The columns of U, V, X and Y will just be the vectors u_i, v_i, x_i and y_i computed by the Level 2 algorithm. Let $U_i = [u_1, \ldots, u_i]$, and define V_i, X_i and Y_i similarly. We wish to compute these four matrices for $i = b$. Assuming U_i, V_i, X_i and Y_i have been computed, we show how to compute U_{i+1}, V_{i+1}, X_{i+1}, and Y_{i+1}. By assumption A_i, if we were to compute it, would be $A - U_i X_i^T - Y_i V_i^T$. We use the notation $A(:, k)$ to mean the kth column of A and $A(k, :)$ to mean the kth row of A. We compute as follows:

    (1) Compute the $i+1$st column of A_i: $z = A(:, i+1) - U_i \cdot (X_i(i+1, :))^T - Y_i \cdot (V_i(i+1, :))^T$ (two matrix–vector multiplies).
    (2) Compute u_{i+1} from z.
    (3) $x_{i+1}^T = 2[u_{i+1}^T \cdot A - (u_{i+1}^T \cdot U_i) \cdot X_i^T - (u_{i+1}^T \cdot Y_i) \cdot V_i^T]$ (five matrix–vector multiplies).
    (4) Compute the $i + 1$st row of A_i: $w = A(i + 1, :) - U_i(i + 1, :) \cdot X_i^T - Y_i(i + 1, :) \cdot V_i^T$ (two matrix–vector multiplies).
    (5) Compute v_{i+1} from w.
    (6) $y_{i+1} = 2[A \cdot v_{i+1} - U_i \cdot (X_i^T \cdot v_{i+1}) - Y_i \cdot (V_i^T \cdot v_{i+1})$ (five matrix–vector multiplies).

When we have computed U_b, V_b, X_b and Y_b, we update $A = A - U_b \cdot X_b^T - Y_b \cdot V_b^T$ with two matrix–matrix multiplications. Then we repeat the process on the remainder of A. Note that we access all of A only twice in the displayed algorithm, to compute $u_{i+1}^T \cdot A$ and $A \cdot v_{i+1}$. The other matrix–vector multiplies deal with smaller matrices.

The need to choose a block size b occurs throughout LAPACK. The optimal b depends on the algorithm, matrix dimension, and machine architecture. Furthermore, on multiprocessor machines, possibly conflicting issues of individual processor performance and overall load balancing must be reconciled. A discussion of these issues and a suggestion for a methodology to overcome this problem can be found in Reference 6. Determining optimal, or near optimal, block sizes for different environments is a major research topic for the LAPACK project.

4. BENCHMARKS

The first version of LAPACK software was released for beta-testing in April 1989. This software included software for general, positive definite, and symmetric indefinite systems and for QR decomposition without pivoting.

In Tables 2–4 we present results for which most or all of the BLAS were optimized for the particular architecture. SGETRF is the LAPACK routine for triangular factorization of a general matrix with partial pivoting, SPOTRF performs Cholesky factorization of a positive definite symmetric matrix, and SGEQRF does QR factorization without pivoting. Also shown are SGEMV (matrix–vector multiply) and SGEMM (matrix–matrix multiply), since these are the 'speed limits' for the algorithms written in terms of the Level 2 BLAS and Level 3 BLAS, respectively. All codes were run in single precision (32 bits on the Convex and 64 bits on the Cray). All results are in Mflops.

Table 2 gives the results for the Convex C210, with an algorithm block size of $n_b = 1$. As the table shows, there is no difference between the Level 2 and Level 3 BLAS versions. Since matrix–vector and matrix–matrix multiply are equally fast on this machine in their current implementations, nothing is gained by going to the Level 3 BLAS.

Tables 3 and 4 give results for the Cray Y-MP for one and eight processors, respectively. Here $n_b = 64$ for SGETRF and SPOTRF and $n_b = 16$ for SGEQRF. The maximum speed of a single processor of a Cray Y-MP is 333 Mflops. Thus, we see that for large-enough matrix dimensions, the single-processor code runs at at 90% efficiency. When all eight processors are used, the code attains 73% to 80% efficiency.

We conclude with some preliminary benchmarks for the SVD code, and compare it to the LINPACK routine SSVDC (see Table 5). We break the LAPACK times down into two parts: reduction to bidiagonal form using Level 2 BLAS (subroutine SGEBD2) and computing the singular values of a bidiagonal matrix (subroutine SBDSQR). As mentioned in Section 3, SGEBD2 performs about $8n^3/3$ flops and SBDSQR only $O(n^2)$. The LINPACK routine SSVDC performs both bidiagonal reduction and bidiagonal SVD, so we only have one set of data for it.

These tests were done on a single processor of a Cray Y-MP. The rows labeled 'Total' mean total LAPACK time or megaflops. The 'Speed-up' is of LAPACK over LINPACK. The most interesting data is in Table 6. SGEBD2 runs over 90 times faster than SBDSQR for $n = 400$. So even though SGEBD2 is performing vastly more flops that SBDSQR, it takes 0.6 seconds compared to SBDSQR's 1.4 seconds. Extrapolating SBDSQR's time to grow proportionally to n^2 and SGEBD2's to n^3, we expect them to take the same

Table 2. LAPACK on a Convex C210

Routine	Matrix dimension				
	32	64	128	256	512
SGEMV	34	43	47	47	47
SGEMM	38	44	47	47	47
SGETRF	6	12	21	30	36
SPOTRF	8	20	33	40	44
SGEQRF	12	21	27	33	38

Table 3. LAPACK on a Cray Y-MP, one processor

Routine	Matrix dimension					
	32	64	128	256	512	1024
SGETRF	40	108	195	260	290	304
SPOTRF	34	95	188	259	289	301
SGEQRF	54	139	225	275	294	301

Table 4. LAPACK on a CRAY Y-MP, eight processors

Routine	Matrix dimension					
	32	64	128	256	512	1024
SGETRF	32	90	205	375	1039	1974
SPOTRF	29	84	273	779	1592	2115
SGEQRF	50	133	328	807	1476	1937

Table 5. SVD (seconds) on a Cray Y-MP, one processor

Routine	Matrix dimension		
	100×100	200×200	400×400
SGEBD2	0.014	0.08	0.60
SBDSQR	0.096	0.36	1.40
Total	0.110	0.44	2.00
SSVDC	0.140	0.58	2.60
Speed-up	1.3	1.3	1.3

Table 6. SVD (Mflops) on a Cray Y-MP, one processor

Routine	Matrix dimension		
	100×100	200×200	400×400
SGEBD2	200	260	280
SBDSQR	3	3	3
Total	27	52	88
SSVDC	22	39	68

time at about $n = 1000$. Thus unless we can significantly speed up the $O(n^2)$ part of the computation, it will dominate the $O(n^3)$ part for rather large n.

For complex data the speed-up of LAPACK over LINPACK improved to 1.6. For $n = 400$, going from real to complex data slowed LAPACK down by a factor of 1.5 and slowed LINPACK down by a factor of 1.9.

We expect further improvements when we benchmark our Level 3 BLAS code for bidiagonal reduction.

5. HIGH-ACCURACY LINEAR ALGEBRA ALGORITHMS

One objective of the LAPACK project is to provide linear algebra algorithms of extremely high accuracy. To discuss the new algorithms, we shall need some notation.

We let H denote the problem for which we seek a solution for some problem; we denote the solution by $f(H)$. For example, $f(H)$ may denote the eigenvalues, eigenvectors, singular values, or singular vectors of the matrix H. If H denotes the pair (A,b), then $f(H)$ may denote the solution of the linear system $Ax = b$, perhaps in a least-squares sense if A is singular or not square. In general, $f(H)$ cannot be computed exactly and hence is approximated by an algorithm whose output we denote $\hat{f}(H)$. We also let ε denote the machine precision.

Analyzing the accuracy of an algorithm $\hat{f}$ for f consists of two parts. First, we use *perturbation theory*, where we bound the difference $f(H + \delta H) - f(H)$ in terms of δH. This part depends only on f and not the algorithm that approximates it. Second, we use *error analysis*, which attempts to show that the computed solution $\hat{f}(H)$ is close to $f(H + \delta H)$ for some bounded δH. Showing that $\hat{f}(H) = f(H + \delta H)$ for some bounded δH is called *backward error analysis*, but is by no means the only way to proceed.

There is a great deal of choice in the measures we choose to bound errors and measure distances. In conventional error analysis as introduced by Wilkinson, we bound $\|f(H + \delta H) - f(H)\|$ in terms of $\|\delta H\|$, and show $\hat{f}(H) = f(H + \delta H)$ where $\|\delta H\| \leq O(\varepsilon)\|H\|$. Here, $\|\cdot\|$ denotes a norm, like the one-norm or Frobenius norm. Typically one proves a formula of the form $\|f(H + \delta H) - f(H)\| \leq \kappa(f,H) \cdot \|\delta H\| + O(\|\delta H\|^2)$, where $\kappa(H)$ is called the *condition number of H with respect to f*. In this formulation, it is easy to see that $\kappa(f,H)$ is simply the norm of the gradient of f at H: $\|\nabla f(H)\|$; other scalings are possible. Thus, combining the perturbation theory and error analysis, one can write

$$\|f(H + \delta H) - f(H)\| \leq O(\varepsilon)\kappa(f,H) \cdot \|H\| + O(\varepsilon^2)$$

The drawback of this approach is that it does not respect the structure of the original data. In particular, if the original data is sparse or graded (large in some entries, small in others), bounding δH only by norm can give very pessimistic results. A trivial example is solving a diagonal system of equations. Each component of the solution is computed to full accuracy by a single divide operation, but the conventional condition number is the ratio of the largest to smallest diagonal entries and may be arbitrarily large.

Instead of bounding δH by its norm $\|\delta H\|$, one may instead use the measure $rel_H(\delta H) \equiv \max_{ij} |\delta H_{ij}|/|H_{ij}|$, the largest relative change in any entry (we use the notation rel_H to indicate the dependence on H). This measure respects sparsity, since δH_{ij} must be zero if H_{ij} is zero, and also grading, since every entry is perturbed by an amount small compared to its magnitude. For example, in the case of diagonal linear equation solving, one can easily see that a perturbation δH of size $rel_H(\delta H)$ in the matrix can only change the solution relatively by $rel_H(\delta H)$ in each component, and that the algorithm is backward stable with $rel_H(\delta H) \leq \varepsilon$. Thus, the new perturbation theory and error analysis with respect to $rel_H(\delta H)$ accurately predict that each component of the solution is computed to full relative accuracy.

We have successfully developed new perturbation theory, algorithms, and error analysis for the measure $rel_H(\delta H)$ for much of numerical linear algebra. We cannot always guarantee to solve problems as though we had a small $rel_H(\delta H)$, but the algorithms can in all cases monitor their accuracy and produce useful error bounds. The algorithms are usually small variations on conventional algorithms, perhaps with a slightly different stopping criterion, although the bidiagonal SVD algorithm has a quite new component. In all cases the algorithms run approximately as fast as their conventional counterparts, sometimes a little slower and sometimes a little faster. Since they are based on the conventional algorithms, all the techniques using the Level 3 BLAS apply to them.

This approach has been applied to linear equation solving[2], linear least-squares problems[3], the bidiagonal SVD[11,9], the tridiagonal symmetric eigenproblem[30,4], the dense symmetric positive definite eigenproblem[12], and the dense definite generalized eigenproblem[4,12]. We have similar but slightly weaker results for the dense SVD and generalized SVD[12]. These algorithms either will be included directly in LAPACK or can be easily constructed by using LAPACK subroutines as 'building blocks'.

We briefly describe the results for the bidiagonal SVD. The standard algorithm[14] computes each singular value σ_i of a bidiagonal matrix B with an error bound $O(\varepsilon)\|B\|_2$. Large singular values, i.e. those near $\|B\|_2$, are therefore computed to high relative accuracy, whereas tiny ones may be computed with no relative accuracy at all. In contrast, our new algorithm can compute each singular value to nearly full precision, no matter how tiny it is. It does this with no degradation in speed on average, and is often faster[11]. It also computes the singular vectors corresponding to groups of nearby tiny singular values much more accurately than the standard algorithm. The proof of this last property relies on the fact that the algorithm is the integer time evaluation of a Hamiltonian differential equation, which may be used to prove that the rounding errors accumulate quite slowly[9].

6. TARGET MACHINES

The LAPACK library will be designed primarily to perform efficiently on machines with a modest number of processors (say, 1–100), each having a powerful vector-processing capability. These machines include all of the most powerful computers currently available and in use for general-purpose scientific computing: Cray-2, Cray X-MP, Cray Y-MP, CYBER 205, Fujitsu VP, IBM 3090/VF, NEC SX, Hitachi S-820, Alliant FX/80, Convex C-1, Convex C-2, Stardent, Sequent Symmetry, Encore Multimax, and BBN Butterfly. We hope that the library will also perform well on a wider class of parallel machines, including the Intel iPSC/860, and NCUBE. On conventional serial machines, the performance of the library is expected to be at least as good as that of the current LINPACK and EISPACK codes. Thus the library will be suitable across the whole range of machines from personal computers to supercomputers to experimental architectures.

We do not claim that the strategy of using Level 2 or Level 3 BLAS will necessarily attain optimal performance on all these machines; indeed, some algorithms can be structured in several different ways, all calling Level 3 BLAS, but with different performance characteristics. In such cases we shall choose the structure that provides the best 'average' performance over the range of target machines. Currently we are limiting machine-dependent optimizations to the BLAS to retain portability across architectures. We encourage vendors to provide implementations of the BLAS kernels that are optimized for their particular architecture. While users are free to develop their own versions of the LAPACK codes, we believe that the possible performance gain will be limited on the more conventional architectures.

On the more experimental architectures (in particular, distributed-memory machines), the restriction of optimization to the BLAS might be too limiting. In particular, it might be advantageous to introduce parallelism at the top-level of the algorithm instead of inside the BLAS. To aid users in experimenting on their particular architecture, the LAPACK codes have been carefully designed in a modular fashion and with the objective of minimizing data movement. Since data movement is the key issue in distributed-memory as well as shared-memory machines, the LAPACK codes should be easily 'tunable' to more experimental architectures.

Several of the algorithms we intend to implement[20] will require more than loop-based parallelism. These algorithms will rely upon the simplified SCHEDULE mechanism[21] to invoke parallelism. These ideas might also be used to express top-level parallelism in a portable fashion. We are also closely following the activities of the Parallel Computing Forum[25] which has been formed by computer vendors, software developers, national laboratories, and universities to exchange technical information and to document agreements on constructs for programming parallel applications for shared-memory multi-processors.

7. FUTURE WORK

Our first software release in April 1989 distributed codes for linear equation solving and QR decomposition to over 20 beta-test sites. Our second release, occurred in April 1990 and includes software for iterative refinement, the non-symmetric eigenproblem, symmetric eigenproblem, and SVD. Banded problems, generalized eigenproblems and the generalized SVD, condition estimation for the eigenproblem, and low-rank updates of various decompositions followed in mid-1991. We expect the final public release in late 1991.

For the longer term, we have identified a number of research directions. First, we are interested in extending our approach to distributed-memory machines. These are more challenging than the shared-memory machines we have been working on, because of the additional cost of communication between different processors and memories. Second, we would like to systematically develop parameterized software that is both portable and efficient. In Section 3 we identified the block size n_b as one such parameter. Other parameters include the access order (which of the six versions of block Gaussian elimination is best) and features of the machine arithmetic (round-off level, overflow and underflow thresholds, presence or absence of guard digits, etc.). Third, we wish to identify features of computer architectures that either help or hinder production of good numerical software. Two examples of helpful features are the ability to access rows and columns of matrices with similar speeds, and friendly error recovery such as the overflow flag in IEEE standard floating-point arithmetic[1]. We also wish to provide performance evaluation tools for new architectures. Finally, we plan to provide C and Fortran 8x versions of the library as well.

ACKNOWLEDGEMENTS

The work is supported by NSF grants ASC-8715728, ASC-9005933 and CCR-8552474, and by DARPA grant F49620-87-C0065.

REFERENCES

1. *IEEE Standard for Binary Floating Point Arithmetic*, ANSI/IEEE, New York, Std 754-1985 edition (1985).
2. M. Arioli, J. Demmel and I. S. Duff, 'Solving sparse linear systems witwh sparse backward error', *SIAM J. Matrix Anal. Appl.*, **10**(2), 165–190, April (1989).
3. M. Arioli, I. S. Duff and P. P. M. de Rijk, 'On the augmented system approach to sparse least-squares problems', *Num. Math.*, **55**, 667–684 (1989).
4. Jesse Barlow and James Demmel. 'Computing accurate eigensystems of scaled diagonally dominant matrices', *SIAM J. Num. Anal.*, **27**(3), 762–791, June (1990).
5. Chris Bischof, James Demmel, Jack Dongarra, Jeremy Du Croz, Anne Greenbaum, Sven Hammarling and Danny Sorensen, 'LAPACK provisional contents', Mathematics and Computer Science Division Report ANL-88-38, Argonne National Laboratory, Argonne, IL, September (1988). (LAPACK Working Note #5.)
6. Christian H. Bischof., 'Adaptive blocking in the QR factorization'. *The Journal of Super-computing*, **3**(3), 193–208 (1989).
7. Christian H. Bischof and Charles F. Van Loan. 'The WY representation for products of Householder matrices', *SIAM Journal on Stat. and Sci. Compt.*, **8**, s2–s13 (1987).
8. Chandler Davis and W. Kahan, 'The rotation of eigenvectors by a perturbation iii', *SIAM Journal on Numerical Analysis*, **7**, 248–263 (1970).
9. P. Deift, J. Demmel, L.-C. Li and C. Tomei, 'The bidiagonal singular values decomposition and Hamiltonian mechanics', Computer Science Dept. Technical Report 458, Courant Institute, New York, NY, July (1989). (To appear in *SIAM J. Num. Anal.*)
10. James Demmel, Jeremy Du Croz, Sven Hammarling and Danny Sorensen. 'Guides for the design of symmetric eigenroutines, SVD, iterative refinement and condition estimation', Mathematics and Computer Science Division Report ANL/MCS-TM-111, Argonne National Laboratory, Argonne, IL, February (1988). (LAPACK Working Note #4.)
11. James Demmel and W. Kahan, 'Accurate singular values of bidiagonal matrices', *SIAM J. Sci. Stat. Comp.*, **11**(5), 873–912, September (1990).
12. James Demmel and K. Veselić. 'Jacobi's method is more accurate than QR'. (To appear in *SIAM J. Matrix Anal. Appl.*)
13. J. Dongarra and D. Sorensen, 'A fully parallel algorithm for the symmetric eigenproblem', *SIAM J. Sci. Stat. Comp.*, **8**(2), 139–154, March (1987).
14. J. J. Dongarra, J. R. Bunch, C. B. Moler and G. W. Stewart, *LINPACK Users' Guide*. SIAM Press, Philadelphia (1979).
15. Jack Dongarra, Jeremy Du Croz, Iain Duff and Sven Hammarling, 'A set of Level 3 basic linear algebra subprograms', *ACM TOMS*, **16**(1), 1–18 March 1990.
16. Jack Dongarra, Jeremy Du Croz, Iain Duff and Sven Hammarling, 'A proposal for a set of level 3 basic linear algebra subprograms', *SIGNUM Newsletter*, **22**(3), 2–14, February (1987).
17. Jack Dongarra, Jeremy Du Croz, Sven Hammarling and Richard J. Hanson, 'An extended set of fortran basic linear algebra subroutines', *ACM Transactions on Mathematical Software*, **14**(1), 1–17, March (1988).
18. Jack Dongarra and Eric Grosse, 'Distribution of mathematical software by electronic mail', *Communications of the ACM*, **30**(5), 403–407 (1987).

19. Jack Dongarra, Sven Hammarling and Danny Sorensen, 'Block reduction of matrices to condensed forms for eigenvalue computations', *Journal of Computational and Applied Mathematics*, **27**, 215–227 (1989).
20. Jack Dongarra and Danny Sorensen, 'A fully parallel algorithm for the symmetric eigenvalue problem', *SIAM Journal on Stat. and Sci. Compt.*, **8**(2), s139–s154 (1987).
21. Jack Dongarra and Danny Sorensen, 'A portable environment for developing parallel programs', *Parallel Computing*, **5**(1&2), 175–186 (1987).
22. Jack J. Dongarra, Jeremy Du Croz, Sven Hammarling and Richard J. Hanson, 'An extended set of Fortran basic linear algebra subprograms', *ACM Transactions on Mathematical Software*, **14**(1), 1–17 (1988).
23. Jack J. Dongarra and Iain S. Duff, 'Advanced computer architectures', Technical Report CS-89-90, University of Tennessee (1989).
24. Jeremy Du Croz, Private communication (1987).
25. The Parallel Computing Forum, *PCF Fortran: Language Definition*. Kuck and Associates, Champaign, IL (1988).
26. K. Gallivan, R. Plemmons and A. Sameh, 'Parallel algorithms for dense matrix computations', *SIAM Review*, **32**, 54–135 (1990).
27. B. Garbow, J. Boyle, J. Dongarra and C. Moler. *Matrix Eigensystem Routines — EISPACK Guide Extension*. Vol. 51 of *Lecture Notes in Computer Science*, Springer Verlag, New York (1977).
28. Gene H. Golub and Charles F. Van Loan, *Matrix Computations*, 2nd edn, The Johns Hopkins Press, Baltimore, MD (1989).
29. Kai Hwang and Fayé A. Briggs, *Computer Architecture and Parallel Processing*, McGraw-Hill, New York (1984).
30. W. Kahan, 'Accurate eigenvalues of a symmetric tridiagonal matrix', Computer Science Dept. Technical Report CS41, Stanford University, Stanford, CA, July (1966). (Revised June 1968.)
31. C. Lawson, R. Hanson, D. Kincaid and F. Krogh, 'Basic linear algebra subprograms for fortran usage', *ACM Transactions on Mathematical Software*, **5**, 308–323 (1979).
32. S.-S. Lo, B. Phillipe and A. Sameh, 'A multiprocessor algorithm for the symmetric eigenproblem', *SIAM J. Sci. Stat. Comp.*, **8**(2), 155–165 (1987).
33. Robert Schreiber and Charles Van Loan, 'A storage efficient WY representation for products of Householder transformations', *SIAM Journal on Stat. and Sci. Compt.*, **10**(1), 53–57 (1989).
34. A. Van Der Sluis, 'Condition numbers and equilibration of matrices', *Numerische Mathematik*, **14**, 14–23 (1969).
35. B. Smith, J. Boyle, J. Dongarra, B. Garbow, Y. Ikebe, V. Klema and C. B. Moler, *Matrix Eigensystem Routines — EISPACK Guide*, 2nd edn, Springer-Verlag, New York (1976).
36. Per Stenström, 'Reducing contention in shared-memory multiprocessors', *IEEE Computer*, **21**(11), 26–37 (1988).
37. Harold Stone, *High-Performance Computer Architecture*, Addison-Wesley, Reading, MA (1987).

CONCURRENCY: PRACTICE AND EXPERIENCE, VOL. 3(6), 667–685 (DECEMBER 1991)

Numerical simulation of incompressible fluid flows

GEORGE ANAGNOSTOU
Ocean Engineering
MIT, Cambridge, MA, USA

YVON MADAY
Laboratoire d'Analyse Numerique
Université Pierre et Marie Curie, Paris, France

ANTHONY T. PATERA
Mechanical Engineering
MIT, Cambridge, MA, USA

PAUL F. FISCHER
California Institute of Technology
Pasadena, CA, USA

EINAR M. RØNQUIST
Nektonics
Cambridge, MA, USA

SUMMARY

In this paper we discuss temporal, spatial, and architectural aspects of the numerical simulation of time-dependent incompressible fluid flows. In particular, we consider: high-order operator-integration-factor time-splitting methods; sliding-mesh spectral mortar-element spatial discretizations; and data-parallel distributed-memory medium-grained parallel solution techniques. Numerous flow examples are presented.

1. INTRODUCTION

Recent advances in numerical algorithms and parallel architectures have rendered many previously intractable problems in incompressible fluid mechanics amenable to meaningful analysis. Unfortunately, a great number of fundamentally and practically important flows remain beyond the reach of current computational procedures, primarily because of the intrinsic complexity of fluid mechanical phenomena. This complexity takes four forms: state complexity; scale complexity; constitutive complexity; and geometric complexity. We briefly describe each category:

(1) complexity refers to the sensitivity of nonlinear problems to initial conditions and other data. A common example of a flow which exhibits state complexity is thermal convection in an enclosure. State complexity creates numerical difficulty by requiring that a large number of calculations be performed in order to fully understand the solution space and associated stability regions.

(2) Scale complexity refers to the presence of a broad range of spatial or temporal scales. The most common example of *global* scale complexity is turbulence, in which instability and global nonlinearity give rise to a broad range of dynamically important wave numbers; an example of *local* scale complexity is the high Prandtl number forced convection boundary layer. Scale complexity creates numerical difficulty by requiring that a large number of degrees of freedom be retained in order to resolve the dynamically important flow structures.

(3) Constitutive complexity refers to the existence of many different physical phenomena in a single flow. Examples of constitutive complexity range from convection–diffusion coupling to surface tension–inertia coupling to multiple-

1040–3108/91/060667–19$09.50
Received 23 October 1990
Accepted 23 September 1991

relaxation-frequency rheology in non-Newtonian fluids. Constitutive complexity creates numerical difficulties in two ways: first, by creating state complexity (e.g. multi-parameter bifurcations), or parametric scale complexity (e.g. capillary waves on the ocean surface); second, by introducing 'mixed' mathematical forms that preclude the use of special solution strategies.

(4) Geometric complexity refers to the complicated geometrical configurations in which flows typically evolve; indeed, many flows evolve in *time-dependent* geometries, either prescribed or free. Complex domains create numerical difficulty in three ways: first, by creating geometrical and topological problems in the mesh generation and discretization process; second, by requiring that many degrees-of-freedom be retained in order to resolve the geometry and geometry-induced flow phenomena; and third, by precluding the use of the many efficient solvers based on symmetry or separability.

We contend that *high-order* methods that are *decoupling* are particularly appropriate for efficient (resource-minimal) solution of fluid flow problems exhibiting these complexities. *High-order* methods ensure that, when required, increased accuracy can be achieved at relatively low marginal cost; that is, the size of the computational problem is determined primarily by the physical problem, and not by numerical convergence properties. *Decoupling* is critical in that it strives to ensure that, in some sense, the computational time required to solve a problem $\mathcal{P}$ with several constituent 'subproblems' $\mathcal{P}_k$ (e.g., spatial or temporal scales, flow regions) is no greater than max $\mathcal{T}_k$, where $\mathcal{T}_k$ is the time required to solve the individual subproblem $\mathcal{P}_k$; non-decoupling methods can result in solution times of $\sum_k \mathcal{T}_k$ or worse. In this paper we describe temporal, spatial, and architectural approaches illustrative of the high-order decoupling theme.

The organization of the paper is as follows. In Section 2 we discuss high-order operator-integration-factor time-splitting methods for convection-Stokes decoupling in the Navier–Stokes equations; in Section 3, we describe minimally constrained sliding-mesh spectral mortar-element spatial discretizations applied to impeller mixer flows; lastly, in Section 4, we describe data-parallel distributed-memory medium-grained parallel solution techniques.

2. INTEGRATION-FACTOR TEMPORAL DECOUPLING

We consider in this paper the time-dependent incompressible Navier–Stokes equations in a domain Ω,

$$\frac{\partial \mathbf{u}}{\partial t} + \mathbf{u} \cdot \nabla \mathbf{u} = -\frac{1}{\rho}\nabla p + \nu \nabla^2 \mathbf{u} + \mathbf{f} \quad in \ \Omega \tag{1}$$

$$\nabla \cdot \mathbf{u} = 0 \ in \ \Omega \tag{2}$$

$$\mathbf{u} = 0 \ on \ \partial\Omega \tag{3}$$

where $\mathbf{u}(\mathbf{x}, t)$ is the velocity, $\mathbf{x}$ is position, t is time, $p(\mathbf{x},t)$ is the pressure, ρ is the density, and ν is the kinematic viscosity (or inverse Reynolds number). Dirichlet conditions are assumed on the domain boundary $\partial\Omega$. The incompressible Navier–Stokes equations are general enough to be applicable to a wide range of phenomena, yet specific enough to constitute an efficient solution procedure.

We next assume some stable spatial discretization of (1)–(3)[1]

$$\frac{d\underline{\mathbf{u}}_h}{dt} + \underline{C}_h(\underline{\mathbf{U}}_h)\underline{\mathbf{u}}_h = \frac{1}{\rho}\underline{\mathbf{D}}_h{}^T p_h + \nu \underline{L}_h \underline{\mathbf{u}}_h + \underline{\mathbf{f}}_h \qquad in \ \Omega \tag{4}$$

$$\underline{\mathbf{D}}_h \cdot \underline{\mathbf{u}}_h = 0 \qquad in \ \Omega \tag{5}$$

where $\underline{\mathbf{u}}_h$ refers to the algebraic (e.g. nodal) representation of a discretization $\mathbf{u}_h$ characterized by a 'mesh-spacing' parameter h, p_h is the associated pressure, $\underline{C}_h, \underline{\mathbf{D}}_h$, and $\underline{L}_h$ are the convection, gradient, and Laplacian matrices, respectively, and superscript T denotes transpose. Note that: all essential boundary conditions (3) are absorbed within the matrix definitions; for simplicity of exposition, the mass matrix is assumed to be the identity operator; for purposes of subsequent temporal discretization, we restrict the integration interval of (4) to $t_1 < t < t_2$, and write the quadratically non-linear convection operator as $\underline{C}_h(\underline{\mathbf{U}}_h)\underline{\mathbf{u}}_h$, where $\underline{\mathbf{U}}_h = \underline{\mathbf{u}}_h$ for the continuous-time case. Equations (4) and (5) can be summarized as

$$\frac{d\underline{\mathbf{u}}_h}{dt} + \underline{C}_h(\underline{\mathbf{U}}_h)\underline{\mathbf{u}}_h = \underline{S}_h \underline{\mathbf{u}}_h \qquad in \ \Omega \tag{6}$$

where $\underline{S}_h$ represents the discrete Stokes operator and associated boundary conditions.

The choice of temporal discretization is dictated by accuracy and stability requirements, as well as by consideration of the work required to invert the implicit spatial operators. As regards the latter, first, we claim that only those parts of an equation which can be solved rapidly (i.e. faster than time-like) should be treated implicitly, with all other operators handled explicitly; second, we claim that, certainly in three space dimensions, *iterative solvers* must be utilized owing to the bandwidth and parallelization problems associated with Gaussian elimination. As there are, to date, very few iterative approaches for the solution of non-symmetric problems that offer the robustness or performance of corresponding solvers for symmetric systems[2], many temporal discretizations of (6) are based upon explicit treatment of the convection operator and implicit treatment of the symmetric Stokes problem. One such (second-order) scheme is the following modified Adams-Bashforth/Backward Differentiation method[3,28],

$$\frac{3\underline{\mathbf{u}}_h^{n+1} - 4\underline{\mathbf{u}}_h^n + \underline{\mathbf{u}}_h^{n-1}}{2\Delta t} + \sum_{l=0}^{2} \alpha_l' \underline{C}_h(\underline{\mathbf{u}}_h^{n-l})\underline{\mathbf{u}}_h^{n-l} = \underline{S}_h \underline{\mathbf{u}}_h^{n+1} \tag{7}$$

where $\underline{\mathbf{u}}_h^n = \underline{\mathbf{u}}_{h\Delta t}(\mathbf{x}, t^n)$, $t^n = n\Delta t$, Δt is the timestep, and α_l' are the modified Adams–Bashforth coefficients. A consistent third-order method is readily derived from the Backward-Differentiation family as well.

The method (7) will be stable as $h \to 0$, $\Delta t \to 0$ only for $\Delta t < C_1 \min_\Omega \{|h|/|u|\}$. This Courant stability condition typically yields time steps, Δt, that are significantly smaller than required from accuracy considerations, even for time-dependent flows. Furthermore, this relatively small time step applies to both the convection *and* the Stokes operators; given that the Stokes operator is more expensive to *invert* than the convection operator is to *evaluate*, the virtues of semi-implicit time-stepping are at least partially lost owing to this strong temporal coupling between the convection and Stokes contributions. It is, therefore, clearly of interest to develop numerical schemes which more effectively decouple the numerical treatment of the convection term and the Stokes problem. We now describe such a (second-order) method.

To begin we take $t_1 = t^{n-1}$, $t_2 = t^{n+1}$, and linearize the convection operator by choosing $\underline{U}_h = \underline{U}_h^{\{n+1\}}$, where $\underline{U}_h^{\{n+1\}}$ is an approximation of $\underline{u}_h(t)$ over the time interval $[t^{n-1}, t^{n+1}]$ based on linear extrapolation of $\underline{u}_h^{n-1}$ and $\underline{u}_h^n$. We next introduce $\underline{Q}_h^{\{n+1\}}(t)$, the operator-integration-factor associated with the linearized convection operator,

$$\underline{Q}_h^{\{n+1\}}(t^{n+1}) = \underline{I} \tag{8}$$

$$\frac{d\underline{Q}_h^{\{n+1\}}}{dt'} = \underline{Q}_h^{\{n+1\}} \underline{C}_h(\underline{U}_h^{\{n+1\}}(t')) \qquad t < t' < t^{n+1} \tag{9}$$

where $\underline{I}$ is the identity matrix. It can then be shown[5] that $\underline{Q}_h^{\{n+1\}}(t)\underline{u}_h(t) = \tilde{\underline{u}}_h(t^{n+1})$, where

$$\frac{d\tilde{\underline{u}}_h}{dt'} = -\underline{C}_h(\underline{U}_h^{\{n+1\}}(t'))\tilde{\underline{u}}_h \qquad t < t' < t^{n+1} \tag{10}$$

$$\tilde{\underline{u}}_h(t' = t) = \underline{u}_h(t) \tag{11}$$

The matrix $\underline{Q}$ can be thought of as the influence or response matrix of the convection system, or, equivalently, as a Floquet matrix; note that it coincides with the usual exponential matrix only if $\underline{U}_h$ is not a function of time. Linearization of (6) is critical for proper consistency; fortunately, for the quadratically non-linear convection operator a simple linearization is available.

From the above definitions one transforms the linearized form of (6) in the usual integration-factor fashion (e.g., for a scalar equation) to give

$$\frac{d}{dt}\left\{\underline{Q}_h^{\{n+1\}}\underline{u}_h\right\} = \underline{Q}_h^{\{n+1\}}\underline{S}_h\underline{u}_h \tag{12}$$

which is then discretized by the second-order Backward Differentiation scheme

$$\frac{3\underline{u}_h^{n+1} - 4\underline{Q}_h^{\{n+1\}}(t^n)\underline{u}_h^n + \underline{Q}_h^{\{n+1\}}(t^{n-1})\underline{u}_h^{n-1}}{2\Delta t} = \underline{S}_h\underline{u}_h^{n+1} \tag{13}$$

The $\underline{Q}_h^{\{n+1\}}(t^n)\underline{u}_h^n$, $\underline{Q}_h^{\{n+1\}}(t^{n-1})\underline{u}_h^{n-1}$ are then determined by (at least second-order) multi-stage Runge–Kutta approximation[3] of (10) and (11) with a subcycle timestep $\Delta s < \Delta t$, where Δs is determined by the usual Courant condition. A third-order scheme is readily derived as well. The essence of the decoupling is that no convection appears in (13), thereby allowing large time steps for the Stokes problem; no pressure appears in (10) and (11), thereby allowing inexpensive explicit treatment of convection.

We make several comments concerning the operator-integration-factor approach. First, for the convection problem the operator-integration-factor approach is equivalent to a high-order synthesis of previous characteristic[6] and subcycling approaches[7], as described in detail in[5]. Second, the operator-integration-factor approach is, in fact, much more general than the convection–Stokes decoupling described here. To yield high-order convergence, however, the operator split apart, say A, must satisfy $Av = 0$ on $\partial\Omega$ for all admissible v; if this condition is not satisfied there will be an initial-condition compatibility problem in the subproblem (10) and (11). Fortunately, this hypothesis holds for the convection operator. Third, we note that there *is* a restriction on Δt even in (13), related to the sharpening of gradients in the convection step (10); this condition is, however, much weaker, and much less mesh-dependent, than the usual Courant condition.

We illustrate application of the technique by considering natural convection flow in the annular enclosure shown in Figure 1 at a Rayleigh number of 10,000. The problem is solved by a third-order scheme similar to (13), with a time step, Δt, 16 times larger than that required for stability by the semi-implicit scheme (7). The spatial discretization is the $I\!\!P_N \times I\!\!P_{N-2}$ conforming spectral element approximation[8,9]; the Stokes solver is a Uzawa conjugate–gradient/conjugate–gradient nested iteration[10]. Owing to the significant reduction in the number of Stokes (pressure) solves required, the operator-integration-factor approach attains the same final time of integration as the semi-implicit scheme (7) at one-tenth the computational effort. The fact that the operator-integration-factor approach is high-order in time is critical, in that it ensures that these computational savings—effected by increases in the timestep, Δt—are achieved without compromising the accuracy of the solution. A more detailed discussion of this issue is given in[5,4].

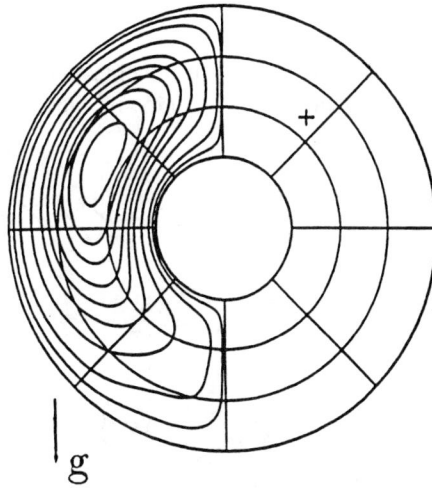

Figure 1. *Streamlines of steady natural convection flow in an annular enclosure at a Rayleigh number of* $Ra = g\beta\Delta TD^3/\alpha\nu = 10,000$, $Pr = \nu/\alpha = 0.71$, *where g is the acceleration of gravity, β is the thermal expansion coefficient, ΔT is the temperature elevation of the inner cylinder, D is the diameter of the outer cylinder, and ν and α are the momentum and thermal diffusivities, respectively. The inner cylinder is of diameter D/3*

We close this section by remarking that the operator-integration-factor scheme addresses only one issue of complexity arising from convection–diffusion coupling—namely, the complication of the mathematical operators. Although the method does eliminate the mesh dependence of the diffusion–convection timescale ratio, this ratio remains at $1/\nu$ for closed-streamline or periodic flows. Thus, although giving order-of-magnitude improvements, the operator-integration-factor approach does not obviate the need for better steady-state solvers to eliminate parametric stiffness.

3. MORTAR-METHOD SPATIAL DECOUPLING

In order to treat the many forms of spatial heterogeneity arising in complex flows, it is critical to develop spatial discretizations that are as local, and as decoupled, as possible. Decoupled discretizations can, for example, effect local refinement in boundary layers without tensor-product mesh propagation, or ease the mesh-generation and mesh-evolution process in time-dependent configurations. Local spatial discretizations are typically low-order, and it thus remains a challenge to construct schemes that are both relatively local *and* exhibit high-order convergence. In this section we describe a locally structured, globally unstructured highly decoupled spatial discretization which achieves spectral convergence rates.

3.1. Time-independent configurations

To begin, we consider the heat equation for $u(\mathbf{x}, t)$

$$\frac{\partial u}{\partial t} = \nabla^2 u + f \qquad in \ \Omega \tag{14}$$

$$u = 0 \qquad on \ \partial\Omega \tag{15}$$

where $\overline{\Omega} = \overline{\Omega}^{(1)} \cup \overline{\Omega}^{(2)}$ is the stationary ($\omega = 0$) impeller-in-chamber geometry shown in Figure 2. The variational statement of (14) and (15) is: Find $u \in H_0^1(\Omega)$ such that

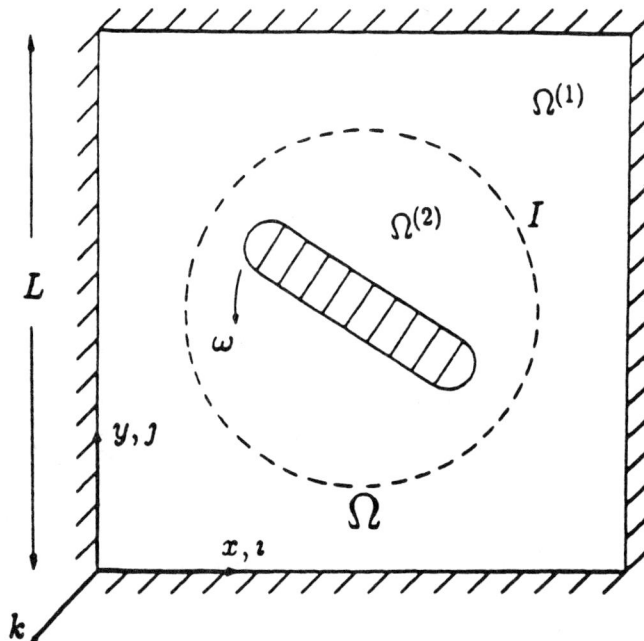

Figure 2. Geometry of the impeller mixer, comprising a square mixing chamber and a semi-circular-tipped impeller

$$(v, u_t) = -(\nabla v, \nabla u) + (v, f) \qquad \forall v \in H_0^1(\Omega) \qquad (16)$$

where $H_0^1(\Omega) = \{v \in H^1(\Omega), v|_{\partial\Omega} = 0\}$ and $(\cdot, \cdot)$ is the usual L^2 inner product. By integration by parts the form (16) already requires one less derivative than (14); however, this does not always provide sufficient flexibility, as we now describe.

If we choose to discretize (14) and (15) by a conforming spectral element method[11,8,9], we first break the domain into (possibly deformed) quadrangles $\Omega^{(q)k}$, $\overline{\Omega}^{(q)} = \bigcup_{k=1}^{K(q)} \overline{\Omega}^{(q)k}$ as shown in Figure 3. We next define the spectral element spaces

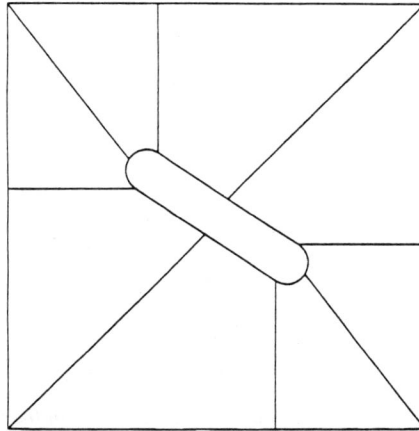

Figure 3. Conforming spectral element discretization of the impeller mixer

$$X_h = \left\{ v|_{\Omega^{(q)k}} \in I\!\!P_N(\Omega^{(q)k}) \right\} \cap H_0^1(\Omega) \qquad (17)$$

where $I\!\!P_N(\Omega^{(q)k})$ refers to the space of all polynomials over $\Omega^{(q)k}$ of order $\leq N$ in both local co-ordinates. The spectral element equations are then: Find $u_h \in X_h$ such that

$$(v, u_{ht})_h = -(\nabla v, \nabla u_h)_h + (v, f)_h \qquad \forall v \in X_h \qquad (18)$$

where $(\cdot, \cdot)_h$ refers to N^{th} order Gauss-Lobatto-Legendre tensor-product quadrature of the continuous L^2 inner product. The discrete statement is completed by specification of a tensor product Gauss-Lobatto-Legendre Lagrangian interpolant basis for representation of u_h; the nodal points and associated dependent-variable values will be denoted $\underline{x}$ ($=x_p$) and $\underline{u}_h$, respectively. The spectral element discretization is locally structured for efficiency, globally unstructured for geometric flexibility, and relatively decoupled between subdomains. Furthermore, the method is high-order, with spectral convergence as $N \to \infty$, and exponential convergence for sufficiently smooth problems[8,12].

It is clear, however, that a preferred decomposition of the mixer domain is as shown in Figure 4, with each object (impeller and chamber) meshed *independently*, and subsequently brought together. Unfortunately, for this choice of $\Omega^{(q)k}$, $u_h \in X_h$ is equivalent to the requirement that $u_h|_I$ be a *global* N^{th}-order polynomial over I, where $I = \partial\Omega^{(1)} \cap \partial\Omega^{(2)}$. This restriction greatly increases the coupling of the discrete equations, while simultaneously decreasing the accuracy of the method. In order to exploit the decomposition of Figure 4 the functional requirements (17) must be relaxed in order to maintain local error estimates and minimal coupling. To this end, we consider the mortar element method[13–16], in which functional glue, or 'mortar', is introduced to permit non-conforming discretizations.

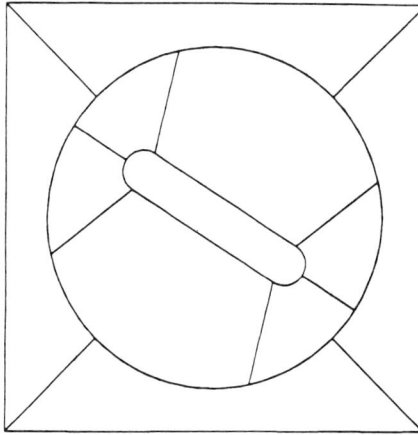

Figure 4. Nonconforming spectral mortar-element discretization of the impeller mixer; the chamber and impeller flow regions are meshed independently, and subsequently brought together

To begin, we define the 'skeleton' of mortars

$$S = \bigcup_{m=1}^{M} \overline{\gamma}^m \tag{19}$$

where $S = I$, and each mortar γ^m coincides with some (open) edge $\Gamma^{(1)kj}$, $j = 1,\ldots,4$, of some element $k = 1,\ldots,K^{(1)}$ in $\Omega^{(1)}$, with $\gamma^m \cap \gamma^n = \emptyset$. We then define the set $E_I^{(2)}$ of all couples (k, j) such that $\Gamma^{(2)kj} \cap I$ is non empty, and the set $V_I^{(2)}$ of all couples (k, j) such that some vertex $v^{(2)kj}$, $j = 1,\ldots,4$, of some element $k = 1,\ldots,K^{(2)}$ lies on I. We then define the nonconforming space as

$$W = \{ \ \phi \in C^0(S), \ \phi|_{\gamma^m} \in I\!\!P_N(\gamma^m)\} \tag{20}$$

$$X_h^* = \{ \ v \in L^2(\Omega); \ v|_{\Omega^{(q)k}} \in I\!\!P_N(\Omega^{(q)k}); \tag{21}$$

$$\exists \phi \in W \text{ such that:}$$

$$v^{(1)}|_I = \phi;$$

$$\int_{\Gamma^{(2)kj}} (v^{(2)} - \phi)\psi \, ds = 0 \qquad \forall \psi \in I\!\!P_{N-2}(\Gamma^{(2)kj}),$$

$$\forall \{k,j\} \in E_l^{(2)};$$

$$v^{(2)}(v^{(2)kj}) = \phi(v^{(2)kj}) \qquad \forall (k,j) \in V_l^{(2)} \qquad \}$$

where $v^{(q)} = v|_{\Omega^{(q)}}$. The resulting method is given by: Find $u_h \in X_h^*$ such that

$$(v, u_{h\,t})_h = -(\nabla v, \nabla u_h)_h + (v, f)_h \qquad \forall v \in X_h^* \qquad (22)$$

The method is optimal as regards stability, approximation, and consistency, and is local not only in approximation error, but also in that, unlike Lagrange-multiplier methods, only degrees of freedom in Ω^k, Ω^l such that $\overline{\Omega}^k \cap \overline{\Omega}^l$ is non-empty couple algebraically.

3.2. Time-dependent configurations

We now describe the case where the geometry is time-dependent, using as an example the problem of Figure 2 with the impeller now rotating with non-zero angular velocity ω. It is clear that one (unacceptable) solution to the resulting mesh-generation problem is a complete remeshing of Ω at each time step. A much preferred solution, both from implementation and efficiency considerations, is a sliding-mesh solution, in which nodal points in $\Omega^{(1)}$ remain fixed, but nodal points $\mathbf{x}_q^{(2)} \in \Omega^{(2)}$ move with the impeller,

$$\frac{d\mathbf{x}_q^{(2)}}{dt} = \omega \mathbf{k} \times (\mathbf{x} - \mathbf{x}_c) \qquad (23)$$

where $\mathbf{k}$ is the unit vector $i \times j$, $\mathbf{x}=xi + yj$, and $\mathbf{x}_c$ denotes the center of the impeller. Note that (23) is not a change of reference frame, but rather a change of basis, or mapping. The mortar method is critical in providing the proper matching, (20) and (21), between 'decoupled', autonomously evolving meshes.

The final set of equations for the heat equation (14) in the time-dependent rotating impeller configuration are[15,17]: Find $u_h \in X_h^*(t)$ such that

$$(v, u_h)_{h\,t} - (v\,\omega \mathbf{k} \times (\mathbf{x} - \mathbf{x}_c), \nabla u_h)_h = -(\nabla v, \nabla u_h)_h + (v, f)_h \qquad \forall v \in X_h^*(t) \qquad (24)$$

where $X_h^*(t)$ is given by (20) and (21), with the time argument referring to the fact that $\Omega^{(2)k}$, $E_l^{(2)}$, and $V_l^{(2)}$ are now evolving according to (23). The second term on the left-hand side of (24) is the Lagrangian–Eulerian term resulting from the time-dependent basis.

It can be shown that the method (24) incurs errors no larger than those of the standard non-conforming discretization. Rather than review these results here, we instead demonstrate that the method is sufficiently robust and efficient to perform calculations of physical interest. The following calculations are based on Navier–Stokes extensions of (24) combined with the (semi-implicit) temporal discretizations described in Section 2.

3.3. Impeller mixing

We consider the problem of Figure 2 with rotating impeller, for which the non-dimensional equations are

$$\frac{\partial \hat{\mathbf{u}}}{\partial t} + \hat{\mathbf{u}} \cdot \nabla \hat{\mathbf{u}} = -\frac{1}{\rho}\nabla \hat{p} + \frac{1}{R}\nabla^2 \hat{\mathbf{u}} \qquad \text{in } \Omega(t) \tag{25}$$

$$\nabla \cdot \hat{\mathbf{u}} = 0 \qquad \text{in } \Omega(t) \tag{26}$$

$$\hat{\mathbf{u}} = 0 \qquad \text{on } \partial\Omega \cap \partial\Omega^{(1)} \tag{27}$$

$$\hat{\mathbf{u}} = \mathbf{k} \times (\mathbf{x} - \mathbf{x}_c) \qquad \text{on } \partial\Omega \cap \partial\Omega^{(2)} \tag{28}$$

$$\frac{\partial \hat{T}}{\partial \hat{t}} + \hat{\mathbf{u}} \cdot \nabla \hat{T} = \frac{1}{R\,Pr}\nabla^2 \hat{T} \qquad \text{in } \Omega(t) \tag{29}$$

$$\frac{\partial \hat{T}}{\partial \hat{n}} = 0 \qquad \left\{ \begin{array}{l} \text{on } \partial\Omega \cap \partial\Omega^{(2)} \\ \text{vertical } \partial\Omega \cap \partial\Omega^{(1)} \end{array} \right. \tag{30}$$

$$\hat{T} = \left\{ \begin{array}{ll} 0 & \text{top} \\ 1 & \text{bottom} \end{array} \right\} \text{ walls of } \partial\Omega \cap \partial\Omega^{(1)} \tag{31}$$

where the circumflex denotes non-dimensional variables. Here $\hat{\mathbf{u}} = \mathbf{u}/\omega L$, $\hat{\mathbf{x}} = \mathbf{x}/L$, $\hat{t} = \omega t$, $\hat{T} = (T - T_0)/(T_1 - T_0)$, $R = \omega L^2/\nu$, and $Pr = \nu/\alpha$, where L is the chamber side length, T_1 and T_0 are the bottom and top wall temperatures, respectively, and ν and α are the momentum and thermal diffusivities, respectively. The two quantities of interest are the heat transfer rate (Nusselt number) and dissipation (power consumption)

$$Nu = -\int_0^1 \frac{\partial \hat{T}}{\partial \hat{y}}(\hat{x}, \hat{y} = 0)\, d\hat{x} \tag{32}$$

$$\Phi = \frac{1}{2R}\int_\Omega (\nabla \hat{\mathbf{u}} + \nabla \hat{\mathbf{u}}^T) \cdot (\nabla \hat{\mathbf{u}} + \nabla \hat{\mathbf{u}}^T)\, d\hat{x} \tag{33}$$

respectively, and their time averages (for the steady-periodic state), $< Nu >$ and $< \Phi >$. Note the impeller is of length $L/2$ and thickness $L/10$, with the last $L/10$ of each tip of the impeller represented by a semi-circle of diameter $L/10$.

At very low Reynolds numbers, for example, $R = 1$ ($Pr = 1$) the problem reduces to a quasi-steady Stokes/conduction problem, for which we find $< Nu >= 0.85$, $< \Phi >= 0.47$; the Nusselt number is less than unity owing to the insulating effect of the impeller. The velocity vector field is shown in Figure 5. At higher Reynolds numbers, $R = 1000$, we notice that, at least for this two-dimensional calculation, the velocity vector field, Figure 6, is quite similar to the Stokes solution. This might be expected given the relatively small departure from azimuthal symmetry of the square chamber. However, the temperature field, Figure 7, departs significantly from the conduction solution owing to the fact that the temperature boundary conditions (31) break azimuthal symmetry. This results in high heat transfer rates, as is well known from studies of enhancement by 'interrupted' boundary layers. We find, at $R = 1000$, $< \Phi >= 0.0073$, $< Nu >= 2.7$. Although higher Reynolds numbers, three-dimensional calculations, and perhaps turbulence models are

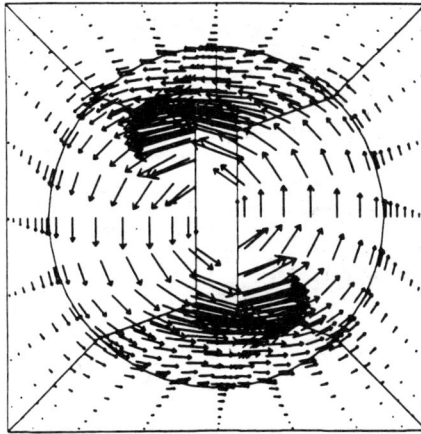

Figure 5. Velocity vectors at one instant in time (that is, one impeller location) for the steady-periodic solution at $R = 1$

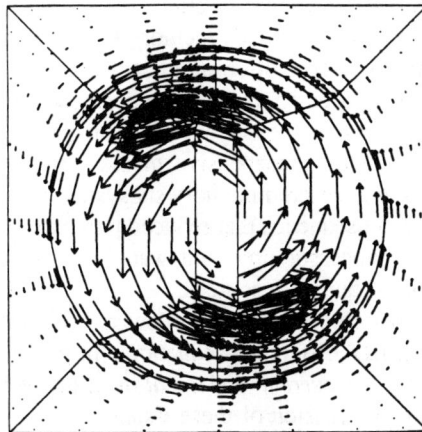

Figure 6. Velocity vectors at one instant in time for the steady-periodic solution at $R = 1000$. The solution resembles the Stokes solution owing to the near-azimuthal symmetry of the mixing chamber

required before comparisons with real impellers[18] can be made, these preliminary calculations already indicate possible avenues of optimization.

Other applications of sliding meshes include the study of rotor–stator interactions, the analysis of propellers and propulsion systems, and the free motion of bodies in internal and external flows. Previous work on sliding meshes has been low-order, and has been applied either to structural problems[19], or to fluid flows in which the interface I occurs in an Euler, not Navier–Stokes, region of the flow[20,21]; high-order Navier–Stokes results, are, to our knowledge, new.

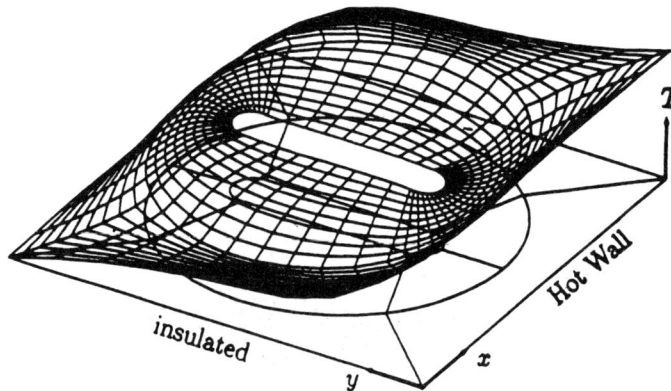

Figure 7. Temperature distribution at one instant in time at $R = 1000$, $Pr = 1$. The temperature distribution deviates appreciably from the conduction solution (essentially $T = 1 - \hat{y}$) owing to the non-azimuthally symmetric boundary conditions on the temperature

4. PARALLEL DECOUPLING

In this section we describe parallel solution of (conforming) spectral element Navier–Stokes discretizations on distributed-memory medium-grained parallel machines. Distributed-memory multi–processors offer significant economic advantages over serial machines: first, M commodity processors each operating at a speed s/M cost significantly less than a single special-purpose processor operating at speed s; second, multiple paths to memory permit relatively slow, inexpensive memory to effect the same aggregate bandwidth as an expensive single shared-memory subsystem. These economic advantages are further enhanced by the consequence that reduced purchase cost permits departmental supercomputers, for which processor time and wall-clock time are synonymous, thus leading to better utilization of human resources.

The availability of fast, cost-efficient machines does not necessarily imply their efficient utilization for solution of partial differential equations. In particular, algorithms must be devised that are sufficiently *concurrent* and *local* to effectively exploit the available resources. We now turn to a discussion of these issues.

4.1. Native processor

We first describe the performance of the (conforming) spectral element algorithms presented in the previous sections on a 'native' data-parallel architecture, that is, an architecture which is ideally matched to our particular algorithmic requirements. To begin, K spectral elements are partitioned amongst $M < K$ independent processor/memory units, $P_1, \ldots, P_M$, as shown in Figure 8. (Our terminology will be two-dimensional; however, the methods readily extend to three space dimensions.) We denote the set of all elements $E = \{1, \ldots, K\}$, and the set of elements associated with processor P_q as $E_q = \{\ldots\}$, with $E = \bigcup_q E_q$, and $E_p \bigcap E_q = \emptyset$ for $p \neq q$; we assume load balance in the sense that all processors have an equal number of elements. The communication network of the native parallel processor is assumed to satisfy two constraints:

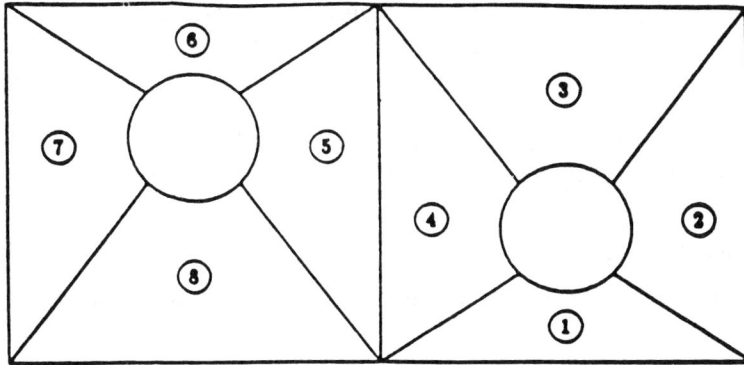

(a)

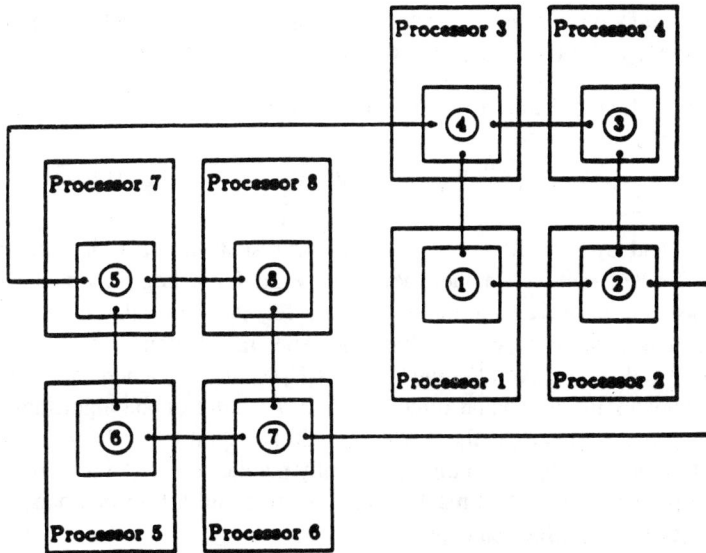

(b)

Figure 8. (a) Spectral element decomposition for a multiply connected domain, with elements numbers in ◯. (b) Associated 'native' parallel processor

(1) a distinct, direct link must exist between two processors P_p and P_q for each distinct pair of elements (m,n) $m \in E_p$, $n \in E_q$ that share an edge;

(2) a summation of M values distributed over M processors must be performed in $O(\log M)$ communication steps (or less).

These two requirements relate directly to the two communication constructs central to our algorithms.

We characterize the 'hardware' associated with the processors and sparse communication networks in Figure 8 by a basic clock cycle for calculation, δ, and the time-per-word required to send m words across a direct link, $\Delta(m)$. It is assumed that data transfer can occur simultaneously over all distinct links. The ratio Δ/δ is denoted $\sigma(m)$; $\sigma(m)$ is assumed to be a decreasing function of m, with $\sigma(1)$ appreciably greater than $\sigma(\infty)$ due to message startup overhead. Messages travelling more than one link (or 'hop') can be penalized in terms of both longer transmission time and potential contention; contention represents network imbalance/saturation, and arises when more than one potentially parallel communication requires the same link.

4.2. Parallel algorithms

The spectral element iterative algorithms comprise, to leading order, three essential operations:

(1) evaluation of residuals within an element, with computational work (number of operations) W_R per spectral element;
(2) summation of residuals between elements sharing edges, with W_S data per edge;
(3) vector reduction, or inner product calculations (e.g. to determine new search directions), with order-unity data communicated per processor.

The resulting 'wall-clock' time for solution on M processors, τ_M, can then be written

$$\tau_M = c_4 \left\{ c_1 \delta \frac{K}{M} W_R + c_2 \Delta(W_S) W_S + c_3 \Delta(1) \log_2 M \right\} \qquad (34)$$

where c_1, c_2, and c_3 are order unity, and c_4 represents number of iterations and/or time steps. This equation is, in fact, generally valid for a large class of substructure discretizations and iterative solution strategies; for the particular case of conjugate gradient iterative solution of elliptic (Poisson) spectral element spatial discretizations $W_R \sim O(N^{d+1})$, $W_S \sim O(N^{d-1})$, and $c_4 \sim O(K_1 N)$ in $\mathbb{R}^d$, where K_1 is the number of spectral elements in one spatial direction. A key feature of the algorithms presented earlier in this paper, for example the convection–Stokes splitting of Section 2, is that they improve performance while remaining intrinsically parallelizable. An in-depth analysis of (34), with empirical fits to actual machine data, is given in[22]; in this paper we restrict ourselves to several essential features.

First, the dominant term in (34) scales as $1/M$ owing to the concurrency and locality intrinsic to our parallel algorithms; this concurrency and locality derive first, from the use of iterative solvers, and second, from the natural (numerical) granularity afforded by a single spectral element. The ratio $W_R/W_S \gg 1$ reflects the fact that most data required by processor P_q are, in fact, resident on processor P_q; furthermore, any data transfer that is required is local in physical, if not processor, space, leading to highly parallel communication. The hierarchy $W_R \gg W_S \gg 1$ ensures that, even in the presence of realistic $\sigma \gg 1$, reasonable parallel efficiencies can be obtained. Here (same-algorithm) parallel speed-up and efficiency are defined in the usual fashion, $S_M = \tau_1/\tau_M$ and $\eta = S_M/M$, respectively. Note τ_1 is calculated by extrapolation of a least-squares fit of computational performance on M' processors for several $M' > 1$; memory limitations prohibit direct measurement of τ_1 in most cases.

Second, we note that the balance between the $1/M$ and $\log M$ terms in (34) yields the speed-up-optimal number of processors for a particular problem, M_{opt}. It is immediately apparent that M_{opt} scales with K (problem size), confirming that our algorithm is, indeed, medium-grained; that is, as the problem size grows, M increases, but the number of degrees of freedom per processor remains large—N^d for spectral elements in $\boldsymbol{R}^d$, with N, the polynomial order, $O(10)$ in most applications. It follows that roughly constant computer time τ can be achieved for all problems by scaling M with K; this, not arbitrarily large speed-up for a fixed problem, is a realizable goal of parallel processing[23]. Note that the use of Jacobi iteration, rather than conjugate gradient iteration, eliminates the majority of the $\log_2 M$ operations in (34). However, c_4 for Jacobi iteration is roughly the square of that for conjugate gradient iteration, illustrating a typical compromise between parallel efficiency and overall performance.

4.3. Intel vector hypercube implementation

We have implemented our parallel spectral element iterative Navier–Stokes solvers on $M = 2^D$-node Intel vector hypercubes, the iPSC/1-VX/dD and its successor, the iPSC/2-VX/dD. The iPSC/1-VX is a 286-based system with store-and-forward message-passing; the iPSC/2-VX is a 386-based system with pipelined communication routing. In both cases the same vector hardware is used, capable of a peak speed of 10 Mflops/board. The two machines differ primarily in scalar speed and communication speed and robustness, with the iPSC/2 representing a significant improvement in both capabilities due to advances in technology and architecture. These MIMD Intel message-passing hypercubes are clearly similar to our model system of Figure 8, and therefore represent a relatively simple port, in 'single-program-multiple-data' fashion, of the virtual-parallel-processor code which embodies the native system described in Section 4.1. Although hypercube networks do honor our log M communication requirement, they may not honor the nearest-neighbor requirement; mapping issues are discussed in detail in[24,25].

To illustrate the performance of the spectral element–hypercube algorithm–archictecture coupling we consider solution of the three-dimensional steady-Stokes problem in the complex duct geometry shown in Figure 9(a). The flow is periodic in the flow direction, with no-slip boundary conditions imposed on all solid walls. The discretization parameter is taken to be $h = (K = 32, N = 10)$, corresponding to 80,000 degrees of freedom. The problem is solved on $M=16$ processors using the Uzawa conjugate gradient/conjugate gradient nested iteration procedure describe in the context of the Navier–Stokes equations in Section 2. The results of the calculation are shown in Figure 9(b) in terms of the velocity field at the midplane of the channel. We note that the duct cylinder problem does not correspond to a Cartesian or regular mesh, and, inasmuch exercises the full generality of our parallel constructs[22,25].

The iPSC/2-VX/d4 obtains the solution to the problem of Figure 9 in approximately 130 seconds, with a parallel efficiency of $\eta = 0.75$. The non-vector iPSC/2-/d4 obtains the solution in 5760 seconds, but with a parallel efficiency of $\eta = 0.99$. From this comparison we draw two conclusions. First, vectorization (or pipelining) internal to the hypercube nodes is critical to performance; the nested parallel/vector unstructured/structured hierarchy of the spectral element discretization is ideally suited for the task. Second, parallel efficiency is not a reliable measure by which to compare different machines (or, for that matter, algorithms); the non-vector machine achieves high efficiency due to a decrease in σ brought about by an increase in δ, not a decrease in Δ. We note that the iPSC/1-VX/d4 obtains the solution in 360 seconds with an efficiency

(a)

(b)

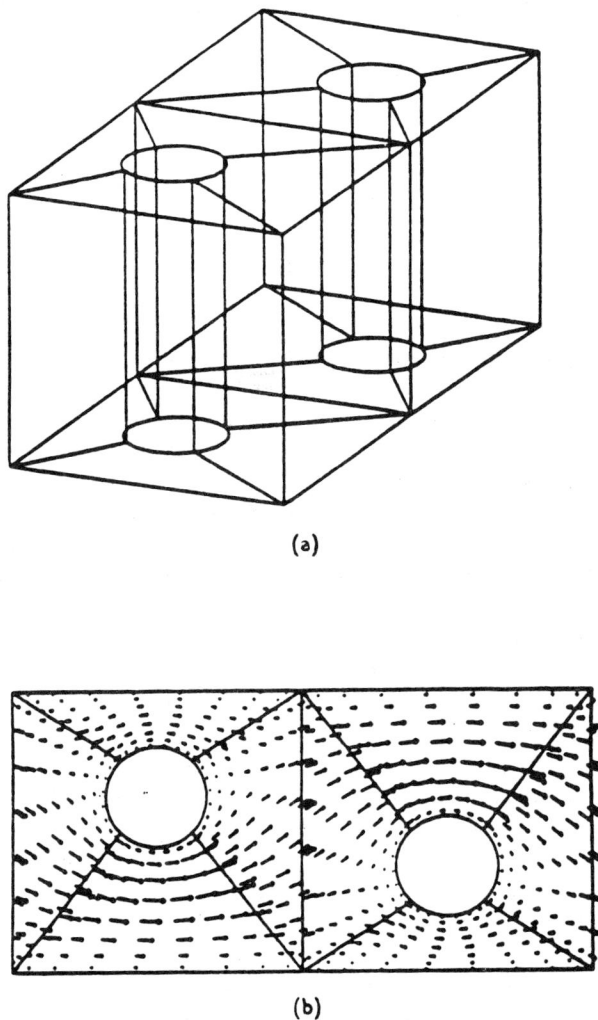

Figure 9. (a) Computational domain comprising $K = 32$ spectral elements (only eight are shown for clarity) for the steady Stokes problem of flow past two cylinders in a duct. (b) Velocity vectors at the midplane of the domain

of $\eta = 0.25$; the improvement in efficiency of the iPSC/2-VX/d4 with respect to the iPSC/1-VX/d4 is 'real' in the sense that it is brought about by an effective decrease in Δ, and thus results in a decrease in computation time.

We can avoid some of the inconsistencies and ambiguities associated with parallel efficiency comparisons of algorithm–architecture couplings by turning to a more rational (s,e) characterization; here s is speed measured in Mflops (millions of floating-point operations/second), and $e = s/fC$, where C is the cost of the machine, and f is the fraction of the machine requisitioned. An increase in s represents a decrease in computation time, whereas an increase in e represents a decrease in direct computer costs. Mflops are determined by comparative timings based on a conservative standard

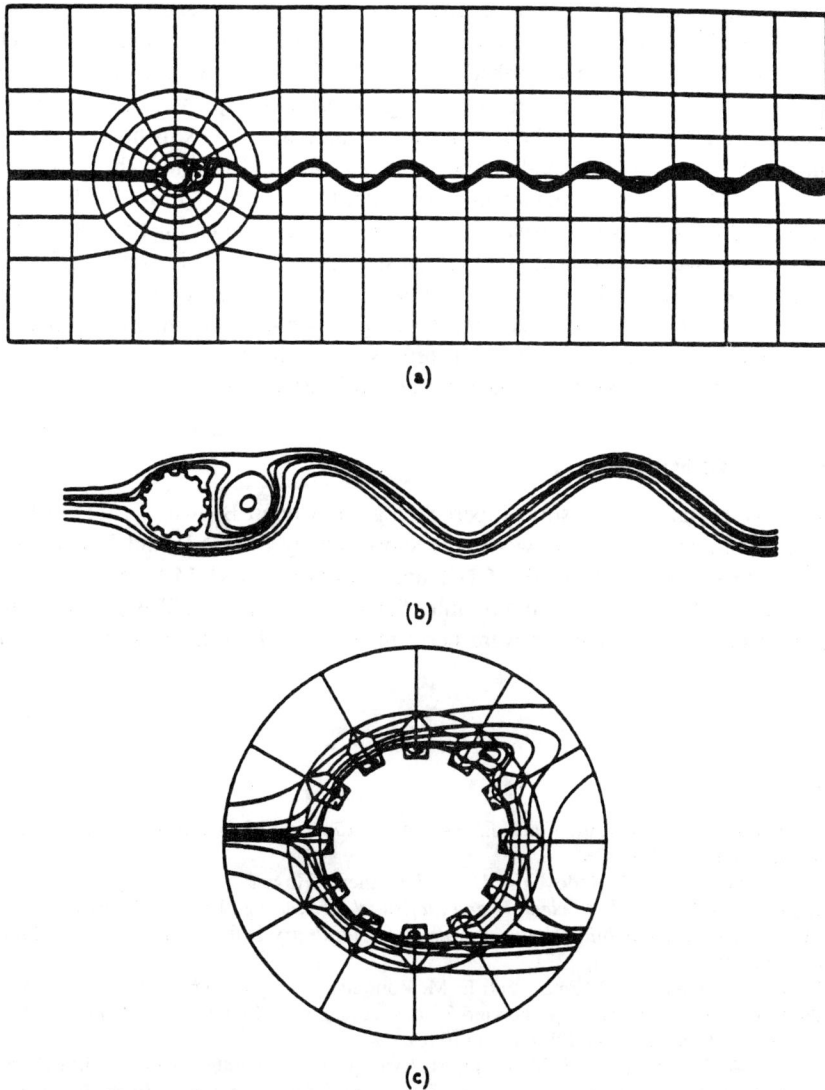

Figure 10. Flow past a grooved ('roughened' cylinder) at $Re_D = 200$: (a) vortex street and spectral element discretization; (b) and (c) enlarged views revealing broad range of scales present in the flow. Non-conforming approximations will provide a more efficient discretization for this multi-scale flow

of 0.1 Mflops for a MICROVAX II. For the calculation of Figure 9 the iPSC/2-VX/d4 achieves ($s = 44$ Mflops, $e = 12 \times 10^{-5}$ Mflops/\$), whereas the non-vector iPSC/2-/d4 achieves a very uninteresting ($s = 1$ Mflops, $e = 0.5 \times 10^{-5}$ Mflops/\$). Most importantly, the same calculation on the CRAY 2/4-256($M=1$) achieves approximately ($s = 66$ Mflops, $e = 1.7 \times 10^{-5}$ Mflops/\$); this result indicates that properly designed numerical algorithms can solve real problems on parallel processors at serial-supercomputer speeds, using only a fraction of serial-supercomputer resources.

More detailed descriptions and analyses of our parallel algorithms are given in[22,26,27,25]. Numerous Intel vector hypercube Navier–Stokes calculations, such as that shown in Figure 10, are described in[26] and [25]. Our current parallel work is focussed on two areas. First, we are embarking on parallel implementation of the non-conforming discretizations described in Section 3; although (34) still holds in the non-conforming case, generalized parallel constructs are required to effect the edge–mortar transfers. Second, we are implementing our algorithms on the new i860-based Intel hypercube. Scaling predictions—based on (34) and i860 data indicating fivefold decreases in δ and $\Delta(1)$ over the iPSC/2-VX—suggest expected 32-node i860 performance on Navier–Stokes calculations of close to 400 Mflops, at a resource efficiency of $e = 6 \times 10^{-4}$ Mflops/$. Initial tests with the i860 hypercube are, indeed, encouraging; a fairly *unoptimized* Stokes code on a 16-processor machine achieves ($s = 83$ Mflops, $e = 21 \times 10^{-5}$ Mflops/$) on the problem described in Figure 9.

ACKNOWLEDGEMENTS

We would like to thank Professors Gilbert Strang and Robert Brown of MIT for helpful suggestions and comments. This work was supported by the ONR and DARPA under Contract N00014-89-J-1610, by the ONR under Contract N00014-88-K-0188, by the NSF under Grant ASC-8806925, and by Intel Scientific Computers. The non-conforming sliding-mesh impeller calculations were performed on the MIT Supercomputer Facility CRAY-2.

REFERENCES

1. V. Girault and P. A. Raviart, *Finite Element Approximation of the Navier–Stokes Equations*, Springer Verlag, Berlin, 1986.
2. N. M. Nachtigaal, S. C. Reddy and L. N. Trefethen, 'How fast are non-symmetric matrix iterations', *SIAM Journal of Scientific and Statistical Computing* (1990), submitted.
3. C. W. Gear, *Numerical Initial Value Problems for Ordinary Differential Equations*, Prentice Hall, Englewood Cliffs, NJ, 1971.
4. L. W. Ho, Y. Maday, A. T. Patera and E. M. Rønquist, 'A high-order Lagrangian-decoupling method for the incompressible Navier–Stokes equations', *Computer Methods in Applied Mechanics and Engineering*, **80**, 65–90 (1990).
5. Y. Maday, A. T. Patera and E. M. Rønquist, 'An operator-integration-factor splitting method for time-dependent problems: application to incompressible fluid flow', *Journal of Scientific Computing*, **5**, 263–292 (1990).
6. O. Pironneau, 'On the transport-diffusion algorithm and its application to the Navier–Stokes equations', *Numerische Mathematik*, **38**, 309–332 (1982).
7. P. M. Gresho, S. T. Chan, R. L. Lee and C. D. Upson, 'A modified finite element method for solving the time-dependent incompressible Navier–Stokes equations, Part 1: Theory', *International Journal of Numerical Methods in Fluids*, **4**, 557–598 (1984).
8. Y. Maday and A. T. Patera, 'Spectral element methods for the incompressible Navier–Stokes equations', in *State of the Art Surveys on Computational Mechanics*, A.K. Noor (ed.), ASME, New York, 1989, pp. 71–143.
9. E. M. Rønquist, 'Optimal spectral element methods for unsteady three-dimensional incompressible Navier–Stokes equations', Ph.D. thesis, MIT, Cambridge, MA, 1988.
10. Y. Maday, D. I. Meiron, A. T. Patera and E. M. Rønquist, 'Analysis of iterative methods for the steady and unsteady Stokes problem: application to spectral element discretizations', *SIAM Journal of Scientific Statistical Computing* (1990), submitted.

11. A. T. Patera, 'A spectral element method for fluid dynamics: laminar flow in a channel expansion', *Journal of Computational Physics*, **54**, 468–488 (1984).
12. C. Canuto, M. Y. Hussaini, A. Quarteroni and T. A. Zang, *Spectral Methods in Fluid Dynamics*, Springer Verlag, Berlin, 1988.
13. C. Bernardi, N. Debit and Y. Maday, 'Coupling finite element and spectral methods: first results', *Mathematics of Computation*, **54**, 21–39 (1990).
14. Y. Maday, C. Mavriplis and A. T. Patera, 'Nonconforming mortar element methods: application to spectral discretizations', in *2nd International Symposium on Domain Decomposition Methods*, T. Chan (ed.), SIAM, Philadelphia, pp. 392–418.
15. G. Anagnostou, Y. Maday, C. Mavriplis and A. T. Patera, 'On the mortar element method: generalizations and implementation, in *3rd International Symposium on Domain Decomposition Methods*, R. Glowinski (ed.), SIAM, Philadelphia, 1990, pp. 157–173.
16. C. Bernardi, Y. Maday and A. T. Patera, 'A new nonconforming approach to domain decomposition: the mortar element method', Publications du Laboratoire D'Analyse Numerique, No. R 89027, 1990.
17. G. Anagnostou, 'Nonconforming sliding spectral element methods for the unsteady incompressible Navier-Stokes equations', Ph.D. Thesis, MIT, Cambridge, MA, 1990.
18. M. F. Edwards and P. Ayazi-Shamlou, Heat transfer in agitated vessels at low Reynolds numbers', in *Low Reynolds Number Flow Heat Exchangers*, S. Kakac, R. K. Shah and A. E. Bergles (eds), Hemisphere Publishers, Washington, New York, London, 1983, pp. 795–812.
19. J. O. Hallquist, G. L. Goudreau and D. J. Benson, 'Sliding interfaces with contact impact in large-scale Lagrangian calculations', *Computer Methods in Applied Mechanics and Engineering*, **51**, 107–137 (1985).
20. J. T. Oden, S. J. Robertson, T. Strouboulis, P. Devloo, L. W. Spradley and H. B. McConnaughey, 'Adaptive and moving mesh finite element methods for flow interaction problems', in *6th International Symposium on Finite Element Methods in Flow Problems*, M.O. Bristeau (ed.), Antibes, France, 1986, pp. 339–343.
21. K. L. Gundy-Burlet and M. M. Rai, 'Two-dimensional computations of multi-stage compressor flows using a zonal approach', AIAA Paper 89-2452, 1989.
22. P. F. Fischer and A. T. Patera, 'Parallel spectral element solution of the Stokes problem', *Journal of Computational Physics*, **92**, 380–421 (1990).
23. J. L. Gustafson, G. R. Montry and R. E. Benner, 'Development of parallel methods for 1024-processor hypercube, *SIAM Journal of Scientific and Statistical Computing*, **9**, 609–638 (1988).
24. G. Anagnostou, D. Dewey and A. T. Patera, 'Geometry-defining processors for engineering design and analysis', *The Visual Computer*, **5**, 304–315 (1989).
25. P. F. Fischer, 'Spectral element solution of Navier–Stokes equations on high-performance distributed-memory parallel processors', Ph.D. Thesis, MIT, Cambridge, MA, 1989.
26. P. F. Fischer and A. T. Patera, 'Parallel spectral element methods for the incompressible Navier–Stokes equations', in *Solution of Super-Large Problems in Computational Mechanics*, J. H. Kane and A. D. Carlson (eds), Plenum Publishers, New York, 1990, to appear.
27. P. F. Fischer, L. W. Ho, G. E. Karniadakis, E. M Rønquist and A. T. Patera, 'Recent advances in parallel spectral element simulation of unsteady incompressible flows, *Computer Structures*, **30**, 217–231 (1988).
28. L. W. Ho and A. T. Patera, 'A Legendre spectral element method for simulation of unsteady incompressible viscous free surface flows', *Computer Methods in Applied Mechanics and Engineering* (1990), to appear.

CONCURRENCY: PRACTICE AND EXPERIENCE, VOL. 3(6), 687–698 (DECEMBER 1991)

The use of the CAPE Environment in the simulation of rock fracturing

M.G. NORMAN,* J.R. HENDERSON,† I.G. MAIN† AND D.J. WALLACE‡*

University of Edinburgh
James Clerk Maxwell Building
Mayfield Road
Edinburgh EH9 3JZ, UK

SUMMARY

The Cellular Automaton Programming Environment (CAPE) was developed as a programming paradigm specific tool for simulation of physical systems by cellular automata (CAs) on the Meiko Computing Surface. CAPE is structured in a way that allows application-specific elements to be replaced whilst retaining the core of the tool.

One of the applications areas where CAPE has been used is in the initial stages of a project which is studying the complex non-linear processes of fracture evolution and fluid flow in geological materials. We describe the programming abstraction provided by CAPE, primarily concentrating on the approach that is taken to reducing the application programmer's initial exposure to issues in parallel computing. We give a brief description of the geological processes that have been simulated, and consider the problems that are associated with this application of CAPE.

1. INTRODUCTION

The Cellular Automaton Programming Environment was developed to allow the writing of Cellular Automaton (CA) codes to run on a distributed memory MIMD architecture (a multicomputer) viz. the Meiko Computing Surface. A description of the use of CAPE in simulating a simple lattice gas model is be found in White and Mackay[1].

CAPE provides a paradigm-specific interface to the Computing Surface for regular decomposition of regular grid-based problems. It is similar in a number of ways to the CrOS and CUBIX parallel programming environments (see Fox *et al.*[2]), but has a number of features more closely tailored to CA applications. In addition, CAPE provides a graphical user interface (GUI) for the display of macroscopic properties of the evolving system.

Section 2 of the paper describes a CA-based approach to the modelling of geophysical fracture mechanics. Section 3 gives a view of the abstraction provided to the CAPE programmer, and the way that different CA models can be programmed inside it. In Section 4 we explain in detail the steps that were taken to allow the initial porting of the geophysical code. Finally, we consider the way in which the abstraction that is provided by CAPE supports the programmer of a simple CA application, and the way in which it begins to break down for more complicated computations, such as those that are required in the geophysical application.

---

*Edinburgh Parallel Computing Centre
†Department of Geology & Geophysics
‡Department of Physics

1040–3108/91/060687–12$06.00
©1991 by John Wiley & Sons, Ltd.

Received 23 October 1990
Accepted 20 August 1991

2. THE APPLICATION

2.1. Background

Arguably the highest priority in the study of seismology is to provide some means of predicting the occurrence of potentially damaging earthquakes. Following the recent upsurge in interest in the dynamics of non-linear systems, it has been recognized that earthquakes may in fact be an example of a *chaotic* system and therefore inherently unpredictable. If this is the case then it may not be immediately fruitful to attempt to study the occurrence of individual earthquakes, and it may instead be of more value to study the phenomenon of *seismicity*, or the statistical characteristics of an ensemble of earthquakes.

For some time it has been recognized that the parameters which describe seismicity in a region show a spatial and temporal evolution which may be associated with the process of the generation of large earthquakes. For example, one of the most common means of describing the pattern of seismicity in a given area is the value b in the Gutenberg–Richter relation:

$$\log N = a - bm$$

where N is the number of earthquakes in a given time of magnitude greater than m. Smith[3] has demonstrated that the value of b in New Zealand has shown a systematic change connected with the occurrence of large earthquakes, and Wyss[4] and Wyss *et al.*[5] have suggested that changes in the b-value in the Parkfield area support the prediction of a large ($m > 5.7$) earthquake in that area in the next few years.

A means of describing the spatial distribution of seismicity follows from the recognition that many natural objects or systems are not well described by the familiar figures of geometry, but are better described in terms of fractals[6]. The fractal geometries of various aspects of fault systems have been investigated.

It is the purpose of our project to develop a simple model of the failure process based on fracture mechanics, and to show that such a model may be used to predict some general relationships between the parameters of seismicity which are in agreement with results derived from studies of both naturally occurring earthquakes and rock fracture in the laboratory. We base our model on studies of rock fracture (e.g. Meredith *et al.*[7]), which suggest the presence of both positive and negative feedback mechanisms. One of the properties we wish to model is the evolution of the fractal dimension during the fracturing process. This question is discussed in Section 5.2.

2.2. Description of the model and its fracture-mechanical basis

We consider a 'fault' to be an isolated two-dimensional feature composed of an array of elements of differing strengths. The whole fault is subject to a uniform remote stress (that is a stress that is applied externally to the system), but locally the stress may be modified by the existence of cracks. By 'crack' we mean an element, or series of elements, whose strength is exceeded by the local stress. We specifically examine two effects which occur as the remote stress is increased: the effect of introducing an isolated crack into the fault, and the effect on crack evolution of the interaction of nearby cracks.

When a crack is introduced into a material under stress, the stress field in the vicinity of the crack is modified. In the early stages of damage, crack growth is not continuous, and appears to stop when the stress has been locally relieved. It is unlikely to be the cause of dynamic failure. The stability of this quasi-static state of damage is due to the negative feedback between the increase in crack length and the local stress intensity. The dominant process leading to rock failure in compression is now known to be crack interaction. The stress intensity at the tip of a crack is increased by the presence of a neighbour, and the stress in the intervening region is also increased. This corresponds to a positive feedback in the crack's growth process, eventually leading to a runaway instability.

The equations governing cracking of materials are extremely complicated even for regular geometries, or for simple interactions, and we cannot hope to solve the detailed physical problems. Instead we seek to create a model which conserves the essential physical ideas of the processes we believe to be operating. Experience with a one-dimensional model suggests that realistic results can be obtained using simplified versions of the governing equations, and we wish to extend our modelling to two dimensions. An ideal approach for calculating the development of such a simplified model is provided by the use of a cellular automaton, with *nearest-neighbour* rules for the crack interactions, on a very large array. We believe that our simplifications will be valid if we consider the statistical behaviour of the system, but in order to do this we need to consider a very large model—significantly larger than is feasible on a conventional sequential machine.

We begin with a two-dimensional array, each element of which is assigned a value which represents the 'strength' of the fault element. We also define a *remote stress*, that is a stress which is applied externally to the system. A fault element is deemed to have failed when its strength is exceeded by the stress acting upon it. The local stress depends upon the remote stress and also the local presence of 'cracks', or failed elements. We consider the stress acting upon an element to be a product of the remote stress and some *stress amplification factor*. The value of this stress amplification factor depends upon the number of nearest neighbours which have failed. In cases where this number of failed nearest neighbours is small, the stress amplification factor is less than 1.0. When the number of failed nearest neighbours is high, the stress amplification factor is greater than 1.0. At each iteration the remote stress is increased, and the effect upon the 'fault' lattice calculated until a crack crosses the whole 'fault' (analogous to the *infinite cluster* of percolation theory). In this way we produce a model of a system in which, during periods where the density of 'cracks' is low, a negative feedback process operates, whereas during periods where 'crack' density is high a positive feedback process dominates.

The ultimate aim of our work is to understand the process of fracturing which gives rise to the observed spatial and temporal evolution of seismicity, and to develop quantitative predictive tools which can be applied to rock fracturing phenomena on a large range of scales.

3. THE CAPE ENVIRONMENT

3.1. History

CAPE was developed for a specific brief:

- The environment was to be capable of supporting a wide range of CA programs.
- CA programs were to be written in Fortran.

- CA programs were to run on a multicomputer, specifically on the Meiko Computing Surface.
- The same Fortran CA program was to run on a sequential machine.
- The program was to provide an interface via a pre-existing windows-based graphical user interface (GUI).

The time scales of CAPE's development were restricted. The project took about 20 weeks for two recent graduates, with some limited supervision. This included time for preparation of documentation, which is to be found in White and Mackay[8,9] and White and Norman[10].

3.2. Design philosophy

The motivation behind CAPE was the observation that much sequential code development is incremental. Old codes are re-worked or added to. Moreover, GUI development can often be seen as a separate activity from scientific programming. In sequential programming, libraries may be used to provide reusable code fragments such as GUIs. Parallel programming suffers from the problem that such libraries need to provide *parallel* interfaces. CAPE is one approach to providing re-usable functionality whereby programming is performed inside an environment within which layers can be replaced as the program changes, but the innermost layers of which—that is those coming closest to the hardware—stay constant. It contrasts with other approaches, such as self-configuring parallel libraries (e.g. see Norman[11]), architecture-independent languages (e.g. see Skillicorn[12]), or even automatic parallelization (e.g. see Zima *et al.*[13]).

3.3. Interacting with CAPE via the GUI

CAPE is supplied with a working FHP[14] cellular automaton lattice gas program running inside the environment. It is possible to interact with the program without modification by supplying configuration files and data files on which it is to compute, and by use of the GUI.

Conceptually, CAPE communicates with the GUI through a data base with a locking protocol. Both the GUI and CAPE can write to or read from the data base, but there exist critical regions during which the data base is locked. Information such as the position of the mouse cursor, the position and size of the windows and tokens indicating information which the user requires to be displayed in the windows are placed initially in the data base from the startup file, and can be modified by the GUI, which runs on a master processor. From time to time the CAPE program may query the contents of the data base, and subsequently perform operations on the basis of the information contained within. Most often this will consist of refreshing the windowing system with averaged displays of the current state of the system being simulated. CAPE can also pass information about the progress of the simulation, perhaps numeric or textual, into the data base for display by the GUI.

3.4. The basic abstraction

Figure 1 shows how CAPE works on the multicomputer. As far as the applications programmer is concerned, CAPE is a *single program multiple data* (SPMD) program.

There are a number of SPMD applications processes, each of which is assigned a contiguous part of the data space being simulated. In addition, there is a master process which handles communications with the user of the program and with the file-system, and where the data structures associated with the windowing system reside. There is also a graphics process.

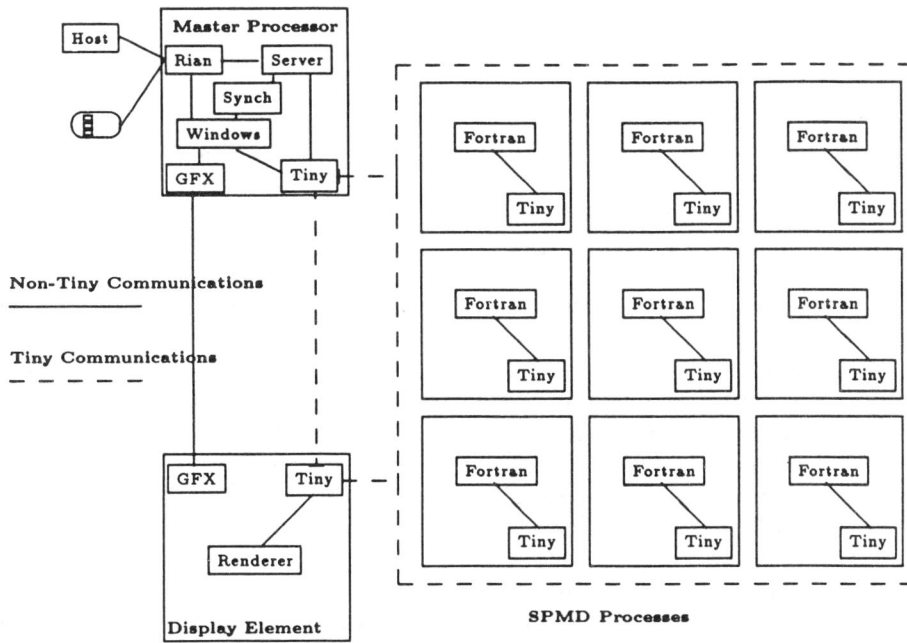

Figure 1. The process structure of CAPE

CAPE was written inside an occam harness which provides buffering and interprocess communication facilities on top of the *Tiny*[15] message passing system. The applications programmer does not normally see this level. He merely starts up the environment and then loads the compiled Fortran SPMD image, which does not require recompilation to run on a different number of processors.

Each of the SPMD processes is, by default, mapped to a distinct processor in such a way that the localities in the decomposition are matched exactly to the localities in the physical processor network. The master process is mapped to a processor which is connected to the host environment and the graphics process is mapped to a processor which forms part of a dedicated display element with attached video screen. All interprocess communication is *via* the Tiny message passing system except for the link between the master and the host (which runs Meiko File-System protocols) and the direct link between the master and the graphics processor which runs Meiko's GFX protocols. The three remaining links into the graphics processor run Tiny protocols to a process which writes directly into videoRAM.

3.5. The SPMD abstraction

The abstraction provided to the CA programmer is that he is writing a whole cellular automaton program at each of his SPMD processes. Two primitives have been provided to handle boundary conditions, one to send boundaries and one to receive boundaries. In the centre of the data space they swap boundaries across divisions in the assignment of data to processes. At the edges of the data space they can provide either fixed or cyclic boundary conditions. Send calls copy messages to buffers and set up lightweight processes to perform asynchronous pairwise exchanges. Receive calls rendezvous with the lightweight processes and copy messages out of buffers. The application programmer does not see this level of concurrency.

To continue the distributed data abstraction, file system primitives have been provided to allow an arbitrary number of processes each to appear to be writing a complete file, but actually to be contributing to a composite file containing their records—interleaved so that they appear to have been written as a single large file from a single process. As well as interleaved write we provide interleaved read and thus the same file can be written and read back by CAPE programs running on different numbers of processes. In addition, it is possible to read and write records such as file headers so that, although every process makes a call, there is only one header in the file.

The graphics calls follow the same pattern as the file system calls. The calls to query from, or to set values into, the data base that is shared with the GUI are made at every process and respectively return the same value at each process, or set a single value in the GUI. Calls that draw part of a window are called simultaneously at each process, but draw into locations on the screen which are dependent upon the partition of data amongst the processors. The use of a data base for interaction between the GUI and CAPE appears cumbersome. It would be more natural for the application to service *interrupts* from the GUI. In the case of a loosely synchronous parallel program such as CAPE, where exact synchrony occurs only periodically, there are complications with interrupts which happen between synchronizations, since the timing of interrupts with respect to other interprocess communications is non-deterministic and does not necessarily interrupt all processes in the same state. This breaks the SPMD abstraction.

Finally, to complete the distributed data abstraction, CAPE provides a single example of the class of *scan* operations (see Blelloch[16]) in the form of a global sum procedure which adds up an array of values at each process and returns, at every process, the sum of all such sums.

In contrast to the above, CAPE provides some functionality which allows the programmer to think in global data space rather than in terms of the local partition of the data. For example, CAPE provides functions to set values at locations in partitioned arrays. These are called at every process, and values are set only in processes which have been assigned the relevant portion of the main array.

3.6. Performance

The performance of CAPE was given in[1]. An FHP simulation was run, firstly on a lattice of 400×400 sites (see Table 1), and then on a lattice of 800×800 sites (see Table 2). Small lattice sizes were used in order to allow the simulation to be run on both small and large domains. All timings are in seconds.

Table 1. Timings for 400×400 lattice

Processor grid	Time for update	Time for averages	Time for display
2×2	2.0	7.1	6.0
4×4	0.55	1.7	2.1
8×8	0.17	0.5	1.6

Table 2. Timings for 800×800 lattice

Processor grid	Time for update	Time for averages	Time for display
2×2	7.8	28.0	13.0
4×4	2.0	7.0	5.0
8×8	0.53	1.9	3.3

From these timings, the speed-up on a CA simulation from 4 processors to 64 processors is 11.7 (73% efficient) on the 400×400 lattice, and 14.7 (92% efficient) on the 800×800 lattice. This difference is to be expected as the communications overhead is proportionally greater on the smaller lattice.

For efficiency, it is best only to update the display after a number of time steps. There is a trade-off between efficiency and the ability to see how the lattice gas is evolving.

4. MODIFICATIONS TO THE SUPPLIED PROGRAM

The basic loop in the supplied CAPE program consists of

```
Set up
Loop over{
      Send edges
      Update centre
      Receive edges
      Update edges
      Propagate
      And, once every few loops{
            Query database
            Display or dump lattice
      }
}
Finish
```

CAPE has been used (in an application which is *not* described by White and Mackay[1,8,9]) to generate promotional material for a manufacturer of stoppers for non-refillable Scotch whisky bottles. In this case, the modifications made by the applications programmer were simply to the code that set the barriers within the system, and this involved only changing the set up phase.

The majority of CAPE users wish to simulate something other than the straight FHP lattice gas model that is provided. We describe the steps that were required for the initial port of the geophysical application.

Modifications were made to the three areas of the CAPE code.

4.1. Changes to the `Set Up`

The original FHP setup code was removed and replaced with a small routine to read in an array from a file using CAPE-specific calls to read the header and the lattice. The lattice was generated off-line.

4.2. Changes to the `Update`

The CA model was originally developed on a sequential mainframe. This sequential code was put, with no modification, into the centre of a loop. No changes were made to the edge-swapping code except to make sure that the right arrays were passed around.

4.3. Changes to the `Display`

The calls that read the data base which is shared with the GUI, and those which perform synchronizations between processes were left alone. The calls which generate rasters were modified to associate tokens in the data base with different arrays in the model. This modification was performed inside the loop which steps through windows in the display, and handles the problem of scaling to arbitrary size.

4.4. The result of the changes

Figure 2 shows a display that was produced after the aforementioned modifications were made. It shows a population of 'cracks' growing on a 'fault' (whose strength was initially generated using a Brownian walk). The example shown is from a relatively small grid (512 × 512), but in future CAPE will allow the analysis of development of cracks on a much larger scale.

The titles on the display in Figure 2 are misleading. The window entitled 'Lattice Density' shows the cracks growing in the system after 23 time-steps. Black areas of the display have failed. The strength is shown at each point on the lattice on a scale from dark grey (low strength) to white (high strength). The window entitled 'Lattice Flow Speed' shows the initial strengths in the system.

4.5. Generality problems

The misleading window labels are a result of fixing *a priori* the meaning to the GUI of tokens in the data base that are shared between the GUI and the application. This is undoubtedly a 'mis-feature', and could be easily corrected.

The common feature of all the modifications that were made to the FHP code, which is possibly a function of the specifics of CAPE's engineering, but may be a feature of the paradigm-specific approach, was that modifications were made in *inner* loops. In principle it might be possible for the CAPE subroutines to take inner-loop subroutines as arguments. In practice, it was not clear at the time of CAPE's development, which

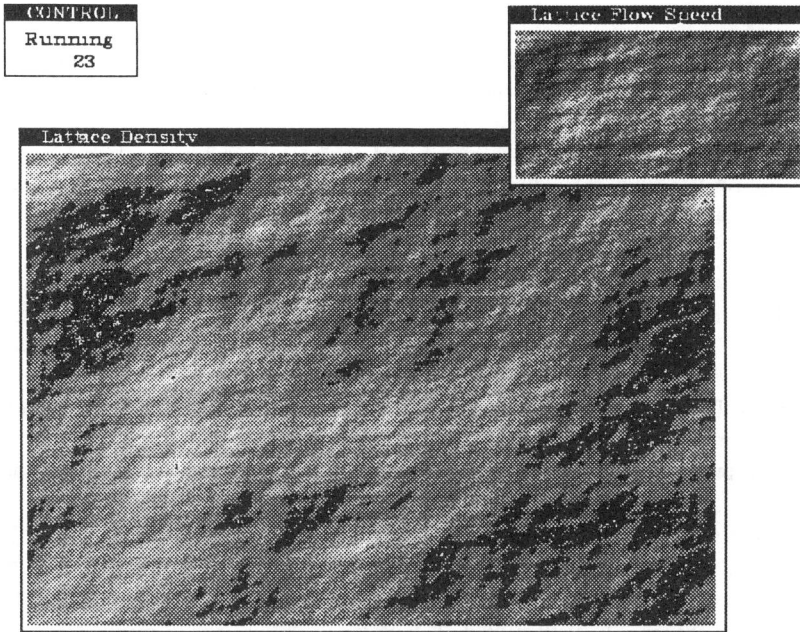

Figure 2. A simulation of 'cracks' growing on a 'fault'; see text for explanation of window labels

inner loops would be required to be modified, and had decisions been made prematurely, generality would have been lost in a similar way to that exhibited in the window labeling code.

5. MORE COMPLEX MODIFICATIONS

5.1. Load balancing

One question which arises in the modifications performed above is *load balancing*. Cracked areas require almost no further computation, so a processor which is assigned to an area which rapidly becomes severely cracked will be underemployed in comparison to processors which are dealing with, say, interactions between numerous smaller cracks. Increased efficiency could be achieved by developing a strategy for sharing the work load in a more equitable manner.

Partitioning of the data space between processes is implicit in the CAPE communications primitives. Substantial modifications would have to be made to CAPE if it were to deal with irregular meshes such as those considered by Williams[17], or with irregular partitionings. On the other hand, mapping of processes to processors is performed by the configuration level of the occam program. It would be relatively simple to perform scattered spatial mapping of processes (see, for example, Nicol and Saltz[18]) at a finer granularity to allow statistical load balance.

5.2. The computation of the fractal dimension

Although the evolution of the system proceeds by time-stepping of a globally computed interaction between adjacent processes, the analysis of the system must be performed on global properties of localized structures.

For example, one of the fundamental properties of the system under simulation is the fractal dimension of the crack ensemble. Two strategies are commonly used to calculate this quantity. In the first strategy one finds the frequency of occurrence of cracks of different sizes, and fits a straight line to a graph of the logarithm of frequency of occurrence against logarithm of crack size. The second strategy involves 'box-counting'. One overlays the array with a grid of boxes, and finds the fraction of boxes containing cracked elements. This is carried out for a large range of box sizes, and the fractal dimension is again found by fitting a straight line to a graph of the data.

Working within the SPMD abstraction, the applications programmer would naturally perform fractal dimension computation on each of the process-allocated partitions of the data, and then perform some special boundary computation to integrate the subcomputations.

When calculating the frequency of occurrence of cracks of different sizes, it is necessary to identify cracks which are continuous across the boundaries of the data partition. This simply involves a list merge operation, which can be implemented with *scans* similar to the global sum. Unfortunately it is not programmed in CAPE and the application programmer would be required to write the code. For efficient implementation, the scan operations require knowledge of locality, or more specifically of locality within the processor network to which the computation has been mapped. This does not fit naturally within the CAPE abstraction.

In the case of the calculation of fractal dimension by 'box-counting', complications arise if one of the analysis boxes spans two or more partitions of the data. This clearly occurs when the analysis box size is greater then the partition size. It also occurs if the partition size is not an integral number of times bigger than the analysis box size. In either case, the application programmer must modify his code to accommodate the fact that some operations can occur simultaneously in all processes, while some require specific interactions between processes. Again this does not fit naturally with the CAPE abstraction.

6. CONCLUDING REMARKS

There are specific failings in CAPE in that the graphical user interface is not programmable, and that the structuring of the subroutine calls and the excessive use of COMMON has made it difficult to understand how to fit in application-specific subroutines.

In the wider sense, however, the most important problem with CAPE, and an important general point for the development of paradigm-specific approaches to parallel programming, is that the abstraction that is provided by CAPE is *too* simple to use. Indeed, a number of concepts inherent in CAPE only became clear to some of the authors of this paper during the preparation of the manuscript. Although initially this leads to an easy life for the application programmer, it means that when the abstraction begins to break down, the programmer finds it difficult to understand how to continue programming his application. It is fair to say that the documentation for CAPE gives limited help in this direction.

With the above caveats in mind it is still, however, clear that CAPE has provided a useful environment within which development and application of CA models has been carried out. Furthermore, it provides a rare example of multicomputer code which has been used in more than one program.

ACKNOWLEDGEMENTS

The Edinburgh Parallel Computing Centre is a multidisciplinary project supported by major grants from the Department of Trade and Industry, the Computer Board, and the Science and Engineering Research Council. CAPE was developed under a Partnership agreement between EPCC and Shell Research B.V. & Shell Expro Ltd. M.G. Norman is supported by the SERC Contract B18534: Novel Architecture Computing Research. J.R. Henderson is supported by a NERC research studentship.

REFERENCES

1. M. White and E. Mackay, 'CAPE - a cellular automaton programming environment', in *Parallel Processing for Fluid Flow: Methods and Systems*, British Computer Society (1990), pp. 1–12.
2. G.C. Fox, M.A. Johnson, G.A. Lyzenga, S.W. Otto, J.K. Salmon and D. Walker, *Solving Scientific Problems on Concurrent Processors*, Prentice Hall, NJ (1988).
3. W.D. Smith, 'Evidence for precursory changes in the frequency-magnitude b–value', *Geophysical Journal of the Royal Astronomical Society*, **86**, 815–838 (1986).
4. M. Wyss, 'Changes of mean magnitude of Parkfield seismicity: a part of the precursory process?', *Geophysical Research Letters*, in press (1991).
5. M. Wyss, P. Bodin and R.E. Habermann, 'Seismic quiescence at Parkfield: an independent indication of an imminent earthquake', *Nature*, **345**, 426–428 (1990).
6. B Mandelbrot, *Les Objets Fractals*, Editions Flammarion, Paris (1975).
7. P.G. Meredith, I. Main and C. Jones, 'Temporal variations in seismicity during quasi-static and dynamic rock failure', *Tectonophysics*, **175**, 249–268 (1990).
8. M. White and E. Mackay, 'CAPE user guide', Technical Report ECSP-UG-16, Edinburgh Parallel Computing Centre (1989).
9. M. White and E. Mackay, 'CAPE programmer's guide', Technical Report ECSP-UG-17, Edinburgh Parallel Computing Centre (1989).
10. M. White and M.G. Norman, CAPE cellular automata and beyond...', Technical Report ECSP-TN-39, Edinburgh Parallel Computing Centre (1989).
11. M.G. Norman, 'A parallel graphics utility for parallel programs', in L. Freeman and C. Phillips (eds), *Applications of Transputers*, IOS, Amsterdam (1989).
12. D.B. Skillicorn, 'Architecture-independent parallel computation', *IEEE Computer*, **23**, 38–50 (1990).
13. H.P. Zima, H.J. Bast and H.M. Gerndtm, 'SUPERB—a tool for semi-automatic MIMD/SIMD Parallelization', *Parallel Computing*, **6**, 1–18 (1988).
14. U. Frisch, B. Hasslacher and Y. Pomeau, 'Lattice gas automata for the Navier–Stokes equation', *Physical Review Letters*, **56**, 1505 (1986).
15. Lyndon J. Clarke and Greg Wilson. 'Tiny: an efficient routing harness for the Inmos Transputer', *Concurrency: Practice and Experience*, 3(3), 221–245 (1991).
16. G.E. Blelloch, 'Scans as primitive parallel operations', *IEEE Transactions on Computing*, C-**38**, 1526–1538 (1989).

17. Roy D. Williams, 'DIME: a programming environment for unstructured triangular meshes on a distributed-memory parallel processor', Technical Report C3P-502, CalTech Concurrent Computation Project.
18. D.M. Nicol and J.H. Saltz, 'An analysis of scatter decomposition', *IEEE Transactions on Computing*, **C-39**, 1337–1345 (1990).

Analysis of multidimensional images on the Connection Machine* system

GIAMPIERO MARCENARO AND MASSIMO TISTARELLI

DIST, University of Genoa
via Opera Pia 11a
16145 Genoa, Italy

SUMMARY

The Connection Machine* (CM) has been demonstrated to be an efficient and fast computational engine for the solution of many problems related to image processing. The high-level parallelism of the CM naturally fits to many large-scale data intensive applications.

In this paper the implementation of parallel algorithms for the analysis of multidimensional images on the CM is presented. Different aspects in the analysis of multidimensional images are considered. In the field of artificial vision, the implementation of algorithms for the filtering of image sequences (both in space and time) and the estimation of the optical flow is described and some results in terms of accuracy and computation time are presented.

The processing of three-dimensional images is investigated in the field of biomedical engineering. In this case the goal is the development of algorithms for the 3-D reconstruction of human body segments and their visualization.

The parallel implementations exploit the fine grain parallelism allowed by the CM, processing each point of the data on a different processor. This mechanism is allowed by the possibility of dynamically reconfiguring the connectivity of the CM nodes and of defining a huge number of virtual processors. Moreover, as the CM processors operate on one-bit data, it is possible to tune the number of bits for each data point to match the accuracy required by the application.

1. INTRODUCTION

Computer vision has been generally regarded as the extraction of information from images, aimed at the interpretation of the observed scene. Much of the information, however, cannot be derived from a single picture, while it requires the dynamic evolution of the data stream versus time. Everyday experience shows how movements are important in the perception and understanding of the world. Sometimes, the movement of an object is an essential requirement for recognition (for example, to recognize if the surface of a lake is frozen, the absence of water movements on the surface must be observed). Movements of the observer, purposively planned, can induce an enormous amount of information about the structure of the environment and the contained objects[1–4].

Many researchers have addressed the geometric properties of image motion, such as displacement of image features versus time or, more generally, the instantaneous velocity of the image brightness[5–11].

One important consideration in vision is the representation adopted for a given feature. A natural way of representing image velocity is the *optical flow*, which is a 2-D vector field representing the instantaneous velocity for each image point. The optical flow is

*Connection Machine is a trademark of Thinking Machines Co.

1040–3108/91/060699–15$07.50
Received 23 October 1990
Accepted 26 August 1991

generally regarded as a good approximation of the 2-D motion field, that is the perspective projection onto the image plane of the true 3-D velocity field.

Among the possible applications of the recovered velocity field is the computation of the 'time-to-collision' (TTC)[12]. In the case of a moving observer, like an autonomous moving robot, it represents the elapsed time before the impact with an obstacle along its pathway. In order to reliably compute the TTC, the optical flow must be precisely determined, and also fast enough to allow time for planning a motion strategy to avoid the collision (even if the obstacle is also moving toward the robot). It is obvious that the minimal computational speed is dictated by both the velocity of the robot and its reaction time. The time required for the computation of the flow field and consequently the TTC, should be within an order of magnitude of the sampling rate of the imaging device. The same assumption is not as imperative for other visual tasks like object recognition[13] or scene segmentation, but it is strictly necessary for interpreting a dynamically changing scenario.

The Connection Machine (CM) has been demonstrated to be an efficient and fast computational engine for the solution of many vision problems. Within the paradigm of dynamic vision, the algorithm to be implemented must be as fast as possible.

In this paper, a system based on the CM computer is developed which is capable of computing the optical flow from image sequences at near real time, as they are grabbed from a sensor. The key components of the system (besides the CM itself) are:

- a fast I/O interface that allows loading images into the CM as they are acquired;
- a massively parallel implementation that maps naturally onto the CM architecture.

The analysis of *magnetic resonance* (MR) data is a formidable problem, again, because of the amount of data to be processed. A 3-D imaging technique is described, referring to MR data at the human body organ level.

3-D imaging tecniques have wide applications in the field of tomographic data processing of human body organs. The technique described in this paper refers to data acquired from a human body organ according to a direct 3-D MR acquisition method. In this case, the biological volume can be considered, in principle, as sampled through a voxel grid: the MR signal is directly taken in 3-D from each voxel and stored in the memory of the computer. Therefore, we deal with a full 3-D method, from the original acquisition up to the last processing step. 3-D processing includes 3-D edge detection, volumetric segmentation and surface rendering and animation. The surface detection algorithm described in this work is based on the detection of peaks in the first derivative of the 3-D image brightness. Surface detection and volumetric segmentation are performed directly in the spatial frequency domain, and only subsequently are the processed data transformed via an inverse Fourier transform, before the volume rendering. It must be noticed that this technique takes full advantage of the possibility offered by MR of performing 3-D volumetric acquisition directly.

The 3-D processing system has been implemented on the Connection Machine system, including the surface extraction in the frequency domain and the 3-D volumetric representation and segmentation of human body segments.

The paper is organized according to the following schema:

- the architecture and functionality of the CM are briefly reviewed, with the more salient features for image processing purposes being pointed out;

- the algorithm used for the computation of the optical flow is described in Section 2 and 3, together with an outline of its structure and the definition of how it has been implemented on the CM;
- in Section 4 the experiments performed on real image sequences are presented, together with an analysis of the performance in terms of both accuracy and computational speed. These results are also compared with similar ones obtained running the algorithm on serial computers;
- in Section 5 the application of parallel image processing to 3-D MR surface reconstruction is presented. An algorithm for 3-D surface reconstruction processing data in the frequency domain is also presented;
- some experiments performed on real MR data are presented in Section 6;
- in the conclusions the features of the systems are summarized outlining the future developments of this work.

1.1. Brief overview of the Connection Machine system

The Connection Machine is a fine-grained massively parallel computer, composed of up to 65536 one-bit processors[14]. The CM is a single instruction, multiple data (SIMD) architecture; each processor executes independently, on the data stored in its local memory, a common instruction stream, shared with all the other processors. This behaviour is particularly useful in processing a large amount of data (like images), where each data element is subject to the same transformation.

The processors themselves are serial processors, with one-bit ALU and single-bit-wide local memory. In the CM-2 model each processor is equipped with up to 32,768 bytes of read/write memory. The user can handle variables of any length in bits.

The data processors are arranged in a 12-dimensional Boolean hypercube. The CM allows two communication modes between processors: broadcast, and grid-based nearest-neighbor communication. The global communication utilizes special hardware (the router) to perform parallel message sending among the processors.

The grid communication is an efficient way to exchange data between near-neighbor processors. In grid-based communication, the CM processors can be seen as a dynamic reconfigurable mesh of processors. The processors network can be dynamically configured as an N-dimensional cube. This feature is especially useful for processing images. In fact, using iconic representations and local computations, it is always possible to embed the data for the processing into an N-cube topology. The assembly language of the CM is called *Paris* (PARallel Instruction Set). It is possible to use Paris calls within a serial Lisp or C program. In this case we refer to the program as having been written in *Lisp-Paris* and *C-Paris* respectively.

The virtual processor mechanism permits each processor to simulate many processors, operating on different blocks of its local memory. Virtual processors are invisible to the user, and 'simply' make the machine to seem large enough to fit the given application. It is possible to define a map between the real processors in the CM and the configured virtual processors. The ratio between the real machine size and the number of virtual processors is named the virtual processor ratio (vp-ratio).

In the described experiments, an 8K machine (8192 processors) has been used, requiring a vp-ratio of 1:8, for processing images with a resolution of 256×256 pixels. On a full 64K CM-2, the times noted for each task would be reduced by a factor of 8.

This is possible because no additional overhead is introduced by increasing the number of processors, but synchronization and communication between processors is performed by dedicated hardware (which is increased when processors are added).

2. COMPUTING OPTICAL FLOW

The computation of the optical flow field is one of the most interesting topics in computer vision. Many algorithms have been proposed for this purpose and many others are currently being studied. Among them a gradient technique has been used, mainly for two reasons:

- All the computations are done locally on the images, while token-matching algorithms and other techniques often require more 'global' computations.
- Few convolutions and derivatives (both in space and time) are required and all can be performed in integer arithmetics. No feature extraction is needed, nor other preprocessing stages as in most feature-matching techniques[11].

The implemented algorithm has been originally proposed by Torre and his associates[8] and further developed for applications on real world images [10]. The basic idea is that of imposing the stationarity of the image intensity gradient $\nabla E(x,y,t)$ over time:

$$\frac{d}{dt}\nabla E = 0 \tag{1}$$

This relation leads to a vector equation in the two components of the flow field $\mathbf{V}(x,y) = (u(x,y), v(x,y))$:

$$\mathbf{H}\,\mathbf{v} = -\nabla\mathbf{I_t} \tag{2}$$

where $\mathbf{H}$ is the Hessian (with respect to the spatial coordinates) of the image intensity and the subscript $\mathbf{t}$ denotes the partial temporal derivative.

The two components of $\mathbf{v}$ can be recovered from equation (2) whenever $det\,\mathbf{H}\,(I(x,y,t))$ is different from zero. Written explicitly, equation (2) becames:

$$\begin{cases} u\frac{\partial^2 I}{\partial x^2} + v\frac{\partial^2 I}{\partial x\,\partial y} = -\frac{\partial^2 I}{\partial x\,\partial t} \\ u\frac{\partial^2 I}{\partial x\,\partial y} + v\frac{\partial^2 I}{\partial y^2} = -\frac{\partial^2 I}{\partial y\,\partial t} \end{cases} \tag{3}$$

As has been shown in[15], the system of equations is well-conditioned only if the determinant of the Hessian of the image brightness is 'large' and the ratio between its minimum and maximum eigenvalue is close to unity.

2.1. Structure of the algorithm

In order to obtain an estimate of the velocity field v, the following steps are performed:

(i) convolution of the image sequence with a 2-D or 3-D Gaussian operator; this step is required to make the image sequence smooth in space and/or in time, for the subsequent derivative computations and to reduce image noise;

(ii) computation of the partial derivatives of the central image of the sequence; as the derivatives are computed using five points support, it is generally the third image of the set, unless temporal smoothing is also performed, in which case the time span of the Gaussian must be added;

(iii) selection of the processors for which both the determinant of the Hessian is greater than a fixed threshold and the condition number is close to unit;

(iv) evaluation of the optical flow from (3).

In order to perform (i) the images are first loaded into the CM memory. The CM processor grid is first set as a 2-D regular grid with the same width and height of the images; each processor stores all the pixels of the image sequence at a given spatial location. The convolutions are performed using 32-bit integer arithmetic and the results are stored in 17-bit fields. The first- and second-order derivatives are computed using 32-bit signed integers and this only involves arithmetic shifts and adds. The results are stored in 22-bit fields. The size of the output fields is obtained considering 8-bit input images and a precision of three digits in the output of the filtering stage.

Owing to quantization errors and image noise (changes in the illumination conditions or object and/or camera acceleration are regarded as 'noise') the recovered optic flow can still be affected by errors. A final filtering of the two components of the velocity field with a *box-car* operator reduces the errors, smoothing the flow. The operator is simply a unitary filter, the output being, for each image point, the average of the intensity values in an $N \times N$ neighborhood (corresponding to the size of the mask). Assigning one pixel to each CM processor, this filtering can be implemented very easily using scan operations[16]. It requires only two global scans with addition (two elementary parallel instructions on the CM) and four arithmetic operations performed in parallel by each processor. Even if a Gaussian operator seems most appropriate for regularization, it has been shown that Gaussian filtering attenuates too much the velocity amplitudes, leading to underestimated measurements. For this reason it is preferable to avoid the final smoothing of the flow field or to use a simpler filter.

2.2. Implementation

The algorithm has been implemented in C-Paris, avoiding functions calls and grouping all CM instructions in fast macros. The computations use integer arithmetic whenever possible; only the flow field, obtained from equation (2), is computed in floating point. Solving the same equations using integer arithmetic improves the speed by only 5% in a machine without a floating-point accelerator.

The most time-consuming operation is the spatio-temporal Gaussian convolution, which is performed as a cascade of 1-D convolutions. Each convolution is computed directly as sum of products, adopting bit shifts whenever possible. Fast convolution algorithms are described in full detail in [16]. In this paper the authors show that it is sometimes better (depending on the size of the convolution kernel) to perform a cascade of 1-D convolutions than adopting a recursive algorithm (generally based on the application of 2-D kernels of small size). Therefore, as the size of the smoothing filters is variable, we decided to perform convolution only using the separability property of the Gaussian operator.

As for the temporal filtering, it is worth noting that the Gaussian operator is non-causal, therefore each frame is actually weighted with both its 'past' and 'future'. This is an undesirable effect as it implies a longer delay with respect to causal filters, while an image processed at time T should not be much correlated with subsequent images and such correlation is not even needed for computing the flow field. Finally a causal operator should have a smaller (actually more or less a half) temporal support, involving fewer computations. In order to verify the effectiveness of such a conjecture, several experiments were run, smoothing the sequence in time with a half-Gaussian mask. This function works, but it is probably one of the worst causal functions, in terms of frequency response, that one could use. But, without considering the discontinuity of the operator, the output can be regarded as a weighting function of the current image and the preceding ones, where the more distant image in time has the lower weight. The results obtained using this operator do not differ very much from those obtained from a full temporal Gaussian, while the application of this causal filter results in a 20% improvement in computation speed.

The algorithm for the computation of the optic flow operates in two phases: at the startup a number of images equal to the size of the temporal filter are loaded in the CM and convolved in space and time. The partial derivatives and then the optic flow are computed for the central image of the set (it should be the second to the last image, in the case of a causal temporal filter; the last two frames constitute the overlap needed by the derivative mask which uses a support of five frames). For each new image grabbed by the sensor and loaded into the CM only one 3-D convolution is computed both in space and time, and a new optic flow is estimated. The overall performance of the algorithm is given by the time needed for the convolution of one frame plus the computation of derivatives and the solution of equation (1).

The CM processors are configured as a 2-D grid array, each processor storing pixels of different frames, at a given spatial location. More complex geometries have been tested, such as 3-D arrays of processors, but this turned out to be less efficient, since most of the computations are performed locally on a single image (spatial convolution and derivatives and the actual estimation of the flow field). Moreover, using different geometries for the different processes, one introduces an overhead for sending the data among processors, according to the different configurations of the network.

3. OUTLINE OF THE REAL-TIME IMAGE PROCESSING SYSTEM

The computation of the optical flow represents an example of the possible applications of the CM for dynamic scene analysis. In order to fully take advantage of the computational power of the CM system, it is necessary to provide a high I/O throughput with the image grabber, which cannot be achieved with a conventional front-end interface. A special I/O board may be employed for high-speed transfers between the CM memory and a frame grabber hosted on the front-end machine. The complete system is depicted in Figure 1.

In summary the system will be composed of the following parts:

- CM-2 computational engine, with 32K or 64K processors and floating-point unit;
- VME I/O interface, a special-purpose VME board, hosted by the front-end computer and connected directly to the CM I/O bus, which allows transfer rates up to the speed of the VME bus;

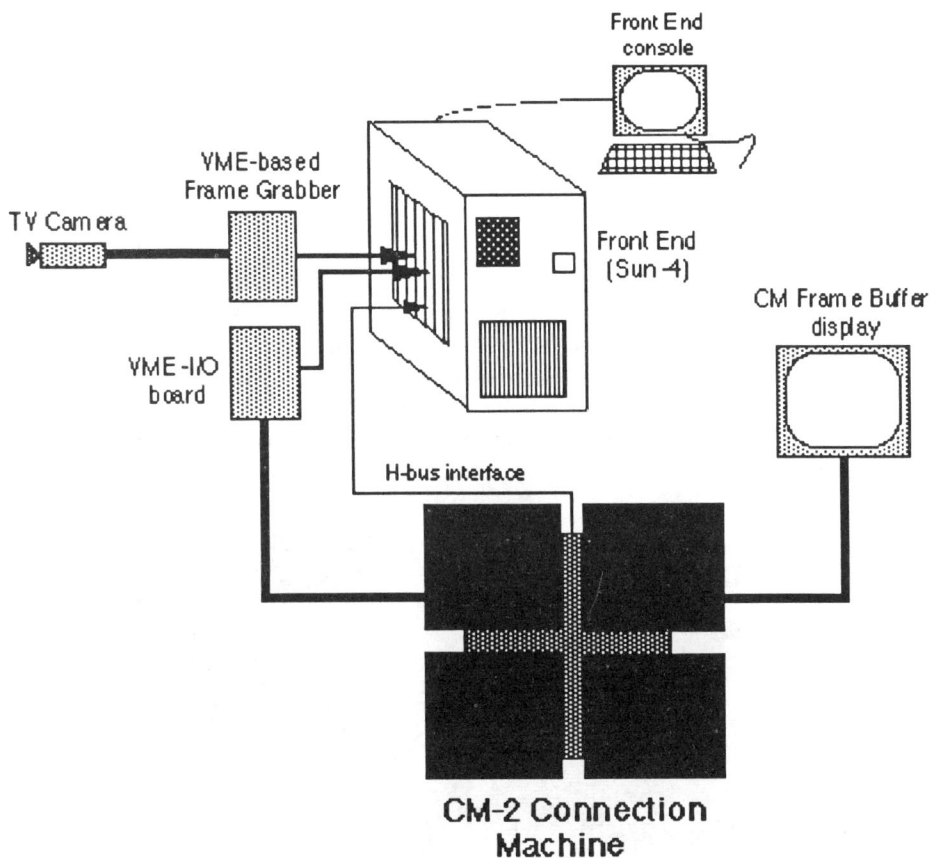

Figure 1. Schematic representation of the real-time image-processing system based on the CM-2 Connection Machine

- the front-end computer, which is a VME-based machine, typically a Sun-4[1] workstation; it hosts the frame grabber and the VME I/O board. The front-end communicates with the CM via the standard interface and controls the image acquisition and transfer to the CM memory via the VME I/O board;
- CM frame buffer, 1024 × 1024 pixels with 24 bits per pixels, it is hosted by the CM and allows very fast visualization of the results of processing.

The transfer rate of the images through the VME I/O board should be only limited by the access time of the frame grabber image memory. In the case of a Datacube Max-Video[2] board it is approximately 1150 nsec. for each block read from the frame buffer.

The computation of the optic flow requires 400 ms on an 8K CM-2 with floating-point unit, using a virtual processor (vp) ratio of 1:8 (the images are 256 × 256 pixels).

---

[1] Sun-4 is a trademark of SUN Microsystems.

[2] Max-Video is a trademark of Datacube Inc.

Running the program on a 64K machine, using a vp ratio of 1:1, the processing time drops to about 50 ms, which corresponds to a frequency of 20 flow fields per second. Hence it is possible to predict a throughput of one optic flow every two frames.

4. EXPERIMENTAL RESULTS

The system outlined in the previous section has been implemented as a C-Paris program running on an 8K CM-2 connected to a Sun-4 front-end. In order to simulate the image acquisition process, the images are first loaded onto the front-end from files and then transferred into the CM memory through the sequencer. The images used are 256 × 256 pixels with 8 bits of resolution in intensity; the vp ratio of the configured CM is 1:8.

The image in Figure 2 represents a flat picture (a portrait of the 'Apollo di Velo' statue) translating horizontally along a direction parallel to the image plane; the background is static as well as the cube in the foreground. The picture was moved using an electrical rail at a speed of 20 cm/s, resulting in an overall displacement on the image plane of about 2.4 pixels.

Figure 2. First image of a sequence of 15, acquired during a parallel translation of a picture of the 'Apollo di Velo' statue. The size of the images is 256 × 256 pixels; the cube in the foreground and the background are stationary

The sequence was processed by the program; the standard deviation σ of the temporal Gaussian was set to 1, corresponding to a temporal support of 9 frames. Different trials were made, varying the sigma of the spatial Gaussian; the timings corresponding to the experiments are shown in Table 1. The reported results correspond to the computation of the spatial and temporal convolution of all the images in the sequence with the Gaussian operators, and the computation of one optical flow. In Table 2 the actual mean and standard deviation of the flow field computed varying the sizes of the spatial and temporal Gaussian filters are presented. The table shows the effect of the smoothing filters and,

Table 1. Timings required on a Connection Machine using a 1:8 vp-ratio, to compute a spatio-temporal convolution and the optical flow, with a temporal σ equal to 1, and varying the spatial kernel

Spatial σ	Convolution time (ms)	Optic flow time (ms)	Global time (ms)
1.5	200	130	330
2.0	260	130	390
2.5	320	130	450
4.0	460	130	590

Table 2. Statistics of the optical flows computed from the sequence of Apollo. The data refer to repeated measures performed varying the size of the spatial and temporal Gaussian. The real overall mean displacement is 2.4. The mean and standard deviation of the optic flow are computed within a window containing the moving portrait

σ_s	σ_t	Mean of **V**	σ of **V**
1.5	—	2.1	2.4
2.0	—	2.2	1.6
4.0	1.0	2.4	0.1
1.5	1.0	2.3	0.5
2.0	1.0	2.4	0.6

in particular, demonstrates that a smoothing of the flow field is not required to obtain a good estimate of the image displacement vectors. In fact, the smoothing of the flow greatly attenuates the amplitude of the vectors, leading to underestimated measurements. For this reason it is evident that a temporal filtering of the sequence is usually sufficient and gives better results, without degrading the performance of the system. In Figure 3 some examples of computed optical flows are presented.

In order to evaluate the performance of the system with respect to other computers, the same experiment illustrated was run on a Sun-4 and a DEC Vax 8600[3] workstation. The timings for the computation of the optic flow within the different environments are summarized in Table 3.

Table 3. Comparison between the timings required on different computing systems to execute a spatio-temporal convolution and compute the optic flow. The results are from experiments performed on the sequence of Apollo. The spatial and temporal σ of the Gaussian operator were set to 2.0 and 1.0, respectively

Operation	CM-2 vp-ratio 1:8 timing (s)	Sun-4 timing (s)	Vax 8600 timing (s)
convolution	0.26	50.3	33.05
optic flow	0.13	17.5	13.78
global	0.39	67.8	46.83

[3] DEC Vax is a trademark of Digital Equipment Corp.

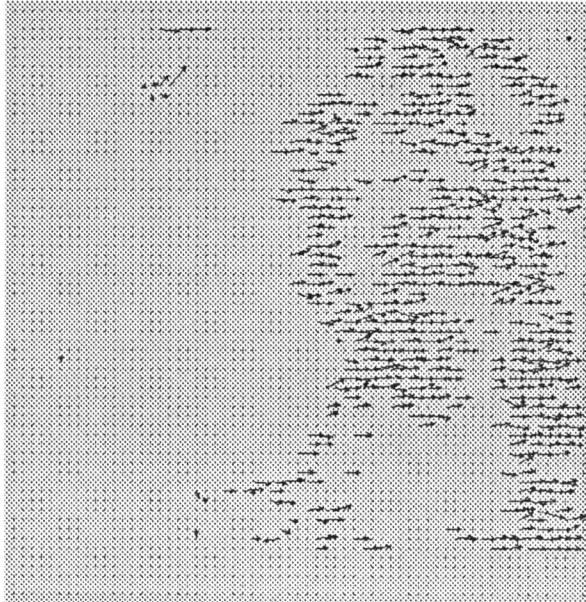

(a)

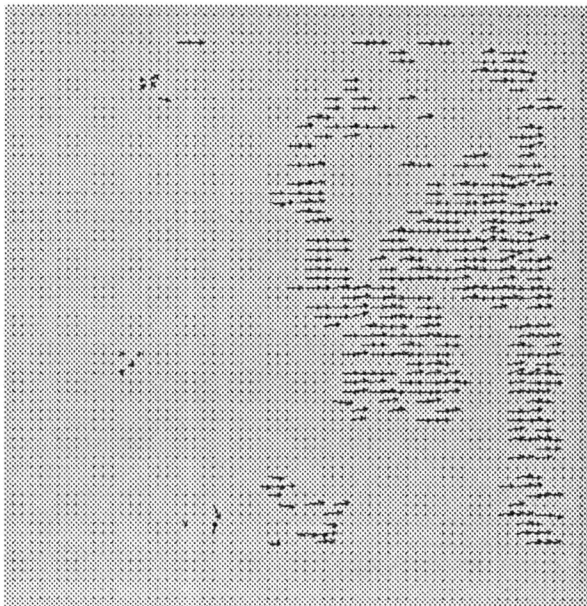

(b)

Figure 3. (a) Optical flow computed after filtering the sequence with a Gaussian operator with spatial σ equal to 2 and temporal σ of 1. (b) Optical flow computed after filtering the sequence with a Gaussian operator with spatial σ equal to 4 and temporal σ of 1

5. SURFACE DETECTION FROM 3-D MR DATA

Owing to the large amount of data involved, the analysis of 3-D magnetic resonance (MR) images requires a very high computing power, which cannot ordinarily be solved, within an acceptable time, with conventional serial computers. Moreover, the computing time increases with the accuracy required for the results.

Image-processing techniques for edge detection (or surface detection in images of higher dimension) have been extensively studied in the last 30 years. They are generally based on first- or second-order derivatives of the image intensity. Differentiation is usually performed by means of a regularization filtering followed by a discrete convolution with a small derivative kernel (an example of this approach has been presented in a previous section). It is well-known that the convolution of an image with a mask is equivalent to the scalar product of the Fourier transform of the image with the Fourier transform of the mask.

Since any MR system generates image data directly in the frequency domain[4] [17] and the inverse Fourier transform is a following step, it is possible to process data directly in the frequency domain without introducing discretization and noise due to the inverse transform.

Surfaces corresponding to boundaries of human body segments are extracted from 3-D MR data by using a technique based on the detection of peaks in the first-order derivative. Derivatives and low-pass filtering are performed in the frequency domain, but data is transformed in the space domain to detect surfaces in space. 3-D surfaces can be visualized by using standard ray tracing algorithms[18].

By processing data directly in the frequency domain, accuracy is greatly increased because raw data is not affected by discretization errors due to the hardware inverse Fourier transform.

5.1. Structure of the algorithm

Edges can be detected from images (of any dimensionality) by taking the local maximum value of the first derivative or the zero-crossings in the second derivative. In the 3-D image the intensity gradient is given by:

$$\frac{\partial f}{\partial x} \cdot vers(\mathbf{x}) + \frac{\partial f}{\partial y} \cdot vers(\mathbf{y}) + \frac{\partial f}{\partial z} \cdot vers(\mathbf{z}) \tag{4}$$

where f represents the intensity value of a given voxel at position (x,y,z). Considering the image in the frequency domain this is equivalent to:

$$j\omega_x F(\omega_x,\omega_y,\omega_z) \cdot vers(\omega_x) + j\omega_y F(\omega_x,\omega_y,\omega_z) \cdot vers(\omega_y) + j\omega_z F(\omega_x,\omega_y,\omega_z) \cdot vers(\omega_z) \tag{5}$$

---

[4] Data from human body segments is acquired by detecting different points as having different resonance frequencies.

F represents the Fourier transform of the intensity f. Finally the modulus of the derivative in the frequency domain results:

$$\sqrt{-(\omega_x^2 + \omega_y^2 + \omega_z^2)F^2} = Fj\sqrt{\omega_x^2 + \omega_y^2 + \omega_z^2} \qquad (6)$$

The computation of the derivative in the space domain becomes a simple arithmetic operation on the Fourier coefficients.

The system implemented on the Connection Machine is structured in the following way:

- The CM processors are first set as a regular 3-D grid with the same dimensions of the data volume. Each processor stores the value of the image brightness, while the grid axes correspond to $(\omega_x, \omega_y, \omega_z)$ in the frequency space. Raw MR data are loaded into the CM memory, each processor takes a single data value;
- for each processor (corresponding to a different spatial frequency) the value of $\sqrt{\omega_x^2 + \omega_y^2 + \omega_z^2}$ is evaluated and stored in a 64-bit field;
- for each processor the stored raw MR data is multiplied by the computed frequency modulus;
- data is translated in the space domain by applying a library function to perform an inverse Fourier transform on the resulting data volume;

At the beginning each processor stores a voxel of the image at a given spatial frequency. The result is the spatial derivative of the 3-D image in the space domain. The derivative operations are performed using 128-bit float complex arithmetic and the results are stored in 128-bit complex fields.

An experiment has been carried out on real data acquired from a human knee. Raw MR data has been stored in a $128 \times 128 \times 128$ volume. In Figure 4 a slice from the data volume transformed in the space domain is shown. In Figure 5 the result obtained by applying the surface-detection algorithm is presented. Only one slice, corresponding to the original data in Figure 4, is shown. It is worth noting that the detected surfaces correspond to edges in the 2-D slice. In Figure 6 a 3-D representation of the surface of the bone is presented. It has been obtained by applying a standard ray-tracing algorithm to visualize the recovered surfaces.

6. CONCLUSIONS

Two basic applications of the Connection Machine have been presented, the former concerning artificial vision, the latter 3-D MR data processing. Both cases present similar aspects, the central tenet being the processing of multidimensional images. In the first case we deal with sequences of images in time, while in the case of MR data a 3-D volume is processed, representing a 3-D image of a human body segment.

These applications are tackled using similar techniques. In both cases, in fact, it is possible to process data:

- with local operations only, generally at the pixel level;
- assigning to each processor a single data value;

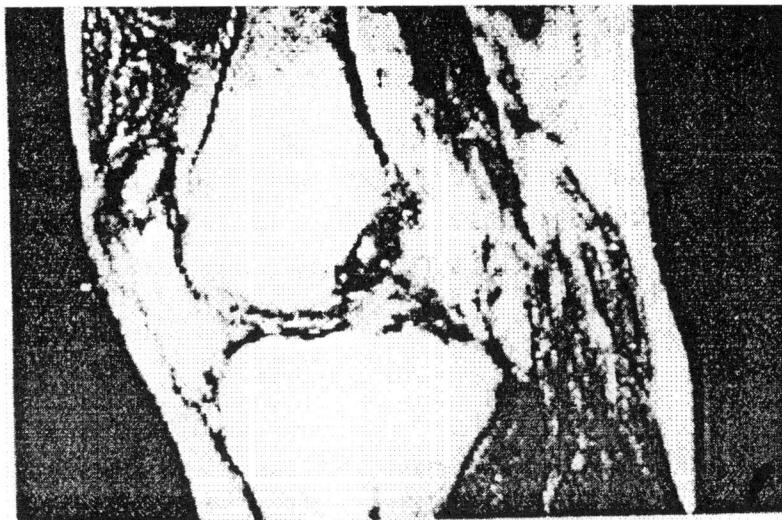

Figure 4.   2-D reslicing of a standard reconstructed 3-D MR acquisition

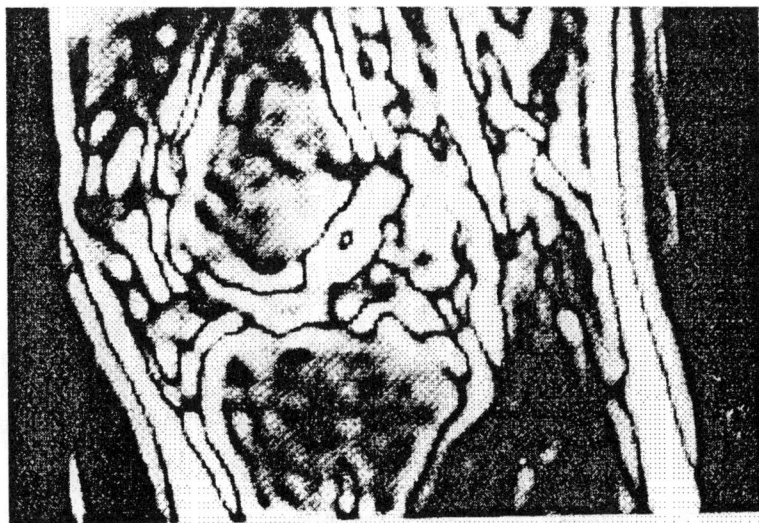

Figure 5.   2-D reslicing of a frequency filtered and reconstructed 3-D MR acquisition

The advantage of this approach is the possibility of arranging the CM processor as a regular *N*-dimensional grid associating one processing element to one data element. This makes it possible to implement very easily parallel programs from serial algorithms. Moreover, because of the locality of the operations, only nearest-neighborhood communications are used, resulting in a more efficient and faster use of the CM architecture.

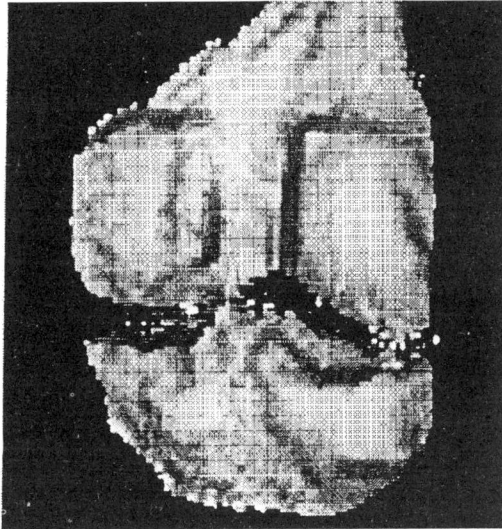

Figure 6. 3-D surface rendering of knee bone using ray-tracing technique

As a matter of fact the Boolean hypercube architecture of the Connection Machine is not used very much. It is our opinion, in fact, that many low-level vision and image-processing applications can be solved by making use of simple nearest-neighborhood communications without requiring any more complex communication schema. As concerns the analysis of MR tomographic images, a system for processing 3-D data from human body segments has been presented. The algorithm makes possible 3-D surface extraction from volumetric, raw MR data. This is obtained by processing data directly in the frequency domain, as it is obtained from the MR acquisition system. Data processing in the frequency domain has at least two advantages:

- discretization errors due to the limited support of the derivation mask are avoided;
- the derivative operation in the frequency domain (a product of the Fourier coefficient by its frequency) is much simpler and can be easily implemented on a highly parallel computer involving only operations within each single element. In the extreme case, each processor could operate on one single voxel.

The regions extracted from the MR volume can be processed with standard ray-tracing algorithms[18] to obtain a full 3-D representations of the organs. The computing power of the CM allows the user to completely interact with the processing and the final rendering, in real-time. It could then be possible to simulate in-body navigations in real-time.

REFERENCES

1. G. Sandini and M. Tistarelli, 'Active tracking strategy for monocular depth inference over multiple frames', *IEEE Transactions on PAMI*, **PAMI-12** (1), 13–27 (1990).
2. A. Bandopadhay, J.Y. Aloimonos and I. Weiss, 'Active vision', *International Journal of Computer Vision*, **1**, 333–356 (1988).

3. D.J. Coombs, 'Tracking objects with eye movements', *Proceedings of Topical Meeting on Image Understanding and Computer Vision*, pp. Tua3-1 - Tua3-4. North Falmouth, Cape Cod, MA, June 12–14 (1989), pp. Tua3-1–Tua3-4.
4. P. Morasso, G. Sandini and M. Tistarelli, 'Active vision: integration of fixed and mobile cameras', *NATO ASI on Sensors and Sensory Systems for Advanced Robots*, Vol. F43, Springer-Verlag, New York (1988), pp. 449–462.
5. B.K.P. Horn and B.G. Shunk, 'Determining optical flow', *Artificial Intelligence*, **17**, 185–204 (1981).
6. E.C. Hildreth, *The Measurement of Visual Motion*, MIT Press, Cambridge, MA (1983).
7. H.H. Nagel, 'On the estimation of optical flow: relations between different approaches and some new results', *Artificial Intelligence*, **33**, 299–324 (1987).
8. S. Uras, F. Girosi, A. Verri and V. Torre, 'A computational approach to motion perception', *Biological Cybernetics*, **60**, 69–87 (1988).
9. H. Bulthoff, J.J. Little and T. Poggio, 'A parallel algorithm for real-time computation of optical flow', *Nature*, **337**, 549–553 (1989).
10. E. DeMicheli, G. Sandini, M. Tistarelli and V. Torre, 'Estimation of visual motion and 3D motion parameters from singular points', *Proceedings of IEEE International Workshop on Intelligent Robots and Systems*, Tokyo, Japan, IEEE Computer Society Press (1988), pp. 543–549.
11. J.J. Little and A. Verri 'Analysis of differential and matching techniques for optical flow', *Proceedings of IEEE International Workshop on Visual Motion*, March 20–22, Irvine, CA, IEEE Computer Society Press (1988).
12. M. Tistarelli, 'Computing optical flow and depth from motion on the connection machine', *Proceedings of the SPIE/IEEE International Conference on Applications of Artificial Intelligence VIII*, Orlando, FA, SPIE **1293**, 114–127 (1990).
13. L.W. Tucker, C. Feynman and D. Fritzsche, 'Object recognition using the Connection Machine', *Proceedings of IEEE International Conference on Computer Vision and Pattern Recognition*, IEEE Computer Society Press (1988), pp. 871–878.
14. Thinking Machines Co., 'CM-2 Technical Summary', Thinking Machines Corp., Cambridge, MA, Technical report (1989).
15. P. Baraldi, E. DeMicheli, G. Radonich and V. Torre, 'The recovery of motion and depth from optical flow', *Proceedings of Topical Meeting on Image Understanding and Computer Vision*, North Falmouth, Cape Cod, MA, June 12–14 (1989), pp. Tua2-1–Tua2-4.
16. J.J. Little, G.E. Blelloch and T.A. Cass, 'Algorithmic techniques for computer vision on a fine-grained parallel machine', *IEEE Transactions on PAMI*, **PAMI-11**, 244–256 (1989).
17. W.S. Hinsaw and A.H. Lent, 'An introduction to NMR imaging: from the Bloch equation to the imaging equation', *Proceedings of the IEEE*, **71**, 338–350 (1983).
18. H.C. Delany, 'Ray tracing on a Connection Machine', Thinking Machine Corp., Technical Report VZ88-3 (1988).

Aeroelastic applications of the Connection Machine

SLOBODAN R. SIPCIC[1] AND THOMAS WESTBROOK[2]

[1]*Assistant Professor*
[2]*Graduate Student*
Department of Aerospace and Mechanical Engineering
Boston University
Boston, MA, USA

SUMMARY

This paper describes the implementation of a dynamical systems approach to aeroelastic analysis using the Connection Machine model 2 (CM-2). Through numerical simulation, the regions of harmonic and chaotic behavior in the λ, R_x (velocity, in-plane load) plane have been examined in detail. These regions are of interest in evaluation of the fatigue life of fluttering plates. The CM-2 computer architecture allows the removal of many of the previous simplifying and limiting assumptions regarding the prediction of the stability regions maps. Owing to its high-speed prediction capability, the CM-2, with framebuffer, offers 'real-time' display of the solution as it evolves during the prediction process. This feature gives insight into the fundamental way in which the solution evolves. This is essential in defining the scenarios describing roads to chaotic behavior of the dissipative dynamical systems.

1. INTRODUCTION

Fundamentally, aeroelasticity combines the fields of aerodynamics and elasticity. Simultaneous interaction of an elastic structure and aerodynamics forces leads to a complex and fascinating variety of dynamical behavior. In the previous work of Sipcic and Morino[1] and Sipcic[2] the aeroelastic evolution equations were studied using conventional computers stressing individual solution curves and their properties. Here the emphasis will be on families of such curves, and hence with the global behavior of the system. The analysis is based on the qualitative theory of dynamical systems and bifurcation theory. Those unfamiliar with the field will find Hirsch and Smale's book[3] an excellent introduction. More advanced concepts are discussed in Guckenheimer and Holmes[4], and Ruelle[5].

The use of single-processor supercomputers with vector processor facilities for the qualitative analysis of aeroelastic systems has been discussed by Moon and Li[6], and Dowell and Ilgamov[7]. They studied initial condition problems of buckled beams using the forced Duffing's equation. The interest herein is on realistic multidimensional aeroelastic systems. The highlight of this paper is not the algorithm and its applications, rather it is the process of implementing the algorithm on the Connection Machine.

2. FORMULATION OF THE PROBLEM

First, some definitions are needed. Consider systems whose behavior, expressed in terms of state vector $x = x(t) \in U \subset \Re^n$ is in some way controlled by external variables. The

1040–3108/91/060715–10$05.00
Received 23 October 1990
Revised 4 June 1991

latter are collected in a control parameter μ; one can often take $\mu \in \Re^m$. The family of differential equations

$$\frac{dx}{dt} = f_\mu(x), \qquad x \in U \subset \Re^n, \qquad \mu \in \Re^m \tag{1}$$

generates a flow $g^t(x)$ on U. Given a initial condition $x(0) = x_0 \in U$, a solution curve, or orbit starting at x_0 is the set of points

$$\bigcup_{t \geq 0} g^t(x_0) \tag{2}$$

The classical approach to the analysis of the differential equations (1) is based on individual solution curves and their properties (see Figure 1). Here we are concerned with families of such curves, and hence with the global behavior of the flow $g^t : U \to \Re^n$ for all $x \in U$ (see Figure 2).

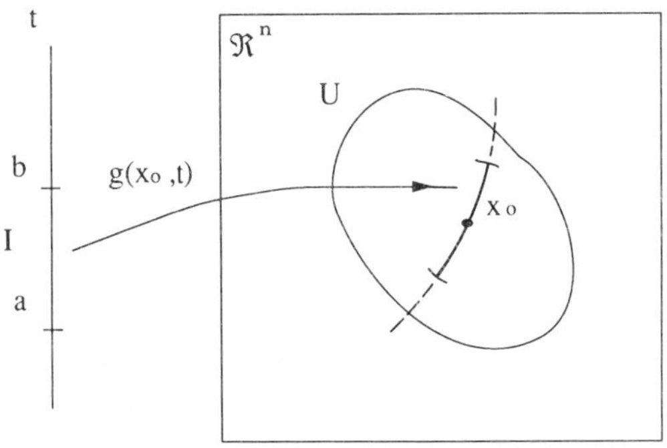

Figure 1.   The solution curve

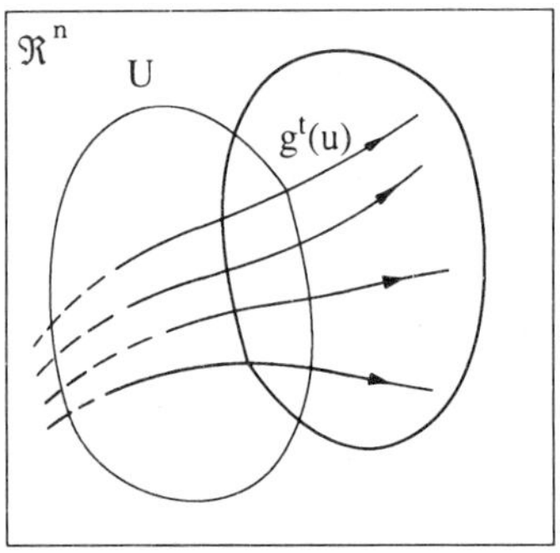

Figure 2.   The flow g^t

We shall deal exclusively with dissipative systems, i.e., systems with internal friction, such that volume carried by the flow g^t decreases in state space. The state space in this case can be pictured as densely filled with flow lines defined by equation (1) which approaches the attractors $\mathcal{A}$ in U as $t \to \infty$. The structure of the collection of attracting sets $\mathcal{A}$ in U is clearly important; we wish to know what qualitative solution types exist and in particular to classify the ways in which $\mathcal{A}$ might change with μ. This aim is clearly felt throughout the literature on dynamical systems; see, for example, Guckenheimer and Holmes[4].

3. CONNECTION MACHINE IMPLEMENTATION

The problem is inherently parallel and, as such, extremely suitable for the implementation on the CM-2. A brief description of the algorithm is given here (for more details see Sipcic and Deutsch[8]). The algorithm is composed of four stages

1. Initialization,
2. Integration,
3. Classifying attractors,
4. Postprocessing.

During initialization the state space, $U \subset \Re^n$, and the parameter space, $\mu \in P \subset \Re^m$, are defined. Each virtual processor is provided with an initial point x_0, and control parameter μ. Two distinctive analyses are possible. In the first analysis the emphasis is on the collection of attracting sets and their basins of attraction. In this case the state space U should be mapped onto the portion of the CM-2 to which the user is currently attached, and control parameter μ should be kept fixed during the whole duration of an experiment (see Figure 2). If we are interested in the changes of the attractors as the control parameters are varied, than the parameter space P should be mapped onto the CM-2 and the flow $g_\mu^t(x_0)$ on U should be generated (see Figure 3).

Once each virtual processor is provided with the initial point x_0 and the control parameter μ, the flow defined by equation (1) will be generated by using a fourth order Runge–Kutta algorithm with the constant step size. The criterion used to classify the types of the attractors encountered relies on the information about the long-time average of the flow g^t

$$\overline{g}(x_0) = \frac{1}{T} \int_0^T g^t(x_0) \, dt, \qquad x_0 \in U \tag{3}$$

Two simple schemes the trapezoidal rule, and Simpson's rule are used for the numerical integration. Note that the long-time average of the flow on some attractors, such as fixed-point or periodic orbits, converges to a point.

The algorithm used to determine the various attractors, which represent the asymptotic behavior of certain classes of solutions, utilizes the information about the long-time average of the flow and is based on the definition of the non-wandering sets. A point p

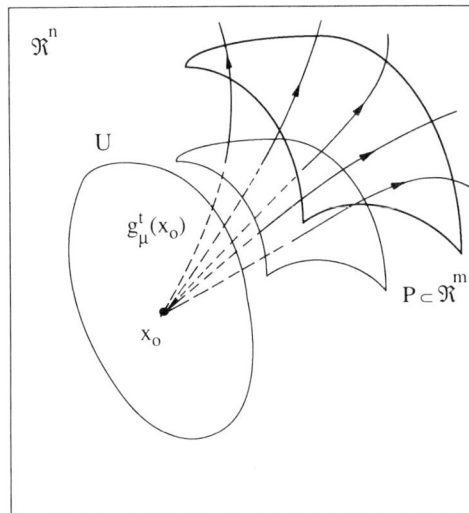

Figure 3. The flow g_μ^t

is called non-wandering for the flow g^t if, for any neighborhood Ω of p, there exists arbitrarily large t such that

$$g^t(\Omega) \cap \Omega \neq \emptyset \qquad (4)$$

Using geometrical language we say that a non-wandering point lies on or near orbits which come back within a specified distance of themselves. The non-wandering set is a set of all such points. Fixed points and periodic orbits are clearly non-wandering.

Studying attractors amounts to neglecting transient behavior, therefore we have considered only the stages of the system after it has attained some sort of 'internal equilibrium'. In other words, we analyze the motion on $\mathcal{A}$ or on parts of $\mathcal{A}$, assuming that the orbits which tend to $\mathcal{A}$ but are not in it behave similarly to those in $\mathcal{A}$, at least after sufficient lapse of time. The strategy for classifying the attractors is than as follows. Each virtual processor continuously checks the convergence of the averaged flow; the convergence of the averaged flow is a criterion for the elimination of the initial transient. The processor which has encountered convergence of the averaged flow then continues to search for the non-wandering orbit by choosing one point on the orbit and then checking if it is a non-wandering point for the flow. Using geometrical language we are checking if the point chosen lies on or near orbits which come back within a specified distance of themselves a specified number of times—in our applications, one hundred times. We are, however, far from able to define any complete classification of attractors. What is presented is a more modest approach which leads to a classification of some non-trivial attractors, which have the additional feature that they arise as modification of trivial attractors as the control parameter is changed.

In the postprocessing stage the user is given the power to point a mouse at a certain location in the state space and either blow up that region or request additional information, such as long-time histories, phase plane plots, and spectra of the responses.

The above algorithm has been embedded in the Dynamica-1 code. The version of the code described in this paper is programmed entirely in the Fortran-PARIS language. (The CM-Fortran version of the code, Dynamica-2, will be available in the near future.)

4. AEROELASTIC EQUATION

As an example we will examine the motion of an elastic panel subjected to an axial load, R_x, and a fluid flow of the velocity λ along its surface (see Figure 4). Dynamics of the plate is essentially governed by one-dimensional version of the von Karman equations for a thin plate, along with the simply supported boundary conditions. Using a Galerkin method we view the system of the equations and the boundary conditions as a flow defined on a Hilbert space, H, and choose an orthonormal basis ϕ_j for H. Assuming that the vertical plate deformation is given as a linear combination

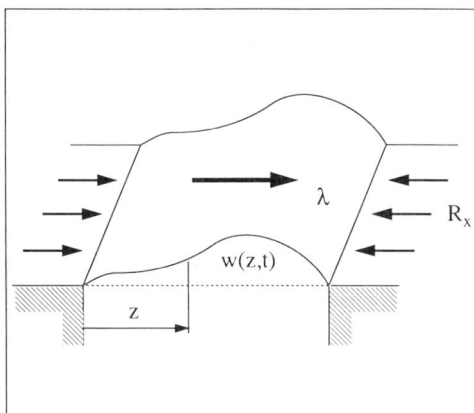

Figure 4. Panel flutter

$$w(z,t) = \sum_{j=1}^{\infty} a_j(t)\phi_j(z) \tag{5}$$

formally produces an infinite system of second-order ordinary differential equations for the unknown coefficients a_j. Truncation of this system by setting all of the modes $a_j, j > n$ to be zero produces a finite-dimensional dynamical system of the form given by equation (1), with $x = \{\dot{a}_1 \ldots \dot{a}_n a_1 \ldots a_n\}^T \in \Re^{2n}$, and $\mu = \{R_x \; \lambda\}^T$. For the details of the derivation see Sipcic[2].

For the sake of clarity, before addressing the general results, the key types of responses are introduced from a physical point of view. Three stable fixed points may be obtained in the phase plane $(w, \dot{w})$, (with w being the plate's vertical displacement at a given point, e.g. $z = 0.75$). The first fixed point corresponds to the undeformed position, the other two to the up-buckled or down-buckled plate position. The stable plate motion, generally speaking, consists of vibrations around the up-buckled and down-buckled positions, and the 'snapping through' motion. Finally, there is the possibility of chaotical response as well.

5. APPLICATION

The applications are designed to illustrate the capability of the method to determine the collection of attracting sets and in particular to classify the ways in which attracting sets might change with a control parameter. Consider the two-parameter family of aeroelastic problems equation (1), with parameters λ, R_x. The grid will be configured as two-dimensional, with shape 128×64. In what follows we will assume six-mode expansion, (equation (5)), i.e. the state space is twelve-dimensional. Each processor will follow the flow line from the same initial point x_0 for one value of the parameters (see Figure 3). We will associate a shade of grey to the different non-wandering sets recognized by each processor. Since the virtual processors are organized into a two-dimensional grid, the image within the CM-2 will be organized one pixel per virtual processor.

6. CLASSIFYING ATTRACTORS

The collection of the attracting sets is given in Figure 5(a). The regions 1 and 2 correspond to the stable fixed points. The regions 3 and 4 correspond to the simple harmonic motion, and more complicated periodic motion, respectively. In Figure 5(b) the regions of period multiplied orbits have been presented; note that region 5 corresponds to a period one motion. The limit cycles maximum size (corresponding to the amplitude of the periodic response) and the time needed to complete a cycle (corresponding to the frequencies of the periodic response) are given in Figures 5(c) and (d) respectively. These results are known from previous numerical simulation studies of Dowell and Ilgamov. The new interesting results occur at the boundaries between these subspaces (black colored regions). These regions correspond to the strange attractors. That this system has strange attractors is not new. What is new and interesting, however, is the size, distribution and fine structure of these subspaces. Let us examine these issues in the following subsections.

7. CHANGES OF THE ATTRACTORS-ROADS TO CHAOS

Upon examination of Figure 5(a) one may notice that the stable fixed point $x = 0$ changes to a stable limit cycle through Hopf bifurcation at the boundary between regions 2 and 3. The most interesting transitions occur when the parameters cross the boundaries between the limit cycle attractors and the strange attractors (black colored regions). In order to study the transition let us zoom into region 'A' of Figure 5(a), the result is given in Figure 6. Examining the structure of the attracting sets in Figure 6(a) at the boundary between the region of simple harmonic responses (region 3) and chaotic responses (black colored region) (see detail 'A' in Figure 6(a)), one finds the sequences of the period-doubling bifurcations culminating in chaos. The results of the calculation of the six neighboring processors from the region 'A', given in Figure 7, further supports this conclusion. Similar transitions occur at the boundary between the more complicated limit cycle attractor (region 4) and strange attractor (black colored region) (see Figure 6(b)).

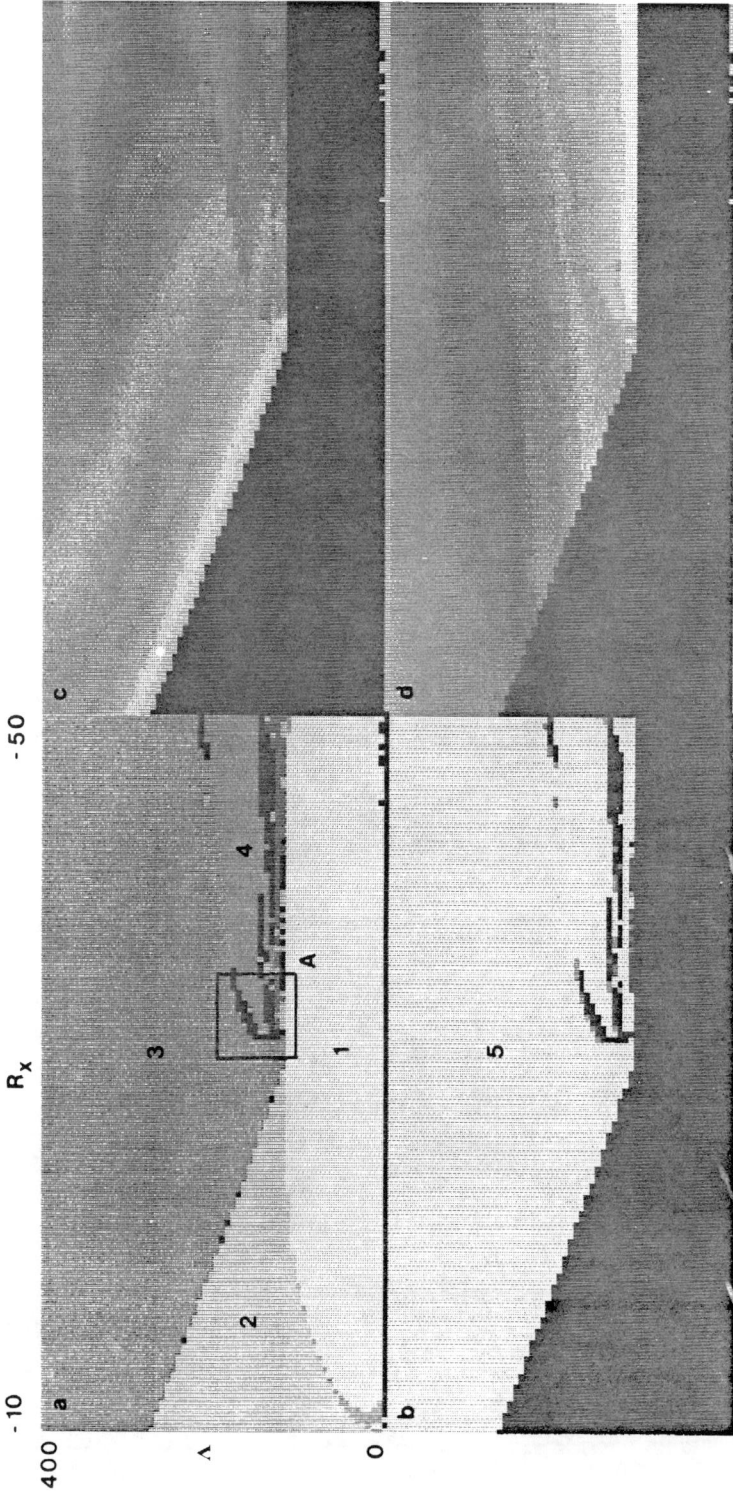

Figure 5. Two-parameter (λ, R_x) analysis. (a) Classification of the attractors. (b) Regions of the multiple period motion. (c) Amplitudes of the periodic motions. (d) Frequencies of the periodic motions

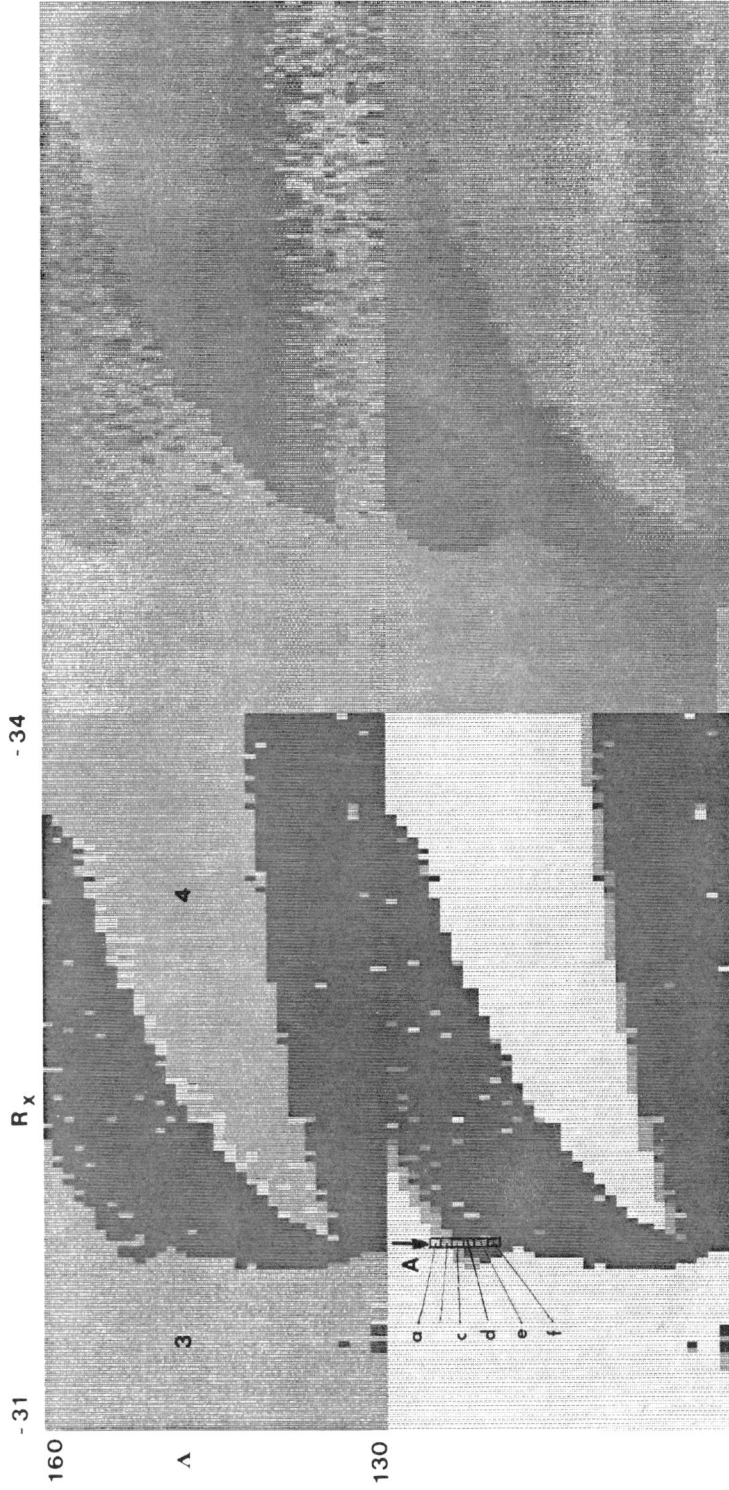

Figure 6. Zoomed region 'A' of Figure 5

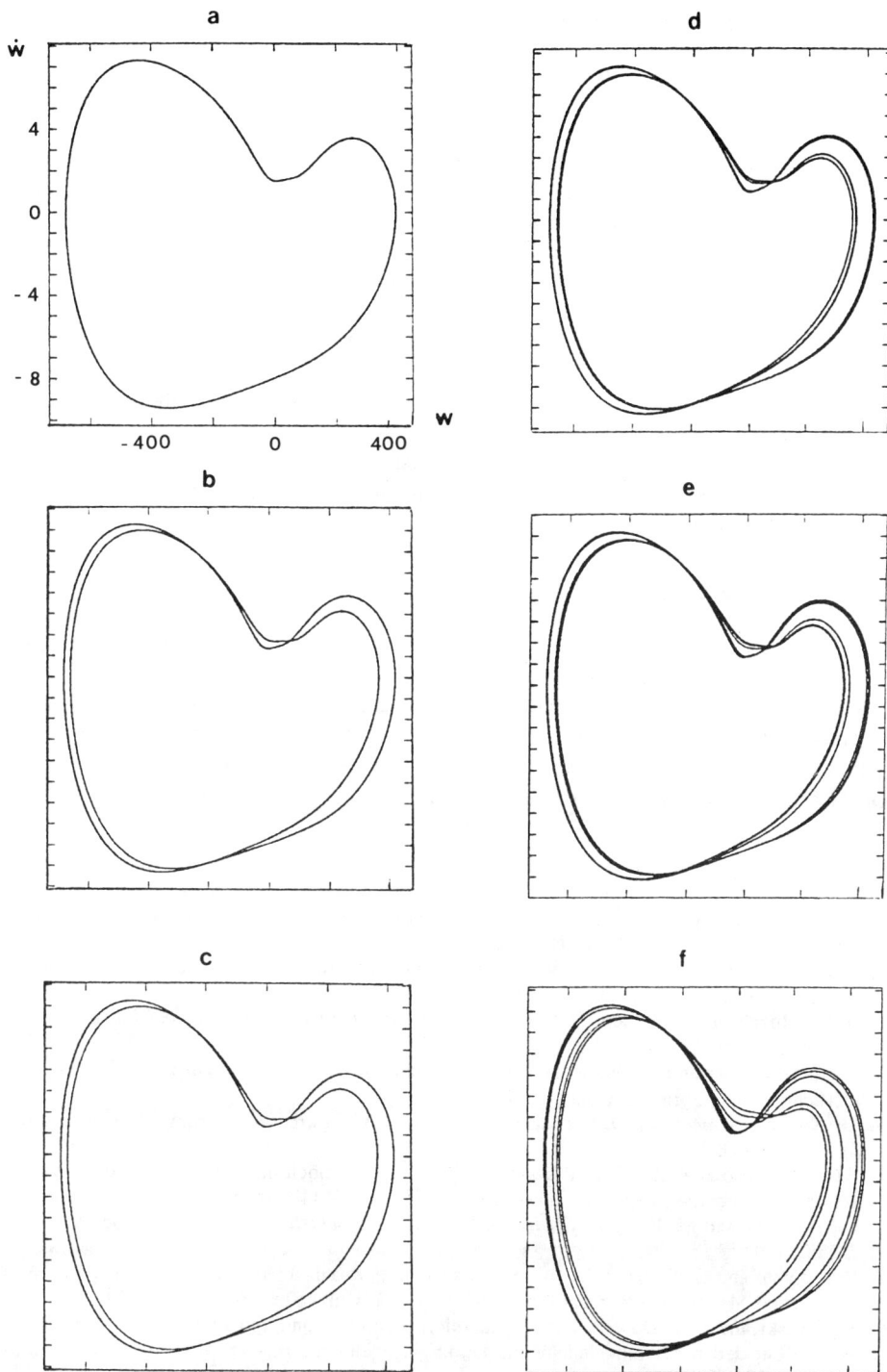

Figure 7. Cascade of period doubling bifurcations

8. CONCLUDING REMARKS

An approach to the analysis of the evolution equation (1) is presented. It is based on the qualitative theory of dynamical systems, and it utilizes the advantages of the CM-2, namely its the high-speed prediction capability, and its ability to perform visualization as part of the processing cycle, using a high-speed framebuffer. The method is capable of determining the collection of the attracting sets and in particular of classifying the ways in which attracting sets might change with a control parameter.

In order to understand the benefits of parallel processing, note that 125×64 pixels map, given in Figure 5(a), would require about one month of the front-end VAX 6410 computation, about 36 hours on a Floating Point System's FPS-164 connected to an IBM 3081 (see Pezeski, and Dowell[9]), compared to approximately 3 hours of CPU time on the CM-2.

Although the initial motivation for this paper was to highlight the algorithm, its implementation on the Connection Machine, and performance obtained, the results of the applications are of practical interest to aeroelasticians involved in the fatigue analysis. Identification of the entire pockets of chaos, frequency and amplitude analysis has been made possible by the method designed for this unique machine.

ACKNOWLEDGEMENTS

Research sponsored by the Air Force Office of Scientific Research (AFSC), under Contract No. F49620-86-C-0040, and NASA Langley Research Center, under Contract NAG-1-934. The United States Government is authorized to reproduce and distribute reprints for governmental purposes notwithstanding any copyright notation herein. The author wishes to thank Professor Luigi Morino of the University of Rome, and Dr. David Deutsch of Boston University for valuable discussions on this work.

REFERENCES

1. R.S. Sipcic and L. Morino, 'Dynamical behavior of the fluttering panel on a maneuvering airplane', *AIAA Journal*, **29**, 1304–1312 (1991).
2. R.S. Sipcic, 'Chaotic response of fluttering panel the influence of maneuvering', *Nonlinear Dynamics*, **1**, 243–264 (1990).
3. M.W. Hirsch and S. Smale, *Differential Equations, Dynamical Systems and Linear Algebra*, Academic Press, London (1974).
4. J. Guckenheimer and P. Holmes, *Nonlinear Oscillations, Dynamical Systems, and Bifurcations of Vector Fields*, Springer-Verlag, New York (1983).
5. D. Ruelle, *Elements of Differentiable Dynamics and Bifurcation Theory*, Academic Press, London (1989).
6. F.C. Moon and B.X. Li, 'Fractal basin boundaries and homoclinic orbits for periodic motion in a two well potential', *Physical Review Letters*, **55**, 1439–1442 (1985).
7. E.H. Dowell and M. Ilgamov, *Studies in Nonlinear Aeroelasticity*, Springer-Verlag, New York (1988).
8. R.S. Sipcic and D. Deutsch, 'A dynamical system approach for the aeroelastic analysis on the Connection Machine', Technical Report 89-1, Boston University, Boston, MA (1990).
9. C. Pezeski and E.H. Dowell, 'An examination of initial condition maps for the sinusoidally excited buckled beam modeled by the Duffing's equation', *Journal of Sound and Vibration*, **117**, 219–232 (1987).

CONCURRENCY: PRACTICE AND EXPERIENCE, VOL. 3(6), 725–739 (DECEMBER 1991)

Achievements and prospects for parallel computing

GEOFFREY C. FOX

Northeast Parallel Architectures Center
Syracuse University
Syracuse, New York 13244, USA

SUMMARY

Parallel computing works for the majority of large-scale computations. The development of parallel hardware designs has been largely transferred to industry, while universities continue major research efforts into better software environments. We describe a classification of problems and how different software models are needed for portable user-friendly, high-performance implementations on parallel machines. The education of a new generation of computational scientists will be a major challenge to our universities.

1. INTRODUCTION

In 1981, I listened to a Physics colloquium given by Carver Mead at Caltech. Carver was a pioneer in the development of VLSI, and explained how developments in this technology would inevitably lead to parallel computers. At the time, we were using our relatively new VAX11/780 to perform crude quantum chromodynamics (QCD) simulations with week-long runs. That talk changed my career, as I realized that QCD would naturally run in parallel. While waiting for the initial 64-node 8086-8087-based hypercube to be completed, I realized that we (now a collaboration with Carver's colleague, Chuck Seitz, in the Caltech Computer Science Department) had a machine that appeared to be generally useful in science. Thus was born the Caltech Concurrent Computation Program (C^3P) which, from 1983 to 1990, investigated the question:

> Is the hypercube (and later more general parallel architectures) effective in numerically intensive scientific and engineering calculations?

I have described the history of C^3P elsewhere[1,2] with the culmination[3] that in 1989 (eight years after believing Carver's dream), we finally obtained parallel computers that were truly supercomputers. In a series of articles, I have described some highlights of the fifty significant applications we built for the hypercube[4,5,3,6]. Here, I will concentrate on other areas—hardware, software and education—but I emphasize that these were each built on the experience of

> Using Real Hardware with Real Software to Solve Real Problems

Indeed, this motto will continue to be a guiding principle in the new program that I am setting up at Syracuse University.

Invited Talk at International Conference on Parallel Computing: Achievements, Problems and Prospects, Anacapri, Italy, 3–9 June 1990.

1040–3108/91/060725–15$07.50
Received May 1991
Accepted August 1991

The research of C^3P taught me several lessons.

- Parallel computing works for essentially all computationally intense problems.
- Computation will grow in importance—fed by high-performance parallel computers—and will 'change the world'—in academia, industry, day-to-day life and government applications.
- We need to develop new educational approaches to train the next generation of scientists who will have the interdisciplinary skills to exploit new computers for new problems.

My time at Caltech, and in particular with C^3P, were immensely rewarding and Caltech was one of the very few universities where a program like C^3P could have succeeded. Now, we know both that parallel computers work and how to exploit them for leading-edge academic applications. The new challenges are different. We must make parallel computing available to a broad range of users both in academia and, more importantly, in the real world of industry—only in this way will it enter the mainstream of computing. This principle underlies my vision of the future of parallel computing. Correspondingly, at Syracuse University, we will have a new program with some similarities with C^3P. It will be interdisciplinary but with a different focus—the Syracuse Center for Computational Science will emphasize education and the integration of parallel computing into industry.

This paper has three major sections describing respectively, the status and prospects for hardware, software and education. We will see my focus on applications in the chapter on software, which we discuss from this point of view.

2. HARDWARE PROSPECTS

Parallel computers were surveyed by Paul Messina for this conference[44], and I will just make a few general remarks. University and industry research has developed the basic principles of parallel computer hardware, and this knowledge has been successfully transferred to industry which can be expected to produce future hardware. The time for large-scale machines to be designed and built in universities has passed.

Existing machines can be classified into three broad architectural areas: MIMD distributed memory or multicomputers; SIMD distributed memory; MIMD shared memory or multiprocessors. My interest is in the first two—distributed memory—machines which can be expected to realize the highest and most cost-effective performance. Shared memory machines will certainly be important in the near future, and this software (as opposed to hardware) structure will be of great importance even on distributed memory hardware.

There are several effective large-scale distributed memory machines now available; the Connection Machine CM-2, INTEL i860, and NCUBE2 custom hypercube all having multi-gigaflop peak performance. We should also mention the Butterfly TC2000, which can be viewed as a shared memory machine, but is better thought of as a distributed memory machine with a switch interconnect that gives, in particular, low latency. It is not clear if this design can produce the high (peak) performance of the other distributed memory architetures. Smaller (in size and price) systems include those based on transputers, and the SIMD AMT DAP and Maspar machines. Although all these machines are very usable, many of them have rather clear design or implementation flaws.

Table 1. Communication and calculation parameters

Machine	t_{flop} node floating-point time (μs)	t_{comm}/t_{flop} communication time/64-bit word (measured in units of a typical node floating-point time)	t_{lat}/t_{flop} message latency
Transputer system			
—Direct (no routing)	2	2.2	13
—Express (routing software)	2	2.8	300
INTEL i860 Express	0.1	60	1400
NCUBE 1 Express	7	2	100

These are in the areas of communication bandwidth and latency, input/output subsystems including the host or interface computer. More generally, system integration needs to be improved. The communication issues can be illustrated with the measurements shown in Table 1[7–9].

We would expect future systems to be able to achieve t_{comm}/t_{flop} (typical node to node communication time per word/typical floating point node calculation time) in range $1 \rightarrow 10$ which is the value needed for general applicability of the machine. However, even the current i860 based INTEL systems with the high value of $t_{comm}/t_{flop} \sim 60$ perform well on many applications.

The issue of latency is less clear and cannot be separated from questions of network topology or node interconnection. Often these points, latency and topology, are treated separately with more attention being given to the interconnection scheme. We now find in current machines, interconnects using meshes, hypercubes, and switches with or without automatic routing hardware. These have all been successful and there is no convincing argument in favor of any one interconnect scheme. Most theoretical studies use unrealistic message-passing models, such as random message traffic which is a poor representation of the highly correlated communication needs in scientific computation. Further, the current systems have too few nodes to allow decisive experiments which could distinguish different interconnect methods. Even less is known about latency which deserves greater study, and this one of the areas where further research is needed to refine the architecture of future machines.

There is no uniquely good machine, as is illustrated by the current commercial systems which are all broadly successful. We can expect architectural diversity to continue within the design space indicated by today's existing and planned machines. Such a range of machines implies that the software must be portable and insensitive to changes in topology, granularity (number of nodes, memory per node), latency and if possible the choice between SIMD and MIMD. To motivate our research in algorithms, applications and software, we can imagine what one of the year 2000 teraflop computers will look like. It could have perhaps $N \sim 10,000$ nodes, each realizing some 200 megaflops. Maybe the architecture would be hierarchical; perhaps a 1024-element hypercube, with each element consisting of around ten processors sharing the same memory system. Such machines will exist before the year 2000 but at higher price and with technology trade-offs (for example, are optical interconnects cost-effective?) which will affect the architecture and hence 'balance' and 'generality' of the machine. We can expect that some or all of today's parallel computer companies will grow as the field matures; new enterprises will be formed and traditional computer manufacturers will move into the field. In particular, Digital and IBM, with their systems integration experience, may be major players. This growth is currently limited by software tools and the need to increase the number of industrial applications that run on parallel machines.

In the above, we have discussed 'conventional' parallel machines. These will be the top of the line supercomputers and will get unbelievable performance on most problems. In particular, special-purpose machines, such as those in high-energy physics (QCD) and computational fluid dynamics, will no longer be cost-effective. Major special-purpose hardware will only be justified in areas like neural networks, which use a radically distinct computational methodology.

3. SOFTWARE

The greatest challenge, and least agreement among practitioners, is found in software support for parallel computers. We will discuss this in the context of the layered structure shown in Figure 1, and introduced to me by Ken Kennedy of the Center for Research in Parallel Computation. Of the four layers, the uncertainty centers on the third, namely, on

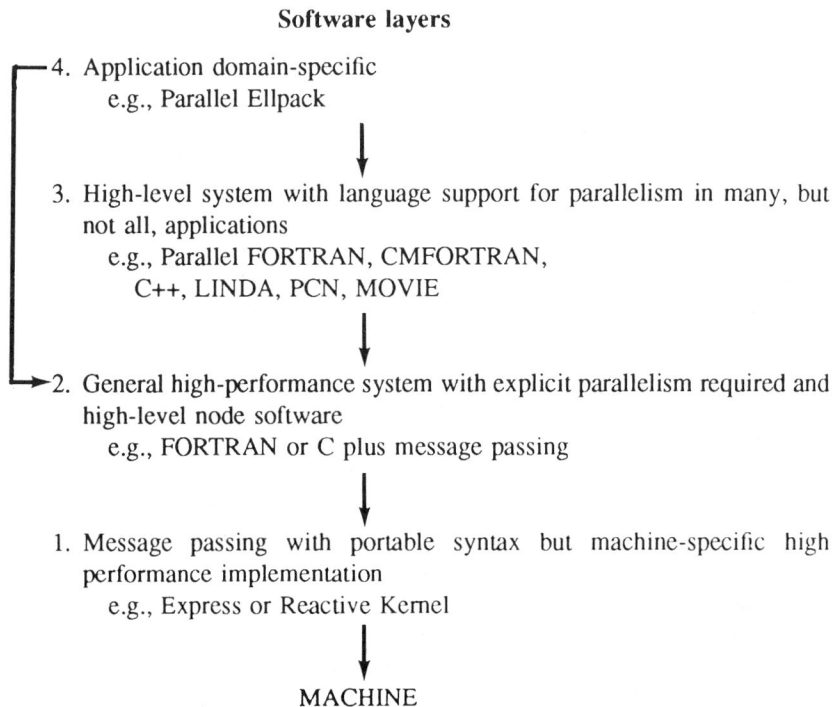

Software layers

4. Application domain-specific
   e.g., Parallel Ellpack

3. High-level system with language support for parallelism in many, but not all, applications
   e.g., Parallel FORTRAN, CMFORTRAN,
   C++, LINDA, PCN, MOVIE

2. General high-performance system with explicit parallelism required and high-level node software
   e.g., FORTRAN or C plus message passing

1. Message passing with portable syntax but machine-specific high performance implementation
   e.g., Express or Reactive Kernel

MACHINE

Figure 1. Software layers for parallel computers

high-level relatively general systems such as Parallel FORTRAN. This level is challenging to define and implement as it must satisfy the conflicting demands of generality in application and high (reasonable) performance which will scale to a variety of current and future architectures. Before returning to this, let us quickly discuss the other levels. We should first note that we will not discuss the support software that is critical for a reasonable environment; this includes debuggers, libraries, performance evaluation and visualization tools. These are important, but not the subject of this paper.

The top layer, with software systems such as NASTRAN (finite elements) and CHARMM (molecular dynamics), is particularly important in industry. These systems will certainly be at least as important for parallel systems, especially as there is an even greater need to shield the user from the immature parallel computers. However, it inevitably will take some time to produce these systems. This work will be accelerated when standards are established for the lower levels, two and three. FORTRAN and C, plus message passing (level two), are clearly effective in giving high-performance implementations on MIMD distributed machines. Indeed, essentially all successful work, including the some fifty hypercube applications we did within C^3P at Caltech, has used this approach. As long as you parameterize the number of nodes, this software is formally portable; and the same program will run on the NCUBE and INTEL hypercubes, a network of workstations, and even multi-headed IBM 3090s and CRAY vector Supercomputers. This portability is supported by the commercial system, *Express*, for level-one software which is the outgrowth of our CrOS software developed at Caltech[10]. However, this portability does not preserve performance; each machine involves different optimizations in the message passing and node programs to reflect trade-offs for

- granularity (number of nodes)
- communication bandwidth and latency (1)
- interconnect topology
- overlap (or not) of communication and calculation
- node architecture

We can illustrate this with our QCD (high-energy physics) calculations on the hypercube. The original code developed for the Cosmic Cube in 1983 was run with little change on the later Mark II (JPL) and commercial NCUBE-1 hypercubes. However, substantial changes were needed when it was used on the more powerful (500 megaflops on 128 nodes) Mark III (JPL) hypercube. The relatively higher communication latency implied substantial rearrangement of the message passing and a reordering of the algorithm to allow communication to be blocked into a smaller number of larger messages. The poor compiler required assembly language coding of key parts of the node program to exploit the WEITEK XL vector floating-point unit. We never did exploit the possible overlap of communication and calculation which was available on the Mark III. This would have increased performance by 25% and was possible in principle, but clumsy to implement. We believe that these optimizations in (1) above, can be performed by appropriate compilers, and this is a minimal goal for the higher level-three software systems.

There are many message passing systems, including:

occam	(Inmos)
Reactive Kernel/Cosmic Environment	(Caltech)
Express	(ParaSoft, Caltech)
Trollius	(Cornell, Ohio State)
Tiny	(Edinburgh)
Vertex	(NCUBE)
NX	(INTEL)

These offer comparable functionality with different trade-offs in the area of portability, performance and collective (higher-level) communication support. The latter includes broadcast and its generalizations, and the various primitives for data shuffling developed particularly by Ho[11,12] and others[13–17]. Further work is needed to define the more sophisticated primitives, but it should soon be possible to agree on a standard message-passing interface which would provide a portable base on which to build the higher-level software.

As illustrated in Figure 2, we view software as a map of a problem onto a computer. As such, it is sensitive to the architecture (structure) of both problem and computer. My goal would be software specialized (optimized) for a broad class of problem architectures which is designed to run portably on all parallel architectures. We will illustrate this idea a little later.

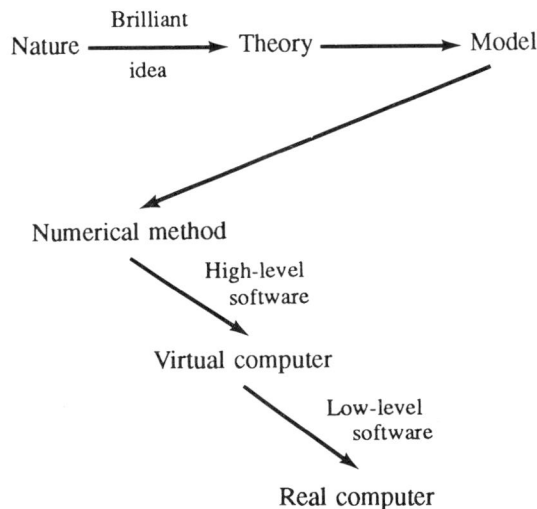

Figure 2   Computation and simulation as a series of maps

We would like to develop a classification of problem architectures and present here a simple division of problems into three classes, each of which presents different software challenges and solutions (at level three). Previously, we have introduced the concept of the spatial and temporal aspects of a problem. We can, rather, generally view a computation as an algorithm performed on the many elements of a data set; the algorithm is repeated corresponding to an increasing iteration count or the simulation of the data set for increasing time. The structure (often called computational graph) of the data set and algorithm we will refer to as the spatial structure of the problem. We call the nature of iteration, recursion, or time simulation, as the temporal structure. We described in [18] three distinct temporal structures: synchronous, loosely synchronous and asynchronous. Synchronous problems are characterized by identical algorithms being applied to all points in their data set. Loosely synchronous problems do not have a tight lockstep with microscopic synchronization, but rather macroscopic time synchronization. An example is a simulation evolving from t to $t + \delta t, t + 2\delta t$ with different algorithms at each data point, but natural synchronization at the beginning and end of each time step. Asynchronous problems have no natural synchronization in the time evolution of the different data points.

In Table 2, we introduce three problem architectures which are imaginatively labeled Classes I, II and III. These classes are not clearly defined and merge into each other. Further, a given application may consist of several components which fall into different classes. From our point of view, FORTRAN 90 is not regarded as the natural language for SIMD computers. Rather, it is the natural language for synchronous (SIMD) Class I problems[19]. One can, in fact, implement this language efficiently on SIMD and MIMD machines. This portability between SIMD and MIMD has been implemented for the analogous language C*[20], the functional language crystal[21], and we are currently implementing a FORTRAN 90 to F77+MP (MP = message passing) preprocessor for MIMD machines[22]. We expand on this later.

Table 2. Three problem architectures

Class	Temporal structure	Spatial structure	Examples	Natural parallel software	Natural parallel machine
I	Synchronous	Regular static	Finite difference QCD Matrix algebra	FORTRAN 90D[23] (CMFORTRAN)	SIMD distributed memory
II	Loosely synchronous	Irregular dynamic	Finite elements with adaptive irregular[24] mesh Cluster approach N-body Problem[25,26]	PARTI[27–29] Extensions of FORTRAN 90D?	MIMD distributed memory
III	Asynchronous	Loosely coupled	Event-driven simulation Computer chess Real time Control system Transaction analysis	Functional Decompositions Object-oriented systems LINDA[30] STRAND[31] PCN[32] MOVIE[33]	Distributed computer networks MIMD shared memory

Class III problems consist of irregular problems with no time synchronization. These are, in principle, very hard to parallelize as is illustrated by the major efforts devoted to parallelizing event-driven simulations[34]. This class can be parallelized when the parts are independent or loosely coupled and so synchronization overheads are small.

The loose coupling makes these problems suitable for distributed systems (e.g., networks of workstations) which have lower communication bandwidth and higher latency than the dedicated parallel machines. The powerful (and hence higher software overhead) programming environments for distributed computers are natural here; an object-oriented formalism is one obvious possibility.

The situation with Class II problems is less clear and a major research area for us. We have described in[25] the astrophysical N-body simulation with the $N \log N$ Barnes–Hut clustering method. It is not easy either to implement on SIMD machines or to code in FORTRAN 90. We can understand this as stemming from the fact that the algorithm's data structure is an irregular dynamic tree. This cannot be represented in FORTRAN 90 which only has array and vector data structures. We are currently investigating if adding extra (e.g., tree) data structures to FORTRAN 90 will allow one to address the N-body problem and other applications (e.g., quicksort) with a recursive or divide and conquer architecture. Saltz and his colleagues at NASA ICASE have shown that FORTRAN can be used for irregular finite element (more generally sparse matrix) problems with extensions to handle pointers[27,29]. Similarly, FORTRAN 90 with vector value subscripts can handle at least some of these problems[35,36]; correspondingly, the Connection Machine can run these problems successfully[37]. We can understand these successes as reflecting that an array, albeit an array of pointers (addresses), is an appropriate data structure. FORTRAN 77/90D is FORTRAN augmented by those possible additional data structures and parallel decomposition constructs that will have some general utility. We expect that most (scientific) problems in Class I and II will be elegantly expressed in FORTRAN 90D. With similar extensions implemented as 'user hints', we should be able to parallelize F77 codes in these classes. Ken Kennedy's group at Rice is building this FORTRAN 77D compiler for distributed memory parallel machines[23,38]; this will either produce directly F77+MP or possibly more usefully FORTRAN 90D.

CMFORTRAN implements the essential parallel constructs in FORTRAN 90 and also the *forall* statement. We include the latter in FORTRAN 90D and can illustrate its importance with a typical chemical reaction[39,40] or potential calculation. This involves an 'embarrassingly parallel' (Class III) calculation of the values of matrix elements combined with (Class I) matrix algebra (multiplication, inversion and eigenvalues). These two steps may be represented respectively by the *forall* and natural parallel array constructs in FORTRAN 90D. We need decomposition statements in FORTRAN 90D and these are extensions of the LAYOUT and ALIGN commands of CMFORTRAN. These instruct the compiler how to break up (either statically or dynamically) the arrays over the nodes[23].

Above, we have described how FORTRAN 90 provides a possible high-level language for Class I, and extensions may extend its utility into Class II. A major goal is to examine further applications to understand which features cannot be expressed in one of these ways and so provide a test suite of 'skeletons in the programming language closet'. These (like the irregular finite element and N-body problems) are the applications for which we need new languages. We do not really need new ways of expressing matrix multiplication and Laplace's equation; what we know now is sufficient. Nevertheless, many new language projects are tested and perhaps motivated by these unrealistic problems. I hope that our classification of problems and its refinement will focus the development of parallel languages and environments on the difficult problems that need to be solved.

Many problems are best regarded as built of several modules which can be considered as belonging to one of the three classes discussed above. This more general and important case is discussed in[41]. We conclude by illustrating the parallelization of FORTRAN 90 for four small Class I problems.

4. EXPERIMENTS WITH FORTRAN 90 ON MIMD MULTICOMPUTERS

These results come from the joint project[38] between Rice University (Ken Kennedy's group) and my research group at Syracuse. We are building a library of problems designed to test languages and parallelizing compilers. For each problem, we build several versions; in particular,

(P1) FORTRAN 77
(P2) FORTRAN 90D (CMFORTRAN)
(P3) Hand-coded FORTRAN 77 + Message Passing
(P4) 'What we think a parallelizing compiler could produce for a MIMD multicomputer from FORTRAN 77 (P1)'
(P5) 'What we think a parallelizing compiler could produce for a MIMD multicomputer from FORTRAN 90 (P2)'

We are using the results of these experiments to build the compilers that realize our expectations for (P4) and (P5).

Our results in Tables 3A, 3B, 3C, 3D are only preliminary but already interesting.

Table 3A. Gaussian elimination (256 × 256 matrix)

	Execution time (seconds) v. number of Processors on iPSC2 hypercube				
	1	2	4	8	16
(P3) Original hand-coded F77+MP	85.4	58.1	31.1	16.0	8.42
(P5) F77+MP from FORTRAN 90	80.0	50.2	26.6	13.8	7.72
(P3) Revised hand-coded F77+MP	73.4	50.1	26.9	13.8	7.53

Table 3B. N-body simulation (1024 particles)

	Execution time (seconds) v. number of Processors on iPSC2 hypercube				
	1	2	4	8	16
(P3) Hand-coded F77+MP	71.7	35.9	17.9	8.98	4.83
(P5) F77+MP from FORTRAN 90	139.6	69.1	35.5	18.1	9.40

Table 3C. Fast Fourier transform (16384 points)

	Execution time (seconds) v. number of Processors on iPSC2 hypercube				
	1	2	4	8	16
(P3) Original hand-coded F77+MP	36.8	23.3	14.2	8.32	4.82
(P3) Optimized hand-coded F77+MP	13.0	6.67	3.42	1.75	0.91
(P5) Optimized F77+MP from FORTRAN 90	18.8	10.1	5.36	2.84	1.50

Table 3D. Climate modeling code[42]

Implementation	Size of code (lines)	Machine	Performance (megaflops)
Original C Code	1500	CRAY X-MP (1 C.P.U.)	~ 1
(P2) FORTRAN 90	600	CM-2 (8 K)	66
(P5) F77 produced by hand from FORTRAN 90	1500	CRAY Y-MP (1 C.P.U.)	20
(P5) F77+MP by hand from FORTRAN 90	1650	NCUBE-1 16 node hypercube	3.3
		NCUBE-2 16 node hypercube	20
		INTEL i860 16 node hypercube	80

For a problem with a simple topology, LU decomposition in Table 3A, the FORTRAN 90 code produced essentially as good a code as the direct FORTRAN 77+ Message Passing. Indeed, the 'automatic' FORTRAN 90 procedure pointed out a possible improvement in our handed codes F77+MP; this is the difference between lines one and three of Table 3A. In Table 3B, our current automatic approach for the N-body problem loses a factor of two compared to the best parallel implementation; this is due to inefficient communication and one may need to change the FORTRAN 90 implementation to allow the compiler to optimize this. In this sense, the user will need to understand some issues of parallelism, even when writing 'explicitly parallel' code as with FORTRAN 90. Note the example in Table 3B is the simple $O(N^2)$ algorithm and not the more interesting and challenging $O(N(\log N))$ approach discussed earlier. In Table 3C, we find a 50% degradation in performance on the FFT for the FORTRAN 90 approach. This indicates that FORTRAN 90 does not optimally support the hierarchical data structures found in the FFT. As already discussed, we expect that the final FORTRAN 90D language will include new data structures—over and above the arrays and vectors in FORTRAN 90. We already mentioned a possible 'tree' data structure needed for the Class II clustering approach for the N-body problem.

Finally in Table 3D, we come to a 'real', albeit small in code size, problem. The original climate modeling code has been used in production[43] on CRAY and SUN computers. We saw in this project an interesting division of labor. The first rewriting from C to FORTRAN 90 was performed by the application expert. The further conversions into FORTRAN 77 and FORTRAN 77+ Message Passing were performed by 'computer scientists' without deep knowledge of the application[42]. In this case, we believe that no automatic method could have parallelized the original C code, but that our planned automatic approach would be able to perform the MIMD parallelization from FORTRAN 90. The result of this project is a portable code running well on the CRAY, Connection Machine and hypercubes. Note that we even improved the sequential performance (line one versus line three of Table 3D) by an order of magnitude. The original C code made extensive use of pointers which had several repercussions. It made vectorization hard on the CRAY; it made the code impossible to automatically parallelize as the 'structure of problem' was expressed in dynamic pointer values; it made the code hard to port except by the domain expert.

Our initial experiments are sufficiently encouraging that we believe that a language like FORTRAN 90 will become an efficient vehicle for Class I applications. We also hope that it can be extended with higher-level data structures to accommodate the more complex 'problem architectures' seen in Class II problems.

5. COMPUTATIONAL SCIENCE EDUCATION

The emergence of computation as a fundamental methodology implies major changes in our educational system which will challenge our universities, community colleges, and schools in the next decade[6]. Computers are being used in schools, even at the kindergarten level. This is necessary, but not sufficient. We need not only to teach students how to program, but instill the understanding that computing is fundamental and will change the nature of both their careers and their day-to-day life. Computing, like the traditional reading, writing and arithmetic is a key enabling skill whose use and *understanding* permeates all other activities. Looking at applicants for graduate school (in Physics at Caltech), I saw few students who viewed computers as anything but a rather tiresome tool. Why is this when most of them come from prestigious undergraduate institutions where the very latest computers abounded? The reason may be that such students are typically not given any courses that treat computation as fundamental and exciting. They are taught by faculty whose vision of computing comes from a time when computers were a useful but unexciting tool. This will change.

The Federal High Performance Computing Initiative developed the concept of interdisciplinary teams to tackle the grand challenges and their implementations on parallel machines. This idea was part of my Caltech Concurrent Computation Program but interestingly enough, something else happened as well. Namely, the majority of the research was performed by interdisciplinary individuals who combined the skills of a computer scientist with those of an application area such as Physics or Chemistry. It is this phenomenon that inspired much of my thoughts on computational science. You may argue that 'jack of all trades, master of none' implies that interdisciplinary scientists are not competitive. I believe this is a valid concern, but the negative conclusion can be avoided. I propose that Computational Science should be an interdisciplinary program with degrees given in the traditional fields. Undergraduates, Masters or PhD students will get degrees in the Computational Science Program such as

- 'Undergraduate degree in Physics in the Computational Science Program' (in my point of view, this is a long way of saying an undergraduate degree in Computational Physics)
- 'Masters in Chemistry with a minor in Computer Science'
- 'PhD in Computer Science with a Masters Degree in Economics'

Computational Science students will need new curricula, and this will require cooperation and understanding from the traditional disciplines. For instance, the requirements for a degree in Physics within the Computational Science Program may require fewer base Physics courses than the traditional Physics degree, with this reduction made up by a set of computational courses. There are typically electives in any set of course requirements and so these reductions in the base (in our example, Physics) academic area need not be significant. In some institutions and some departments, these changes may not be accepted, and a different implementation of Computational Science will be needed. We must gain experience as to what works and what doesn't. Students will enter a program in Computational Science with a variety of aspirations and skills. For instance, freshman undergraduates may initially be interested in Physics, but later decide to graduate in Computer Science. We need a good set of courses to accommodate the different initial skills and allow a student to switch from a focus on Computer Science to one on an application area—or vice versa. Not only are such curricula in their infancy but, as found while teaching at Caltech, the lack of relevant books is a severe handicap. We must develop the curricula, books and the needed educational software.

A Chemist graduating from the Computational Science program will be well-grounded in Chemistry, but will have a broad knowledge of Computer Science. The latter will enable the Chemist to use computers and new computer science techniques more effectively than a Chemist without the computational science background. Thus, he or she will be a better Chemist, and in this way the interdisciplinary scientist is not handicapped. A Computer Scientist graduating in our new program will have a sound basis in Computer Science and an understanding of the computational needs and algorithms of one or more application areas. The latter knowledge will enable our Computer Scientist to develop better compilers, debuggers and visualization aids because he or she understands the needs of the applications.

Thus, I believe that Computational Science is an exciting and viable area which can be implemented within the existing academic framework. I intend to pursue this vigorously at Syracuse. In particular, we will develop the new courses (definition, notes, books, software). We will work with the international community to establish common guidelines for the teaching of Computational Science and build a consensus that it is important.

6. CONCLUSIONS

Technology has opened several new opportunities, both in research and education. We are at the beginning of changes which will have profound implications for academia, industry and society. Parallel computing, discussed here, is only one part of this revolution.

I would like to thank Paul Messina and his colleagues, especially Almerico Murli from the University of Naples, for their warm hospitality and an excellent conference. This work was supported by the Department of Energy (Applied Mathematical Sciences— Grant: DE-FG03-85ER25009), Joint Tactical Fusion Program Office, and the National Science Foundation under Cooperative Agreement No. CCR-8809165; the Government has certain rights in this material.

REFERENCES

1. G. C. Fox, 'Questions and unexpected answers in concurrent computation,' in J. J. Dongarra (ed.), *Experimental Parallel Computing Architectures*, Elsevier Science Publishers, North-Holland (1987), pp. 97–121. (Caltech Report C3P-288.)
2. G. C. Fox, 'The hypercube and the Caltech Concurrent Computation Program: a microcosm of parallel computing', in B. J. Alder (ed.), *Special Purpose Computers*. Academic Press, New York (1988), pp. 1–140. (Caltech Report C3P-422.)
3. G. C. Fox, 'Parallel computing comes of age: Supercomputer level parallel computations at Caltech', *Concurrency: Practice and Experience*, 1(1), 63–103 (1989). (Caltech Report C3P-795.)
4. G. C. Fox, 'Experience on the hypercube', Technical Report C3P-716, California Institute of Technology, February 1989.
5. G. C. Fox, '1989—the first year of the parallel supercomputer', Technical Report C3P-769, California Institute of Technology, March 1989. Paper presented at the Fourth Conference on Hypercubes, Concurrent Computers and Applications.
6. G. C. Fox, 'Applications of parallel supercomputers: scientific results and computer science lessons', in M. A. Arbib and J. A. Robinson (eds), *Natural and Artificial Parallel Computation*, MIT Press, Cambridge, MA (1990), chap. 4, pp. 47–90, SCCS-23. (Caltech Report C3P-806b.)
7. T. H. Dunigan, 'Performance of the intel ipsc/860 hypercube', Technical Report ORNL/TM-11491, Oak Ridge National Laboratory, 1990.
8. L.-R. Hu and G. S. Stiles, 'Fluid dynamics on EXPRESS: an evaluation of a topology-independent parallel programming environment', in D. L. Fielding (ed.), *Transputer Research and Applications 4*, IOS Press, Amsterdam (1990).
9. R. D. Williams, 'Express: portable parallel programming', Technical Report C3P-944, California Institute of Technology, October 1990. Presented at Cray User Group, Austin, Texas.
10. G. C. Fox, M. A. Johnson, G. A. Lyzenga, S. W. Otto, J. K. Salmon and D. W. Walker, *Solving Problems on Concurrent Processors*, Vol. 1, Prentice Hall, Englewood Cliffs, NJ (1988).
11. C.-T. Ho and S. L. Johnsson, 'Distributed routing algorithms for broadcasting and personalized communication in hypercubes', in *Proceedings of IEEE 1986 International Conference on Parallel Processing* (1986), pp. 640–648, IEEE Press, Los Alamitos, CA.
12. C.-T. Ho, 'Optimal Communication Primitives and Graph Embeddings', PhD thesis, Yale University, May 1990.
13. G. Fox and W. Furmanski, 'Communication algorithms for regular convolutions and matrix problems on the hypercube', in M. T. Heath (ed.), *Hypercube Multiprocessors*, SIAM, Philadelphia (1987), pp. 223–238. (Caltech Report C3P-329.)
14. G. C. Fox and W. Furmanski, 'Hypercube algorithms for neural network simulation the Crystal_Accumulator and the Crystal_Router', in G. C. Fox (ed.), *The Third Conference on Hypercube Concurrent Computers and Applications*, Vol. 1, ACM Press, New York (1988), pp. 714–724. (Caltech Report C3P-405b.)
15. G. C. Fox and W. Furmanski, 'Optimal communication algorithms for regular decompositions on the hypercube', in G. C. Fox (ed.), *The Third Conference on Hypercube Concurrent Computers and Applications*, Vol. 1, ACM Press, New York (1988), pp. 648–713. (Caltech Report C3P-314b.)
16. Q. F. Stout and B. Wager, 'Intensive hypercube communication I: prearranged communication in link bound machines', Technical Report CRL-TR-9-87, University of Michigan, 1987.

17. L. G. Valiant, 'General purpose parallel architectures', Technical report, Harvard University, January 1988.

18. G. C. Fox, 'What have we learnt from using real parallel machines to solve real problems?', in G. C. Fox (ed.), *The Third Conference on Hypercube Concurrent Computers and Applications*, Vol. 2, ACM Press, New York (1988), pp. 897–955. (Caltech Report C3P-522.)

19. G. C. Fox, 'FortranD as a portable software system for parallel computers', Technical Report SCCS-91, Syracuse University, June 1991. Published in the Proceedings of Supercomputing USA/Pacific 91, held in Santa Clara, CA. CRPC–TR91128.

20. M. J. Quinn and P. J. Hatcher, 'Data-parallel programming on multicomputers', *IEEE Software*, pp. 69–76 (1990).

21. M. Chen, J. Li and Y. Choo, 'Compiling parallel programs by optimizing performance', *Journal of Supercomputing*, 2, 171–207 (1988).

22. M.-Y. Wu and G. C. Fox, 'Compiling Fortran 90 programs for distributed memory MIMD parallel computers', *Syracuse Center for Computational Science—Technical Report* No. SCCS-88 (1991).

23. G. C. Fox, S. Hiranandani, K. Kennedy, C. Koelbel, U. Kremer, C.-W. Tseng and M.-Y. Wu, 'Fortran D language specification', Technical Report SCCS-42c, Rice Center for Research in Parallel Computation; CRPC-TR90079, April 1991.

24. R. D. Williams, 'Supersonic flow in parallel with an unstructured mesh', *Concurrency: Practice and Experience*, 1(1), 51–62 (1989). (See manual for this code in Caltech Report, C^3P-861 (1990).) (Caltech Report C3P-636b.)

25. G. C. Fox, P. Hipes and J. Salmon, 'Practical parallel supercomputing: examples from chemistry and physics', in *Proceedings of Supercomputing '89*, ACM Press, New York (1989), pp. 58–70. IEEE Computer Society and ACM SIGARCH, Reno, NV. (Caltech Report C3P-818.)

26. J. Salmon, *Parallel Hierarchical N-Body Methods*. PhD thesis, California Institute of Technology, December 1990.

27. H. Berryman, J. Saltz and J. Scroggs, 'Execution time support for adaptive scientific algorithms on distributed memory machines', *Concurrency: Practice and Experience*, 1991. Accepted for publication.

28. J. Saltz, R. Mirchandaney, R. Smith, D. Nicol and K. Crowley, 'The PARTY parallel runtime system', in *Proceedings of the SIAM Conference on Parallel Processing for Scientific Computing*. Los Angeles, CA, SIAM, Philadelphia (1987).

29. J. Saltz, H. Berryman and J. Wu, 'Multiprocessor and runtime compilation', *Concurrency: Practice and Experience*, 1990. Submitted for publication.

30. D. Gelernter, 'Multiple tuple spaces in Linda', in *Proceedings of Parallel Architectures and Languages Europes*, Vol. 2, Springer-Verlag, LNCS (1989), p. 366.

31. I. Foster and S. Taylor, *Strand: New concepts in Parallel Programming*, Prentice Hall, Englewood Cliffs, NJ (1990).

32. K. Chandy and S. Taylor, 'A primer for program composition notation', Technical Report CRPC-TR90056, California Institute of Technology, June 1990.

33. W. Furmanski, 'MOVIE and map separates', Technical Report SCCS-82, Syracuse University, April 1991. JTF Semiannual Coordination Meeting.

34. F. Wieland, L. Hawley, A. Feinberg, M. DiLoreto, L. Blume, J. Ruffles, P. Reiher, B. Beckman, P. Hontalas, S. Bellenot and D. Jefferson, 'The performance of a distributed combat simulation with the time warp operating system', *Concurrency: Practice and Experience*, 1(1), 35–50 (1989). (Caltech Report C3P-798.)

35. S. L. Johnsson and K. K. Mathur, 'Experience with the conjugate gradient method for stress analysis on a data parallel supercomputer', Technical report, Thinking Machines Corporation, 1990.

36. K. K. Mathur and S. L. Johnsson, 'The finite element method on a data parallel computing system', *Int. J. of High-Speed Computing*, 1(1), 29–44 (1989). (Department of Computer Science, Yale University, Technical Report YALEU/DCS/RR-742, Thinking Machines Corporation, Technical Report CS89-2.)

37. G. C. Fox, 'Hardware and software architectures for irregular problem architectures', in *ICASE Workshop on Unstructured Scientific Computation on Scalable Microprocessors*, October 1990.

Held in Nags Head, North Carolina. SCCS-111.

38. M.-Y. Wu and G. C. Fox, 'Test suite and performance for Fortran90 compilers', *Syracuse Center for Computational Science—Technical Report* No. SCCS-40 (1990)

39. Y.-S. M. Wu, S. A. Cuccaro, P. G. Hipes and A. Kuppermann, 'Quantum mechanical reactive scattering using a high-performance distributed-memory parallel computer', Technical Report C3P-860, California Institute of Technology, January 1990. Accepted for publication in *Chemical Physics Letters*.

40. P. Hipes, C. Winstead, M. Lima and V. McKoy, 'Studies of electron-molecule collisions on the Mark IIIfp hypercube', Technical Report C3P-909, California Institute of Technology, April 1990. Published in Proceedings of the Fifth Distributed Memory Computing Conference, April 9–12, Charleston, SC, IEEE.

41. G. C. Fox, 'Parallel problem architectures and their implications for portable parallel software systems', Technical Report C3P-967, Northeast Parallel Architectures Center, May 1991. CRPC-TR91120, SCCS-78, Presentation at DARPA Workshop, Providence, RI, February 28, 1991.

42. C. L. Keppenne, M. Ghil, G. C. Fox, J. W. Flower, A. Kolawa, P. N. Papaccio, J. J. Rosati, J. F. Shepanski, F. G. Spadaro and J. O. Dickey, 'Parallel processing applied to climate modeling', Technical Report SCCS–22, Syracuse University, November 1990.

43. C. L. Keppenne, 'Bifurcations, Strange Attractors and Low-Frequency Atmospheric Dynamics', PhD thesis, Université Catholique de Louvain, 1989.

44. P. C. Messina, 'Parallel computing in the 1980s—one person's view', *Concurrency: Practice and Experience*, **3**(6), 501–524 (1991).

Author Index

Concurrency
PRACTICE AND EXPERIENCE

AIMS AND SCOPE

Recent developments in technology have stimulated the development of **concurrent** computers. These machines consist of a collection of processors connected in a network—or alternatively a collection of processors sharing access to a common memory. These include both general purpose MIMD and SIMD architectures and special purpose systems such as neural networks. Optical and dataflow hardware can be expected in the future. There are now several commercially available concurrent computers and an increasing number of microprocessor chips specifically designed to permit the construction of parallel computers varying in size from PC add-in boards with a few processors up to 64000-processor supercomputers.

These machines are being successfully applied in a wide range of application areas especially in science and engineering. This is producing a substantial amount of practical experience in those problems which parallelize well and the features of hardware and systems software needed to use concurrency effectively. There are also new computational methods, such as cellular automata and massively parallel neural networks, which are particularly suited to concurrent execution. At present, there is no journal that brings this work together. Results, if published at all, are scattered throughout specialized technical journals. This journal will therefore focus on practical experience with concurrent machines, especially:

- Concurrent solutions to specific problems
- Concurrent algorithms and computational methods
- Programming environments, operating systems, and tools
- New languages
- Performance design, analysis, models and results

The papers will all have a practical or phenomenological emphasis.

Updated information—The practical experience central to the journal will evolve more rapidly than the basic concurrent algorithms and approaches. Thus, we will consider for publication short addenda to previously published papers which provide significant and clearly presented additional practical experience, e.g. performance of a new parallel computer, that naturally augments the published paper.

EDITOR

Professor Geoffrey C. Fox, *Northeast Parallel Architectures Centre, Syracuse University, 111 College Place, Syracuse, NY 13244-4100, U.S.A.*
Telephone: (315) 443 1723; Fax: (315) 443 1973; e-mail: gcf@nova.npac.syr.edu.

ASSOCIATE EDITORS

Professor A. J. G. Hey, *Department of Electronics and Computer Science, University of Southampton, Southampton SO9 5NH, U.K.*
Dr Paul Messina, *California Institute of Technology, Mail Stop 158-79, Pasadena, CA 91125, U.S.A.*

EDITORIAL BOARD

WILEY
Publishers Since 1807

Chichester · New York · Brisbane · Toronto · Singapore

CPEXEI 3 1–742 (1991)
ISSN 1040–3108

COPYING OF ARTICLES

Printed and bound in Great Britain by Galliard (Printers) Ltd., Great Yarmouth, Norfolk

CONCURRENCY: PRACTICE AND EXPERIENCE, VOL. 3, iii–vii (1991)

Volume Contents

Indexed or abstracted by 'Cambridge Scientific Abstracts', 'Computing Reviews', 'Data Processing Digest' and 'INSPEC'.

Concurrency
PRACTICE AND EXPERIENCE

Notes for Authors

Initial Submission. In the first instance, all text should be submitted as hardcopy, conventionally mailed, by fax or by e-mail to Professor Geoffrey C. Fox, Department of Computer Science and Physics, Room 3-131 NPAC, 111 College Place, Syracuse, NY 13244-4100, U.S.A. Telephone: (315) 443 1723; Fax: (315) 443 1973; e-mail: gcf@nova.npac.syr.edu. or Professor Anthony J. G. Hey, Department of Electronics and Computer Science, University of Southampton, Southampton SO9 5NH, U.K. (ajgh@ecs.soton.ac.uk). Telephone: (703) 595 000, ext. 2069. Hardcopy submissions should include three copies of the manuscript. All submissions should include the contact author's name; e-mail and street address; and telephone, fax, and telex numbers. It would be convenient if submissions from the United Kingdom be sent to Professor Hey.

Submission of Accepted Papers. All accepted papers should be submitted to the Editor or Associate Editors in final form with original artwork for illustrations. Preferably, authors should submit a machine-readable version of their paper along with one "master" hardcopy (see notes below) and a $5\frac{1}{4}$" floppy disk of their accepted manuscript. Alternately, authors may submit their papers by e-mail to the above address.

Submission of Electronically Readable Manuscripts. Machine-readable submissions are preferred in TeX. Specific macros which have been specially designed to conform to the journal 'house-style' are available from the publisher (Baffins Lane, Chichester, West Sussex PO19 1UD, U.K.) or the Editor and can be sent e-mail. (Note: these macros will *not* produce the final appearance of the paper. Double line spaces have been deliberately introduced so that papers are easier to copyedit. The publisher will adjust the line spacing when setting the paper.) Authors are urged to use these macros rather than creating their own so that considerable time and effort can be saved during the production process.

1. All electronically readable manuscripts must be accompanied by:
   (a) a hardcopy of the paper generated by the file submitted on disk;
   (b) original artwork for illustrations or Postscript files with a hardcopy (see illustration instructions below).
2. Submission of TeX files using macros in the 'house-style' would be preferred in *all* cases. If authors attempt to use any other macros or deviations of TeX (e.g. LaTeX), the Publisher shall reimpose house style macros, possibly causing a delay in publication.
3. If authors use *any other* typesetting software, the disk supplied should not contain any control codes (i.e. a straight ASCII file), but the hardcopy of the paper should indicate any specific and special layout or formatting requirements (e.g. bold, italic, special characters, etc.).
4. All items of artwork or illustrative material should be clearly identified on the back, in pencil, with the author's name and figure number.
5. The position of each figure should be clearly identified in the text and the figure legend should follow it. (Note: The amount of lettering on a drawing should be reduced as far as possible by transferring it to the legend.)
6. Halftone illustrations are to be restricted in number to the minimum necessary. Good glossy bromide prints should accompany the manuscript and should not be attached to manuscript pages. Photographs should be enlarged to permit clear reproduction in halftone after reduction. If words or numbers are to appear on a photograph, two prints should be sent, the lettering being clearly indicated on one print only.
7. Original line drawings (not photocopies) should be submitted suitable for immediate reproduction. Drawings should be about twice the final size and the lettering must be clear and 'open' and must be large enough to be reduced in the same proportion. If this is not possible, the lettering should be provided on an overlay.
8. If illustrations are available in Postscript form, they should be supplied on disk when the manuscript is submitted accompanied by hardcopies. If corrections are required to the illustration, they will be indicated on page proofs and authors would be expected to resubmit a corrected Postscript file. The figure caption should *not* be included in the Postscript files.

Tables
1. Tables should be numbered consecutively and titled. All table columns should have an explanatory heading. Tables should not repeat data which are available elsewhere in the paper, e.g. in a line diagram.
2. Table legends should appear at the start of the table.

NB. The information reproduced above, plus referee forms, copyright transfer forms and lists of journal papers, can be obtained by electronic mail. Please send the message *send help* to citlib.caltech.edu.

General Notes

1. Only original papers will be accepted, and copyright in published papers will be vested in the publisher. (NOTE: Because of recent changes in copyright laws the transfer of copyright from author to publisher, previously implicit in the submission of a manuscript, must now be explicitly transferred to enable the publisher to ensure maximum dissemination of the author's work. A copy of the Publishing Agreement to be used for *Concurrency: Practice and Experience* is reproduced in each volume. Additional copies are available from the journal editor or from the publisher, or contributors may photocopy the agreement from this journal. A copy of this agreement, signed by the author, must accompany every article submitted for publication.)
2. The publisher will do everything possible to ensure prompt publication. It will therefore be appreciated if submitted text and illustrations conform from the outset to the style of the journal. The full postal address should be given for the author who will check proofs, along with e-mail, fax, telephone and telex numbers where possible. Corrected page proofs must be returned to the publisher within three days to minimise the risk of the author's contribution having to be held over to a later issue.
3. It is the author's responsibility to obtain written permission to quote material which has appeared in another publication.
4. Twenty-five offprints of each paper and one copy of the journal issue in which it appears will be provided free of charge. Additional offprints may be purchased on the order form which will be supplied to the author.
5. Submitted material will not be returned to authors following publication unless the material is accompanied by a request to do so when it is first submitted to the publisher.
6. Authors should follow the *Oxford English Dictionary* if using English spelling, and *Webster's New World Dictionary* if using American spelling.
7. Authors should write concisely.
8. Manuscripts should be typed double-spaced with wide margins, on one side of the paper only and submitted in duplicate, unless accompanied by a machine readable copy.
9. The title should be brief, typed on a separate sheet and the author's name should be typed on the line below the title; the affiliation and address should follow on the next line. In the case of co-authors their respective addresses should be clearly indicated. Correspondence and proofs for corrections will be sent to the first-named author, unless otherwise requested.
10. The body of the manuscript should be preceded by a Summary (maximum length 200 words) which should be a summary of the entire paper not of the conclusions alone.
11. The paper should be reasonably subdivided into sections and, if necessary, subsections. Numbering of these should be avoided wherever possible.
12. Distinctions should be made between capital and lower case letters; between the letter O and zero; between the lower case letter 'L', the number one and prime; between K and kappa, and Greek letters, or mathematical and unusual symbols should be identified separately in the margin.
13. Unless submitted in machine-readable form, program material should be applied as originals on plain paper, and will be reproduced photographically to avoid errors. A distinct black image must be supplied. Copies of programs produced on raster devices are acceptable only if the devices have a resolution greater than or equal to 300 dots/inch. The 'house-style' is to set programs in a fixed pitch 9 on 11 point Courier typewriter font to ease problems of vertical alignment. The editor and publishers do not accept responsibility for the correctness of published programs.
14. References to published literature should be quoted in the text by sequential numbers in square brackets and grouped together at the end of the paper in numerical order. Journal titles should be quoted in full.

   For example:
   1. C. Bigelow, 'Typeface protection', *Postscript Language Journal,* **1**, 28-31 (1987).
   2. J. E. Saltzer, 'Runoff', in *The Compatible Time-sharing System,* Cambridge, Mass. (1965).

Illustrations

1. Colour ilustrations will only be reproduced in colour at the author's expense.
2. Each illustration should be produced on a separate sheet and submitted with the final manuscript.

PUBLISHING AGREEMENT